ACCA

PAPER F6

TAXATION (UK)

FA 2011

S T U D Y   T E X T

BPP Learning Media is the **sole ACCA Platinum Approved Learning Partner – content** for the ACCA qualification. In this, **the only Paper F6 study text to be reviewed by the examiner:**

- We **discuss** the **best strategies** for studying for ACCA exams
- We **highlight** the **most important elements** in the syllabus and the **key skills** you will need
- We **signpost** how each chapter links to the syllabus and the study guide
- We **provide** lots of **exam focus points** demonstrating what the examiner will want you to do
- We **emphasise key points** in regular **fast forward summaries**
- We **test your knowledge** of what you've studied in **quick quizzes**
- We **examine your understanding** in our **exam question bank**
- We **reference** all the important topics in our **full index**

BPP's **i-Pass** and **i-Learn** products also support this paper.

FOR EXAMS IN JUNE AND DECEMBER 2012

LEARNING MEDIA

First edition March 2007
Sixth edition October 2011

Printed text ISBN 9781 4453 7762 9
(Previous ISBN 9780 7517 9417 5)
e text ISBN 9781 4453 7585 4

British Library Cataloguing-in-Publication Data
A catalogue record for this book
is available from the British Library

Published by

BPP Learning Media Ltd
BPP House, Aldine Place
London W12 8AA

www.bpp.com/learningmedia

Printed in the United Kingdom

We are grateful to the Association of Chartered Certified Accountants for permission to reproduce past examination questions. The suggested solutions in the exam answer bank have been prepared by BPP Learning Media Ltd, unless otherwise stated.

Your learning materials, published by BPP Learning Media Ltd, are printed on paper sourced from sustainable, managed forests.

Contents

A note about copyright

Dear Customer

What does the little © mean and why does it matter?

Your market-leading BPP books, course materials and e-learning materials do not write and update themselves. People write them: on their own behalf or as employees of an organisation that invests in this activity. Copyright law protects their livelihoods. It does so by creating rights over the use of the content.

Breach of copyright is a form of theft – as well as being a criminal offence in some jurisdictions, it is potentially a serious breach of professional ethics.

With current technology, things might seem a bit hazy but, basically, without the express permission of BPP Learning Media:

- Photocopying our materials is a breach of copyright

- Scanning, ripcasting or conversion of our digital materials into different file formats, uploading them to facebook or emailing them to your friends is a breach of copyright

You can, of course, sell your books, in the form in which you have bought them – once you have finished with them. (Is this fair to your fellow students? We update for a reason.) But the e-products are sold on a single user licence basis: we do not supply 'unlock' codes to people who have bought them second hand.

And what about outside the UK? BPP Learning Media strives to make our materials available at prices students can afford by local printing arrangements, pricing policies and partnerships which are clearly listed on our website. A tiny minority ignore this and indulge in criminal activity by illegally photocopying our material or supporting organisations that do. If they act illegally and unethically in one area, can you really trust them?

Helping you to pass – the ONLY F6 Study Text reviewed by the examiner!

BPP Learning Media – the sole Platinum Approved Learning Partner - content

As ACCA's **sole Platinum Approved Learning Partner – content**, BPP Learning Media gives you the **unique opportunity** to use **examiner-reviewed** study materials for the 2012 exams. By incorporating the examiner's comments and suggestions regarding the depth and breadth of syllabus coverage, the BPP Learning Media Study Text provides excellent, **ACCA-approved** support for your studies.

The PER alert!

Before you can qualify as an ACCA member, you do not only have to pass all your exams but also fulfil a three year **practical experience requirement** (PER). To help you to recognise areas of the syllabus that you might be able to apply in the workplace to achieve different performance objectives, we have introduced the '**PER alert**' feature. You will find this feature throughout the Study Text to remind you that what you are **learning to pass** your ACCA exams is **equally useful to the fulfilment of the PER requirement**.

Tackling studying

Studying can be a daunting prospect, particularly when you have lots of other commitments. The **different features** of the text, the **purposes** of which are explained fully on the **Chapter features** page, will help you whilst studying and improve your chances of **exam success**.

Developing exam awareness

Our Texts are completely **focused** on helping you pass your exam.

Our advice on **Studying F6** outlines the **content** of the paper, the **necessary skills** the examiner expects you to demonstrate and any **brought forward knowledge** you are expected to have.

Exam focus points are included within the chapters to highlight when and how specific topics were examined, or how they might be examined in the future.

Using the Syllabus and Study Guide

You can find the syllabus and Study Guide on pages xiii – xv of this Study Text

Testing what you can do

Testing yourself helps you develop the skills you need to pass the exam and also confirms that you can recall what you have learnt.

We include **Questions** – lots of them – both within chapters and in the **Exam Question Bank**, as well as **Quick Quizzes** at the end of each chapter to test your knowledge of the chapter content.

Chapter features

Each chapter contains a number of helpful features to guide you through each topic.

Topic list

Topic list	Syllabus reference

Tells you what you will be studying in this chapter and the relevant section numbers, together the ACCA syllabus references.

Introduction

Puts the chapter content in the context of the syllabus as a whole.

Study Guide

Links the chapter content with ACCA guidance.

Exam Guide

Highlights how examinable the chapter content is likely to be and the ways in which it could be examined.

 FAST FORWARD

Summarises the content of main chapter headings, allowing you to preview and review each section easily.

Examples

Demonstrate how to apply key knowledge and techniques.

Key terms

Definitions of important concepts that can often earn you easy marks in exams.

Exam focus points

Tell you when and how specific topics were examined, or how they may be examined in the future.

 PER alert

This is a new feature that gives you a useful indication of syllabus areas that closely relate to performance objectives in your Practical Experience Requirement (PER).

Question

Give you essential practice of techniques covered in the chapter.

Chapter Roundup

A full list of the Fast Forwards included in the chapter, providing an easy source of review.

Quick Quiz

A quick test of your knowledge of the main topics in the chapter.

Exam Question Bank

Found at the back of the Study Text with more comprehensive chapter questions. Cross referenced for easy navigation.

Studying F6

As the name suggests, this paper examines the basic principles of taxation. This is a very important area for certified accountants as many areas of practice involve a consideration of taxation issues. It also provides a foundation for P6: Advanced Taxation which will be chosen by those who work in a tax environment.

The F6 examiner

The examiner for this paper is **David Harrowven**. He has been the examiner for this paper since 2007 and a tax examiner with the ACCA since 1991. The examiner is looking for students to show that they have a solid understanding of the UK tax system and the main taxes which are income tax, corporation tax, national insurance contributions, capital gains tax, inheritance tax and value added tax. Mr Harrowven has written several articles in *Student Accountant*, including one on his approach to the paper (February 2011 issue), two on Inheritance Tax (October and November 2010 issues), overseas aspects of Corporation Tax (March 2011 issue), VAT (February 2011 issue – Part 1) and on Finance Act 2011 (September 2011 issue). Make sure you read these articles to gain further insight into what the examiner is looking for.

1 What F6 is about

The UK tax system

The syllabus introduces the rationale behind – and the functions of – the tax system.

The taxes

It then covers the **main UK taxes** which apply to individuals and businesses.

Income tax and corporation tax cover the widest areas of the syllabus, forming the basis for questions 1 and 2 totalling 55% of the marks. Value added tax (VAT) is likely to be covered in one of these questions, in which case at least 10 of the 55 marks will be awarded for VAT, although it is possible that a separate question on VAT will be included instead. Chargeable gains (either personal or corporate) will be covered in question 3, for which 15 marks will be available. Inheritance tax could be examined in either of questions 4 or 5 for a maximum of 15 marks. National insurance may be examined in any question on income tax or corporation tax.

You will be expected to have a detailed knowledge of these taxes, but **no previous knowledge is assumed**. You should **study the basics** carefully and **learn the proforma computations**. It then becomes straightforward to complete these by slotting in figures from your detailed workings.

As well as being able to calculate tax liabilities you will be expected to explain the basis of the calculations and how a taxpayer can minimise or defer tax liabilities

Compliance

The final part of the syllabus covers the **compliance obligations** of the taxpayer. Although not a major part of the syllabus it is likely to form an element in one or more questions in the exam. A knowledge of tax is incomplete without an understanding of how the tax is collected.

2 What skills are required?

- Be able to **integrate** knowledge and understanding from across the syllabus to enable you to complete detailed computations of tax liabilities.

- Be able to **explain** the underlying principles of taxation by providing a simple summary of the rules and how they apply to the particular situation.

- Be able to **apply** tax planning techniques by identifying available options and testing them to see which has the greater effect on tax liabilities.

3 How to improve your chances of passing

Study the **entire** syllabus – all the questions in the exam are **compulsory**. This gives the examiner the opportunity to test all major areas of the syllabus on every paper.

Practise as many questions as you can under **timed conditions** – this is the best way of developing good exam technique. Make use of the **Question Bank** at the back of this Text. **BPP's Practice and Revision Kit** contains numerous exam standard questions (many of them taken from past exam papers) as well as three mock exams for you to try.

Answer selectively – the examiner will expect you to consider carefully what is relevant and significant enough to include in your answer. Don't include unnecessary information.

Present your answers in a **professional** manner – use subheadings and leave spaces between paragraphs, make sure that your numerical workings are clearly set out. Even if you make a mistake in your calculations, you will still gain marks if you show that you understand the principles involved.

Answer all parts of the question – leaving out a five mark part may be the difference between a pass and a fail.

The exam paper

The syllabus is assessed by a **paper-based examination**. The **time allowed** is 3 hours with 15 minutes reading and planning time.

The paper will be **predominantly computational** and will have **five questions**, all of which will be **compulsory**.

- **Question one** will focus on **income tax** and **question two** will focus on **corporation tax**. The two questions will be for a total of **55 marks**, with **one of the questions being for 30 marks** and the **other being for 25 marks**.

- **Question three** will focus on **chargeable gains (either personal or corporate)** and will be for **15 marks**.

- **Questions four and five** will be on **any area of the syllabus**, can **cover more than one topic,** and will be for **15 marks**.

There will always be at a **minimum of 10 marks on value added tax**. These marks will normally be included within question one or question two, although there might be a separate question on value added tax.

There will always be between **5 and 15 marks on inheritance tax**. Inheritance tax can be included within questions three, four or five.

National insurance contributions will not be examined as a separate question, but may be examined in any question involving income tax or corporation tax.

Groups and **overseas aspects of corporation tax** may be examined in **question two**, **question four or question five**.

A small element of chargeable gains could be included in questions other than question three.

Inheritance tax could be examined in **question four or question five** for a maximum of **15 marks**.

Any of the five questions might include **the consideration of issues relating to the minimisation or deferral of tax liabilities.**

Taxation (UK) (F6)
June & December 2012

This syllabus and study guide is designed to help with planning study and to provide detailed information on what could be assessed in any examination session.

THE STRUCTURE OF THE SYLLABUS AND STUDY GUIDE

Relational diagram of paper with other papers

This diagram shows direct and indirect links between this paper and other papers preceding or following it. Some papers are directly underpinned by other papers such as Advanced Performance Management by Performance Management. These
links are shown as solid line arrows. Other papers only have indirect relationships with each other such as links existing between the accounting and auditing papers. The links between these are shown as dotted line arrows. This diagram indicates where you are expected to have underpinning knowledge and where it would be useful to review previous
learning before undertaking study.

Overall aim of the syllabus

This explains briefly the overall objective of the paper and indicates in the broadest sense the capabilities to be developed within the paper.

Main capabilities

This paper's aim is broken down into several main capabilities which divide the syllabus and study guide into discrete sections.

Relational diagram of the main capabilities

This diagram illustrates the flows and links between the main capabilities (sections) of the syllabus and should be used as an aid to planning teaching and learning in a structured way.

Syllabus rationale

This is a narrative explaining how the syllabus is structured and how the main capabilities are linked. The rationale also explains in further detail what the examination intends to assess and why.

Detailed syllabus

This shows the breakdown of the main capabilities (sections) of the syllabus into subject areas. This is the blueprint for the detailed study guide.

Approach to examining the syllabus

This section briefly explains the structure of the examination and how it is assessed.

Study Guide

This is the main document that students, tuition providers and publishers should use as the basis of their studies, instruction and materials.

Examinations will be based on the detail of the study guide which comprehensively identifies what could be assessed in any examination session.

The study guide is a precise reflection and breakdown of the syllabus. It is divided into sections based on the main capabilities identified in the syllabus. These sections are divided into subject areas which relate to the sub-capabilities included in the detailed syllabus. Subject areas are broken down into sub-headings which describe the detailed outcomes that could be assessed in examinations. These outcomes are described using verbs indicating what exams may require students to demonstrate, and the broad intellectual level at which these may need to be demonstrated
(*see intellectual levels below).

Learning Materials

ACCA's Approved Learning Partner - content (ALP-c) is the programme through which ACCA approves learning materials from high quality content providers designed to support study towards ACCA's qualifications.

ACCA has one Platinum Approved Learning Partner content which is BPP Learning Media. In addition, there are a number of Gold Approved Learning Partners - content.
For information about ACCA's
Approved Learning Partners - content, please go ACCA's Content Provider Directory.

The Directory also lists materials by Subscribers, these materials have not been quality assured by ACCA but may be helpful if used in conjunction with approved learning materials. You will also find details of Examiner suggested Additional Reading which may be a useful supplement to approved learning materials.

ACCA's Content Provider Directory can be found here –
http://www.accaglobal.com/learningproviders/al pc/content_provider_directory/search/.

Relevant articles will also be published in Student Accountant.

INTELLECTUAL LEVELS

The syllabus is designed to progressively broaden and deepen the knowledge, skills and professional values demonstrated by the student on their way through the qualification.

The specific capabilities within the detailed syllabuses and study guides are assessed at one of three intellectual or cognitive levels:

Level 1:   Knowledge and comprehension
Level 2:   Application and analysis
Level 3:   Synthesis and evaluation

Very broadly, these intellectual levels relate to the three cognitive levels at which the Knowledge module, the Skills module and the Professional level are assessed.

Each subject area in the detailed study guide included in this document is given a 1, 2, or 3 superscript, denoting intellectual level, marked at the end of each relevant line. This gives an indication of the intellectual depth at which an area could be assessed within the examination. However, while level 1 broadly equates with the Knowledge module, level 2 equates to the Skills module and level 3 to the Professional level, some lower level skills can continue to be assessed as the student progresses through each module and level. This reflects that at each stage of study there will be a requirement to broaden, as well as deepen capabilities. It is also possible that occasionally some higher level capabilities may be assessed at lower levels.

LEARNING HOURS

The ACCA qualification does not prescribe or recommend any particular number of learning hours for examinations because study and learning patterns and styles vary greatly between people and organisations. This also recognises the wide diversity of personal, professional and educational circumstances in which ACCA students find themselves.

Each syllabus contains between 23 and 35 main subject area headings depending on the nature of the subject and how these areas have been broken down.

GUIDE TO EXAM STRUCTURE

The structure of examinations varies within and between modules and levels.

The Fundamentals level examinations contain 100% compulsory questions to encourage candidates to study across the breadth of each syllabus.

The Knowledge module is assessed by equivalent two-hour paper based and computer based examinations.

The Skills module examinations are all paper based three-hour papers. The structure of papers varies from ten questions in the *Corporate and Business Law* (F4) paper to four 25 mark questions in *Financial Management* (F9). Individual questions within all Skills module papers will attract between10 and 30 marks.

The Professional level papers are all three-hour paper based examinations, all containing two sections. Section A is compulsory, but there will be some choice offered in Section B.

For all three hour examination papers, ACCA has introduced 15 minutes reading and planning time.

This additional time is allowed at the beginning of each three-hour examination to allow candidates to read the questions and to begin planning their answers before they start writing in their answer books. This time should be used to ensure that all the information and exam requirements are properly read and understood.

During reading and planning time candidates may only annotate their question paper. They may not write anything in their answer booklets until told to do so by the invigilator.

The Essentials module papers all have a Section A containing a major case study question with all requirements totalling 50 marks relating to this case. Section B gives students a choice of two from
three 25 mark questions.

Section A of each of the Options papers contains 50-70 compulsory marks from two questions, each attracting between 25 and 40 marks. Section B will offer a choice of two from three questions totalling 30-50 marks, with each question attracting
between 15 and 25 marks.

The pass mark for all ACCA Qualification examination papers is 50%.

GUIDE TO EXAMINATION ASSESSMENT

ACCA reserves the right to examine anything contained within the study guide at any examination session. This includes knowledge, techniques, principles, theories, and concepts as specified.

For the financial accounting, audit and assurance, law and tax papers except where indicated otherwise, ACCA will publish *examinable documents* once a year to indicate exactly what regulations and legislation could potentially be assessed within identified examination sessions.

For paper based examinations regulation *issued* or legislation *passed* on or before 30th September annually, will be assessed from June 1st of the following year to May 31st of the year after. Please refer to the examinable documents for the paper for more information.

Regulation issued or legislation passed in accordance with the above dates may be examinable even if the *effective* date is in the future.

The term issued or passed relates to when regulation or legislation has been formally approved.

The term effective relates to when regulation or legislation must be applied to an entity transactions and business practices.

The study guide offers more detailed guidance on the depth and level at which the examinable documents will be examined. The study guide should therefore be read in conjunction with the examinable documents list.

Syllabus

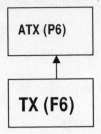

ATX (P6)

TX (F6)

AIM

To develop knowledge and skills relating to the tax system as applicable to individuals, single companies, and groups of companies.

On successful completion of this paper candidates should be able to:

A Explain the operation and scope of the tax system

B Explain and compute the income tax liabilities of individuals

C Explain and compute the corporation tax liabilities of individual companies and groups of companies

D Explain and compute the chargeable gains arising on companies and individuals

E Explain and compute the inheritance tax liabilities of individuals

F Explain and compute the effect of national insurance contributions on employees, employers and the self employed

G Explain and compute the effects of value added tax on incorporated and unincorporated businesses

H Identify and explain the obligations of tax payers and/or their agents and the implications of non-compliance

RELATIONAL DIAGRAM OF MAIN CAPABILITIES

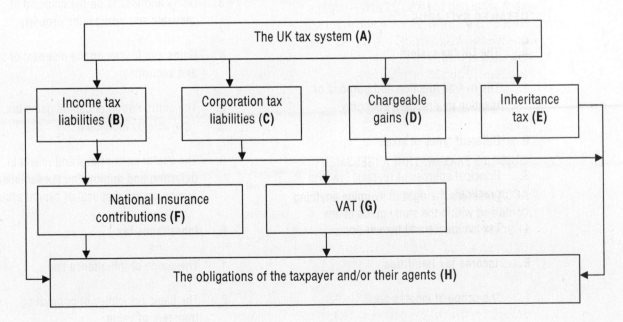

RATIONALE

The syllabus for Paper F6, *Taxation,* introduces candidates to the subject of taxation and provides the core knowledge of the underlying principles and major technical areas of taxation as they affect the activities of individuals and businesses.

Candidates are introduced to the rationale behind – and the functions of – the tax system. The syllabus then considers the separate taxes that an accountant would need to have a detailed knowledge of, such as income tax from self-employment, employment and investments, the corporation tax liability of individual companies and groups of companies, the national insurance contribution liabilities of both employed and self employed persons, the value added tax liability of businesses, and the chargeable gains arising on disposals of investments by both individuals and companies.

Having covered the core areas of the basic taxes, candidates should be able to compute tax liabilities, explain the basis of their calculations, apply tax planning techniques for individuals and companies and identify the compliance issues for each major tax through a variety of business and personal scenarios and situations.

DETAILED SYLLABUS

A. The UK tax system

1. The overall function and purpose of taxation in a modern economy

2. Different types of taxes

3. Principal sources of revenue law and practice

4. Tax avoidance and tax evasion

B. Income tax liabilities

1. The scope of income tax

2. Income from employment

3. Income from self-employment

4. Property and investment income

5. The comprehensive computation of taxable income and income tax liability

6. The use of exemptions and reliefs in deferring and minimising income tax liabilities

C. Corporation tax liabilities

1. The scope of corporation tax

2. Taxable total profits

3. The comprehensive computation of corporation tax liability

4. The effect of a group corporate structure for corporation tax purposes

5. The use of exemptions and reliefs in deferring and minimising corporation tax liabilities

D. Chargeable gains

1. The scope of the taxation of capital gains

2. The basic principles of computing gains and losses.

3. Gains and losses on the disposal of movable and immovable property

4. Gains and losses on the disposal of shares and securities

5. The computation of capital gains tax payable by individuals

6. The use of exemptions and reliefs in deferring and minimising tax liabilities arising on the disposal of capital assets

E. Inheritance tax

1. The scope of inheritance tax

2. The basic principles of computing transfers of value

3. The liabilities arising on chargeable lifetime transfers and on the death of an individual

4. The use of exemptions in deferring and minimising inheritance tax liabilities

5. Payment of inheritance tax

F. National insurance contributions

1. The scope of national insurance

2. Class 1 and Class 1A contributions for employed persons

3. Class 2 and Class 4 contributions for self-employed persons

G. Value added tax

1. The scope of value added tax (VAT)

2. The VAT registration requirements

3. The computation of VAT liabilities

4. The effect of special schemes

H. The obligations of taxpayers and/or their agents

1. The systems for self-assessment and the making of returns

2. The time limits for the submission of information, claims and payment of tax, including payments on account

3. The procedures relating to compliance checks, appeals and disputes

4. Penalties for non-compliance

APPROACH TO EXAMINING THE SYLLABUS

The syllabus is assessed by a three-hour paper-based examination.

Assessment: Taxation (UK)

The paper will be predominantly computational and will have five questions, all of which will be compulsory.

- Question one will focus on income tax and question two will focus on corporation tax. The two questions will be for a total of 55 marks, with one of the questions being for 30 marks and the other being for 25 marks.

- Question three will focus on chargeable gains (either personal or corporate) and will be for 15 marks.

- Questions four and five will be on any area of the syllabus, can cover more than one topic, and will be for 15 marks.

There will always be at a minimum of 10 marks on value added tax. These marks will normally be included within question one or question two, although there might be a separate question on value added tax.

There will always be between 5 and 15 marks on inheritance tax. Inheritance tax can be included within questions three, four or five.

National insurance contributions will not be examined as a separate question, but may be examined in any question involving income tax or corporation tax.

Groups and overseas aspects of corporation tax may be examined in either question two, question four or question five.

A small element of chargeable gains may be included in questions other than question 3.

Any of the five questions might include the consideration of issues relating to the minimisation or deferral of tax liabilities.

BPP LEARNING MEDIA

Study Guide

A   THE UK TAX SYSTEM

1.   The overall function and purpose of taxation in a modern economy

a) Describe the purpose (economic, social etc) of taxation in a modern economy.[2]

2.   Different types of taxes

a) Identify the different types of capital and revenue tax.[1]

b) Explain the difference between direct and indirect taxation.[2]

3.   Principal sources of revenue law and practice

a) Describe the overall structure of the UK tax system.[1]

b) State the different sources of revenue law.[1]

c) Appreciate the interaction of the UK tax system with that of other tax jurisdictions.[2]

4.   Tax avoidance and tax evasion

a) Explain the difference between tax avoidance and tax evasion.[1]

b) Explain the need for an ethical and professional approach.[2]

Excluded topics

- *Anti-avoidance legislation.*

B   INCOME TAX LIABILITIES

1.   The scope of income tax

a) Explain how the residence of an individual is determined.[1]

Excluded topics

- *The treatment of a person who comes to the UK to work or a person who leaves the UK to take up employment overseas.*

- *Foreign income, non-residents and double taxation relief.*

- *Income from trusts and settlements.*

2.   Income from employment

a) Recognise the factors that determine whether an engagement is treated as employment or self-employment.[2]

b) Recognise the basis of assessment for employment income.[2]

c) Compute the income assessable.[2]

d) Recognise the allowable deductions, including travelling expenses.[2]

e) Discuss the use of the statutory approved mileage allowances.[2]

f) Explain the PAYE system.[1]

g) Identify P11D employees.[1]

h) Compute the amount of benefits assessable.[2]

i) Explain the purpose of a dispensation from HM Revenue & Customs.[2]

k) Explain how charitable giving can be made through a payroll deduction scheme.[1]

Excluded topics

- *The calculation of a car benefit where emission figures are not available.*

- *The exemption for zero emission company motor cars.*

- *Share and share option incentive schemes for employees.*

- *Payments on the termination of employment, and other lump sums received by employees.*

3   Income from self-employment

a)   Recognise the basis of assessment for self-employment income.[2]

b)   Describe and apply the badges of trade.[2]

c)   Recognise the expenditure that is allowable in calculating the tax-adjusted trading profit.[2]

d)   Recognise the relief that can be obtained for pre-trading expenditure.[2]

e)   Compute the assessable profits on commencement and on cessation.[2]

f)   Change of accounting date
   i)   Recognise the factors that will influence the choice of accounting date.[2]
   ii) State the conditions that must be met for a change of accounting date to be valid.[1]
   iii) Compute the assessable profits on a change of accounting date.[2]

g)   Capital allowances
   i)   Define plant and machinery for capital allowances purposes.[1]
   ii) Compute writing down allowances, first-year allowances and the annual investment allowance.[2]
   iii) Compute capital allowances for motor cars, including motor cars already owned at 6 April 2009 (1 April 2009 for companies).[2]
   iv) Compute balancing allowances and balancing charges.[2]
   v)   Recognise the treatment of short life assets.[2]
   vi) Explain the treatment of assets included in the special rate pool.[2]

h)   Relief for trading losses
   i)   Understand how trading losses can be carried forward.[2]
   ii) Explain how trading losses can be carried forward following the incorporation of a business.[2]
   iii) Understand how trading losses can be claimed against total income and chargeable gains.[2]
   iv) Explain and compute the relief for trading losses in the early years of a trade.[1]
   v)   Explain and compute terminal loss relief.[1]

i)   Partnerships and limited liability partnerships
   i)   Explain how a partnership is assessed to tax.[2]
   ii) Compute the assessable profits for each partner following a change in the profit sharing ratio.[2]
   iii) Compute the assessable profits for each partner following a change in the membership of the partnership.[2]
   iv) Describe the alternative loss relief claims that are available to partners.[1]
   v)   Explain the loss relief restriction that applies to the partners of a limited liability partnership.[1]

Excluded topics

- *The 100% allowance for expenditure on renovating business premises in disadvantaged areas, flats above shops and water technologies.*

- *Capital allowances for industrial buildings, agricultural buildings, patents, scientific research and know how.*

- *Enterprise zones.*

- *Investment income of a partnership.*

- *The allocation of notional profits and losses for a partnership.*

- *Farmers averaging of profits.*

- *The averaging of profits for authors and creative artists.*

- *Loss relief for shares in unquoted trading companies.*

4.   Property and investment income

a)   Compute property business profits.[2]

b)   Explain the treatment of furnished holiday lettings.[1]

c)   Describe rent-a-room relief.[1]

d) Compute the amount assessable when a premium is received for the grant of a short lease.[2]

e) Understand how relief for a property business loss is given.[2]

f) Compute the tax payable on savings income.[2]

g) Compute the tax payable on dividend income.[2]

h) Explain the treatment of individual savings accounts (ISAs) and other tax exempt investments.[1]

Excluded topics

- *The deduction for expenditure by landlords on energy-saving items.*

- *Junior ISAs.*

5 The comprehensive computation of taxable income and income tax liability

a) Prepare a basic income tax computation involving different types of income.[2]

b) Calculate the amount of personal allowance available generally, and for people aged 65 and above.[2]

c) Compute the amount of income tax payable.[2]

d) Explain the treatment of interest paid for a qualifying purpose.[2]

e) Explain the treatment of gift aid donations.[1]

f) Explain the treatment of property owned jointly by a married couple, or by a couple in a civil partnership.[1]

Excluded topics

- *The blind person's allowance and the married couple's allowance.*

- *Tax credits.*

- *Maintenance payments.*

- *The income of minor children.*

6. The use of exemptions and reliefs in deferring and minimising income tax liabilities

a) Explain and compute the relief given for contributions to personal pension schemes, using the rules applicable from 6 April 2011.[2]

b) Describe the relief given for contributions to occupational pension schemes, using the rules applicable from 6 April 2011.[1]

c) Explain how a married couple or a couple in a civil partnership can minimise their tax liabilities.[2]

Excluded topics

- *The conditions that must be met in order for a pension scheme to obtain approval from HM Revenue & Customs.*

- *The enterprise investment scheme.*

- *Venture capital trusts.*

C   CORPORATION TAX LIABILITIES

1.   The scope of corporation tax

a)   Define the terms 'period of account', 'accounting period', and 'financial year'.[1]

b)   Recognise when an accounting period starts and when an accounting period finishes.[1]

c)   Explain how the residence of a company is determined.[2]

Excluded topics

- *Investment companies.*

- *Close companies.*

- *Companies in receivership or liquidation.*

- *Reorganisations.*

- *The purchase by a company of its own shares.*

- *Personal service companies.*

2.   Taxable total profits

a)   Recognise the expenditure that is allowable in calculating the tax-adjusted trading profit.[2]

b)   Explain how relief can be obtained for pre-trading expenditure.[1]

c)   Compute capital allowances (as for income tax).[2]

d)   Compute property business profits.[2]

e)   Explain the treatment of interest paid and received under the loan relationship rules.[1]

f)   Explain the treatment of gift aid donations.[2]

g)   Understand how trading losses can be carried forward.[2]

h)   Understand how trading losses can be claimed against income of the current or previous accounting periods.[2]

i)   Recognise the factors that will influence the choice of loss relief claim.[2]

j)   Explain how relief for a property business loss is given.[1]

k)   Compute taxable total profits.[2]

Excluded topics

- *Research and development expenditure.*

- *Non-trading deficits on loan relationships.*

- *Relief for intangible assets.*

3.   The comprehensive computation of corporation tax liability

a)   Compute the corporation tax liability and apply marginal relief.[2]

b)   Explain the implications of receiving franked investment income.[2]

4.   The effect of a group corporate structure for corporation tax purposes

a)   Define an associated company and recognise the effect of being an associated company for corporation tax purposes.[2]

b)   Define a 75% group, and recognise the reliefs that are available to members of such a group.[2]

c)   Define a 75% capital gains group, and recognise the reliefs that are available to members of such a group.[2]

d)   Compare the UK tax treatment of an overseas branch to an overseas subsidiary.[2]

e)   Calculate double taxation relief.[2]

f)   Explain the basic principles of the transfer pricing rules.[2]

Excluded topics

- *Relief for trading losses incurred by an overseas subsidiary.*

- *Consortia.*

- *Pre-entry gains and losses.*

- *The anti-avoidance provisions where arrangements exist for a company to leave a group.*

- *The tax charge that applies where a company leaves a group within six years of receiving an asset by way of a no gain/no loss transfer.*

- *Controlled foreign companies.*

- *Foreign companies trading in the UK.*

- *Expense relief in respect of overseas tax.*

- *Election for the exemption of profits from an overseas branch.*

- *Transfer pricing transactions not involving an overseas company.*

5. **The use of exemptions and reliefs in deferring and minimising corporation tax liabilities:**

   The use of such exemptions and reliefs is implicit within all of the above sections 1 to 4 of part C of the syllabus, concerning corporation tax.

D   CHARGEABLE GAINS

1. **The scope of the taxation of capital gains**

a) Describe the scope of capital gains tax.[2]

b) Explain how the residence and ordinary residence of an individual is determined.[2]

c) List those assets which are exempt.[1]

Excluded topics

- *Assets situated overseas and double taxation relief.*

- *Partnership capital gains.*

2. **The basic principles of computing gains and losses.**

a) Compute capital gains for both individuals and companies.[2]

b) Calculate the indexation allowance available to companies.[2]

c) Explain the treatment of capital losses for both individuals and companies.[1]

d) Explain the treatment of transfers between a husband and wife or between a couple in a civil partnership.[2]

e) Compute the amount of allowable expenditure for a part disposal.[2]

f) Explain the treatment where an asset is damaged, lost or destroyed, and the implications of receiving insurance proceeds and reinvesting such proceeds.[2]

Excluded topics

- *Small part disposals of land.*

- *Losses in the year of death.*

- *Relief for losses incurred on loans made to traders.*

- *Negligible value claims.*

3. **Gains and losses on the disposal of movable and immovable property**

a) Identify when chattels and wasting assets are exempt.[1]

b) Compute the chargeable gain when a chattel is disposed of.[2]

c) Calculate the chargeable gain when a wasting asset is disposed of.[2]

d) Compute the exemption when a principal private residence is disposed of.[2]

e) Calculate the chargeable gain when a principal private residence has been used for business purposes.[2]

f) Identify the amount of letting relief available when a principal private residence has been let out. [2]

Excluded topics

- *The disposal of leases and the creation of sub-leases.*

4. Gains and losses on the disposal of shares and securities

a) Calculate the value of quoted shares where they are disposed of by way of a gift. [2]

b) Explain and apply the identification rules as they apply to individuals and to companies, including the same day, nine day, and 30 day matching rules. [2]

c) Explain the pooling provisions. [2]

d) Explain the treatment of bonus issues, rights issues, takeovers and reorganisations. [2]

e) Explain the exemption available for gilt-edged securities and qualifying corporate bonds. [1]

Excluded topics

- *A detailed question on the pooling provisions for shares as they apply to limited companies.*

- *The small part disposal rules applicable to rights issues.*

- *Substantial shareholdings.*

- *Gilt-edged securities and qualifying corporate bonds other than the fact that they are exempt.*

5. The computation of capital gains tax payable by individuals

a) Compute the amount of capital gains tax payable. [2]

6. The use of exemptions and reliefs in deferring and minimising tax liabilities arising on the disposal of capital assets

a) Explain and apply entrepreneurs' relief as it applies to individuals. [2]

b) Explain and apply rollover relief as it applies to individuals and companies. [2]

c) Explain and apply holdover relief for the gift of business assets. [2]

d) Explain and apply the incorporation relief that is available upon the transfer of a business to a company. [2]

Excluded topics

- *Reinvestment relief.*

- *Entrepreneurs' relief for associated disposals.*

E   INHERITANCE TAX

1. The scope of inheritance tax

a) Describe the scope of inheritance tax. [2]

b) Identify and explain the persons chargeable. [2]

Excluded topics

- *Pre 18 March 1986 lifetime transfers.*

- *Transfers of value by close companies.*

- *Domicile, deemed domicile, and non-UK domiciled individuals.*

- *Trusts.*

2. The basic principles of computing transfers of value

a) State, explain and apply the meaning of transfer of value, chargeable transfer and potentially exempt transfer. [2]

b) Demonstrate the diminution in value principle. [2]

c) Demonstrate the seven year accumulation principle taking into account changes in the level of the nil rate band. [2]

Excluded topics

- *Excluded property.*

- *Related property.*

- *The tax implications of the location of assets.*

- *Gifts with reservation of benefit.*

- *Associated operations.*

3. **The liabilities arising on chargeable lifetime transfers and on the death of an individual**

a) Understand the tax implications of chargeable lifetime transfers and compute the relevant liabilities. [2]

b) Understand the tax implications of transfers within seven years of death and compute the relevant liabilities. [2]

c) Compute the tax liability on a death estate. [2]

d) Understand and apply the transfer of any unused nil rate band between spouses.[2]

Excluded topics

- *Specific rules for the valuation of assets (values will be provided).*

- *Business property relief.*

- *Agricultural relief.*

- *Relief for the fall in value of lifetime gifts.*

- *Quick succession relief.*

- *Double tax relief.*

- *Variation of wills and disclaimers of legacies.*

- *Grossing up on death.*

- *Post mortem reliefs.*

- *Double charges legislation.*

4. **The use of exemptions in deferring and minimising inheritance tax liabilities**

a) Understand and apply the following exemptions:
   i) small gifts exemption[2]
   ii) annual exemption[2]
   iii) normal expenditure out of income[2]
   iv) gifts in consideration of marriage[2]
   v) gifts between spouses.[2]

Excluded topics

- *Gifts to charities.*

- *Gifts to political parties.*

- *Gifts for national purposes.*

5. **Payment of inheritance tax**

a) Identify who is responsible for the payment of inheritance tax. [2]

b) Advise on the due date for payment of inheritance tax. [2]

Excluded topics

- *Administration of inheritance tax other than listed above.*

- *The instalment option for the payment of tax.*

- *Interest and penalties.*

F NATIONAL INSURANCE CONTRIBUTIONS

1. The scope of national insurance

a) Describe the scope of national insurance.[1]

2. Class 1 and Class 1A contributions for employed persons

a) Compute Class 1 NIC.[2]

b) Compute Class 1A NIC.[2]

Excluded topics

- *The calculation of directors' national insurance on a month by month basis.*

- *Contracted out contributions.*

3. Class 2 and Class 4 contributions for self-employed persons

a) Compute Class 2 NIC.[2]

b) Compute Class 4 NIC.[2]

Excluded topics

- *The offset of trading losses against non-trading income.*

G VALUE ADDED TAX

1. The scope of value added tax (VAT)

a) Describe the scope of VAT.[2]

b) List the principal zero-rated and exempt supplies.[1]

2. The VAT registration requirements

a) Recognise the circumstances in which a person must register for VAT.[2]

b) Explain the advantages of voluntary VAT registration.[2]

c) Explain the circumstances in which pre-registration input VAT can be recovered.[2]

d) Explain how and when a person can deregister for VAT.[1]

e) Explain the conditions that must be met for two or more companies to be treated as a group for VAT purposes, and the consequences of being so treated.[1]

3. The computation of VAT liabilities

a) Explain how VAT is accounted for and administered.[2]

b) Recognise the tax point when goods or services are supplied.[2]

c) List the information that must be given on a VAT invoice.[1]

d) Explain and apply the principles regarding the valuation of supplies.[2]

e) Recognise the circumstances in which input VAT is non-deductible.[2]

f) Compute the relief that is available for impairment losses on trade debts.[2]

g) Explain the circumstances in which the default surcharge, a penalty for an incorrect VAT return, and default interest will be applied.[1]

h) Explain the treatment of imports, exports and trade within the European Union.

Excluded topics

- *VAT periods where there is a change of VAT rate.*

- *Partial exemption.*

- *In respect of property and land: leases, do-it-yourself builders, and a landlord's option to tax.*

- *Penalties apart from those listed in the study guide.*

4. The effect of special schemes

a) Describe the cash accounting scheme, and recognise when it will be advantageous to use the scheme.[2]

b) Describe the annual accounting scheme, and recognise when it will be advantageous to use the scheme.[2]

c) Describe the flat rate scheme, and recognise when it will be advantageous to use the scheme.[2]

Excluded topics

- *The second-hand goods scheme.*
- *The capital goods scheme.*
- *The special schemes for retailers.*

H THE OBLIGATIONS OF TAX PAYERS AND/OR THEIR AGENTS

1. The systems for self-assessment and the making of returns

a) Explain and apply the features of the self-assessment system as it applies to individuals.[2]

b) Explain and apply the features of the self-assessment system as it applies to companies, including the use of iXBRL.[2]

2. The time limits for the submission of information, claims and payment of tax, including payments on account

a) Recognise the time limits that apply to the filing of returns and the making of claims.[2]

b) Recognise the due dates for the payment of tax under the self-assessment system.[2]

c) Compute payments on account and balancing payments/repayments for individuals.[2]

d) Explain how large companies are required to account for corporation tax on a quarterly basis.[2]

e) List the information and records that taxpayers need to retain for tax purposes.[1]

Excluded topics

- *The payment of CGT by annual instalments.*

3. The procedures relating to *compliance checks*, appeals and disputes

a) Explain the circumstances in which HM Revenue & Customs can make a compliance check into a self-assessment tax return.[2]

b) Explain the procedures for dealing with appeals and disputes.[1]

4. Penalties for non-compliance

a) Calculate late payment interest.[2]

b) State the penalties that can be charged.[2]

SUMMARY OF CHANGES TO F6 (UK)

ACCA periodically reviews it qualification syllabuses so that they fully meet the needs of stakeholders such as employers, students, regulatory and advisory bodies and learning providers.

The main areas that have been added to the syllabus are shown in table 1 below:

Table 1 – Additions to F6 (UK)

Section and subject area	Syllabus content
B3 Income from self-employment – *Excluded topics*	Industrial buildings allowance (IBA)
B4 Property and investment income – *Excluded topics*	Junior ISAs
C4 Group Structure – *Excluded topics*	Profits from overseas branch

The main areas that have been added to the syllabus are shown in Table 2 below:

Table 2 – Deletions from F6 (UK)

Section and subject area	Syllabus content
B3g)vii) Income from self-employment	Industrial buildings allowance (IBA)
B3g)viii) Income from self-employment	IBA
B3 Income from self-employment – *Excluded topics*	40% FYA
B3 Income from self-employment – *Excluded topics*	Apportionment of AIA
B3 Income from self-employment – *Excluded topics*	Calculation of IBA
B3 Income from self-employment – *Excluded topics*	Additional loss relief
B4 Property and investment income – *Excluded topics*	Pension additional tax charge
B4 Property and investment income – *Excluded topics*	Anti-forestalling provisions
C2 Taxable total profits – *Excluded topics*	Extended loss relief
C3c) The comprehensive computation of corporation tax liability	Exemptions and reliefs (as repetition of C5)
C3 The comprehensive computation of corporation tax liability – *Excluded topics*	The corporate venturing scheme
C4 Group Structure – *Excluded topics*	Overseas dividends
D2 Computing gains and losses – *Excluded topics*	Disposals prior to 23 June 2010
D6 Use of exemptions – *Excluded topics*	Entrepreneurs' relief qualifying limits prior to 22 June 2010

The main areas that have been amended or clarified in the syllabus are shown in Table 3 below:

Table 3 – Amendments to F6 (UK)

Section and subject area	Amendment
Approach to examining	Groups and overseas aspects can also be examined in question 4
Approach to examining	A small element of chargeable gains could be included in questions other than question 3
B6a) Use of exemptions	Pensions rules will only be examined from 6 April 2011
E3 The liabilities arising on a chargeable lifetime transfers and on the death of an individual – *Excluded topics*	Double grossing up on death amended to Grossing up on death
F3g) The computation of VAT liabilities	A serious misdeclaration penalty replaced with a penalty for an incorrect VAT return
H1b) Corporate self-assessment	Use of iXBRL
H3a) Procedures relating to compliance checks	'Enquiry' changed to 'compliance check' to agree to HMRC terminology
H4 a) Penalties for non-compliance	Interest on overdue tax replaced with late payment interest

Analysis of past papers

The table below provides details of when each element of the syllabus has been examined and the question number and section in which each element appeared. Further details can be found in the Exam Focus Points in the relevant chapters. Note that Inheritance Tax was added to the syllabus in 2011.

Covered in Text chapter		June 2011	Dec 2010	June 2010	Dec 2009	Dec 2008	June 2008
	UK TAX SYSTEM						
1	Introduction to the UK tax system			**4b**			
	INCOME TAX AND AND NATIONAL INSURANCE CONTRIBUTIONS						
2	The computation of taxable income and the income tax liability	1a	1a	1a, 2d	1c	1a	1b, 1c
3	Employment income		1a			1a	1a
4	Taxable and exempt benefits. The PAYE system		1a, 4			1a	1a
5	Pensions		1a		5		
6	Property income				1a		
7	Computing trading income	1a		1b	1b, 4a		1a
8	Capital allowances			2c			
9	Assessable trading income				1a		
10	Trading losses		5				
11	Partnerships and limited liability partnerships			1b		4	
12	National insurance contributions	1b	4	1c, 2d	4b	1b	
	CHARGEABLE GAINS FOR INDIVIDUALS						
13	Computing chargeable gains	3b			3, 4c		3
14	Chattels and the principal private residence exemption		3		3c		
15	Business reliefs	3a,3b	3		3a, 3b		3
16	Shares and securities	3b	3				
	TAX ADMINISTRATION FOR INDIVIDUALS						
17	Self assessment and payment of tax for individuals	1a	1b	4	1c, 1d		4
	INHERITANCE TAX						
18	Inheritance tax	5	n/a	n/a	n/a	na/	n/a

Covered in Text chapter		June 2011	Dec 2010	June 2010	Dec 2009	Dec 2008	June 2008
	CORPORATION TAX						
19	Computing taxable total profits	2a	2a, 4	2a	2a, 5b	2a	2a, 5
20	Computing the corporation tax liability	2a	2a,4	5	2a	3a	5
21	Chargeable gains for companies		3	3a, 3b		3a, 3b	
22	Losses			2a	5	2a	
23	Groups			2b			
24	Overseas matters for companies		2a		2a		2a
25	Self assessment and payment of tax by companies	2b				2a	
	VALUE ADDED TAX						
26	An introduction to VAT	4a	2b	1d	2b	2b	2b
27	Further aspects of VAT	4b-e	2b	1d	2b	2b	

UK tax system

1

Introduction to the UK tax system

Topic list	Syllabus reference
1 The overall function and purpose of taxation in a modern economy	A1(a)
2 Different types of taxes	A2(a), (b)
3 Principal sources of revenue law and practice	A3(a)-(c)
4 Tax avoidance and tax evasion	A4(a), (b)

Introduction

We start our study of tax with an introduction to the UK tax system.

First we consider briefly the purpose of raising taxes, both economic and social. We next consider the specific UK taxes, both revenue and capital, and also direct and indirect.

We see how the collection of tax is administered in the UK, and where the UK tax system interacts with overseas tax jurisdictions.

Finally we highlight the difference between tax avoidance and tax evasion and explain the need for a professional and ethical approach in dealing with tax. In particular, we look at the situation where a client has failed to disclose information to the tax authorities.

When you have finished this chapter you should be able to discuss the broad features of the tax system. In the following chapters we will consider specific UK taxes, starting with income tax.

Study guide

		Intellectual level
A1	**The overall function and purpose of taxation in a modern economy**	
(a)	Describe the purpose (economic, social etc) of taxation in a modern economy.	2
A2	**Different types of taxes**	
(a)	Identify the different types of capital and revenue tax.	1
(b)	Explain the difference between direct and indirect taxation.	2
A3	**Principal sources of revenue law and practice**	
(a)	Describe the overall structure of the UK tax system.	1
(b)	State the different sources of revenue law.	1
(c)	Appreciate the interaction of the UK tax system with that of other tax jurisdictions.	2
A4	**Tax avoidance and tax evasion**	
(a)	Explain the difference between tax avoidance and tax evasion.	1
(b)	Explain the need for an ethical and professional approach.	2

Exam guide

You are unlikely to be asked a whole question on this part of the syllabus. You may, however, be asked to comment on one aspect, such as the difference between tax avoidance and tax evasion or how to act if a client has failed to disclose information to the tax authorities, as part of a question.

1 The overall function and purpose of taxation in a modern economy

FAST FORWARD

Economic, social and environmental factors may affect the government's tax policies.

1.1 Economic factors

In terms of economic analysis, government **taxation represents a withdrawal from the UK economy** while its expenditure acts as an injection into it. So the government's net position in terms of taxation and expenditure, together with its public sector borrowing policies, has an effect on the level of economic activity within the UK.

The government favours longer-term planning, currently publishing and then sticking to three year plans for expenditure. These show the proportion of the economy's overall resources which will be allocated by the government and how much will be left for the private sector.

This can have an effect on demand for particular types of goods, eg health and education on the one hand, which are predominately the result of public spending, and consumer goods on the other, which results from private spending. Changing demand levels will have an impact on employment levels within the different sectors, as well as on the profitability of different private sector suppliers.

Within that overall proportion left in the private sector, **the government uses tax policies to encourage and discourage certain types of activity**.

It **encourages**:

(a) **saving** on the part of the individual, by offering tax incentives such as tax-free Individual Savings Accounts and tax relief on pension contributions

(b) **donations to charities**, through the Gift Aid scheme

(c) **entrepreneurs** who build their own business, through reliefs from capital gains tax

(d) **investment in plant and machinery** through capital allowances;

while it **discourages**:

(a) **smoking** and **alcoholic drinks**, through the duties placed on each type of product;

(b) **motoring**, through fuel duties.

Governments can and do argue that these latter taxes and duties to some extent mirror the extra costs to the country as a whole of such behaviours, such as the cost of coping with smoking related illnesses. However, the Government needs to raise money for spending in areas where there are no consumers on whom the necessary taxes can be levied, such as defence, law and order, overseas aid and the cost of running the government and Parliament.

1.2 Social factors

Social justice lies at the heart of politics, since what some think of as just is regarded by others as completely unjust. Attitudes to the redistribution of wealth are a clear example.

In a free market some individuals generate greater amounts of income and capital than others and once wealth has been acquired, it tends to grow through the reinvestment of investment income received. This can lead to the rich getting richer and the poor poorer, with economic power becoming concentrated in relatively few hands.

Some electors make the value judgement that these trends should be countered by **taxation policies which redistribute income and wealth** away from the rich towards the poor. This is one of the key arguments in favour of some sort of capital gains tax and inheritance tax, taxes which, relative to the revenue raised, cost a great deal to collect.

Different taxes have different social effects:

(a) **Direct taxes** based on income and profits (income tax), gains (capital gains tax) or wealth (inheritance tax) **tax only those who have these resources**.

(b) **Indirect taxes** paid by the consumer (VAT) **discourage spending** and encourage saving. Lower or nil rates of tax can be levied on essentials, such as food.

(c) **Progressive taxes** such as income tax, where the proportion of the income or gains paid over in tax increases as income/gains rise, **target those who can afford to pay**. Personal allowances and the rates of taxation can be adjusted so as to ensure that those on very low incomes pay little or no tax.

(d) Taxes on capital or wealth ensure that that people cannot avoid taxation by having an income of zero and just living off the sale of capital assets.

Almost everyone would argue that taxation should be **equitable** or 'fair', but there are many different views as to what is equitable.

An **efficient tax** is one where the costs of collection are low relative to the tax paid over to the government. The government publishes figures for the administrative costs incurred by government departments in operating the taxation systems, but there are also compliance costs to be taken into account. Compliance costs are those incurred by the taxpayer, whether they be the individual preparing tax returns under the self assessment system or the employer operating the PAYE system to collect income tax or the business collecting value added tax. Some of the more equitable taxes may be less efficient to collect.

1.3 Environmental factors

The taxation system is moving slowly to accommodate the environmental concerns which have come to the fore over the last twenty years or so, especially the concerns about renewable and non-renewable sources of energy and global warming.

Examples of tax changes which have been introduced for environmental reasons are:

(a)   the **climate change levy**, raised on businesses in proportion to their consumption of energy. Its claimed purpose is to encourage reduced consumption;

(b)   the **landfill tax** levied on the operators of landfill sites on each tonne of rubbish/waste processed at the site. Its claimed purpose is to encourage recycling by taxing waste which has to be stored;

(c)   the changes to rules on the lease or purchase of cars, and taxation of **cars and private fuel provided for employees** to be dependent on CO_2 emissions. Its claimed purpose is to encourage the manufacture and purchase of low CO_2 emission cars to reduce emissions into the atmosphere caused by driving.

Only the last of these will be directly felt by individuals, even if the other taxes are passed on by being factored into a business's overheads.

2 Different types of taxes

FAST FORWARD ▶▶

> Central government raises revenue through a wide range of taxes. Tax law is made by statute.

2.1 Taxes in the UK

Central government raises revenue through a wide range of taxes. Tax law is made by **statute.**

The main taxes, their incidence and their sources, are set out in the table below.

Tax	Suffered by	Source
Income tax	**Individuals** **Partnerships**	Capital Allowances Act 2001 (CAA 2001); Income Tax (Earnings and Pensions) Act 2003 (ITEPA 2003); Income Tax (Trading and Other Income) Act 2005 (ITTOIA 2005); Income Tax Act 2007 (ITA 2007)
Corporation tax	**Companies**	CAA 2001 as above, Corporation Tax Act 2009 (CTA 2009), Corporation Tax Act 2010 (CTA 2010)
Capital gains tax	**Individuals** **Partnerships** **Companies** (which pay tax on capital gains in the form of corporation tax)	Taxation of Chargeable Gains Act 1992 (TCGA 1992)
Inheritance tax	**Individuals** **Trustees**	Inheritance Tax Act 1984 (IHTA 1984)
Value added tax	**Businesses**, both incorporated and unincorporated	Value Added Tax Act 1994 (VATA 1994)

You will also meet National Insurance. **National insurance is payable by employers, employees and the self employed.**

Further details of all these taxes are found later in this Text.

The other taxes referred to in the previous section, such as landfill tax, are not examinable at F6.

Finance Acts are passed each year, incorporating proposals set out in the **Budget**. They make changes which apply mainly to the tax year ahead. **This Study Text includes the provisions of the Finance Act 2011**. This is the Finance Act **examinable in June and December 2012**.

2.2 Revenue and capital taxes

Revenue taxes are those charged on income. In this Text this covers:

(a) **income tax,**
(b) **corporation tax**, and
(c) **national insurance**.

Capital taxes are those charged on capital gains or on wealth. In this Text this covers:

(a) **capital gains tax** and
(b) **inheritance tax.**

2.3 Direct and indirect taxes

Direct taxes are those charged on **income, gains and wealth**. **Income tax, national insurance, corporation tax, capital gains tax** and **inheritance tax** are **direct taxes**. Direct taxes are collected directly from the taxpayer.

Indirect taxes are those **paid by the consumer to the supplier** who then passes the tax to the Government. **Value added tax** is an indirect tax.

3 Principal sources of revenue law and practice

FAST FORWARD

> Tax is administered by HM Revenue and Customs (HMRC).

3.1 The overall structure of the UK tax system

The **Treasury** formally imposes and collects taxation. The management of the Treasury is the responsibility of the Chancellor of the Exchequer. **The administrative function for the collection of tax is undertaken by Her Majesty's Revenue and Customs (HMRC).**

The HMRC staff are referred to in the tax legislation as **'Officers of the Revenue and Customs'**. They are responsible for supervising the self-assessment system and agreeing tax liabilities. Officers who collect tax may be referred to as **receivable management officers**. These officers are local officers who are responsible for following up amounts of unpaid tax referred to them by the **HMRC Accounts Office.**

The **Revenue and Customs Prosecutions Office (R&CPO)** provides legal advice and institute and conducts criminal prosecutions in England and Wales where there has been an investigation by HMRC.

Tax appeals are heard by the **Tax Tribunal** which is made up of **two tiers:**

(a) **First Tier Tribunal**, and
(b) **Upper Tribunal**

The **First Tier Tribunal deals with most cases** other than complex cases. The **Upper Tribunal deals with complex cases** which either involve an important issue of tax law or a large financial sum. The Upper Tribunal **also hears appeals** against decisions of the First Tier Tribunal. We look at the appeals system in more detail later in this Text.

3.2 Different sources of revenue law

As stated above, taxes are imposed by statute. This comprises not only **Acts of Parliament** but also regulations laid down by **Statutory Instruments**. Statute is interpreted and amplified by **case law**.

HM Revenue and Customs also issue:

(a) **Statements of practice**, setting out how they intend to apply the law

(b) **Extra-statutory concessions**, setting out circumstances in which they will not apply the strict letter of the law where it would be unfair. Following the case of *R v HM Commissioners of Inland Revenue ex p Wilkinson (2005)* which clarified the scope of HM Revenue and Custom's power to make extra-statutory concessions, a number of concessions have been withdrawn and instead their effect given statutory force by statutory instrument..

(c) A wide range of **explanatory leaflets**

(d) **Business economic notes**. These are notes on particular types of business, which are used as background information by HMRC and are also published

(e) **Revenue and Customs Brief**. This is gives HMRC's view on specific points

(f) The **Internal Guidance**, a series of manuals used by HMRC staff

(g) **Working Together**, for tax practitioners

A great deal of information and HMRC publications can be found on the HM Revenue and Customs Internet site (www.hmrc.gov.uk).

Although the HMRC publications do not generally have the force of law, some of the VAT notices do where power has been delegated under regulations. This applies, for example, to certain administrative aspects of the cash accounting scheme.

3.3 The interaction of the UK tax system with that of other tax jurisdictions

3.3.1 The European Union

Membership of the European Union has a significant effect on UK taxes although there is not yet a general requirement imposed on the EU member states to move to a common system of taxation or to harmonise their individual tax systems. The states may, however, agree jointly to enact specific laws, known as '**Directives**', which provide for a common code of taxation within particular areas of their taxation systems.

The most important example to date is **VAT**, where the UK is obliged to pass its laws in conformity with the rules laid down in the European legislation. The VAT Directives still allow for a certain amount of flexibility between member states, eg in setting rates of taxation. There are only limited examples of Directives in the area of Direct Taxes, generally concerned with cross-border dividend and interest payments and corporate reorganisations.

However, under the EU treaties, member states are also obliged to permit freedom of movement of workers, freedom of movement of capital and freedom to establish business operations within the EU. These treaty provisions have '**direct effect**', ie a taxpayer is entitled to claim that a UK tax provision is ineffective because it **breaches one or more of the freedoms** guaranteed under European Law.

The European Court of Justice has repeatedly held that taxation provisions which discriminate against non-residents (ie treat a non-resident less favourably than a resident in a similar situation) are contrary to European Law, unless there is a very strong public interest justification.

There are provisions regarding the **exchange of information** between European Union Revenue authorities.

3.3.2 Other countries

The UK has entered into **double tax treaties** with various countries, such as the USA. These contain rules which prevent income and gains being taxed twice, but often include non-discrimination provisions, preventing a foreign national from being treated more harshly than a national. There are also usually rules for the **exchange of information** between the different Revenue authorities.

Even where there is no double tax relief, the UK tax system gives some relief for foreign taxes paid.

4 Tax avoidance and tax evasion

FAST FORWARD Tax avoidance is the legal minimisation of tax liabilities, tax evasion is illegal.

4.1 Tax evasion

Tax evasion consists of seeking to pay too little tax by deliberately misleading HMRC by either:

(a) **suppressing information to which they are entitled** (eg failing to notify HMRC that you are liable to tax, understating income or gains or omitting to disclose a relevant fact, eg that business expenditure had a dual motive), or

(b) **providing them with deliberately false information** (eg deducting expenses which have not been incurred or claiming capital allowances on plant that has not been purchased).

Tax evasion is illegal. Minor cases of tax evasion have generally been settled out of court on the payment of penalties. However, there is now a **statutory offence of evading income tax**, which enables such matters as deliberate failure to operate PAYE to be dealt with in magistrates' courts.

Serious cases of tax evasion, particularly those involving fraud, will continue to be the subject of **criminal prosecutions** which may lead to **fines and/or imprisonment on conviction.**

4.2 Tax avoidance

Tax avoidance is more difficult to define.

In a very broad sense, it could include **any legal method of reducing your tax burden**, eg taking advantage of tax shelter opportunities explicitly offered by tax legislation such as ISAs. However, the term is more commonly used in a more narrow sense, to denote ingenious arrangements designed to produce unintended tax advantages for the taxpayer.

The effectiveness of tax avoidance schemes has often been examined in the courts. Traditionally the tax rules were applied to the legal form of transactions, although this principle was qualified in later cases. It was held that the Courts could disregard transactions which were preordained and solely designed to avoid tax.

Traditionally, the response of HMRC has been to seek to mend the **loopholes** in the law as they come to their attention. In general, there is a presumption that the effect of such changes should not be backdated.

There are **disclosure obligations** on promoters of certain tax **avoidance schemes**, and on taxpayers, to provide details to HMRC of any such schemes used by the taxpayer. This enables HMRC to introduce anti avoidance measures at the earliest opportunity.

4.3 The distinction between avoidance and evasion

The distinction between tax evasion and tax avoidance is generally clear cut, since tax avoidance is an entirely legal activity and does not entail misleading HMRC.

However, care should be taken in giving advice in some circumstances. For example, a taxpayer who does not return income or gains because he wrongly believes that he has successfully avoided having to pay tax on them may, as a result, be guilty of tax evasion.

4.4 The need for an ethical and professional approach

FAST FORWARD

If a client makes a material error or omission in a tax return, or fails to file a tax return, and does not correct the error, omission or failure when advised, the accountant should cease to act for the client, inform HMRC of this cessation and make a money laundering report.

Under self assessment, all taxpayers (whether individuals or companies) are responsible for disclosing their taxable income and gains and the deductions and reliefs they are claiming against them.

Many taxpayers arrange for their accountants to prepare and submit their tax returns. **The taxpayer is still the person responsible for submitting the return and for paying whatever tax becomes due**: the accountant is only acting as the taxpayer's agent.

The practising accountant often acts for taxpayers in their dealings with HMRC and situations can arise where the accountant has concerns as to whether the taxpayer is being honest in providing information to the accountant for onward transmission.

How the accountant deals with such situations is a matter of **professional judgement**, but in deciding what to do, the accountant will be expected to uphold the standards of the Association of Chartered Certified Accountants. He must act **honestly** and **objectively**, with **due care and diligence**, and showing the highest standards of **integrity**.

If an accountant learns of a material error or omission in a client's tax return or of a **failure to file a required tax return**, the accountant has a responsibility to **advise the client of the error, omission or failure** and **recommend that disclosure be made to HMRC**.

If the client, after having had a reasonable time to reflect, does not correct the error, omission or failure or authorise the accountant to do so on the client's behalf, the accountant should **inform the client in writing that it is not possible for the accountant to act for that client.**

The accountant should also **notify HMRC that the accountant no longer acts for the client but should not to provide details of the reason for ceasing to act**.

An accountant whose client refuses to make disclosure to HMRC, after having had notice of the error, omission or failure and a reasonable time to reflect, **must also report the client's refusal and the facts surrounding it to the Money Laundering Reporting Officer within the accountancy firm or to the appropriate authority (Serious Organised Crime Agency (SOCA)) if the accountant is a sole practitioner**.

Accountants who suspect or are aware of tax evasion activities by a client may themselves commit an offence if they do not report their suspicions. The accountant must not disclose to the client, or any one else, that such a report has been made if the accountant knows or suspects that to do so would be likely to prejudice any investigation which might be conducted following the report as this might constitute the criminal offence of 'tipping-off'.

Chapter Roundup

- Economic, social and environmental factors may affect the government's tax policies.
- Central government raises revenue through a wide range of taxes. Tax law is made by statute.
- Tax is administered by HM Revenue and Customs (HMRC).
- Tax avoidance is the legal minimisation of tax liabilities, tax evasion is illegal.
- If a client makes a material error or omission in a tax return, or fails to file a tax return, and does not correct the error, omission or failure when advised, the accountant should cease to act for the client, inform HMRC of this cessation and make a money laundering report.

Quick Quiz

1   What is the difference between a direct and an indirect tax?

2   What is an Extra Statutory Concession?

3   Tax avoidance is legal. TRUE /FALSE?

4   You work for a firm of accountants. A few weeks ago, you prepared a tax return for Serena. Serena has now told you that she forgot to include some bank interest in the return but that she does not intend to tell HMRC of the omission.

     Which ONE of the following actions should you NOT take?

     A   Inform Serena in writing that it is not possible for you to act for her

     B   Inform HMRC that you are no longer acting for Serena

     C   Inform HMRC about the details of Serena's omission

     D   Report Serena's refusal to disclose the omission to HMRC and the facts surrounding it to your firm's Money Laundering Reporting Officer

Answers to Quick Quiz

1   A direct tax is one charged on income or gains; an indirect tax is paid by a consumer to the supplier, who then passes it to HMRC.

2   An Extra Statutory Concession is a relaxation by HMRC of the strict rules where their imposition would be unfair.

3   True. Tax avoidance is legal; tax evasion is illegal.

4   C

    You are not required to inform HMRC about the details of Serena's omission.

P
A
R
T

B

Income tax and national insurance contributions

The computation of taxable income and the income tax liability

Topic list	Syllabus reference
1 The scope of income tax	B1(a)
2 Computing taxable income	B5(a)
3 Various types of income	B4(f), (g), B5(a)
4 Tax exempt income	B4(h)
5 Deductible interest	B5(d)
6 Allowances deductible from net income	B5(b)
7 Computing tax payable	B5(c)
8 Gift Aid	B5(e)
9 Jointly held property	B5(f) B6(c)

Introduction

In the previous chapter we considered the UK tax system generally. Now we look at income tax, which is the tax applied on the income individuals make from their jobs, their businesses and their savings and investments. We consider the scope of income tax and see how to collect together all of an individual's income in a personal tax computation, and we also see which income can be excluded as being exempt from tax.

Next we look at the circumstances in which interest paid can be deducted in the income tax computation.

Each individual is entitled to a personal allowance, and only if that is exceeded will any tax be due. Older taxpayers are entitled to a higher allowance, the age allowance.

We then learn how to work out the tax on the individual's taxable income, and we see how donations to charity under the gift aid scheme can save tax.

Finally we consider how income from property held jointly by married couples or civil partners is allocated for tax purposes.

In later chapters, we look at particular types of income in more detail.

Study guide

		Intellectual level
B1	**The scope of income tax**	
(a)	Explain how the residence of an individual is determined.	1
B4	**Property and investment income**	
(f)	Compute the tax payable on savings income.	2
(g)	Compute the tax payable on dividend income.	2
(h)	Explain the treatment of individual savings accounts (ISAs) and other tax exempt investments.	1
B5	**The comprehensive computation of taxable income and income tax liability**	
(a)	Prepare a basic income tax computation involving different types of income.	2
(b)	Calculate the amount of personal allowance available generally, and for people aged 65 and above.	2
(c)	Compute the amount of income tax payable.	2
(d)	Explain the treatment of interest paid for a qualifying purpose.	2
(e)	Explain the treatment of gift aid donations.	1
(f)	Explain the treatment of property owned jointly by a married couple, or by a couple in a civil partnership.	1
B6	**The use of exemptions and reliefs in deferring and minimising income tax liabilities**	
(c)	Explain how a married couple or a couple in a civil partnership can minimise their tax liabilities.	2

Exam guide

It is very likely that you will have to prepare an income tax computation in your exam. You should familiarise yourself with the layout of the computation, and the three types of income: non-savings, savings and dividends. It is then a simple matter of slotting the final figures into the computation from supporting workings for the different types of income.

Gift aid donations are likely to feature regularly. You will come across the technique of increasing the basic rate and higher rate limits again when you deal with pensions later in this Text.

1 The scope of income tax

An individual may be resident and/or ordinarily resident in the UK. His liability to UK income tax will be determined accordingly.

1.1 Introduction

A taxpayer's **residence and ordinary residence** have important consequences in establishing the tax treatment of his UK and overseas income and capital gains.

1.2 Residence

An individual is resident in the UK for a given tax year if, in that tax year, he satisfies either of the following criteria.

(a) **He is present in the UK for 183 days or more.**

(b) He makes substantial annual visits to the UK. **Visits averaging 91 days or more a year for each of four** or more consecutive years will usually make the person resident for each of these tax years (for someone emigrating from the UK, the four years are reduced to three).

If days are spent in the UK because of exceptional circumstances beyond the individual's control (such as illness), those days are ignored for the purposes of the 91 day rule (but not for the 183 day rule above).

Generally, an individual is present in the UK on a particular day if he is in the UK at midnight.

1.3 Ordinary residence

A person who is resident in the UK will be ordinarily resident in the UK where his residence in the UK is of a habitual nature. Ordinary residence implies a greater degree of permanence than residence.

A person who is resident in the UK and who goes abroad for a period which does not include a complete tax year is regarded as remaining resident and ordinarily resident in the UK throughout the period of absence.

1.4 Tax consequences

Generally, a UK resident is liable to UK income tax on his UK and overseas income whereas a non-UK resident is liable to UK income tax only on income arising in the UK.

Exam focus point

The taxation of the overseas income of a UK resident and the taxation of non-UK residents is outside the scope of your syllabus.

2 Computing taxable income

In a personal income tax computation, we bring together income from all sources, splitting the sources into non-savings, savings and dividend income.

 PER alert

This section relates to your PER requirement:
19   Evaluate and compute taxes payable

An individual's income from all sources is brought together (aggregated) in a personal tax computation. Three columns are needed to distinguish between non-savings income, savings income and dividend income. Here is an example. All items are explained later in this Text.

RICHARD: INCOME TAX COMPUTATION 2011/12

	Non-savings income £	Savings income £	Dividend income £	Total £
Income from employment	46,600			
Building society interest		1,000		
National Savings & Investments interest		400		
UK dividends			1,000	
Total income	46,600	1,400	1,000	
Less interest paid	(2,000)			
Net income	44,600	1,400	1,000	47,000
Less personal allowance	(7,475)			
Taxable income	37,125	1,400	1,000	39,525

	£	£
Income tax		
Non savings income		
£35,000 × 20%		7,000
£2,125 × 40%		850
		7,850
Savings income		
£1,400 × 40%		560
Dividend income		
£1,000 × 32.5%		325
Tax liability		8,735
Less tax suffered		
Tax credit on dividend income	100	
PAYE tax on salary (say)	7,500	
Tax on building society interest	200	
		(7,800)
Tax payable		935

Key term

> **Total income** is all income subject to income tax. Each of the amounts which make up total income is called a component. **Net income** is total income after deductible interest and trade losses. **Taxable income** is net income less the personal allowance or age allowance. The **tax liability** is the amount of tax charged on the individual's income. **Tax payable** is the balance of the liability still to be settled in cash.

Income tax is charged on **taxable income**. Non-savings income is dealt with first, then savings income and then dividend income.

For non-savings income, income up to £35,000 (the basic rate limit) is taxed at the basic rate (20%), income between £35,000 and £150,000 (the higher rate limit) at the higher rate (40%) and any remaining income at the additional rate (50%). We will look at the taxation of the other types of income later in this chapter.

The remainder of this chapter gives more details of the income tax computation.

3 Various types of income

3.1 Classification of income

All income received must be **classified** according to the nature of the income. This is because different computational rules apply to different types of income. The main types of income are:

(a)   **Income from employment and pensions**
(b)   **Profits of trades, professions and vocations**
(c)   **Income from property letting**
(d)   **Savings and investment income, including interest and dividends.**

The rules for computing employment income, profits from trades, professions and vocations and property letting income will be covered in later chapters. These types of income are **non-savings income**. Pension income is also non-savings income.

FAST FORWARD

> An individual may receive interest net of 20% tax suffered at source. The amount received must be grossed up by multiplying by 100/80 and must be included gross in the income tax computation. Dividends are received net of a 10% tax credit and must be grossed up for inclusion in the tax computation.

3.2 Savings income

3.2.1 What is savings income?

Savings income is interest. Interest is paid on bank and building society accounts, on Government securities, such as Treasury Stock, and on company debentures and loan stock.

Interest may be paid net of 20% tax or it may be paid gross.

3.2.2 Savings income received net of 20% tax

The following savings income is received net of 20% tax. **This is called income taxed at source.**

(a)   Bank and building society interest paid to individuals
(b)   Interest paid to individuals by unlisted UK companies on debentures and loan stocks

The reason this income is received net of 20% tax is that HMRC initially assumes that all taxpayers are only liable to income tax at the basic rate of 20%. The bank or building society deducts the basic rate tax at source and pays it to HMRC on behalf of the taxpayers. This eliminates the need for a large number of taxpayers to fill out a tax return. There may however be further tax to pay on the savings income, if, for example, the taxpayer is a higher or additional rate taxpayer and so a tax return will have to be completed,

The amount received is grossed up by multiplying by 100/80 and is included gross in the income tax computation. The basic rate tax deducted at source is then deducted in computing tax payable and may be repaid.

Exam focus point

> In examinations you may be given either the net or the gross amount of such income: read the question carefully. If you are given the net amount (the amount received or credited), you should gross up the figure at the rate of 20%. For example, net building society interest of £160 is equivalent to gross income of £160 × 100/80 = £200 on which tax of £40 (20% of £200) has been suffered.

3.2.3 Savings income received gross

Some savings income is received gross, ie without tax having been deducted. Examples are:

(a)   National Savings & Investments interest including interest from Easy Access Savings Accounts (EASAs), Investment Accounts, Income Bonds

(b)   Interest on government securities (these are also called 'gilts')

(c)   Interest from quoted company debentures and loan stock.

3.3 Dividend income

Dividends on UK shares are received net of a 10% tax credit. This means a dividend of £90 has a £10 tax credit, giving gross income of £100 to include in the income tax computation. The tax credit can be deducted in computing tax payable **but it cannot be repaid.**

4 Tax exempt income

4.1 Types of tax exempt investments

This section relates to your PER requirement:
20   Assist with tax planning

Income from certain investments is exempt from income tax. They are therefore useful for tax planning to minimise tax from investments.

In the examination you may be given details of exempt income. You should state in your answer that the income is exempt to show that you have considered it and have not just overlooked it.

4.2 Individual savings accounts

An individual savings account (ISA) is a special tax exempt way of saving. In 2011/12 an individual can invest £10,680 in ISAs, of which up to £5,340 can be held as cash.

The ISA limits will be given to you in the Tax Rates and Allowances in the examination paper.

Funds invested in ISAs can be used to buy stock market investments, such as shares in quoted companies or OEICs, units in unit trusts, fixed interest investments, or insurance policies.

Dividend income and interest received from ISAs is exempt from income tax, whether it is paid out to the investor or retained and reinvested within the ISA. Similarly, capital gains made within an ISA are exempt from capital gains tax.

4.3 Savings certificates

Savings certificates are issued by National Savings and Investments (NS&I). They may be fixed rate certificates or index linked and are for fixed terms of between two and five years. On maturity the profit is tax exempt. This profit is often called interest.

4.4 Premium bonds

Prizes received from premium bonds are exempt from tax.

5 Deductible interest

FAST FORWARD

Deductible interest is deducted from total income to compute net income.

5.1 Interest payments

An individual who pays interest on a loan in a tax year is entitled to relief in that tax year if the loan is for one of the following purposes:

(a)   **Loan to buy plant or machinery for partnership use.** Interest is allowed for three years from the end of the tax year in which the loan was taken out. If the plant is used partly for private use, the allowable interest is apportioned.

(b) **Loan to buy plant or machinery for employment use.** Interest is allowed for three years from the end of the tax year in which the loan was taken out. If the plant is used partly for private use, the allowable interest is apportioned.

(c) **Loan to buy interest in employee-controlled company.** The company must be an unquoted trading company resident in the UK with at least 50% of the voting shares held by employees.

(d) **Loan to invest in a partnership.** The investment may be a share in the partnership or a contribution to the partnership of capital or a loan to the partnership. The individual must be a partner (other than a limited partner) and relief ceases when he ceases to be a partner.

(e) **Loan to invest in a co-operative.** The investment may be shares or a loan. The individual must spend the greater part of his time working for the co-operative.

Tax relief is given by deducting the interest from total income to calculate net income for the tax year in which the interest is paid. It is deducted from **non-savings income first, then from savings income and lastly from dividend income**.

5.2 Example

Frederick is aged 35 and in 2011/12 has taxable trading income of £45,000, savings income of £1,320 (gross) and dividend income of £1,000 (gross).

Frederick pays interest of £1,370 in 2011/12 on a loan to invest in a partnership.

Frederick's net income for 2011/12 is:

	Non-savings income £	Savings income £	Dividend income £	Total £
Total income	45,000	1,320	1,000	
Less: interest paid	(1,370)			
Net income	43,630	1,320	1,000	45,950

6 Allowances deductible from net income

6.1 Personal allowance

FAST FORWARD

All persons are entitled to a personal allowance. It is deducted from net income, first against non savings income, then against savings income and lastly against dividend income. The personal allowance is reduced by £1 for every £2 that adjusted net income exceeds £100,000 and can be reduced to nil.

Once income from all sources has been aggregated and any deductible interest deducted, the remainder is the taxpayer's net income. An allowance, the **personal allowance**, is **deducted from net income**. Like deductible interest, it reduces non **savings income first, then savings income and lastly dividend income**.

All individuals under the age of 65 (including children) **are entitled to the personal allowance of £7,475.** However, if the **individual's adjusted net income exceeds £100,000**, the **personal allowance is reduced by £1 for each £2 by which adjusted net income exceeds £100,000 until the personal allowance is nil (which is when adjusted net income is £114,950 or more).**

Key term

> **Adjusted net income is net income less the gross amounts of personal pension contributions and gift aid donations.**

We will look at personal pension contributions and gift aid donations later in this Text and revisit this topic again then. At the moment, we will look at the situation where net income and adjusted net income are the same amounts.

Question

In 2011/12, Clare receives employment income of £95,000, bank interest of £6,400 and dividends of £6,750.

Calculate Clare's taxable income for 2011/12.

Answer

	Non-savings income £	Savings income £	Dividend income £	Total £
Employment income	95,000			
Bank interest £6,400 x 100/80		8,000		
Dividends £6,750 x 100/90			7,500	
Net income	95,000	8,000	7,500	110,500
Less: personal allowance (W)	(2,225)			
Taxable income	92,775	8,000	7,500	108,275

Working

Net income	110,500
Less income limit	(100,000)
Excess	10,500
Personal allowance	7,475
Less half excess £10,500 × ½	(5,250)
	2,225

Where an individual has an adjusted net income between £100,000 and £114,950, the rate of tax on the income between these two amounts will usually be 60%. This is calculated as 40% (the higher rate on income) plus 20% basic rate tax extra payable as the result of the reduction of the personal allowance. The individual should consider **making personal pension contributions and/or gift aid donations to reduce adjusted net income to below £100,000.**

6.2 Age allowance

Taxpayers aged 65-74 are entitled to an age allowance and taxpayers aged 75 and over are entitled to a higher age allowance. The age allowance is reduced by £1 for every £2 that adjusted net income exceeds £24,000 but is generally not reduced below the amount of the personal allowance.

An individual aged 65-74 receives an age allowance of £9,940 instead of the personal allowance of £7,475.

An individual aged 75 or over receives a higher age allowance of £10,090 instead of the personal allowance of £7,475.

If the individual's adjusted net income exceeds £24,000 the age allowance is reduced by £1 for each £2 by which adjusted net income exceeds £24,000. The age allowance **cannot usually be reduced below the amount of the personal allowance (£7,475).** However, **if the individual has adjusted net income in excess of £100,000,** the **personal allowance will be reduced** as described in Section 6.1 above.

An individual is entitled to the age allowance, or higher age allowance, provided he attains the age of 65 or 75 respectively **before the end of the tax year,** or would have had he not died before his birthday.

Question

Three taxpayers have the following net income for 2011/12.

A   £25,350
B   £33,900
C   £29,210

Calculate their taxable income assuming taxpayers A and B are aged 68 and taxpayer C is aged 78.

Answer

	A	B	C
Taxable income is:	£	£	£
Net income	25,350	33,900	29,210
Less age allowance (W)	(9,265)	(7,475)	(7,485)
Taxable income	16,085	26,425	21,725
Working			
Net income	25,350	33,900	29,210
Less income limit	(24,000)	(24,000)	(24,000)
Excess	1,350	9,900	5,210
Age allowance	9,940	9,940	10,090
Less half excess £1,350/9,990/5,250 × 1/2	(675)	(4,950)	(2,605)
	9,265	4,990	7,485
Minimum		7,475	

7 Computing tax payable

FAST FORWARD

Work out income tax on the taxable income. Deduct the tax credit on dividend income and any income tax suffered at source to arrive at tax payable. The tax credit on dividend income cannot be repaid if it exceeds the tax liability calculated so far. Other tax suffered at source can be repaid.

PER alert

This section relates to your PER requirement:
19   Evaluate and compute taxes payable

7.1 Tax rates

Income tax payable is computed on an individual's taxable income, which comprises net income less the personal allowance or age allowance. The tax rates are applied to taxable income which is non-savings income first, then to savings income and finally to dividend income.

7.1.1 Savings income starting rate

There is a **tax rate of 10% for savings income up to £2,560 (the savings income starting rate limit)**. This rate is called the **savings income starting rate**.

The savings income starting rate only applies where the savings income falls wholly or partly below the starting rate limit. Remember that income tax is charged first on non-savings income. So, in most cases, an individual's non-savings income will exceed the savings income starting rate limit and the savings income starting rate will not be available on savings income.

Part B Income tax and national insurance contributions | **2: The computation of taxable income and the income tax liability**   23

7.1.2 Basic rate

The basic rate of tax is 20% for 2011/12 for both non-savings income and savings income. The basic rate of tax is 10% for 2011/12 for dividend income. The basic rate limit for 2011/12 is £35,000.

Question — Savings income starting rate and basic rate

Joe is aged 55. In 2011/12, he earns a salary of £8,500 from a part-time job and receives bank interest of £4,000. Calculate Joe's tax liability for 2011/12.

Answer

	Non-savings income £	Savings income £	Total £
Employment income	8,500		
Bank interest £4,000 × 100/80		5,000	
Net income	8,500	5,000	13,500
Less: personal allowance	(7,475)		
Taxable income	1,025	5,000	6,025

	£
Income tax	
Non-savings income	
£1,025 × 20 %	205
Savings income	
£(2,560 − 1,025) = 1,535 × 10%	153
£(5,000 − 1,535) = 3,465 × 20%	693
Tax liability	1,051

7.1.3 Higher rate

The higher rate of tax is 40% for 2011/12 for non-savings and savings income. The higher rate of tax is 32.5% for 2011/12 for dividend income. The higher rate limit for 2011/12 is £150,000.

Question — Basic rate and higher rate

Margery is aged 35. In 2011/12, she has employment income of £36,900, receives building society interest of £2,000 and dividends of £9,000. Calculate Margery's tax liability for 2011/12.

Answer

	Non-savings income £	Savings income £	Dividend income £	Total £
Employment income	36,900			
BSI £2,000 × 100/80		2,500		
Dividends £9,000 × 100/90			10,000	
Net income	36,900	2,500	10,000	49,400
Less: personal allowance	(7,475)			
Taxable income	29,425	2,500	10,000	41,925

Income tax

	£
Non-savings income	
£29,425 × 20%	5,885
Savings income	
£2,500 × 20%	500
Dividend income	
£(35,000 − 29,425 − 2,500) = 3,075 × 10%	307
£(10,000 − 3,075) = 6,925 × 32.5%	2,251
Tax liability	8,943

7.1.4 Additional rate

The additional rate of tax is 50% for 2011/12 for non-savings and savings income.

The additional rate of tax is 42.5% for 2011/12 for dividend income.

The additional rate of tax applies to taxable income in excess of the higher rate limit which is £150,000 for 2011/12.

Question   **Additional rate**

In 2011/12, Julian has employment income of £148,000, receives bank interest of £5,000 and dividends of £18,000. Calculate Julian's tax liability for 2011/12.

Answer

	Non-savings income £	Savings income £	Dividend income £	Total £
Employment income	148,000			
Bank interest £5,000 × 100/80		6,250		
Dividends £18,000 × 100/90			20,000	
Taxable income (no personal allowance available)	148,000	6,250	20,000	174,250

	£
Income tax	
Non-savings income	
£35,000 × 20 %	7,000
£(148,000 − 35,000) = 113,000 × 40%	45,200
Savings income	
£(150,000 − 148,000) = 2,000 × 40%	800
£(6,250 − 2,000) = 4,250 × 50%	2,125
Dividend income	
£20,000 × 42.5%	8,500
Tax liability	63,625

7.2 Steps in the income tax computation

We now summarise the steps required in a full income tax computation and then show examples of the different computations you might be asked to prepare in the examination. You have already met all the steps separately earlier in this chapter.

Step 1 **The first step in preparing a personal tax computation is to set up three columns**
One column for non-savings income, one for savings income and one for dividend income. Add up income from different sources. The sum of these is known as 'total income'. Deduct deductible interest and trade losses to compute 'net income'. Deduct the personal allowance or age allowance to compute 'taxable income'.

Step 2 **Deal with non-savings income first**
Any non-savings income up to the basic rate limit of £35,000 is taxed at 20%. Non-savings income between the basic rate limit and the higher rate limit of £150,000 is taxed at 40%. The maximum non-savings income to which the higher rate applies is therefore £(150,000 – 35,000) = £115,000. Any further non-savings income is taxed at 50%.

Step 3 **Now deal with savings income**
If savings income is below the starting rate limit of £2,560, it is taxed at the savings income starting rate of 10% up to the starting rate limit. Savings income between the starting rate limit and the basic rate limit of £35,000 is taxed at 20%. Savings income between the basic rate limit and the higher rate limit of £150,000 is taxed at 40%, so again, the maximum savings income to which the higher rate applies is therefore £(150,000 – 35,000) = £115,000. Any further savings income is taxed at 50%. In most cases, non-savings income and savings income can be added together and tax calculated on the total, provided that the savings income starting rate does not apply.

Step 4 **Lastly, tax dividend income**
If dividend income is below the basic rate limit of £35,000, it is taxed at 10%. Dividend income between the basic rate limit and the higher rate limit of £150,000 (maximum £115,000) is taxed at 32.5%. Any further dividend income is taxed at 42.5%.

Step 5 Add the amounts of tax together. The resulting figure is the **income tax liability**.

Step 6 Next, **deduct the tax credit on dividends**. This tax credit cannot be repaid if it exceeds the tax liability calculated so far.

Step 7 Finally **deduct the tax deducted at source** from savings income such as bank interest and from employment income under the Pay As You Earn (PAYE) scheme. These **amounts can be repaid to the extent that they exceed the income tax liability**.

7.3 Examples: personal tax computations

(a) Kathe has a salary of £16,000 and receives dividends of £4,500.

	Non-savings income £	Dividend income £	Total £
Earnings	16,000		
Dividends £4,500 × 100/90		5,000	
Net income	16,000	5,000	21,000
Less personal allowance	(7,475)		
Taxable income	8,525	5,000	13,525

	£
Income tax	
Non savings income	
£8,525 × 20%	1,705
Dividend income	
£5,000 × 10%	500
Tax liability	2,205
Less tax credit on dividend £5,000 × 10%	(500)
Tax payable	1,705

The dividend income falls below the basic rate limit so it is taxed at 10%.

Some of the tax payable has probably already been paid on the salary under PAYE.

(b)   Jules has a salary of £20,000, business profits of £34,400, net dividends of £6,750 and building society interest of £3,000 net. He is entitled to relief on interest paid of £2,000.

	Non-savings income £	Savings income £	Dividend income £	Total £
Business profits	34,400			
Employment income	20,000			
Dividends £6,750 × 100/90			7,500	
Building society interest £3,000 × 100/80	–	3,750	-	
Total income	54,400	3,750	7,500	
Less interest paid	(2,000)			
Net income	52,400	3,750	7,500	63,650
Less personal allowance	(7,475)			
Taxable income	44,925	3,750	7,500	56,175

Income tax	£
Non savings income	
£35,000 × 20%	7,000
£(44,925 − 35,000) = 9,925 × 40%	3,970
Savings income	
£3,750 × 40%	1,500
Dividend income	
£7,500 × 32.5%	2,437
Tax liability	14,907
Less tax credit on dividend income £7,500 × 10%	(750)
Less tax deducted at source on building society interest £3,750 × 20%	(750)
Tax payable	13,407

Savings income and dividend income fall above the basic rate limit but below the higher rate limit so they are taxed at 40% and 32.5% respectively.

(c)   Jim does not work. He receives net bank interest of £40,000. He is entitled to relief on interest paid of £2,000.

	Savings income £	Total £
Bank interest £40,000 × 100/80/Total income	50,000	
Less interest paid	(2,000)	
Net income	48,000	48,000
Less personal allowance	(7,475)	
Taxable income	40,525	40,525

	£
Savings income	
£2,560 × 10%	256
£(35,000 − 2,560) = 32,440 × 20%	6,488
£5,525 × 40%	2,210
Tax liability	8,954
Less tax deducted at source £50,000 × 20%	(10,000)
Tax repayable	(1,046)

The savings income starting rate applies to the first £2,560 of savings income. The income up to the basic rate limit is then £(35,000 − 2,560) = £32,440.

(d)   Duncan has a salary of £160,000 (PAYE deducted £50,000) and receives dividends of £45,000.

	Non-savings income £	Dividend income £	Total £
Earnings	160,000		
Dividends £45,000 × 100/90		50,000	
Net income/Taxable income	160,000	50,000	210,000

	£
Income tax	
Non savings income	
£35,000 × 20%	7,000
£(150,000 – 35,000) = 115,000 × 40%	46,000
£10,000 × 50%	5,000
Dividend income	
£50,000 × 42.5%	21,250
Tax liability	79,250
Less tax credit on dividend £50,000 × 10%	(5,000)
Less tax deducted under PAYE	(50,000)
Tax payable	24,250

Duncan is not entitled to the personal allowance as his net income exceeds £114,950.

7.4 The complete proforma

Here is a complete proforma computation of taxable income. It is probably too much for you to absorb at this stage, but refer back to it as you come to the chapters dealing with the types of income shown. You will also see how trading losses fit into the proforma later in this study text.

	Non-savings income £	Savings income £	Dividend income £	Total £
Trading income	X			
Employment income	X			
Property business income	X			
Bank/building society interest (gross)		X		
Other interest (gross)		X		
(as many lines as necessary)				
Dividends (gross)			X	
Total income	X	X	X	
Less interest paid	(X)	(X)	(X)	
Net income	X	X	X	X
Less personal allowance	(X)	(X)	(X)	
Taxable income	X	X	X	X

8 Gift Aid

FAST FORWARD

Increase the basic rate limit and the higher rate limit by the gross amount of any gift aid payment to give tax relief at the higher and additional rates.

8.1 Gift aid donations

Key term

One-off and regular charitable gifts of money qualify for tax relief under the **gift aid scheme** provided the donor gives the charity a gift aid declaration.

Gift aid declarations can be made in writing, electronically through the internet or orally over the phone. A declaration can cover a one-off gift or any number of gifts made after a specified date (which may be in the past).

The gift must not be repayable and must not confer any more than a minimal benefit on the donor.

8.2 Tax relief for gift aid donations

A gift aid donation is treated as though it is paid net of basic rate tax (20%). This gives basic rate tax relief when the payment is made. **Additional tax relief for higher rate and additional rate taxpayers is given in the personal tax computation by increasing the donor's basic rate limit and higher rate limit by the gross amount of the gift.** To arrive at the gross amount of the gift you must multiply the amount paid by 100/80. The effect of increasing the basic rate limit is to increase the amount on which basic rate tax is payable and so to adjust the tax liability for the basic rate tax relief already given. This is sometimes called 'extending the basic rate band'. The effect of increasing the higher rate limit is simply to preserve the amount of taxable income on which higher rate tax is payable.

No additional relief is due for basic rate taxpayers. Increasing the basic rate limit is irrelevant as taxable income is below this limit.

Question	Gift Aid with higher rate relief

James earns a salary of £66,000 but has no other income. In 2011/12 he paid £8,000 (net) under the gift aid scheme. Compute James' income tax liability for 2011/12.

Answer

		Non-savings Income £
Salary/Net income		66,000
Less: personal allowance		(7,475)
Taxable income		58,525
Income tax	£	£
Basic rate	35,000 × 20%	7,000
Basic rate (increased limit)	10,000 × 20%	2,000
Higher rate	13,525 × 40%	5,410
	58,525	14,410

Question	Gift Aid with additional rate relief

Matt has trading income of £182,000 in 2011/12. In January 2012, he made a gift aid donation of £12,000 (net). Compute Matt's income tax liability for 2011/12.

Answer

		Non-savings Income £
Taxable income (no PA as income over £114,950)		182,000
Income tax	£	£
Basic rate	35,000 × 20%	7,000
Basic rate (increased limit)	15,000 × 20%	3,000
Higher rate	115,000 × 40%	46,000
Additional rate	17,000 × 50%	8,500
	182,000	64,500

The basic rate limit is increased by the gross amount of the gift (£12,000 × 100/80). The basic rate limit is therefore £(35,000 + 15,000) = £50,000. The higher rate limit is also increased by the gross amount of the gift aid donation and so becomes £(150,000 + 15,000)= £165,000. The higher rate therefore applies to income between £(165,000 – 50,000) = £115,000. The additional rate is applicable to £(182,000 – 165,000) = £17,000.

8.3 Adjusted net income

Adjusted net income is net income less the gross amounts of personal pension contributions and gift aid donations. The restrictions on the personal allowance and age allowance are calculated in relation to adjusted net income.

Question

Adjusted net income

Margaretta earns a salary of £110,000 in 2011/12. In January 2012, she made a gift aid donation of £5,000.

Compute Margaretta's income tax liability for 2011/12.

Answer

		Non-savings income
		£
Salary/Net income		110,000
Less: personal allowance (W)		(5,600)
Taxable income		104,400

Income tax	£	£
Basic rate	35,000 × 20%	7,000
Basic rate (increased limit)	6,250 × 20%	1,250
Higher rate	63,150 × 40%	25,260
	104,400	33,510

Working	£
Net income	110,000
Less: gift aid donation £5,000 × 100/80	(6,250)
Adjusted net income	103,750
Less: income limit	(100,000)
Excess	3,750
Personal allowance	7,475
Less half excess £3,750 × ½	(1,875)
	5,600

9 Jointly held property

Income on property held jointly by married couples and members of a civil partnership is treated as if it were shared equally unless the couple make a joint declaration of the actual shares of ownership.

This section relates to your PER requirement:
20   Assist with tax planning

9.1 Allocation of joint income

If property is held jointly by a married couple or civil partners the income arising from that property is taxed as if it was shared equally between the members of the couple.

Civil partners are members of a same sex couple which has registered as a civil partnership under the Civil Partnerships Act 2004.

This 50:50 split of income from jointly held property applies even if the property is not owned in equal shares, **unless the members of the couple make a joint declaration to HMRC specifying the actual proportion to which each is entitled.**

9.2 Example: joint income

Janet owns 40% of a holiday cottage and John, her husband, owns the other 60%.

If no declaration is made each will be taxed on one half of the income arising when the property is let out.

If a declaration is made, Janet will be taxed on her 40% of the income and John will be taxed on his 60%.

9.3 Tax planning for married couples/civil partners

Where one member of a married couple/civil partnership is a basic rate taxpayer and the other a higher rate taxpayer, income tax liabilities can be minimised by transferring income producing assets from the higher rate taxpayer to the other spouse or civil partner.

If assets are owned jointly but in unequal proportions, then:

(a)   if the taxpayer who pays tax at a higher rate of tax than the other spouse/civil partner owns more than 50% of the asset, no declaration of beneficial interest should be made so that the income is shared equally, or

(b)   if the taxpayer who pays tax at a higher rate of tax than the other spouse/civil partner owns less than 50% of the asset, a declaration of beneficial interest should be made so that the other spouse or civil partner is taxed on their full amount of income at the lower tax rate.

Thus in the above example a declaration is beneficial, for example, if Janet is a higher rate taxpayer whilst John is a basic rate taxpayer or if Janet is an additional rate taxpayer and John is either a higher rate or basic rate taxpayer.

Chapter Roundup

- An individual may be resident and/or ordinarily resident in the UK. His liability to UK income tax will be determined accordingly.

- In a personal income tax computation, we bring together income from all sources, splitting the sources into non-savings, savings and dividend income.

- An individual may receive interest net of 20% tax suffered at source. The amount received must be grossed up by multiplying by 100/80 and must be included gross in the income tax computation. Dividends are received net of a 10% tax credit and must be grossed up for inclusion in the tax computation.

- Deductible interest is deducted from total income to compute net income.

- All persons are entitled to a personal allowance. It is deducted from net income, first against non savings income, then against savings income and lastly against dividend income. The personal allowance is reduced by £1 for every £2 that adjusted net income exceeds £100,000 and can be reduced to nil.

- Taxpayers aged 65-74 are entitled to an age allowance and taxpayers aged 75 and over are entitled to a higher age allowance. The age allowance is reduced by £1 for every £2 that adjusted net income exceeds £24,000 but is generally not reduced below the amount of the personal allowance.

- Work out income tax on the taxable income. Deduct the tax credit on dividend income and any income tax suffered at source to arrive at tax payable. The tax credit on dividend income cannot be repaid if it exceeds the tax liability calculated so far. Other tax suffered at source can be repaid.

- Increase the basic rate limit and the higher rate limit by the gross amount of any gift aid payment to give tax relief at the higher and additional rates.

- Income on property held jointly by married couples and members of a civil partnership is treated as if it were shared equally unless the couple make a joint declaration of the actual shares of ownership.

Quick Quiz

1   When will an individual be resident in the UK?

2   Income tax on non-savings income is charged at _ % below the basic rate limit, at _% between the basic rate limit and the higher rate limit, and at _% above the higher rate limit. Fill in the blanks.

3   Give one type of savings income that is received by individuals net of 20% tax.

4   How is dividend income taxed?

5   If Dennis has taxable income of £35,700 and makes gift aid payments of £400, on how much of his income will he pay higher rate tax?

    A   £200
    B   £300
    C   £400
    D   £500

6   Mike and Matt have registered a civil partnership. Mike owns 25% of an investment property and Matt owns 75%. How will the income be taxed?

Answers to Quick Quiz

1   An individual is resident in the UK if he is here for 183 days or more, or he makes visits to the UK averaging 91 days or more a year for each of four consecutive years.

2   Income tax on non-savings income is charged at **20%** below the basic rate limit, at **40%** between the basic rate limit and the higher rate limit, and at **50%** above the higher rate limit.

3   Bank (or building society) interest.

4   Dividend income below the basic rate limit is taxed at 10%, at 32.5% between the basic rate limit and the higher rate limit , and at 42.5% above the higher rate limit.

5   A. The basic rate limit is increased by £400 × 100/80 = £500 to £35,500. Dennis will be liable to higher rate tax on £35,700 – £35,500 = £200.

6   Mike and Matt will each be taxed on 50% of the income from the investment property unless they make a joint declaration to specify the actual proportions in which case Mike will be taxed on 25% of the income and Matt on 75%.

Now try the questions below from the Exam Question Bank

Number	Level	Marks	Time
Q1	Introductory	12	22 mins
Q2	Examination	15	27 mins
Q3	Examination	15	27 mins

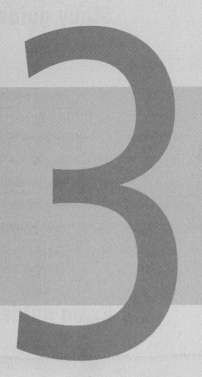

Employment income

Topic list	Syllabus reference
1 Employment and self employment	B2(a)
2 Basis of assessment for employment income	B2(c) B2(b)
3 Allowable deductions	B2(c) B2(d)
4 Statutory mileage allowances	B2(c) B2(e)
5 Charitable donations under the payroll deduction scheme	B2(c) B2(k)

Introduction

In the previous chapter we saw how to construct the income tax computation. Now we start to look in greater detail at the different types of income that people may receive so that the income can be slotted into the computation.

Many people earn money by working. We look at the important distinction between employment and self employment, so that we can consider the way in which people are taxed on the wages or salaries from their jobs.

Sometimes the employee may incur expenses when carrying out his job. We look at the rules determining when these can be deducted from employment income for tax purposes. We also look at the rules covering mileage payments made by employers to employees who use their own cars for business journeys. Finally employees can make tax efficient contributions to charity under the payroll giving scheme.

In the next chapter we look at how benefits received as a result of employment are taxed and at how tax is deducted from employment income under the PAYE system.

Study guide

		Intellectual level
B2	**Income from employment**	
(a)	Recognise the factors that determine whether an engagement is treated as employment or self-employment.	2
(b)	Recognise the basis of assessment for employment income.	2
(c)	Compute the income assessable.	2
(d)	Recognise the allowable deductions, including travelling expenses.	2
(e)	Discuss the use of the statutory approved mileage allowances.	2
(k)	Explain how charitable giving can be made through a payroll deduction scheme.	1

Exam guide

You are very likely to be asked a question concerning at least one aspect of employment taxation in your exam. This could range from a discussion of the distinction between employment and self employment to a full computation of employment income, including benefits.

1 Employment and self employment

FAST FORWARD

Employment involves a contract of service whereas self employment involves a contract for services. The distinction between employment and self employment is decided by looking at all the facts of the engagement.

1.1 Employment income

Employment income includes income arising from an employment under a **contract of service**.

Some people, however, set themselves up in business and carry out work for customers under a **contract for services**.

Before we can calculate employment income, we must be sure that the individual is employed rather than self employed. This can only be decided by looking at all the facts of the engagement.

1.2 Employment and self employment

Exam focus point

Many of the tax rules have come about as a result of legal cases. In the exam you are not required to know the relevant cases. However we have included the case names in the Text for your information.

It can be difficult to distinguish between employment (receipts taxable as earnings) and self employment (receipts taxable as trading income). Employment involves a contract of service, whereas self employment involves a contract for services. Taxpayers tend to prefer self employment, because the rules on deductions for expenses are more generous.

Factors which may be of importance include:

- The degree of control exercised over the person doing the work (a high level of control indicates employment)
- Whether the worker must accept further work (if yes, indicates employment)
- Whether the person who has offered work must provide further work (if yes, indicates employment)
- Whether the worker provides his own equipment (if yes, indicates self-employment)
- Whether the worker is entitled to employment benefits such as sick pay, holiday pay and pension facilities (entitlement indicates employment)
- Whether the worker hires his own helpers (if yes, indicates self-employment)
- What degree of financial risk the worker takes (if high risk, indicates self-employment)
- What degree of responsibility for investment and management the worker has (if most of responsibility the worker's, indicates self-employment)
- Whether the worker can profit from sound management (if can do so, indicates self-employment)
- Whether the worker can work when he chooses (if can do so, indicates self-employment)
- Whether the worker works for a number of different people or organisations (working for just one person or organisation indicates employment)
- The wording used in any agreement between the worker and the person for whom he performs work (but not conclusive about the actual legal relationship between them).

Relevant cases include:

(a)   *Edwards v Clinch 1981*

A civil engineer acted occasionally as an inspector on temporary unplanned appointments.

Held: there was no ongoing office which could be vacated by one person and held by another so the fees received were from self employment not employment.

(b)   *Hall v Lorimer 1994*

A vision mixer was engaged under a series of short-term contracts.

Held: the vision mixer was self employed, not because of any one detail of the case but because the overall picture was one of self-employment.

(c)   *Carmichael and Anor v National Power plc 1999*

Individuals engaged as visitor guides on a casual 'as required' basis were not employees. An exchange of correspondence between the company and the individuals was not a contract of employment as there was no provision as to the frequency of work and there was flexibility to accept work or turn it down as it arose. Sickness, holiday and pension arrangements did not apply and neither did grievance and disciplinary procedures.

A worker's status also affects national insurance contributions (NIC). The self-employed generally pay less than employees. National insurance contributions are covered later in this Text.

2 Basis of assessment for employment income

General earnings are taxed in the year of receipt. Money earnings are generally received on the earlier of the time payment is made and the time entitlement to payment arises.

2.1 Outline of the charge

Employment income includes income arising from an employment under a contract of service and the income of office holders, such as directors. The term 'employee' is used in this Text to mean anyone who receives employment income (ie both employees and directors).

General earnings are an employee's earnings (see key term below) plus the 'cash equivalent' of any taxable non-monetary benefits.

Key term

'Earnings' means any salary, wage or fee, any gratuity or other profit or incidental benefit obtained by the employee if it is money or money's worth (something of direct monetary value or convertible into direct monetary value) or anything else which constitutes a reward of the employment.

Taxable earnings from an employment in a tax year are the general earnings received in that tax year.

2.2 When are earnings received?

General earnings consisting of money are treated as received at the earlier of:

- **The time when payment is made**
- **The time when a person becomes entitled to payment of the earnings.**

If the employee is a **director** of a company, earnings from the company are received on the **earliest** of:

- The earlier of the two alternatives given in the general rule (above)
- The time when the amount is **credited in the company's accounting records**
- **The end of the company's period of account** (if the amount was determined by then)
- The **time the amount is determined** (if after the end of the company's period of account).

    Taxable benefits (see next chapter) are generally treated as received when they are provided to the employee.

The receipts basis does not apply to pension income. Pension income is taxed on the amount accruing in the tax year, whether or not it has actually been received in that year.

2.3 Net taxable earnings

Total taxable earnings less total allowable deductions (see below) **are net taxable earnings of a tax year.** Deductions cannot usually create a loss: they can only reduce the net taxable earnings to nil. If there is more than one employment in the tax year, separate calculations are required for each employment.

3 Allowable deductions

FAST FORWARD

Deductions for expenses are extremely limited. Relief is available for the costs that an employee is obliged to incur in travelling in the performance of his duties or in travelling to the place he has to attend in performance of his duties. Relief is **not** available for normal commuting costs.

3.1 The general rules

Deductions for expenses are extremely limited and are notoriously hard to obtain. Although there are some specific deductions, which are covered below, the general rule is that relief is limited to:

- **Qualifying travel expenses**
- **Other expenses the employee is obliged to incur and pay as holder of the employment which are incurred wholly, exclusively and necessarily in the performance of the duties of the employment.**

3.2 Travel expenses

3.2.1 Qualifying travel expenses

Tax relief is not available for an employee's normal commuting costs. This means relief is not available for any costs an employee incurs in getting from home to his normal place of work. However **employees are entitled to relief for travel expenses that they are obliged to incur and pay in travelling in the performance of their duties or travelling to or from a place which they have to attend in the performance of their duties (other than a permanent workplace).**

3.2.2 Example: travel in the performance of duties

Judi is an accountant. She often travels to meetings at the firm's offices in Scotland returning to her office in Leeds after the meetings. Relief is available for the full cost of these journeys as the travel is undertaken in the performance of her duties.

Question	Relief for travelling costs

Zoe lives in Wycombe and normally works in Chiswick. Occasionally she visits a client in Wimbledon and travels direct from home. Distances are shown in the diagram below:

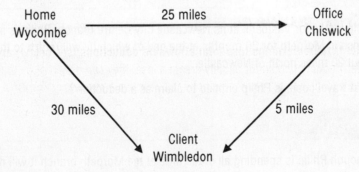

What tax relief is available for Zoe's travel costs?

Zoe is not entitled to tax relief for the costs incurred in travelling between Wycombe and Chiswick since these are normal commuting costs. However, relief is available for all costs that Zoe incurs when she travels from Wycombe to Wimbledon to visit her client.

To prevent manipulation of the basic rule normal commuting will not become a business journey just because the employee stops during the journey to perform a business task (eg to send an e-mail). Nor will relief be available if the journey is essentially the same as the employee's normal journey to work.

3.2.3 Example: normal commuting

Judi is based at her office in Leeds City Centre. One day she is required to attend a 9.00 am meeting with a client whose premises are around the corner from her Leeds office. Judi travels from home directly to the meeting. As the journey is substantially the same as her ordinary journey to work relief is not available.

3.2.4 Site based employees

Site based employees (eg construction workers, management consultants etc) **who do not have a permanent workplace, are entitled to relief for the costs of all journeys made from home to wherever they are working**. This is because these employees do not have an ordinary commuting journey or any normal commuting costs.

3.2.5 Temporary workplace

If an employee is seconded to work at another location for some considerable time, then the question arises as to whether the journey from home to that workplace can become normal commuting. There is a 24 month rule.

Tax relief is available for travel, accommodation and subsistence expenses incurred by an employee who is working at a temporary workplace on a secondment expected to last up to 24 months. If a secondment is initially expected not to exceed 24 months, but it is extended, relief ceases to be due from the date the employee becomes aware of the change.

When looking at how long a secondment is expected to last, HMRC will consider not only the terms of the written contract but also any verbal agreement by the employer and other factors such as whether the employee buys a house etc.

Question   Temporary workplace

Philip works for Vastbank at its Newcastle City Centre branch. Philip is sent to work full-time at another branch in Morpeth for 20 months at the end of which he will return to the Newcastle branch. Morpeth is about 20 miles north of Newcastle.

What travel costs is Philip entitled to claim as a deduction?

Answer

Although Philip is spending all of his time at the Morpeth branch it will not be treated as his normal work place because his period of attendance will be less than 24 months. Thus Philip can claim relief in full for the costs of travel from his home to the Morpeth branch.

3.3 Other expenses

Relief is given for other expenses incurred **wholly, exclusively and necessarily in the performance of the duties** of the employment. The word 'exclusively' strictly implies that the expenditure must **give no private benefit at all**. If it does, none of it is deductible. In practice HMRC may ignore a small element of private benefit or make an apportionment between business and private use.

Whether an expense is 'necessary' is not determined by what the employer requires. The test is **whether the duties of the employment could not be performed without the outlay.**

The following cases illustrate how the requirements are interpreted. Remember you are not expected to know the case names, they are given for information only.

- Sanderson v Durbridge 1955

  The cost of evening meals taken when attending late meetings was not deductible because it was not incurred in the performance of the duties.

- Blackwell v Mills 1945

  As a condition of his employment, an employee was required to attend evening classes. The cost of his text books and travel was not deductible because it was not incurred in the performance of the duties.

- *Lupton v Potts 1969*

  Examination fees incurred by a solicitor's articled clerk were not deductible because they were incurred neither wholly nor exclusively in the performance of the duties, but in furthering the clerk's ambition to become a solicitor.

- *Brown v Bullock 1961*

  The expense of joining a club that was virtually a condition of an employment was not deductible because it would have been possible to carry on the employment without the club membership, so the expense was not necessary.

- *Elwood v Utitz 1965*

  A managing director's subscriptions to two residential London clubs were claimed by him as an expense on the grounds that they were cheaper than hotels.

  The expenditure was deductible as it was necessary in that it would be impossible for the employee to carry out his London duties without being provided with appropriate accommodation. The residential facilities (which were cheaper than hotel accommodation) were given to club members only.

- *Lucas v Cattell 1972*

  The cost of business telephone calls on a private telephone is deductible, but **no part of the line or** telephone **rental charges is deductible**.

- *Fitzpatrick v IRC 1994; Smith v Abbott 1994*

  Journalists could not claim a deduction for the cost of buying newspapers which they read to keep themselves informed, since they were merely preparing themselves to perform their duties.

The cost of clothes for work is not deductible, except for certain trades requiring protective clothing where there are annual deductions on a set scale.

An employee required to work at home may be able to claim a deduction for the additional costs of working from home, such as an appropriate proportion of expenditure on lighting and heating. Employers can pay up to £3 per week without the need for supporting evidence of the costs incurred by the employee. Payments above the £3 limit require evidence of the employee's actual costs.

3.4 Other deductions

Some expenditure is specifically deductible in computing net taxable earnings:

(a) **Contributions to registered occupational pension schemes**

(b) **Subscriptions to professional bodies** on the list of bodies issued by the HMRC (which includes most UK professional bodies such as the ACCA), if relevant to the duties of the employment

(c) Payments for certain liabilities relating to the employment and for insurance against them (see below).

Employees may also claim capital allowances on plant and machinery (other than cars or other vehicles) necessarily provided for use in the performance of those duties. The computation of capital allowances is discussed later in this Text.

3.5 Liabilities and insurance

If a director or employee incurs a liability related to his employment or pays for insurance against such a liability, the cost is a deductible expense. If the employer pays such amounts, there is no taxable benefit.

A liability relating to employment is one which is imposed in respect of the employee's acts or omissions as employee. Thus, for example, liability for negligence would be covered. Related costs, for example the costs of legal proceedings, are included.

For insurance premiums to qualify, the insurance policy must:

(a) Cover only liabilities relating to employment, vicarious liability in respect of liabilities of another person's employment, related costs and payments to the employee's own employees in respect of their employment liabilities relating to employment and related costs, and

(b) It must not last for more than two years (although it may be renewed for up to two years at a time), and the insured person must not be not required to renew it.

4 Statutory mileage allowances

FAST FORWARD

Employers may pay a mileage allowance to employees who use their own car on business journeys. Payments up to the statutory limits are tax free, any excess is taxable, and a deduction can be claimed if the payment is lower.

A single authorised mileage allowance for business journeys in an employee's own vehicle applies to all cars and vans. There is no income tax on payments up to this allowance and employers do not have to report mileage allowances up to this amount. The allowance for 2011/12 is **45p per mile on the first 10,000 miles** in the tax year with **each additional mile over 10,000 miles at 25p per mile.**

The authorised mileage allowance for **employees using their own motor cycle is 24p per mile**. For **employees using their own pedal cycle it is 20p per mile.**

If employers pay less than the statutory mileage allowance, employees can claim tax relief up to that level.

The statutory mileage allowance does not prevent employers from paying higher rates, but any excess will be subject to income tax. There is a similar (but slightly different) system for NICs, covered later in this Text.

Employers can make income tax and NIC free payments of up to 5p per mile for each fellow employee making the same business trip who is carried as a passenger. If the employer does not pay the employee for carrying business passengers, the employee cannot claim any tax relief.

Sophie uses her own car for business travel. During 2011/12, Sophie drove 15,400 miles in the performance of her duties. Sophie's employer paid her a mileage allowance. How is the mileage allowance treated for tax purposes assuming that the rate paid is:

(a)   40p a mile, or
(b)   25p a mile?

Answer

(a)

	£
Mileage allowance received (15,400 × 40p)	6,160
Less: tax free [(10,000 × 45p) + (5,400 × 25p)]	(5,850)
Taxable benefit	310

£5,850 is tax free and the excess amount received of £310 is a taxable benefit.

(b)

	£
Tax free amount [(10,000 × 45p) + (5,400 × 25p)]	5,850
Less: mileage allowance received (15,400 × 25p)	(3,850)
Shortfall	2,000

There is no taxable benefit and Sophie can claim a deduction from her employment income for the shortfall of £2,000.

5 Charitable donations under the payroll deduction scheme

FAST FORWARD

Employees can make tax deductible donations to charity under the payroll deduction scheme. The amount paid is deducted from gross pay.

Employees can make charitable donations under the payroll deduction scheme by asking their employer to make deductions from their gross earnings. The deductions are then passed to a charitable agency which will either distribute the funds to the employees' chosen charities on receipt of their instructions, or provide the employee with vouchers that can be redeemed by the recipient charities.

The donation is an allowable deduction from the employee's earnings for tax purposes. Tax relief is given at source as the employer must deduct the donation from gross pay before calculating PAYE.

Exam focus point

Make sure you understand the difference between how tax relief is given for gift aid donations and how tax relief is given through the payroll deduction scheme.

Chapter Roundup

- Employment involves a contract of service whereas self employment involves a contract for services. The distinction between employment and self employment is decided by looking at all the facts of the engagement.

- General earnings are taxed in the year of receipt. Money earnings are generally received on the earlier of the time payment is made and the time entitlement to payment arises.

- Deductions for expenses are extremely limited. Relief is available for the costs that an employee is obliged to incur in travelling in the performance of his duties or in travelling to the place he has to attend in performance of his duties. Relief is not available for normal commuting costs.

- Employers may pay a mileage allowance to employees who use their own car on business journeys. Payments up to the statutory limits are tax free, any excess is taxable, and a deduction can be claimed if the payment is lower.

- Employees can make tax deductible donations to charity under the payroll deduction scheme. The amount paid is deducted from gross pay.

Quick Quiz

1   On what basis are earnings taxed?

2   In order for general expenses of employment to be deductible, they must be incurred _____, _____and in the performance of the duties of the employment. Fill in the blanks.

3   What relief can Karen claim if she is paid 40p for each mile that she drives her own car on company business and she drives 5,000 miles in 2011/12?

    A   £250
    B   £1,750
    C   £2,000
    D   £2,250

4   Could Karen claim any extra relief if she was accompanied by a work colleague for 1,000 of those miles?

Answers to Quick Quiz

1   Earnings are taxed on a receipts basis.

2   In order for general expenses of employment to be deductible, they must be incurred **wholly, exclusively** and **necessarily** in the performance of the duties of the employment.

3   A. Karen could claim relief of 5,000 x (45 − 40)p = £250. The 40p per mile received would not be taxable.

4   Karen could not claim any extra relief if she was accompanied by a work colleague for 1,000 of those miles. If her employer had made extra payments of up to 5p per mile for those journeys the extra payment would have been tax free.

Now try the question below from the Exam Question Bank

Number	Level	Marks	Time
Q4	Examination	15	27 mins

Taxable and exempt benefits. The PAYE system

Introduction

In the previous chapter we discussed when a worker was an employee and when he was self employed. We then considered the taxation of salaries and wages and the deduction of expenses and charitable donations.

In this chapter we look at benefits provided to employees. Benefits are an integral part of many remuneration packages, but the tax cost of receiving a benefit must not be overlooked. Special rules apply to fix the taxable value of certain benefits.

Finally we look at how tax is deducted from employment income under the PAYE system. Tax is deducted from cash payments, and benefits are dealt with through the PAYE code.

In the next chapter we look at how employees can save for their retirement through pension provision and the tax reliefs available.

Study guide

Exam guide

Benefits are a very important part of employment income and you are likely to come across them in your exam. Most employees these days are P11D employees, but you may need to know which benefits apply to excluded employees. If you come across exempt benefits in a question, note this in your answer to show that you have considered each item.

The PAYE system is a system of deduction of tax at source. You should be able to explain how it collects tax. The forms for the PAYE system are important as are the dates for submission.

1 P11D employees

FAST FORWARD

Most employees are taxed on benefits under the benefits code. 'Excluded employees' (lower paid/non-directors) are only subject to part of the provisions of the code.

1.1 Excluded employees

There is comprehensive legislation which covers the taxation of benefits.

The legislation generally applies to all employees. However, only certain parts of it apply to 'excluded employees'.

An excluded employee is an employee in lower paid employment who is either not a director of a company or is a director but has no material interest in the company ('material' means control of more than 5% of the ordinary share capital) and either:

(a)   He is full time working director, or
(b)   The company is non-profit-making or is established for charitable purposes only.

The term 'director' refers to any person who acts as a director or any person in accordance with whose instructions the directors are accustomed to act (other than a professional adviser).

1.2 Lower paid employment

A lower paid employment is one where earnings for the tax year are less than £8,500. To decide whether this applies, add together the total earnings and benefits that would be taxable if the employee were **not** an excluded employee.

A number of specific deductions must be taken into account to determine lower paid employment. These include contributions to registered pension schemes and payroll charitable deductions. However, general deductions from employment income (see earlier in this Text) are not taken into account.

Question

Tim earns £6,500 per annum working full time as a sales representative at Chap Co Ltd. The company provides the following staff benefits to Tim:

Private health insurance	£300
Company car	£1,500
Expense allowance	£2,000

Tim used £1,900 of the expense allowance on business mileage petrol.

Is Tim an excluded employee?

Answer

No. Although Tim's taxable income is less than £8,500 this is only after his expense claim. The figure to consider and compare to £8,500 is the £10,300 as shown below.

	£
Salary	6,500
Benefits: health insurance	300
car	1,500
expense allowance	2,000
Earnings to consider if Tim is an 'excluded employee'	10,300
Less claim for expenses paid out	(1,900)
Taxable income	8,400

1.3 P11D employees

Employees, including directors, who are not excluded employees may be referred to as 'P11D employees'; the P11D is the form that the employer completes for each such employee with details of expenses and benefits.

2 Benefits taxable on all employees

2.1 Introduction

All employees, including excluded employees, are taxable on the provision of:

- vouchers
- living accommodation.

For excluded employees, other benefits are taxed on their "second-hand value", which is usually nil. The special rules for P11D employees are covered in the next Section.

2.2 Vouchers

If any employee (including an excluded employee):

(a) receives cash vouchers (vouchers exchangeable for cash)
(b) uses a credit token (such as a credit card) to obtain money, goods or services, or
(c) receives exchangeable vouchers (such as book tokens), also called non-cash vouchers

he is taxed on the cost to the employer of providing the benefit, less any amount made good.

The first 15p per working day of meal vouchers (eg luncheon vouchers) is not taxed.

2.3 Accommodation

FAST FORWARD

The benefit in respect of accommodation is its annual value. There is an additional benefit if the property cost over £75,000.

2.3.1 Annual value charge

The taxable value of accommodation provided to an employee (including an excluded employee) is the **rent that would have been payable if the premises had been let at their annual value** (sometimes called 'rateable value'). **If the premises are rented** rather than owned by the employer, then **the taxable benefit is the higher of the rent actually paid and the annual value**.

2.3.2 Additional benefit charge

If a property was bought by the employer for a cost of more than £75,000, an additional amount is chargeable as follows:

(Cost of providing the living accommodation – £75,000) × the official rate of interest at the start of the tax year. The official rate of interest at the start of the 2011/12 tax year is 4%.

Exam focus point

The 'official rate' of interest will be given to you in the exam.

Thus with an official rate of 4%, the total benefit for accommodation costing £95,000 and with an annual value of £2,000 would be £2,000 + £(95,000 – 75,000) × 4% = £2,800.

The **'cost of providing'** the living accommodation is the total of the **cost of purchase and the cost of any improvements made before the start of the tax year** for which the benefit is being computed. It is therefore not possible to avoid the charge by buying an inexpensive property requiring substantial repairs and improving it.

Where the property was acquired more than six years before first being provided to the employee, the **market value when first so provided plus the cost of subsequent improvements** is used as the **cost of providing the living accommodation**. However, unless the actual cost plus improvements up to the start of the tax year in question exceeds £75,000, the additional charge cannot be imposed, however high the market value.

2.3.3 Job related accommodation

There is no taxable benefit in respect of job related accommodation. Accommodation is job related if:

(a)   Residence in the accommodation is necessary for **the proper performance of the employee's duties (as with a caretaker), or**

(b)   The accommodation is provided **for the better performance of the employee's duties** and the employment is of a kind in which it is customary for accommodation to be provided (as with a policeman), or

(c)   The **accommodation is provided as part of arrangements in force because of a special threat to the employee's security.**

Directors can only claim exemptions (a) or (b) if:

(i)   They have no **material interest** ('material' means over 5%) in the company, and
(ii)   Either they are **full time working directors** or the company is **non-profit making or is a charity**.

2.3.4 Contribution by employee

Any contribution paid by the employee is deducted from the annual value of the property and then from the additional benefit.

Question Accommodation

Mr Quinton was provided with a company flat in Birmingham in January 2011. The rateable value of the flat is £1,200. The property cost his employer £125,000, but was valued at £150,000 in January 2011. Mr Quinton paid rent of £500 pa.

What is the taxable benefit for 2011/12 assuming:

(a) His employer purchased the property in 2009, or

(b) His employer purchased the property in 2003, or

(c) Mr Quinton was required to live in the flat as he was employed as the caretaker for the company premises (of which the flat was part).

Answer

		£
(a)	Annual value	1,200
	Less: rent paid	(500)
		700
	Additional amount £(125,000 − 75,000) × 4%	2,000
	Taxable benefit	2,700

		£
(b)	Annual value	1,200
	Less: rent paid	(500)
		700
	Additional amount £(150,000 − 75,000) × 4%	3,000
	Taxable benefit	3,700

As Mr Quinton first moved in more than six years after the company bought the flat, the value at the date he moved in is used.

(c) Job related accommodation: taxable benefit £ nil

3 Benefits taxable on P11D employees

3.1 Introduction

Special rules apply to determine the taxable value of expenses and benefits paid to or provided for P11D employees.

3.2 Expenses

3.2.1 General business expenses

If business expenses on such items as travel or hotel stays are reimbursed by an employer, the reimbursed amount is a taxable benefit for P11D employees. To avoid being taxed on this amount, **an employee must then make a claim to deduct it as an expense** under the rules set out below.

A P11D dispensation may be obtained from HMRC to avoid the need to report expenses and claim a deduction (see later in this Chapter).

Part B Income tax and national insurance contributions │ **4: Taxable and exempt benefits. The PAYE system** 51

3.2.2 Private incidental expenses

When an individual has to spend one or more nights away from home, his employer may reimburse expenses on items incidental to his absence (for example laundry and private telephone calls). **Such incidental expenses are exempt** if:

(a)   The expenses of travelling to each place where the individual stays overnight, throughout the trip, are incurred necessarily in the performance of the duties of the employment (or would have been, if there had been any expenses).

(b)   The total (for the whole trip) of incidental expenses not deductible under the usual rules is no more than £5 for each night spent wholly in the UK and £10 for each other night. If this limit is exceeded, all of the expenses are taxable, not just the excess. The expenses include any VAT.

This incidental expenses exemption applies to expenses reimbursed, and to benefits obtained using credit tokens and non-cash vouchers.

3.2.3 Expenses related to living accommodation

In addition to the benefit of living accommodation itself, P11D **employees are taxed on related expenses paid by the employer**, such as:

(a)   **Heating, lighting or cleaning the premises**
(b)   **Repairing, maintaining or decorating the premises**
(c)   **The provision of furniture (the annual value is 20% of the cost).**

If the accommodation is 'job related', however, the **taxable amount is restricted to a maximum of 10% of the employee's 'net earnings'**. For this purpose, net earnings comprises the total employment income, net of expenses and pension contributions, but excluding these related expenses.

Council tax and water or sewage charges paid by the employer are taxable in full as a benefit unless the accommodation is 'job-related'.

3.3 Cars

FAST FORWARD

Employees who have a company car are taxed on a % of the car's list price which depends on the level of the car's CO_2 emissions. The same % multiplied by £18,800 determines the benefit where private fuel is also provided.

3.3.1 Cars provided for private use

A car provided by reason of the employment to a P11D employee or member of his family or household for private use gives rise to a taxable benefit. 'Private use' includes home to work travel.

A tax charge arises whether the car is provided by the employer or by some other person. The benefit is computed as shown below, even if the car is taken as an alternative to another benefit of a different value.

The starting point for calculating a car benefit is the list price of the car (plus accessories). **The percentage of the list price that is taxable depends on the car's CO_2 emissions.**

3.3.2 Taxable benefit

For cars that emit CO_2 **of between 121g/km and 125g/km (2011/12), the taxable benefit is 15% of the car's list price. This percentage increases by 1% for every 5g/km (rounded down to the nearest multiple of 5) by which CO_2 emissions exceed 125g/km up to a maximum of 35%.** Therefore the 15% rate applies to cars with emissions between 126g/km and 129g/km as these are rounded down to 125g/km. Then, for cars with emissions between 130g/km and 134g/km, the relevant percentage will be 15 + ((130 − 125)/5) = 16% etc.

Exam focus point

The CO_2 baseline figure will be given to you in the tax rates and allowances section of the exam paper.

For cars that emit CO_2 between 76g/km and 120g/km, the taxable benefit is 10% of the car's list price. For cars that emit 75g/km or less, the taxable benefit is 5% of the car's list price.

Diesel cars have a supplement of 3% of the car's list price added to the taxable benefit. The maximum percentage, however, remains 35% of the list price.

3.3.3 List price

The price of the car is the sum of the following items:

(a) **The list price of the car** for a single retail sale at the time of first registration, including charges for delivery and standard accessories. The manufacturer's, importer's or distributor's list price must be used, even if the retailer offered a discount. A notional list price is estimated if no list price was published.

(b) **The price (including fitting) of all optional accessories provided when the car was first provided** to the employee, excluding mobile telephones and equipment needed by a disabled employee. The extra cost of adapting or manufacturing a car to run on road fuel gases is not included.

(c) **The price (including fitting) of all optional accessories fitted later** and costing at least £100 each, excluding mobile telephones and equipment needed by a disabled employee. Such accessories affect the taxable benefit from and including the tax year in which they are fitted. However, accessories which are merely replacing existing accessories and are not superior to the ones replaced are ignored. Replacement accessories which *are* superior are taken into account, but the cost of the old accessory is then deducted.

There is a special rule for **classic cars**. If the car is at least 15 years old (from the time of first registration) at the end of the tax year, and its market value at the end of the year (or, if earlier, when it ceased to be available to the employee) is over £15,000 and greater than the price found under the above rules, that market value is used instead of the price. The market value takes account of all accessories (except mobile telephones and equipment needed by a disabled employee).

Capital contributions made by the employee in that and previous tax years up to a maximum of £5,000 are deducted from the list price. Capital contributions are payments by the employee in respect of the price of the car or accessories for the same car. Contributions beyond the maximum are ignored.

Question
Car benefit (1)

Nigel Issan is provided with a diesel car which had a list price of £22,000 when it was first registered. The car has CO_2 emissions of 188g/km.

You are required to calculate Nigel's car benefit for 2011/12.

Answer

Car benefit £22,000 × 30% (15% + (185 − 125)/5 + 3%) = £6,600

Note that 188 is rounded down to 185 to be exactly divisible by 5.

Robyn is provided with a petrol car which had a list price of £12,000 when it was first registered. The car has CO_2 emissions of 123 g/km.

You are required to calculate Robyn's car benefit for 2011/12.

Answer

Car benefit £12,000 x 15% = £1,800

Note that the 10% car benefit rate only applies if the CO_2 emissions are exactly between 76g/km and 120g/km on petrol cars. In this case, there is no rounding down to be exactly divisible by 5.

3.3.4 Reductions in the benefit

The benefit is reduced on a time basis where a car is first made available or ceases to be made available during the tax year or is incapable of being used for a continuous period of not less than 30 days (for example because it is being repaired).

The benefit is reduced by any payment the user must make for the private use of the car (as distinct from a capital contribution to the cost of the car). The benefit cannot become negative to create a deduction from the employee's income.

Question

Time apportioning benefits

Vicky Olvo starts her employment on 6 January 2012 and is immediately provided with a new petrol car with a list price of £25,000. The car was more expensive than her employer would have provided and she therefore made a capital contribution of £6,200. The employer was able to buy the car at a discount and paid only £23,000. Vicky contributed £100 a month for being able to use the car privately. CO_2 emissions are 253g/km.

You are required to calculate her car benefit for 2011/12.

Answer

	£
List price *	25,000
Less capital contribution (maximum)	(5,000)
	20,000

	£
£20,000 × 35% ** × 3/12 ***	1,750
Less contribution to running costs (£100 × 3)	(300)
Car benefit	1,450

*   The discounted price is not relevant
**   15% + (250 – 125) × 1/5 = 40% restricted to 35% max
***   Only available for 3 months in 2011/12.

3.3.5 Pool cars

Pool cars are exempt. A car is a pool car if **all** the following conditions are satisfied:

(a)   It is used by more than one employee and is not ordinarily used by any one of them to the exclusion of the others

(b)   Any private use is merely incidental to business use

(c)   It is not normally kept overnight at or near the residence of an employee.

3.3.6 Ancillary benefits

There are many ancillary benefits associated with the provision of cars, such as insurance, repairs, vehicle licences and a parking space at or near work. No extra taxable benefit arises as a result of these, with the exception of the cost of providing a driver.

3.4 Fuel for cars

3.4.1 Introduction

Where fuel is provided there is a further benefit in addition to the car benefit.

No taxable benefit arises where either

(a)   **All the fuel provided was made available only for business travel, or**

(b)   **The employee is required to make good, and has made good, the whole of the cost of any fuel provided for his private use.**

Unlike most benefits, a reimbursement of only part of the cost of the fuel available for private use does not reduce the benefit.

3.4.2 Taxable benefit

The taxable benefit is a percentage of a base figure. The base figure for 2011/12 is £18,800. The percentage is the same percentage as is used to calculate the car benefit (see above).

Exam focus point

> The fuel base figure will be given to you in the tax rates and allowances section of the exam paper.

3.4.3 Reductions in the benefit

The fuel benefit is reduced in the same way as the car benefit **if the car is not available for 30 days or more**.

The fuel benefit is also reduced if private fuel is not available for part of a tax year. However, if private fuel later becomes available in the same tax year, the reduction is not made. If, for example, fuel is provided from 6 April 2011 to 30 June 2011, then the fuel benefit for 2011/12 will be restricted to just three months. This is because the provision of fuel has permanently ceased. However, if fuel is provided from 6 April 2011 to 30 June 2011, and then again from 1 September 2011 to 5 April 2012, then the fuel benefit will not be reduced since the cessation was only temporary.

Question   Car and fuel benefit

An employee was provided with a new car costing £15,000 on 6 April 2011. The car emits 176g/km of CO_2. During 2011/12 the employer spent £900 on insurance, repairs and a vehicle licence. The firm paid for all petrol, costing £1,500, without reimbursement. The employee paid the firm £270 for the private use of the car. Calculate the taxable benefits for private use of the car and private fuel.

Answer

Round CO_2 emissions figure down to the nearest 5, ie 175g/km.

Amount by which CO_2 emissions exceed the baseline:

(175 – 125) = 50 g/km

Divide by 5 = 10

Part B Income tax and national insurance contributions | **4: Taxable and exempt benefits. The PAYE system**   **55**

Taxable percentage = 15% + 10% = 25%

	£
Car benefit £15,000 × 25%	3,750
Less contribution towards use of car	(270)
	3,480
Fuel benefit £18,800 × 25%	4,700
Total benefits	8,180

If the contribution of £270 had been towards the petrol the benefit would have been £(3,750 + 4,700) = £8,450 since partial reimbursement of private use fuel does not reduce the fuel benefit.

Note there is no additional benefit for the insurance, repairs and licence costs. The car benefit is deemed to cover all these expenses incurred by the employer.

3.5 Vans and heavier commercial vehicles

If a van (of normal maximum laden weight up to 3,500 kg) **is made available for an employee's private use, there is an annual scale charge of £3,000.** The scale charge covers ancillary benefits such as insurance and servicing. The benefit is scaled down if the van is not available for the full year (as for cars) and is reduced by any payment made by the employee for private use.

There is, however, **no taxable benefit where an employee takes a van home** (ie uses the van for home to work travel) but is not allowed any other private use.

Where private fuel is provided, there is an additional charge of £550. If the van is unavailable for part of the year, or fuel for private use is only provided for part of the year, the benefit is scaled down.

If a commercial vehicle of normal maximum laden weight over 3,500 kg is made available for an employee's private use, but the employee's use of the vehicle is not wholly or mainly private, no taxable benefit arises except in respect of the provision of a driver.

3.6 Beneficial loans

FAST FORWARD

Cheap loans are charged to tax on the difference between the official rate of interest and any interest paid by the employee.

3.6.1 Taxable benefit

Employment related loans to P11D employees and their relatives give rise to a benefit equal to:

(a) **Any amounts written off** (unless the employee has died), and

(b) The excess of the interest based on an official rate prescribed by the Treasury, over any interest actually charged ('taxable cheap loan'). Interest payable during the tax year but paid after the end of the tax year is taken into account.

The following loans are normally not treated as taxable cheap loans for calculation of the interest benefits (but not for the purposes of the charge on loans written off).

(a) A loan on normal commercial terms made in the ordinary course of the employer's money-lending business.

(b) A loan made by an individual in the ordinary course of the lender's domestic, family or personal arrangements.

3.6.2 Calculating the interest benefit

There are two alternative methods of calculating the taxable benefit. The simpler **'average' method** automatically applies unless the taxpayer or HMRC elect for the alternative **'strict' method**. (HMRC normally only make the election where it appears that the 'average' method is being deliberately exploited.) In both methods, the benefit is the interest at the official rate minus the interest payable.

For the purposes of the F6 exam, the official rate of interest is assumed to be 4% throughout 2011/12.

The 'average' method averages the balances at the beginning and end of the tax year (or the dates on which the loan was made and/or discharged if it was not in existence throughout the tax year) and applies the official rate of interest to this average. If the loan was not in existence throughout the tax year only the number of complete tax months (from the 6th of the month) for which it existed are taken into account.

The 'strict' method is to compute interest at the official rate on the actual amount outstanding on a daily basis. However, for exam purposes, it is acceptable to work on a monthly basis.

Question

Loan benefit

At 6 April 2011 a taxable cheap loan of £30,000 was outstanding to an employee earning £12,000 a year, who repaid £20,000 on 6 December 2011. The remaining balance of £10,000 was outstanding at 5 April 2012. Interest paid during the year was £250.

What was the benefit under both methods for 2011/12?

Answer

Average method

	£
$4\% \times \dfrac{30,000 + 10,000}{2}$	800
Less interest paid	(250)
Benefit	550

Alternative method (strict method)

	£
$£30,000 \times \dfrac{8}{12}$ (6 April – 5 December) $\times 4\%$	800
$£10,000 \times \dfrac{4}{12}$ (6 December – 5 April) $\times 4\%$	133
	933
Less interest paid	(250)
Benefit	683

HMRC might opt for the alternative method.

Note. You must always show the workings for the average method. If it appears likely that the taxpayer should or HMRC might opt for the alternative method you will need to show those workings as well.

3.6.3 The de minimis test

The interest benefit is not taxable if the total of all non-qualifying loans to the employee did not exceed £5,000 at any time in the tax year.

A qualifying loan is one on which all or part of any interest paid would qualify for tax relief (see further below).

When the £5,000 threshold is exceeded, a benefit arises on interest on the whole loan, not just on the excess of the loan over £5,000.

3.6.4 Qualifying loans

If the whole of the interest payable on a qualifying loan is eligible for tax relief as deductible interest (as seen earlier in this Text), then no taxable benefit arises. If the interest is only partly eligible for tax relief,

Part B Income tax and national insurance contributions | **4: Taxable and exempt benefits. The PAYE system**

57

then the employee is treated as receiving earnings because the actual rate of interest is below the official rate. He is also treated as paying interest equal to those earnings. This **deemed interest paid may qualify as a business expense or as deductible interest in addition to any interest actually paid.**

Question

Anna, who is single, has an annual salary of £30,000, and two loans from her employer.

(a)   A season ticket loan of £2,300 at no interest

(b)   A loan, 90% of which was used to buy a partnership interest, of £54,000 at 1.5% interest

What is Anna's tax liability for 2011/12?

Answer

	£
Salary	30,000
Season ticket loan (non-qualifying): not over £5,000	0
Loan to buy partnership interest (qualifying): £54,000 × (4 − 1.5 = 2.5%)	1,350
Earnings/Total income	31,350
Less deductible interest paid (£54,000 × 4% × 90%)	(1,944)
Net income	29,406
Less personal allowance	(7,475)
Taxable income	21,931

Income tax

Tax liability £21,931 × 20%	4,386

3.7 Private use of other assets

FAST FORWARD

20% of the value of assets made available for private use is taxable.

When assets are made available for private use to employees or members of their family or household, the taxable benefit is the higher of 20% of the market value when first provided as a benefit to any employee and the rent paid by the employer. The 20% charge is time-apportioned when the asset is provided for only part of the year. The charge after any time apportionment is reduced by any contribution made by the employee.

There is an additional taxable benefit of any other amounts that the employer pays during the tax year relating to the provision of the asset such as running costs.

Bicycles provided for journeys to work, as well as being available for private use, are exempt from the private use benefit rules.

If an asset made available is subsequently acquired by the employee, **the taxable benefit on the acquisition is the *greater* of:**

- The **current market value minus the price paid by the employee.**

- The **market value when first provided minus any amounts already taxed (ignoring contributions by the employee) minus the price paid by the employee.**

This rule prevents tax free benefits arising on rapidly depreciating items through the employee purchasing them at their low second-hand value.

There is an exception to this rule for bicycles which have previously been provided as exempt benefits (see above). The taxable benefit on acquisition is restricted to current market value, minus the price paid by the employee.

3.8 Example: assets made available for private use

A suit costing £400 is purchased by an employer for use by an employee on 6 April 2010. On 6 April 2011 the suit is purchased by the employee for £30, its market value then being £50.

The benefit in 2010/11 is £400 × 20% = £80.

The benefit in 2011/12 is £290, being the *greater* of:

		£
(a)	Market value at acquisition by employee	50
	Less price paid	(30)
		20
(b)	Original market value	400
	Less taxed in respect of use	(80)
		320
	Less price paid	(30)
		290

Question

Bicycles

Rupert is provided with a new bicycle by his employer on 6 April 2011. The bicycle is available for private use as well as commuting to work. It cost the employer £1,500 when new. On 6 October 2011 the employer transfers ownership of the bicycle to Rupert when it is worth £800. Rupert does not pay anything for the bicycle.

What is the total taxable benefit on Rupert for 2011/12 in respect of the bicycle?

Answer

Use benefit	Exempt
Transfer benefit (use MV at acquisition by employee only)	
MV at transfer	£800

3.9 Scholarships

If scholarships are given to members of an employee's family, the **employee is taxable on the cost** unless the scholarship fund's or scheme's payments by reason of people's employments are not more than 25% of its total payments.

3.10 Childcare

FAST FORWARD

Workplace childcare is an exempt benefit. Employer-supported childcare and childcare vouchers are exempt up to £55 per week. Maximum tax relief is limited to £11 per week (the equivalent of £55 x 20%).

The cost of running a **workplace nursery or playscheme is an exempt benefit (without limit).**

Otherwise a certain amount of childcare is tax free if the employer contracts with an approved childcarer or provides childcare vouchers to pay an approved childcarer. The childcare must usually be available to all employees and the childcare must either be registered or approved home-childcare.

Exam focus point

The rules about childcare schemes changed on 6 April 2011 but the old rules still apply to taxpayers who joined a childcare scheme prior to that date. However, the examiner has stated that a question will not be set involving a person who had joined a childcare scheme prior to 6 April 2011.

Part B Income tax and national insurance contributions | **4: Taxable and exempt benefits. The PAYE system** 59

A **£55 per week limit applies to basic rate employees** who use employer-supported childcare schemes or receive childcare vouchers. The amount of tax relief for a basic rate taxpayer is therefore £55 x 20% = £11 per week.

Higher rate and additional rate employees have their tax relief restricted so that it is the equivalent of that received by a basic rate taxpayer. Higher and additional rate employees can therefore receive vouchers tax-free up to £28 per week and £22 per week respectively, each giving £11 of tax relief which is the same amount a basic rate taxpayer would receive.

Exam focus point

The examiner has stated that in an exam question involving childcare, it would be quite clear at what rate a taxpayer was paying tax.

Question

Childcare

Archie is employed by M plc and is paid a salary of £80,000 in 2011/12. He starts receiving childcare vouchers from M plc worth £50 per week for his daughter in June 2011 and receives them for 26 weeks during 2011/12.

What is Archie's employment income for 2011/12?

Answer

	£
Salary (higher rate employee)	80,000
Childcare vouchers £(50 – 28) x 26 weeks	572
Employment income 2011/12	80,572

3.11 Other benefits

FAST FORWARD

There is a residual charge for other benefits, usually equal to the cost to the employer of the benefits.

We have seen above how certain specific benefits are taxed. **There is a sweeping up charge for all other benefits. Under this rule the taxable value of a benefit is the cost of the benefit less any part of that cost made good by the employee to the persons providing the benefit.**

The residual charge applies to any benefit provided for a P11D employee or a member of his family or household, by reason of the employment. There is an exception where the employer is an individual and the provision of the benefit is made in the normal course of the employer's domestic, family or personal relationships.

3.12 Example: other benefits

A private school offers free places to the children of its staff. The marginal cost to the school of providing the place is £2,000 pa, although the fees charged to other pupils is £5,000 pa.

The taxable value of the benefit to the staff is the actual cost of £2,000 per pupil, not the full £5,000 charged to other pupils.

4 Exempt benefits

FAST FORWARD

There are a number of exempt benefits including removal expenses, sporting facilities, meal vouchers and workplace parking.

Various benefits are exempt from tax. These include:

(a) **Entertainment provided to employees by genuine third parties** (eg seats at sporting/cultural events), even if it is provided by giving the employee a voucher.

(b) **Gifts of goods** (or vouchers exchangeable for goods) from third parties (ie not provided by the employer or a person connected to the employer) if the total cost (incl. VAT) of all gifts by the same donor to the same employee in the tax year is £250 or less. If the £250 limit is exceeded, the full amount is taxable, not just the excess.

(c) **Non-cash awards for long service** if the period of service was at least 20 years, no similar award was made to the employee in the past 10 years and the cost is not more than £50 per year of service.

(d) **Awards under staff suggestion schemes** if:

    (i) There is a formal scheme, open to all employees on equal terms.

    (ii) The suggestion is outside the scope of the employee's normal duties.

    (iii) Either the award is not more than £25, or the award is only made after a decision is taken to implement the suggestion.

    (iv) Awards over £25 reflect the financial importance of the suggestion to the business, and either do not exceed 50% of the expected net financial benefit during the first year of implementation or do not exceed 10% of the expected net financial benefit over a period of up to five years.

    (v) Awards of over £25 are shared on a reasonable basis between two or more employees putting forward the same suggestion.

    If an award exceeds £5,000, the excess is always taxable.

(e) **The first £8,000 of removal expenses** if:

    (i) The employee does not already live within a reasonable daily travelling distance of his new place of employment, but will do so after moving.

    (ii) The expenses are incurred or the benefits provided by the end of the tax year following the tax year of the start of employment at the new location.

(f) **Some childcare** (see earlier in this Chapter)

(g) **Sporting or recreational facilities available to employees generally and not to the general public**, unless they are provided on domestic premises, or they consist of an interest in or the use of any mechanically propelled vehicle or any overnight accommodation. Vouchers only exchangeable for such facilities are also exempt, but membership fees for sports clubs are taxable.

(h) **Assets or services used in performing the duties of employment** provided any private use of the item concerned is insignificant. This exempts, for example, the benefit arising on the private use of employer-provided tools.

(i) **Welfare counselling** and similar minor benefits if the benefit concerned is available to employees generally.

(j) **Bicycles or cycling safety equipment** provided to enable employees to get to and from work or to travel between one workplace and another. The equipment must be available to the employer's employees generally. Also, it must be used mainly for the aforementioned journeys.

(k) **Workplace parking**

(l) **Up to £15,000 a year paid to an employee who is on a full-time course lasting at least a year**, with average full-time attendance of at least 20 weeks a year. If the £15,000 limit is exceeded, the whole amount is taxable.

(m) **Work related training** and related costs. This includes the costs of training material and assets either made during training or incorporated into something so made.

(n)   **Air miles** or car fuel coupons obtained as a result of business expenditure but used for private purposes.

(o)   **The cost of work buses and minibuses or subsidies to public bus services.**

A works bus must have a seating capacity of 12 or more and a works minibus a seating capacity of 9 or more but not more than 12 and be available generally to employees of the employer concerned. The bus or minibus must mainly be used by employees for journeys to and from work and for journeys between workplaces.

(p)   **Transport/overnight costs where public transport is disrupted by industrial action,** late night taxis and travel costs incurred where car sharing arrangements unavoidably breakdown.

(q)   The private use of one **mobile phone**. Top up vouchers for exempt mobile phones are also tax free. If more than one mobile phone is provided to an employee for private use only the second or subsequent phone is a taxable benefit valued using the rules for assets made available to employees.

(r)   **Employer provided uniforms** which employees must wear as part of their duties.

(s)   The cost of **staff parties** which are open to staff generally provided that the **cost per head per year (including VAT) is £150 or less**. The £150 limit may be split between several parties. If exceeded, the full amount is taxable, not just the excess over £150.

(t)   **Private medical insurance premiums paid to cover treatment when the employee is outside the UK in the performance of his duties**. Other medical insurance premiums are taxable as is the cost of medical diagnosis and treatment except for routine check ups. Eye tests and glasses for employees using VDUs are exempt.

(u)   **The first 15p per day of meal vouchers (eg luncheon vouchers).**

(v)   **Cheap loans that do not exceed £5,000** at any time in the tax year (see above).

(w)   **Job related accommodation (see above).**

(x)   **Employer contributions towards additional household costs incurred by an employee who works wholly or partly at home**. Payments up to £3 pw (£156 pa) may be made without supporting evidence (see earlier in this Text).

(y)   **Meals or refreshments for cyclists** provided as part of official 'cycle to work' days.

(z)   **Personal incidental expenses** (see earlier in this Text).

Where a voucher is provided for a benefit which is exempt from income tax the provision of the voucher itself is also exempt.

5 P11D dispensations

As we have seen expense payments to P11D employees should be reported to HMRC. They form part of the employee's employment income and a claim must be made to deduct the expenses in computing net employment income.

To avoid this cumbersome procedure **the employer and HMRC can agree for a dispensation to apply to avoid the need to report expenses covered by the dispensation, and the employee then need not make a formal claim for a deduction.**

Dispensations can only apply to genuine business expenses. Some employers only reimburse business expenses, so that a dispensation may be agreed to cover all payments. Other employers may agree to cover a particular category of expenses, such as travel expenses.

A dispensation cannot be given for mileage allowances paid to employees using their own cars for business journeys as these payments are governed by a statutory exemption (see earlier in this Text).

6 The PAYE system

Most tax in respect of employment income is deducted under the PAYE system. The objective of the PAYE system is to collect the correct amount of tax over the year. An employee's PAYE code is designed to ensure that allowances etc are given evenly over the year.

6.1 Introduction

6.1.1 Cash payments

The objective of the PAYE system is to deduct the correct amount of tax over the year. Its scope is very wide. It applies to most cash payments, other than reimbursed business expenses, and to certain non cash payments.

In addition to wages and salaries, PAYE applies to round sum expense allowances and payments instead of benefits. It also applies to any readily convertible asset.

A readily convertible asset is any asset which can effectively be exchanged for cash. The amount subject to PAYE is the amount that would be taxed as employment income. This is usually the cost to the employer of providing the asset.

Tips paid direct to an employee are normally outside the PAYE system (although still assessable as employment income). An exception may apply in the catering trades where tips are often pooled. Here the PAYE position depends on whether a 'tronc', administered by someone other than by the employer, exists.

It is the employer's duty to deduct income tax from the pay of his employees, whether or not he has been directed to do so by HMRC. **If he fails to do this he** (or sometimes the employee) **must pay over the tax which he should have deducted and the employer may be subject to penalties**. Interest will also run from 14 days after the end of the tax year concerned on any underpaid PAYE. Officers of HMRC can inspect employer's records in order to satisfy themselves that the correct amounts of tax are being deducted and paid over to HMRC.

6.1.2 Benefits

PAYE is not normally operated on benefits; instead the employee's PAYE code is restricted (see below).

However, PAYE must be applied to remuneration in the form of a taxable non-cash voucher if at the time it is provided:

(a)   the voucher is capable of being exchanged for readily convertible assets; or

(b)   the voucher can itself be sold, realised or traded.

PAYE must normally be operated on cash vouchers and on each occasion when a director/employee uses a credit-token (eg a credit card) to obtain money or goods which are readily convertible assets. However, a cash voucher or credit token which is used to defray expenses is not subject to PAYE.

6.2 How PAYE works

6.2.1 Operation of PAYE

To operate PAYE the employer needs:

(a)   deductions working sheets

(b)   codes for employees that reflect the tax allowances to which the employees are entitled

(c)   tax tables.

The employer works out the amount of PAYE tax to deduct on any particular pay day by using the employee's code number (see below) in conjunction with the PAYE tables. The tables are designed so that tax is normally worked out on a cumulative basis. This means that with each payment of earnings the running total of tax paid is compared with tax due on total earnings to that date. The difference between the tax due and the tax paid is the tax to be deducted on that particular payday.

National insurance tables are used to work out the national insurance due on any payday.

6.2.2 Records

The employer must keep records of each employee's pay and tax at each pay day. The records must also contain details of National Insurance. The employer has a choice of three ways of recording and returning these figures:

(a)   he may use the official deductions working sheet (P11)
(b)   he may incorporate the figures in his own pay records using a substitute document
(c)   he may retain the figures on a computer.

These records will be used to make a return at the end of the tax year.

6.3 Payment under the PAYE system

Under PAYE income tax and national insurance is normally paid over to HMRC monthly, 14 days after the end of each tax month.

If an employer's average monthly payments under the PAYE system are less than £1,500, the employer may choose to pay quarterly, within 14 days of the end of each tax quarter. Tax quarters end on 5 July, 5 October, 5 January and 5 April. Payments can continue to be made quarterly during a tax year even if the monthly average reaches or exceeds £1,500, but a new estimate must be made and a new decision taken to pay quarterly at the start of each tax year. Average monthly payments are the average net monthly payments due to HMRC for income tax and NICs.

6.4 PAYE codes

An employee is normally entitled to various allowances. Under the PAYE system an amount reflecting the effect of a proportion of these allowances is set against his pay each pay day. To determine the amount to set against his pay the allowances are expressed in the form of a code which is used in conjunction with the Pay Adjustment Table (Table A).

An employee's code may be any one of the following:

L   tax code with basic personal allowance
P   tax code with age 65-74 age allowance
Y   tax code with age 75+ age allowance

The codes BR, DO and OT are generally used where there is a second source of income and all allowances have been used in a tax code which is applied to the main source of income.

Generally, a tax code number is arrived at by deleting the last digit in the sum representing the employee's tax free allowances. Every individual is entitled to a personal tax free allowance of £7,475. The code number for an individual who is entitled to this but no other allowance is 747L.

The code number may also reflect other items. For example, **it will be restricted to reflect benefits, small amounts of untaxed income** and **unpaid tax on income from earlier years.** If an amount of tax is in point, it is necessary to gross up the tax in the code using the taxpayer's estimated marginal rate of income tax.

Question	PAYE codes

Adrian is a 40 year old single man (suffix letter L) who earns £15,000 pa. He has benefits of £560 and his unpaid tax for 2009/10 was £58. Adrian is entitled to a tax free personal allowance of £7,475 in 2011/12.

Adrian is a basic rate taxpayer.

What is Adrian's PAYE code for 2011/12?

	£
Personal allowance	7,475
Benefits	(560)
Unpaid tax £58 × 100/20	(290)
Available allowances	6,625

Adrian's PAYE code is 662L

Codes are determined and amended by HMRC. They are normally notified to the employer on a code list. The employer must act on the code notified to him until amended instructions are received from HMRC, even if the employee has appealed against the code.

By using the code number in conjunction with the tax tables, an employee is generally given 1/52nd or 1/12th of his tax free allowances against each week's/month's pay. However because of the cumulative nature of PAYE, if an employee is first paid in, say, September, that month he will receive six months' allowances against his gross pay. In cases where the employee's previous PAYE history is not known, this could lead to under-deduction of tax. To avoid this, codes for the employees concerned have to be operated on a 'week 1/month1' basis, so that only 1/52nd or 1/12th of the employee's allowances are available each week/month.

6.5 PAYE forms

FAST FORWARD

Employers must complete forms P60, P14, P35, P9D, P11D and P45 as appropriate. A P45 is needed when an employee leaves. Forms P9D and P11D record details of benefits. Forms P60, P14 and P35 are year end returns.

At the end of each tax year, the employer must provide each employee with a form P60. This shows total taxable earnings for the year, tax deducted, code number, NI number and the employer's name and address. **The P60 must be provided by 31 May following the year of assessment.**

Following the end of each tax year, the employer must submit to HMRC:

(a)   by 19 May:

   (i)   **End of year Returns P14** (showing the same details as the P60)
   (ii)   **Form P35** (summary of total tax and NI deducted from all employees)

(b)   by 6 July:

   (i)   **Forms P11D** (benefits etc for directors and employees paid £8,500+ pa)
   (ii)   **Forms P11D(b)** (return of Class 1A NICs (see later in this Text))
   (iii) **Forms P9D** (benefits etc for other employees)

A copy of the form P11D (or P9D) must also be provided to the employee by 6 July. The details shown on the P11D include the full cash equivalent of all benefits, so that the employee may enter the details on his self-assessment tax return. Specific reference numbers for the entries on the P11D are given to assist with the preparation of the employee's self assessment tax return.

When an employee leaves, a form P45 (particulars of Employee Leaving) must be prepared. This form shows the employee's code and details of his income and tax paid to date and is a four part form. One part is sent to HMRC, and three parts handed to the employee. One of the parts (part 1A) is the employee's personal copy.

If the employee takes up a new employment, he must hand the other two parts of the form P45 to the new employer. The new employer will fill in details of the new employment and send one part to HMRC, retaining the other. The details on the form are used by the new employer to calculate the PAYE due on the next payday. If the employee dies a P45 should be completed, and the whole form sent to HMRC.

If an employee joins with a form P45, the new employer can operate PAYE. If there is no P45 the employer still needs to operate PAYE. **The employee is required to complete a form P46**.

If he declares that the employment is his first job since the start of the tax year and he has not received a taxable state benefit, or that it is now his only job but he previously had another job or received a taxable state benefit, the emergency code (747L for 2011/12) applies, on a cumulative basis or week 1/month 1 basis respectively. If the employee declares that he has another job or receives a pension the employer must use code BR.

The P46 is sent to HMRC, unless the pay is below the PAYE and NIC thresholds, and the emergency code applies. In this case no PAYE is deductible until the pay exceeds the threshold.

6.6 Penalties

A form P35 is due on 19 May after the end of the tax year. In practice, a 7 day extension to the due date of 19 May is allowed.

Where a form P35 is late, a penalty of £100 per month per 50 employees may be imposed. This penalty cannot be mitigated. **This penalty ceases 12 months after the due date and a further penalty of up to 100% of the tax (and NIC) for the year which remains unpaid** at 19 April may be imposed. This penalty can be mitigated. HMRC automatically reduce the penalty by concession to the greater of £100 and the total PAYE/NIC which should be reported on the return.

Where a person has fraudulently or negligently submitted an incorrect form P35 the penalty is 100% of the tax (and NIC) attributable to the error. This penalty can be mitigated.

6.7 PAYE settlement agreements

PAYE settlement agreements (PSAs) are arrangements under which employers can make single payments to settle their employees' income tax liabilities on expense payments and benefits which are minor, irregular or where it would be impractical to operate PAYE.

Chapter Roundup

- Most employees are taxed on benefits under the benefits code. 'Excluded employees' (lower paid/non-directors) are only subject to part of the provisions of the code.

- The benefit in respect of accommodation is its annual value. There is an additional benefit if the property cost over £75,000.

- Employees who have a company car are taxed on a % of the car's list price which depends on the level of the car's CO_2 emissions. The same % multiplied by £18,800 determines the benefit where private fuel is also provided.

- Cheap loans are charged to tax on the difference between the official rate of interest and any interest paid by the employee.

- 20% of the value of assets made available for private use is taxable.

- Workplace childcare is an exempt benefit. Employer-supported childcare and childcare vouchers are exempt up to £55 per week. Maximum tax relief is limited to £11 per week (the equivalent of £55 x 20%).

- There is a residual charge for other benefits, usually equal to the cost to the employer of the benefits.

- There are a number of exempt benefits including removal expenses, sporting facilities, meal vouchers and workplace parking.

- Most tax in respect of employment income is deducted under the PAYE system. The objective of the PAYE system is to collect the correct amount of tax over the year. An employee's PAYE code is designed to ensure that allowances etc are given evenly over the year.

- Employers must complete forms P60, P14, P35, P9D, P11D and P45 as appropriate. A P45 is needed when an employee leaves. Forms P9D and P11D record details of benefits. Forms P60, P14 and P35 are year end returns.

Quick Quiz

1   What accommodation does not give rise to a taxable benefit?

2   Mike is provided with a petrol-engined car by his employer throughout 2011/12. The car has a list price of £15,000 (although the employer actually paid £13,500 for it) and has CO_2 emissions of 140g/km. Mike's taxable car benefit is:

    A   £2,430
    B   £2,700
    C   £4,050
    D   £4,500

3   When may an employee who is provided with fuel by his employer avoid a fuel scale charge?

4   To what extent are qualifying removal expenses paid for by an employer taxable?

5   Give an example of a PAYE code.

Answers to Quick Quiz

1   Job related accommodation

2   B. Amount by which CO_2 emissions exceed the baseline is $(140 - 125)$ $= 15 \div 5 = 3 + 15\%$

$= 18\% \times £15,000$

$= £2,700$

3   There is no fuel scale charge if:

(a)   All the fuel provided was made available only for business travel, or
(b)   The full cost of any fuel provided for private use was completely reimbursed by the employee.

4   The first £8,000 of qualifying removal expenses are exempt. Any excess is taxable.

5   747L.

Now try the question below from the Exam Question Bank

Number	Level	Marks	Time
Q5	Examination	15	27 mins

Pensions

Topic list	Syllabus reference
1 Types of pension scheme and membership	B6(a), (b)
2 Contributing to a pension scheme	B6(a), (b)
3 Receiving benefits from pension arrangement	B6(a), (b)

Introduction

In the previous two chapters we have discussed the taxation of employment income. Many employers offer their employees the option of joining an occupational pension scheme, and they may choose instead, or in addition, to take out a personal pension scheme run by a financial institution such as a bank or building society.

Self-employed or non-working individuals can only make provision for a pension using a personal pension scheme.

Whichever type of scheme is chosen the amount of tax relief available is the same. However, the method for giving the relief can be different: contributions to occupational schemes are usually deducted from gross pay before PAYE is calculated whilst contributions to personal pensions are paid net of basic rate tax and further tax relief is given through the personal tax computation. We cover both methods of giving tax relief in detail in this Chapter.

Study guide

		Intellectual level
B6	**The use of exemptions and reliefs in deferring and minimising income tax liabilities**	
(a)	Explain and compute the relief given for contributions to personal pension schemes, using the rules applicable from 6 April 2011.	2
(b)	Describe the relief given for contributions to occupational pension schemes, using the rules applicable from 6 April 2011.	1

Exam guide

Pension contributions can be paid by all individuals and you may come across them as part of an income tax question. You may be required to discuss the types of pension schemes available and the limits on the tax relief due, or you may have to deal with them in an income tax computation. You must be sure that you know how to deal with the two ways of giving relief – contributions to occupational schemes are deducted from earnings whilst contributions to personal pensions are paid net of basic rate tax and further tax relief is given by increasing the basic rate and higher rate limits..

1 Types of pension scheme and membership

FAST FORWARD

An employee may be a member of his employer's occupational pension scheme. Any individual whether a member of an occupational pension scheme or not, can take out a 'personal pension' plan with a financial institution such as an insurance company, bank or building society.

1.1 Introduction

An individual is encouraged by the Government to make financial provision to cover his needs when he reaches a certain age. There are state pension arrangements which provide some financial support, but the Government are keen for individuals to make their own pension provision to supplement their state pensions.

Therefore tax relief is given for private pension provision. This includes both relief for contributions paid into pension schemes during an individual's working life and an exemption from tax on income and gains arising in the pension fund itself.

1.2 Pension arrangements

An individual may make pension provision in a number of ways.

1.2.1 Occupational pension scheme

Key term

Employers may set up an **occupational pension scheme**. Such schemes may either require contributions from employees or be non-contributory. The employer may use the services of an insurance company (an insured scheme) or may set up a totally self administered pension fund.

There are two kinds of occupational pension scheme – earnings-related (**defined benefits arrangements**) and investment-related (**money purchase arrangements**). In a **defined benefits arrangements** – also known as a **final salary scheme** – the pension is generally based on employees' earnings at retirement and linked to the number of years they have worked for the firm.

A **money purchase pension** – also known as a **defined contribution scheme** – does not provide any guarantee regarding the level of pension which will be available. The individual invests in the pension scheme and the amount invested is used to build up a pension.

1.2.2 Personal pensions

> **Personal pensions** are money purchase schemes, which are provided by banks, insurance companies and other financial institutions.

Stakeholder pensions are a particular type of personal pension scheme. They must satisfy certain rules, such as a maximum level of charges, ease of transfer etc.

Any individual (whether employed or not) may join a personal pension scheme.

1.2.3 More than one pension arrangement

An individual may make a number of different pension arrangements depending on his circumstances. For example, he may be a member of an occupational pension scheme and also make pension arrangements independently with a financial provider. If the individual has more than one pension arrangement, the rules we will be looking at in detail later apply to all the pension arrangements he makes. For example, **there is a limit on the amount of contributions that the individual can make in a tax year. This limit applies to all the pension arrangements that he makes, not *each* of them**.

The rules below apply to registered pension schemes, ie those registered with HMRC.

2 Contributing to a pension scheme

> Anyone can contribute to a personal pension scheme, even if they are not earning, subject to the contributions threshold of £3,600 (gross).

2.1 Contributions by a scheme member

Any individual **under the age of 75 can make tax relievable pension contributions** in a tax year.

The maximum amount of contributions attracting tax relief made by an individual in a tax year is the higher of:

(a)   **the individual's relevant UK earnings chargeable to income tax in the year; and**
(b)   **the basic amount (set at £3,600 for 2011/12).**

These figures are gross contributions (see further below).

Relevant UK earnings are broadly employment income, trading income and income from furnished holiday lettings (see later in this Text).

If the individual does not have any UK earnings in a tax year, the maximum pension contribution he can obtain tax relief on is £3,600.

Where an individual contributes to more than one pension scheme, the aggregate of his contributions will be used to give the total amount of tax relief.

2.2 Methods of giving tax relief

> Contributions to personal pension plans are paid net of basic rate tax. Higher/ additional rate relief is given through the personal tax computation. Contributions to occupational pension schemes are usually paid under the net pay scheme.

2.2.1 Pension tax relief given at source

This method will be used where an individual makes a contribution to a pension scheme run by a personal pension provider such as an insurance company.

Relief is given at source by the contributions being deemed to be made net of basic rate tax. This applies whether the individual is an employee, self-employed or not employed at all and whether or not he has taxable income. HMRC then pay an amount of basic rate tax to the pension provider.

Further tax relief is given if the individual is a higher rate or additional rate taxpayer. The relief is given by increasing the basic rate limit and the higher rate limit for the year by the gross amount of contributions for which the taxpayer is entitled to relief. You will recognise this method as the same way in which relief is given for gift aid donations.

Exam focus point

> Make sure your workings show clearly how you have increased the basic rate and higher rate limits. Note the difference between this method and that used for net pay arrangements (see below).

Question

Pension tax relief given at source

Joe has earnings of £60,000 in 2011/12. He pays a personal pension contribution of £7,200 (net). He has no other taxable income.

Show Joe's tax liability for 2011/12.

Answer

	Non savings Income £
Earnings/Net income	60,000
Less PA	(7,475)
Taxable income	52,525

Tax	£
£35,000 × 20%	7,000
£9,000 (7,200 × 100/80) × 20% (increased basic rate limit)	1,800
£8,525 × 40%	3,410
52,525	12,210

Remember that **gross personal pension contributions** are also used to compute **adjusted net income** and that **restrictions on the personal allowance and age allowance** are calculated in relation to adjusted net income.

2.2.2 Net pay arrangements

An occupational scheme will normally operate net pay arrangements.

In this case, the employer will deduct gross pension contributions from the individual's earnings before operating PAYE. The individual therefore obtains tax relief at his marginal rate of tax automatically.

Question

Net pay arrangements

Maxine has taxable earnings of £60,000 in 2011/12. Her employer deducts a pension contribution of £9,000 from these earnings before operating PAYE. She has no other taxable income.

Show Maxine's tax liability for 2011/12.

	Non-savings Income £
Earnings/Total income	60,000
Less pension contribution	(9,000)
Net income	51,000
Less PA	(7,475)
Taxable income	43,525

Tax

	£
£35,000 × 20%	7,000
£8,525 × 40%	3,410
43,525	10,410

This is the same result as Joe in the previous example. Joe had received basic rate tax relief of £(9,000 – 7,200) = £1,800 at source, so his overall tax position was £(12,210 – 1,800) = £10,410.

2.3 Contributions not attracting tax relief

An individual can also make contributions to his pension arrangements which do not attract tax relief, for example out of capital. The member must notify the scheme administrator if he makes contributions in excess of the higher of his UK relevant earnings and the basic amount.

Such contributions do not count towards the annual allowance limit (discussed below) but will affect the value of the pension fund for the lifetime allowance.

2.4 Employer pension contributions

Where the individual is an employee, his **employer may make contributions to his pension scheme** as part of his employment benefits package. Such contributions are **exempt benefits** for the employee.

There is **no limit** on the amount of the contributions that may be made by an employer but **they always count towards the annual allowance** and will also affect the value of the pension fund for the lifetime allowance (see further below).

All contributions made by an employer are made gross and the employer will usually obtain tax relief for the contribution by deducting it as an expense in calculating trading profits for the period of account in which the payment is made.

2.5 Annual allowance

FAST FORWARD

There is an overriding limit on the amount that can be paid into an individual's pension schemes for each tax year. This is called the annual allowance. Unused annual allowance can be carried forward for up to three years.

2.5.1 Introduction

The annual allowance effectively restricts the amount of tax relievable contributions that can be paid into an individual's pension scheme each year. The amount of the annual allowance for 2011/12 is £50,000.

2.5.2 Carry forward of unused annual allowance

Where **an individual is a member of a registered pension scheme** but **does not make contributions of at least the annual allowance in a tax year**, the individual can **carry forward the unused amount of the annual allowance for up to three years**. In any year for which the individual is not a member of a pension scheme, the annual allowance does not apply and so there can be no carry forward.

The annual allowance in the current tax year is treated as being used first, then any unused annual allowance is brought forward from earlier years, using the earliest tax year first. For tax years before 2011/12, a notional £50,000 annual allowance applies to calculate the unused annual allowance in those years.

Question   Carry forward of annual allowance

Ted is a sole trader. His gross contributions to his personal pension scheme have been as follows:

2007/08	£21,000
2008/09	£26,000
2009/10	£46,000
2010/11	£35,000

In 2011/12 Ted has a good trading year and wishes to make a large pension contribution.

(a) What is the maximum gross pension contribution Ted can make in 2011/12 without incurring an annual allowance charge taking into account any brought forward annual allowance?

(b) If Ted makes a gross personal pension contribution of £53,000 in 2011/12, what are the unused annual allowances he can carry forward to 2012/13?

Answer

(a)

	£
Annual allowance 2011/12	50,000
Annual allowance unused in 2008/09 £(50,000 – 26,000)	24,000
Annual allowance unused in 2009/10 £(50,000 – 46,000)	4,000
Annual allowance unused in 2010/11 £(50,000 – 35,000)	15,000
Maximum gross pension contribution in 2011/12	93,000

Note

The unused allowance from 2007/08 cannot be used in 2011/12 as this is more than three years after 2007/08.

(b)

	£
Annual allowance 2011/12 used in 2011/12	50,000
Annual allowance unused in 2008/09 used in 2011/12	3,000
Contribution in 2011/12	53,000

The remaining £(24,000 – 3,000) = £21,000 of the 2008/09 annual allowance cannot be carried forward to 2012/13 since this is more than three years after 2008/09. The unused annual allowances are therefore £4,000 from 2009/10 and £15,000 from 2010/11 and these are carried forward to 2012/13.

2.5.3 Contributions in excess of annual allowance

> An annual allowance charge arises if tax-relievable contributions exceed the available annual allowance.

If tax-relievable pension contributions exceed the annual allowance, there is a charge to income tax based on the individual's taxable income. This will occur if the taxpayer has relevant earnings in excess of the available annual allowance and makes a contribution in excess of the available annual allowance (including any brought forward annual allowance).

The taxpayer is primarily liable for the tax on the excess contribution.

The annual allowance charge is calculated by treating the excess contribution as an extra amount of non-savings income received by the taxpayer. The calculation therefore claws back the tax relief given on the pension contribution.

Question
Annual allowance charge

Jaida had employment income of £240,000 in 2011/12. She made a gross personal pension contribution of £80,000 in 2011/12. She does not have any unused annual allowance brought forward. What is Jaida's income tax liability for 2011/12?

Answer

	Non-savings income £
Employment income	240,000
Excess pension contribution £(80,000 – 50,000) (N1)	30,000
Taxable income (no personal allowance available)	270,000
Tax	
£35,000 × 20%	7,000
£80,000 × 20% (increased basic rate limit)	16,000
£115,000 × 40% (N2)	46,000
£40,000 × 50%	20,000
Tax liability	89,000

Notes

(1) The pension contribution is below Jaida's relevant earnings and so is below the maximum pension contribution on which tax relief can be given, but has exceeded the annual allowance limit of £50,000.

(2) The higher rate limit is increased to £(150,000 + 80,000) = £230,000. This preserves the higher rate band of £(230,000 – 35,000 – 80,000) = £115,000.

Exam focus point

> The examiner has said that questions involving the annual allowance charge will be kept straightforward. For example, no question will be set where there is a partial restriction of the personal allowance or where the annual allowance charge arises in a different tax year to that in which the related tax relief on the pension contributions was given.

3 Receiving benefits from pension arrangements

3.1 Pension benefits

After reaching the minimum pension age of 55, an individual may 'vest' the benefits, ie set aside all or part of the pension fund to provide pension benefits. Normally an individual may take one quarter of his pension fund as a tax free lump sum, and the balance of the fund is usually used to purchase a pension (annual income) often referred to as an annuity. An individual under the age of 75 can usually both make tax-relieved contributions and receive pension benefits.

3.2 The lifetime allowance

FAST FORWARD

An individual is not allowed to build up an indefinitely large pension fund. There is a maximum value for a pension fund called the lifetime allowance.

The amount of the **lifetime allowance for 2011/12 is £1,800,000.**

If the pension fund exceeds the lifetime allowance at the time the benefit starts to be taken ('vested') this will give rise to an income tax charge on the excess value of the fund. The rate of the charge is 55% if the excess value is taken as a lump sum, or 25% if the funds are left In the scheme to provide a pension.

Chapter Roundup

- An employee may be a member of his employer's occupational pension scheme. Any individual whether a member of an occupational pension scheme or not, can take out a 'personal pension' plan with a financial institution such as an insurance company, bank or building society.

- Anyone can contribute to a personal pension scheme, even if they are not earning, subject to the contributions threshold of £3,600 (gross).

- Contributions to personal pension plans are paid net of basic rate tax. Higher/ additional rate relief is given through the personal tax computation. Contributions to occupational pension schemes are usually paid under the net pay scheme.

- There is an overriding limit on the amount that can be paid into an individual's pension schemes for each tax year. This is called the annual allowance. Unused annual allowance can be carried forward for up to three years.

- An annual allowance charge arises if tax-relievable contributions exceed the available annual allowance.

- An individual is not allowed to build up an indefinitely large pension fund. There is a maximum value for a pension fund called the lifetime allowance.

Quick Quiz

1   Martha has UK earnings of £3,000 in 2011/12. What is the maximum actual amount of pension contribution she can pay in 2011/12 to a personal pension?

    A   £2,400
    B   £2,880
    C   £3,000
    D   £3,600

2   Fern joins a registered pension scheme in 2009/10 and makes a gross contribution of £24,000. She had not been a member of registered pension scheme before this time. She does not make any contribution in 2010/11. What is the maximum gross pension contribution Fern can make in 2011/12 without incurring an annual allowance charge taking into account any brought forward annual allowance?

3   What are the consequences of the total of employee and employer pension contributions exceeding the annual allowance?

4   What are the consequences of exceeding the lifetime allowance?

1   B. The maximum gross contribution that Martha can pay is the higher of her relevant earnings (£3,000) and the basic amount (£3,600). She will actually pay £3,600 × 80% = £2,880 to the pension provider.

2   Fern will not be able to use any unused personal allowance from 2008/09 as she was not a member of a registered pension scheme in this year. She has £(50,000 − 24,000) = £26,000 unused from 2009/10 and £50,000 from 2010/11. Her total maximum contribution in 2011/12 without incurring an annual allowance charge is therefore £(26,000 + 50,000 + 50,000) = £126,000.

3   The excess is subject to the annual allowance charge primarily chargeable on the employee.

4   If the lifetime allowance is exceeded the excess is charged at 55% (if taken as a lump sum) or 25% (if taken as a pension).

Now try the questions below from the Exam Question Bank

Number	Level	Marks	Time
Q6	Introductory	6	11 mins
Q7	Examination	15	27 mins

Property income

Topic list	Syllabus reference
1 Property business income	B4(a)
2 Furnished holiday lettings	B4(b)
3 Rent a room relief	B4(c)
4 Premiums on leases	B4(d)
5 Property business losses	B4(e)

Introduction

We have finished looking at an individual's employment income and can turn our attention to other income to be slotted into the tax computation.

We are now going to look at the computation and taxation of the profits of a property letting business. First we see how to work out the profit (you may like to return to this section once you have studied chapters 7 and 8).

Next we look at the special conditions which must be satisfied if a letting is to be treated as a furnished holiday lettings and at the extra tax reliefs available if it is.

We then consider the special relief available to taxpayers who let out rooms in their own homes, rent a room relief.

Finally we see how part of a premium for granting a short lease is taxed as income.

In the following chapters we shall turn our attention to the profits of an actual trade, profession or vocation.

Study guide

		Intellectual level
B4	**Property and investment income**	
(a)	Compute property business profits.	2
(b)	Explain the treatment of furnished holiday lettings.	1
(c)	Describe rent-a-room relief.	1
(d)	Compute the amount assessable when a premium is received for the grant of a short lease.	2
(e)	Understand how relief for a property business loss is given.	2

Exam guide

You are very likely to have to compute property income as part of question. You may find it in the context of income tax or corporation tax – the basic computational rules are the same (apart from interest paid which is not included as an expense when computing property income for corporation tax purposes). Rent a room relief is an important relief for individuals (it does not apply to companies), and the special rules for furnished holiday lettings will only be examined in an income tax context. Remember that property income is non-savings income even though a property portfolio is usually regarded as an investment.

1 Property business income

FAST FORWARD

Property business profits are calculated on an accruals basis.

1.1 Profits of a property business

Income from land and buildings in the UK is taxed as non-savings income.

The profits of the UK property business are computed for tax years. Each tax year's profit is taxed in that year.

1.2 Computation of profits

A taxpayer with UK rental income is treated as running a business, his 'UK property business'. All the rents and expenses for all properties are pooled, to give a single profit or loss. Profits and losses are computed in the same way as trading profits are computed for tax purposes, on an **accruals basis**.

Expenses will often include rent payable where a landlord is himself renting the land which he in turn lets to others. For individuals, interest on loans to buy or improve properties is treated as an expense (on an accruals basis).

Relief is available for irrecoverable rent as an impaired debt.

1.3 Capital allowances

FAST FORWARD

If a residential property is let furnished a wear and tear allowance may be claimed in respect of the furniture. Capital allowances are not available.

Capital allowances are given on plant and machinery used in the UK property business in the same way as they are given for a trading business with an accounting date of 5 April. However, **capital allowances are not normally available on plant or machinery used in a dwelling but someone who lets a furnished property used as a dwelling (residential property) can instead claim the wear and tear allowance.**

If the wear and tear allowance is claimed, the actual cost of furniture is ignored, but an annual allowance is given of **10% of rents**. The rents are first reduced by amounts which are paid by the landlord but are normally a tenant's burden. These amounts include any **water rates** and **council tax** paid by the landlord.

Exam focus point

In the exam look at the question carefully to see if the property is residential and, if so, whether it is let furnished. If so, the landlord is eligible to claim the wear and tear allowance.

Question — Property business income

Over the last few years Peter has purchased several residential properties in Manchester as 'buy to let' investments.

5 Whitby Ave is let out furnished at £500 per month. A tenant moved in on 1 March 2011 but left unexpectedly on 1 May 2012 having paid rent only up to 31 December 2011. The tenant left no forwarding address.

17 Bolton Rd has been let furnished to the same tenant for a number of years at £800 per month.

A recent purchase, 27 Turner Close, has been let unfurnished since 1 August 2011 at £750 per month. Before then, it had been empty whilst Peter redecorated it after its purchase in March 2011.

Pete's expenses during 2011/12 are:

	No 5 £	No 17 £	No 27 £
Insurance	250	250	200
Letting agency fees	–	–	100
Repairs	300	40	–
Redecoration	–	–	500

No 27 was in a fit state to let when Peter bought it but he wanted to redecorate the property as he felt this would allow him to achieve a better rental income.

Water rates and council tax are paid by the tenants.

Calculate Peter's property business income for 2011/12.

Answer

	No 5 £	No 17 £	No 27 £
Accrued income			
12 × £500	6,000		
12 × £800		9,600	
8 × £750			6,000
Less:			
Insurance	(250)	(250)	(200)
Letting agency fees			(100)
Repairs	(300)	(40)	
Redecoration (N)			(500)
Impairment (irrecoverable rent) 3 × £500	(1,500)		
Wear and Tear Allowance			
£(6,000 – 1,500) × 10%	(450)		
£9,600 × 10%		(960)	
Property business income	3,500	8,350	5,200
Taxable property income for 2011/12			£17,050

Note: The redecoration of No.27 is an allowable expense. This is an example of the application of the case of *Odeon Associated Theatres Ltd v Jones 1971* (covered in more detail later in this Text) which showed that the cost of initial repairs to remedy normal wear and tear of a recently acquired asset was an allowable expense. This contrasts with the case of *Law Shipping v. CIR 1921* where the cost of initial repairs to improve an asset recently acquired to make it fit to earn profits was disallowable capital expenditure. The key point in relation to No. 27 is that it was in a fit state to let when acquired.

2 Furnished holiday lettings

FAST FORWARD

Special rules apply to income from furnished holiday lettings. Whilst the income is taxed as normal as property business income, the letting is treated as if it were a trade. Capital allowances are available on the furniture and the income is relevant earnings for pension purposes. However, only carry forward trade loss relief is available.

2.1 Introduction

There are special rules for furnished holiday lettings (FHLs). The letting is treated as if it were a trade. This means that, although the income is taxed as income from a property business, the provisions which apply to actual trades also apply to furnished holiday lettings.

(a)   Capital allowances are available on furniture instead of the 10% wear and tear allowance.

(b)   The income qualifies as relevant earnings for pension relief (see earlier in this Text).

(c)   Capital gains tax rollover relief, entrepreneurs' relief and relief for gifts of business assets are available (see later in this Text).

However, losses from FHLs are not treated as trade losses for relief against general income, early years loss relief and terminal loss relief. If a loss arises on a FHL, the only trade loss relief available is carry forward loss relief by deduction from the first available future profits of the same FHL business. Trading loss reliefs are dealt with later in this Text.

2.2 Conditions

Exam focus point

A FHL must be situated in the UK or in another state within the European Economic Area. However, only FHL situated within the UK are within the F6 syllabus.

The letting must be of furnished accommodation made on a **commercial basis with a view to the realisation of profit**. The property must also satisfy the following three conditions.

(a)   **The availability condition** – the accommodation is available for commercial let as holiday accommodation to the public generally, for **at least 140 days during the year**.

(b)   **The letting condition** – the accommodation is commercially let as holiday accommodation to members of the public for **at least 70 days during the year**. If the **landlord has more than one FHL**, at least one of which satisfies the 70 day rule ('qualifying holiday accommodation') and at least one of which does not, ('the underused accommodation') , he may elect to **average the occupation of the qualifying holiday accommodation and any or all of the underused accommodation**. If the average of occupation is at least 70 days, the under-used accommodation will be treated as qualifying holiday accommodation.

(c)   **The pattern of occupation condition – not more than 155 days in the year** fall during periods of longer term occupation. Longer term occupation is defined as a **continuous period of more than 31 days during which the accommodation is in the same occupation** unless there are abnormal circumstances.

If someone has furnished holiday lettings and other lettings, **draw up two income statements as if they had two separate property businesses**. This is so that the profits and losses can be identified for the special rules which apply to FHLs.

3 Rent a room relief

FAST FORWARD

Rents received from letting a room in the taxpayer's home may be tax free under the rent a room scheme.

3.1 The exemption

If an individual lets a room or rooms, furnished, in his main residence as living accommodation, then a special exemption may apply.

The limit on the exemption is gross rents (before any expenses or capital allowances) of £4,250 a year. This limit is halved if any other person (eg spouse/civil partner) also received income from renting accommodation in the property.

If gross rents are not more than the limit, the rents are wholly exempt from income tax and expenses are ignored. However, the taxpayer may claim to ignore the exemption, for example to generate a loss by taking into account both rent and expenses.

Exam focus point

If you are asked to calculate property income in an exam don't overlook rent a room relief, but be sure to state whether the relief applies.

3.2 Alternative basis

If gross rents exceed the limit, the taxpayer will be taxed in the ordinary way, ignoring the rent a room scheme, unless he elects for the 'alternative basis'. If he so elects, he will be taxable on gross receipts less £4,250 (or £2,125 if the limit is halved), with no deductions for expenses.

An election to ignore the exemption (if gross profits are below £4,250), or an election for the alternative basis (if gross profits exceed £4,250) must be made by the 31 January which is 22 months from the end of the tax year concerned. An election to ignore the exemption applies only for the tax year for which it is made, but an election for the alternative basis remains in force until it is withdrawn or until a year in which gross rents do not exceed the limit.

Question   Rent a room relief

Sylvia owns a house near the sea in Norfolk. She has a spare bedroom and during 2011/12 this was let to a chef working at a nearby restaurant for £85 per week which includes the cost of heating, lighting etc.

Sylvia estimates that her lodger costs her an extra:

£50 on gas
£25 on electricity
£50 on insurance

each year.

How much property income must Sylvia pay tax on?

Sylvia has a choice:

(1)   Under the normal method, she can be taxed on her actual profit:

	£
Rental income	4,420
Less expenses (50 + 25 + 50)	(125)
	4,295

(2)   Under the 'alternative basis':

Total rental income of £85 × 52 = £4,420 exceeds £4,250 limit so taxable income is £170 (ie 4,420 − 4,250) if rent a room relief claimed.

Sylvia would be advised to claim the 'alternative basis'.

4 Premiums on leases

FAST FORWARD

A premium received on the grant of a lease may be partly taxable as property income. If the premium is paid by a trader, a deduction can be made in computing taxable trading profits.

When a premium or similar consideration is received on the grant (that is, by a landlord to a tenant) **of a short lease (50 years or less), part of the premium is treated as property income received in the year of grant.**

The premium taxed as property income is the whole premium, less 2% of the premium for each complete year of the lease, except the first year.

This rule does not apply on the **assignment** of a lease (one tenant selling his entire interest in the property to another).

4.1 Example: income element of premium

Janet granted a lease to Jack on 1 March 2012 for a period of 40 years. Jack paid a premium of £16,000. How much of the premium received by Janet is taxed as property income?

	£
Premium received	16,000
Less 2% × (40 −1) × £16,000	(12,480)
Taxable as property income	3,520

Note that if Janet **owned 40 year lease and assigned it to Jack**, no part of the amount received would be taxed as property income.

4.2 Premiums paid by traders

Where a trader pays a premium for a lease he may deduct an amount when computing his taxable trading profits in each year of the lease. The amount deductible is the figure taxed as property income on the landlord divided by the number of years of the lease.

You may want to look at this point again once you have studied trade profits later in this Text.

4.3 Example: deduction for premium paid by trader

On 1 July 2011 Bryony, a trader, pays Scott, the landlord, a premium of £30,000 for a ten year lease on a shop. Bryony makes up accounts to 31 December each year.

Scott is taxable on property income in 2011/12 of £30,000 – (£30,000 × (10 – 1) × 2%) = £24,600.

Bryony can therefore deduct £24,600/10 = £2,460 in each of the ten years of the lease. She starts with the accounts year in which the lease starts (year ended 31 December 2011) and apportions the relief to the nearest month. Her deduction for 2011/12 is therefore:

1 July 2011 to 31 December 2011: 6/12 x £2,460   £1,230

4.4 Premiums for granting subleases

A tenant may decide to sublet property and to charge a premium on the grant of a lease to the subtenant. This premium is treated as property income in the normal way (because this is a grant and not an assignment, the original tenant retaining an interest in the property). **Where the tenant originally paid a premium for his own head lease, this property income is reduced by:**

$$\text{Property income part of premium for head lease} \times \frac{\text{duration of sublease}}{\text{duration of head lease}}$$

Question   Taxable premium received

Charles granted a lease to David on 1 March 2001 for a period of 40 years. David paid a premium of £16,000. On 1 June 2011 David granted a sublease to Edward for a period of 10 years. Edward paid a premium of £30,000. Calculate the amount treated as property income out of the premium received by David.

Answer

	£
Premium received by David	30,000
Less £30,000 × 2% × (10-1)	(5,400)
	24,600
Less allowance for premium paid	
(£16,000 – (£16,000 × 39 × 2%)) × 10/40	(880)
Premium treated as property income	23,720

5 Property business losses

FAST FORWARD

A loss on a property letting business is carried forward to set against future property business profits.

A loss from a UK property business is carried forward to set against the **first future profits from the UK property business**. It may be carried forward until the UK property business ends, but it must be used as soon as possible.

As explained above, however, FHL losses are dealt with under special rules so that losses from a FHL business must be kept separate and can only be used against profits of the same FHL business.

Chapter Roundup

- Property business profits are calculated on an accruals basis.

- If residential property is let furnished a wear and tear allowance may be claimed in respect of the furniture. Capital allowances are not available.

- Special rules apply to income from furnished holiday lettings. Whilst the income is taxed as normal as property business income, the letting is treated as if it were a trade. Capital allowances are available on the furniture and the income is relevant earnings for pension purposes. However, only carry forward trade loss relief is available.

- Rents received from letting a room in the taxpayer's home may be tax free under the rent a room scheme.

- A premium received on the grant of a lease may be partly taxable as rent. If the premium is paid by a trader, a deduction can be made in computing taxable trading profits.

- A loss on a property letting business is carried forward to set against future property business profits.

Quick Quiz

1   How is capital expenditure relieved for furnished lettings?

2   In order for property to be a furnished holiday letting it must be:

    (a)   available for letting for at least _____ days during the year; and

    (b)   actually let for at least _____ days during the year

    (c)   not let as longer term accommodation for more than _____days in the year (longer term occupation is a continuous period of more than _____days in the same occupation). Fill in the blanks.

3   How much income per annum is tax free under the rent a room scheme?

    A   £2,125
    B   £4,250
    C   £4,500
    D   £7,475

Answers to Quick Quiz

1   Except for furnished holiday lettings where capital allowances are available for the cost of furniture, capital expenditure on furnishings is relieved through the wear and tear allowance. The allowance is equal to 10% of rents less council tax and water rates (if paid by the landlord).

2   In order for property to be a furnished holiday letting it must be:

   (a)   available for letting for at least **140** days during the year; and

   (b)   actually let for at least **70** days during the year

   (c)   not let as longer term accommodation for more than **155** days in the year (longer term occupation is a continuous period of more than **31** days in the same occupation).

3   B. £4,250

Now try the questions below from the Exam Question Bank

Number	Level	Marks	Time
Q8	Examination	15	27 mins

7

Computing trading income

Topic list	Syllabus referenc
1 The badges of trade	B3(b)
2 The adjustment of profits	B3(c)
3 Pretrading expenditure	B3(d)

Introduction

The final figure to slot into the income tax computation is income from self employment (trading income).

We are therefore going to look at the computation of profits of unincorporated businesses. We work out a business's profit as if it were a separate entity (the separate entity concept familiar to you from basic bookkeeping) but, as an unincorporated business has no legal existence apart from its trader, we cannot tax it separately. We have to feed its profit into the owner's personal tax computation.

Later chapters will consider capital allowances, which are allowed as an expense in the computation of profits, the taxation of business profits, and how trading losses can be relieved. We will then extend our study to partnerships, ie to groups of two or more individuals trading together.

Study guide

		Intellectual level
B3	**Income from self-employment**	
(b)	Describe and apply the badges of trade.	2
(c)	Recognise the expenditure that is allowable in calculating the tax-adjusted trading profit.	2
(d)	Recognise the relief that can be obtained for pre-trading expenditure.	2

Exam guide

You are likely to have to compute trading profits at some point in the exam. The computation may be for an individual, a partnership or a company. In each case the same principles are applied. You must however watch out for the adjustments which only apply to individuals, such as private use expenses.

1 The badges of trade

FAST FORWARD

> The badges of trade are used to decide whether or not a trade exists. If one does exist, the accounts profits need to be adjusted in order to establish the taxable profits.

Key term

> A trade is defined in Income Tax Act 2007 only as 'any venture in the nature of trade'. Further guidance about the scope of this definition is found in a number of cases which have been decided by the Courts. This guidance is summarised in a collection of principles known as the **'badges of trade'**. These are set out below. They apply to both corporate and unincorporated businesses.

Exam focus point

> You are not expected to know case names – we have included these below for your information only.

1.1 The subject matter

Whether a person is trading or not may sometimes be decided by examining the subject matter of the transaction. Some assets are commonly held as investments for their intrinsic value: an individual buying some shares or a painting may do so in order to enjoy the income from the shares or to enjoy the work of art. A subsequent disposal may produce a gain of a capital nature rather than a trading profit. But **where the subject matter of a transaction is such as would not be held as an investment** (for example 34,000,000 yards of aircraft linen (*Martin v Lowry 1927*) or 1,000,000 rolls of toilet paper (*Rutledge v CIR 1929*)), **it is presumed that any profit on resale is a trading profit**.

1.2 The frequency of transactions

Transactions which may, in isolation, be of a capital nature will be interpreted as **trading transactions where their frequency indicates the carrying on of a trade.** It was decided that whereas normally the purchase of a mill-owning company and the subsequent stripping of its assets might be a capital transaction, where the taxpayer was embarking on the same exercise for the fourth time he must be carrying on a trade (*Pickford v Quirke 1927*).

1.3 Existence of similar trading transactions or interests

If there is an **existing trade**, then a **similarity to the transaction which is being considered** may point to that transaction having a trading character. For example, a builder who builds and sells a number of houses may be held to be trading even if he retains one or more houses for longer than usual and claims that they were held as an investment (*Harvey v Caulcott 1952*).

1.4 The length of ownership

The courts may infer a venture in the nature of trade where **items purchased are sold soon afterwards**.

1.5 The organisation of the activity as a trade

The courts may infer that a trade is being carried on if the transactions are **carried out in the same manner as someone who is unquestionably trading**. For example, an individual who bought a consignment of whiskey and then sold it through an agent, in the same way as others who were carrying on a trade, was also held to be trading (*CIR v Fraser 1942*). On the other hand, if an **asset has to be sold in order to raise funds in an emergency, this is less likely to be treated as trading**.

1.6 Supplementary work and marketing

When work is done to make an asset more marketable, or **marketing steps are taken to find purchasers**, the Courts will be more ready to ascribe a trading motive. When a group of accountants bought, blended and recasked a quantity of brandy, they were held to be taxable on a trading profit when the brandy was later sold (*Cape Brandy Syndicate v CIR 1921*).

1.7 A profit motive

The absence of a profit motive will not necessarily preclude a tax charge as trading income, but its presence is a strong indication that a person is trading. The purchase and resale of £20,000 worth of silver bullion by the comedian Norman Wisdom, as a hedge against devaluation, was held to be a trading transaction (*Wisdom v Chamberlain 1969*).

1.8 The way in which the asset sold was acquired

If goods are acquired deliberately, trading may be indicated. If goods are acquired unintentionally, for example by gift or inheritance, their later sale is unlikely to be trading.

1.9 Method of finance

If the **purchaser has to borrow money to buy an asset such that he has to sell that asset quickly to repay the loan**, it may be inferred that trading was taking place. This was a factor in the *Wisdom v Chamberlain* case as Mr Wisdom financed his purchases by loans at a high rate of interest. It was clear that he had to sell the silver bullion quickly in order to repay the loan and prevent the interest charges becoming too onerous. On the other hand, taking out a long term loan to buy an asset (such as a mortgage on a house) would not usually indicate that trading is being carried on.

1.10 The taxpayer's intentions

Where a transaction is clearly trading on objective criteria, **the taxpayer's intentions are irrelevant**. If, however, a transaction has (objectively) a dual purpose, the taxpayer's intentions may be taken into account. An example of a transaction with a dual purpose is the acquisition of a site partly as premises from which to conduct another trade, and partly with a view to the possible development and resale of the site.

This test is not one of the traditional badges of trade, but it may be just as important.

2 The adjustment of profits

FAST FORWARD

The net profit in the income statement must be adjusted to find the taxable trading profit.

2.1 Illustrative adjustment

Exam focus point

> The rules relating to profits from trades apply equally to profits from all professions and vocations.

Although the **net profit** shown in the income statement is the starting point in computing the taxable trade profits, many adjustments may be required to calculate the taxable amount.

Exam focus point

> Only international accounting standard terminology is used when presenting accounting information contained within an examination question. This applies for companies, sole traders and partnerships.

Here is an illustrative adjustment of an income statement:

	£	£
Net profit		140,000
Add: expenditure charged in the accounts which is not deductible from trading profits	50,000	
income taxable as trading profits which has not been included in the accounts	30,000	
		80,000
		220,000
Less: profits included in the accounts but which are not taxable as trading profits	40,000	
expenditure which is deductible from trading profits but has not been charged in the accounts (eg capital allowances)	20,000	
		(60,000)
Adjusted taxable trading profit		160,000

You may refer to deductible and non-deductible expenditure as allowable and disallowable expenditure respectively. The two sets of terms are interchangeable.

Exam focus point

> An examination question requiring adjustment to profit will direct you to start the adjustment with the net profit of £XXXX and to deal with all the items listed, indicating with a zero (0) any items which do not require adjustment. Marks will not be given for relevant items unless this approach is used. Therefore students who attempt to rewrite the income statement will be penalised.

2.2 Accounting policies

The fundamental concept is that the profits of the business must be calculated in accordance with generally accepted accounting practice. These profits are subject to any adjustment specifically required for income tax purposes.

2.3 Deductible and non-deductible expenditure

FAST FORWARD

Disallowable (ie non-deductible) expenditure must be added back to the net profit in the computation of the taxable trading profit. Any item not deducted wholly and exclusively for trade purposes is disallowable expenditure. Certain other items, such as depreciation, are specifically disallowable.

2.3.1 Introduction

Certain expenses are specifically disallowed by the legislation. These are covered below. If however a deduction is specifically permitted this overrides the disallowance.

2.3.2 Payments contrary to public policy and illegal payments

Fines and penalties are not deductible. However, **HMRC usually allow employees' parking fines incurred in parking their employer's cars while on their employer's business. Fines relating to traders, however, are never allowed.**

A payment is not deductible if making it constitutes an offence by the payer. This covers protection money paid to terrorists, and also bribes. Statute also prevents any deduction for payments made in response to blackmail or extortion.

2.3.3 Capital expenditure

Capital expenditure is not deductible. This means that depreciation is non-deductible.

Profits and losses on the sale of non-current assets must be deducted or added back respectively. Chargeable gains or allowable losses may be dealt with under capital gains tax (see later in this Text).

The most contentious items of expenditure will often be repairs (revenue expenditure) **and improvements** (capital expenditure).

- **The cost of restoration of an asset by, for instance, replacing a subsidiary part of the asset is revenue expenditure.** Expenditure on a new factory chimney replacement was allowable since the chimney was a subsidiary part of the factory (*Samuel Jones & Co (Devondale) Ltd v CIR 1951*). However, in another case a football club demolished a spectators' stand and replaced it with a modern equivalent. This was held not to be repair, since repair is the restoration by renewal or replacement of subsidiary parts of a larger entity, and the stand formed a distinct and *separate* part of the club (*Brown v Burnley Football and Athletic Co Ltd 1980*).

- **The cost of initial repairs to improve an asset recently acquired to make it fit to earn profits is disallowable capital expenditure.** In *Law Shipping Co Ltd v CIR 1923* the taxpayer failed to obtain relief for expenditure on making a newly bought ship seaworthy prior to using it.

- **The cost of initial repairs to remedy normal wear and tear of recently acquired assets is allowable revenue expenditure.** *Odeon Associated Theatres Ltd v Jones 1971* can be contrasted with the *Law Shipping* judgement. Odeon were allowed to charge expenditure incurred on improving the state of recently acquired cinemas.

Capital allowances may, however, be available as a deduction for capital expenditure from trading profits (see later in this Text).

Two exceptions to the 'capital' rule are worth noting.

(a) **The costs of registering patents and trade marks are deductible**.

(b) **Incidental costs of obtaining loan finance**, or of attempting to obtain or redeeming it, are deductible, other than a discount on issue or a premium on redemption (which are really alternatives to paying interest).

2.3.4 Expenditure not wholly and exclusively for the purposes of the trade

Expenditure is not deductible if it is not for trade purposes (the remoteness test), or if it reflects more than one purpose (the duality test). The private proportion of payments for motoring expenses, rent, heat and light and telephone expenses of a trader is non-deductible. If an exact apportionment is possible, relief is given on the business element. Where the payments are to or on behalf of employees, the full amounts are deductible but the employees are taxed under the benefits code (see earlier in this Text).

The remoteness test is illustrated by the following cases.

- *Strong & Co of Romsey Ltd v Woodifield 1906*
  A customer injured by a falling chimney when sleeping in an inn owned by a brewery claimed compensation from the company. The compensation was not deductible: 'the loss sustained by the appellant was not really incidental to their trade as innkeepers and fell upon them in their character not of innkeepers but of householders'.

- *Bamford v ATA Advertising Ltd 1972*
  A director misappropriated £15,000. The loss was not allowable: 'the loss is not, as in the case of a dishonest shop assistant, an incident of the company's trading activities. It arises altogether outside such activities'.

- Expenditure which is wholly and exclusively to benefit the trades of several companies (for example in a group) but is not wholly and exclusively to benefit the trade of one specific company is not deductible *(Vodafone Cellular Ltd and others v Shaw 1995)*.

- *McKnight (HMIT) v Sheppard (1999)* concerned expenses incurred by a stockbroker in defending allegations of infringements of Stock Exchange regulations. It was found that the expenditure was incurred to prevent the destruction of the taxpayer's business and that as the expenditure was incurred for business purposes it was deductible. It was also found that although the expenditure had the effect of preserving the taxpayer's reputation, that was not its purpose, so there was no duality of purpose.

The **duality test** is illustrated by the following cases.

- *Caillebotte v Quinn 1975*
  A self-employed carpenter spent an average of 40p per day when obliged to buy lunch away from home but just 10p when he lunched at home. He claimed the excess 30p. It was decided that the payment had a dual purpose and was not deductible: a taxpayer 'must eat to live not eat to work'.

- *Mallalieu v Drummond 1983*
  Expenditure by a lady barrister on black clothing to be worn in court (and on its cleaning and repair) was not deductible. The expenditure was for the dual purpose of enabling the barrister to be warmly and properly clad as well as meeting her professional requirements.

- *McLaren v Mumford 1996*
  A publican traded from a public house which had residential accommodation above it. He was obliged to live at the public house but he also had another house which he visited regularly. It was held that the private element of the expenditure incurred at the public house on electricity, rent, gas, etc was not incurred for the purpose of earning profits, but for serving the non-business purpose of satisfying the publican's ordinary human needs. The expenditure, therefore had a dual purpose and was disallowed.

However, the cost of overnight accommodation when on a business trip may be deductible and reasonable expenditure on an evening meal and breakfast in conjunction with such accommodation is then also deductible.

2.3.5 Impaired trade receivables (bad debts)

Only impairment debts incurred wholly and exclusively for the purposes of the trade are deductible for taxation purposes. For example, **loans to employees written off are not deductible** unless the business is that of making loans, or it can be shown that the writing-off of the loan was earnings paid out for the benefit of the trade.

Under FRS 26 *Financial instruments: measurement*, a review of all trade receivables should be carried out to assess their fair value at the balance sheet date and any impairment debts written off. **The tax treatment follows the accounting treatment so no adjustment is required for tax purposes.** As a result of FRS 26, it is less likely that any general provisions will now be seen. In the event that they do arise, increases or decreases in a general provision are not allowable /taxable and an adjustment will need to be made.

If an impairment debt which has been deducted for tax purposes is later recovered, the recovery is taxable so no adjustment is required to the amount of the recovery shown in the income statement.

2.3.6 Unpaid remuneration and employee benefit contributions

If earnings for employees are charged in the accounts but are not paid within nine months of the end of the period of account, the cost is only deductible for the period of account in which the earnings are paid. When a tax computation is made within the nine month period, it is initially assumed that unpaid earnings will not be paid within that period. The computation is adjusted if they are so paid.

Earnings are treated as paid at the same time as they are treated as received for employment income purposes.

Similar rules apply to employee benefit contributions.

2.3.7 Entertaining and gifts

The general rule is that expenditure on entertaining and gifts is non-deductible. This applies to amounts reimbursed to employees for specific entertaining expenses and gifts, and to round sum allowances which are exclusively for meeting such expenses.

There are specific exceptions to the general rule:

- **Entertaining for and gifts to employees are normally deductible** although where gifts are made, or the entertainment is excessive, a charge to tax may arise on the employee under the benefits legislation.

- Gifts to customers not costing more than £50 per donee per year are allowed if they carry a conspicuous advertisement for the business and are not food, drink, tobacco or vouchers exchangeable for goods.

- **Gifts to charities may also be allowed** although many will fall foul of the 'wholly and exclusively' rule above (see further later in this Chapter). If a gift aid declaration is made in respect of a gift, tax relief will be given under the gift aid scheme, not as a trading expense.

2.3.8 Lease charges for cars with CO_2 emissions exceeding 160g/km

There is a restriction on the leasing costs of a car with CO_2 emissions exceeding 160 g/km. 15% of the leasing costs will be disallowed in the adjustment of profits calculation.

Question
Restriction for car leasing costs

Mandy is a sole trader. In May 2011 she leased a car for use in her business. The leasing costs for 2011/12 were £4,000. The car had CO_2 emissions of 171g/km.

What is the amount of the leasing costs that will be disallowed in the adjustment of profits calculation?

Answer

Since the car has CO_2 emissions exceeding 160 g/km, 15% of the leasing costs will be disallowed ie £4,000 x 15% = £600. This disallowed amount will be added back to the net profit assuming the full leasing cost of £4,000 has originally been deducted in calculating the net profit.

2.3.9 Patent royalties and copyright royalties

Patent royalties and copyright royalties paid in connection with an individual's trade are deductible as trading expenses.

2.3.10 National insurance contributions

No deduction is allowed for any national insurance contributions **except for employer's contributions**. For your exam, these are Class 1 secondary contributions and Class 1A contributions (see later in this Text).

2.3.11 Penalties and interest on tax

Penalties and interest on late paid tax are not allowed as a trading expense. For the purpose of your exam, tax includes income tax, capital gains tax, (for companies) corporation tax, and VAT.

2.3.12 Appropriations

Salary or interest on capital paid to a trader are not deductible. A salary paid to a member of the trader's family is allowed as long as it is not excessive in respect of the work performed by that family member.

The private proportion of payments for motoring expenses, rent, heat and light and telephone expenses of a trader is not deductible. Where the payments are to or on behalf of employees, the full amounts are deductible but are taxed on the employees as benefits for income tax.

Payments of the trader's income tax and national insurance contributions are not deductible.

Question	Adjusted taxable trade profits

Here is the income statement of John Dodd, a trader.

INCOME STATEMENT FOR THE YEAR ENDED 31 MAY 2011

	£	£
Gross profit		31,000
Other income		
Bank interest received		500
Expenses		
Wages and salaries	7,000	
Rent and rates	2,000	
Depreciation	1,500	
Motor expenses – cars owned by business	5,000	
Motor expenses – cost of leased car CO_2 emissions 170g/km	2,000	
Entertainment expenses – customers	750	
Office expenses	1,350	
		(19,600)
Finance costs		
Interest payable on overdraft		(1,500)
Net profit		10,400

You ascertain the following:

(a)   Salaries include £1,000 paid to John Dodd's wife who works part time in the business. If John had employed another person to do this work, John would have had to pay at least this amount of salary.

(b)   Motor expenses on cars owned by the business are £3,000 for John Dodd's car used 20% privately and £2,000 for his part-time salesman's car used 40% privately. There is no private use on the leased car.

(c)   There are also capital allowances of £860.

Compute the adjusted taxable trade profit for the year ended 31 May 2011. You should start with the net profit figure of £10,400 and indicate by the use of zero (0) any items which do not require adjustment.

ADJUSTED TAXABLE TRADING PROFIT YEAR TO 31 MAY 2011

		£	£
Net profit			10,400
Add:	wages and salaries	0	
	rents and rates	0	
	depreciation	1,500	
	trader private motor expenses (£3,000 × 20%)	600	
	salesman's car	0	
	leased car cost disallowed (£2,000 × 15%)	300	
	entertainment expenses - customers	750	
	office expenses	0	
	interest payable on overdraft	0	
			3,150
			13,550
Deduct:	bank interest received	(500)	
	capital allowances	(860)	
			(1,360)
Profit adjusted for tax purposes			12,190

Note. The employee's private motor expenses are allowable for the trader but the provision of the car will be taxed on the employee as an income tax benefit. The salary paid to John Dodd's wife is allowed as it is reasonable remuneration for the work actually done.

2.3.13 Subscriptions and donations

The general 'wholly and exclusively' rule determines the deductibility of expenses. Subscriptions and donations are not deductible unless the expenditure is for the benefit of the trade. The following are the main types of subscriptions and donations you may meet and their correct treatments.

- Trade subscriptions (such as to a professional or trade association) are generally deductible.

- Charitable donations are generally deductible only if they are small and to local charities.

- Political subscriptions and donations are generally not deductible.

- When a business makes a gift of equipment manufactured, sold or used in the course of its trade to an educational establishment or for a charitable purpose, nothing need be brought into account as a trading receipt.

2.3.14 Legal and professional charges

Legal and professional charges relating to capital or non-trading items are not deductible. These include charges incurred in acquiring new capital assets or legal rights, issuing shares, drawing up partnership agreements and litigating disputes over the terms of a partnership agreement.

Professional charges are deductible if they relate directly to trading. Deductible items include:

- Legal and professional charges incurred defending the taxpayer's title to non-current assets
- Charges connected with an action for breach of contract
- Expenses of the **renewal** (not the original grant) of a lease for less than 50 years
- Charges for trade debt collection
- Normal charges for preparing accounts/assisting with the self assessment of tax liabilities

Accountancy expenses arising out of an enquiry into the accounts information in a particular year's return are not allowed where the enquiry reveals discrepancies and additional liabilities for the year of enquiry, or any earlier year, which arise as a result of negligent or fraudulent conduct.

Where, however, the enquiry results in no addition to profits, or an adjustment to the profits for the year of enquiry only and that assessment does not arise as a result of negligent or fraudulent conduct, the additional accountancy expenses are allowable.

2.3.15 Interest

Interest paid by an individual on borrowings for trade purposes is deductible as a trading expense on an accruals basis, so no adjustment to the accounts figure is needed.

Individuals cannot deduct interest on overdue tax.

2.3.16 Miscellaneous deductions

Here is a list of various other items that you may meet.

Item	Treatment	Comment
Educational courses for staff	Allow	
Educational courses for trader	Allow	If to update existing knowledge or skills, not if to acquire new knowledge or skills
Removal expenses (to new business premises)	Allow	Only if not an expansionary move
Travelling expenses to the trader's place of business	Disallow	*Ricketts v Colquhoun 1925*: unless an itinerant trader (*Horton v Young 1971*)
Counselling services for employees leaving employment	Allow	If qualify for exemption from employment income charge on employees
Pension contributions (to schemes for employees and company directors)	Allow	If paid, not if only provided for; special contributions may be spread over the year of payment and future years
Premiums for insurance: • against an employee's death or illness • to cover locum costs or fixed overheads whilst the policyholder is ill	Allow	Receipts are taxable
Damages paid	Allow	If not too remote from trade: *Strong and Co v Woodifield 1906*
Improving an individual's personal security	Allow	Provision of a car, ship or dwelling is excluded

2.4 Income taxable as trading income but excluded from the accounts

The usual example is when a trader takes goods for his own use. In such circumstances the selling price of the goods if sold in the open market is added to the accounting profit. If the trader pays anything for the goods, this is left out of the account. In other words, the trader is treated for tax purposes as having made a sale to himself.

This rule does not apply to supplies of services, which are treated as sold for the amount (if any) actually paid (but the cost of services to the trader or his household is not deductible).

2.5 Accounting profits not taxable as trading income

FAST FORWARD

Receipts not taxable as trading profit must be deducted from the net profit. For example, rental income and interest received are not taxable as trading profit. The rental income is taxed instead as property business income, whilst the interest is taxed as savings income.

There are three types of receipts which may be found in the accounting profits but which must be excluded from the taxable trading profit computation. These are:

(a) **Capital receipts**
(b) **Income taxed in another way** (at source or as another type of income)
(c) **Income specifically exempt from tax**

However, compensation received in one lump sum for the loss of income is likely to be treated as income (*Donald Fisher (Ealing) Ltd v Spencer 1989*).

Income taxed as another type of income, for example rental income, is excluded from the computation of taxable trading profits but it is brought back into the income tax computation further down as property business income. Similarly capital receipts are excluded from the computation of taxable trading profits but they may be included in the computation of chargeable gains (see later in this Text).

2.6 Deductible expenditure not charged in the accounts

Amounts not charged in the accounts that are deductible from trading profits must be deducted when computing the taxable trading income. An example is capital allowances.

Capital allowances (see the next Chapter) are an example of deductible expenditure not charged in the accounts.

A second example is **an annual sum which can be deducted by a trader that has paid a lease premium to a landlord who is taxable on the premium as property business income** (see earlier in this Text).

Normally, the amortisation of the lease will have been deducted in the accounts and must be added back as an appropriation of profit.

Question	Adjustment of profits

Here is the income statement of S Pring, a trader.

	£	£
Gross profit		30,000
Other income		
Bank interest received		860
Expenses		
Wages and salaries	7,000	
Rent and rates	2,000	
Depreciation	1,500	
Impairment of trade receivables	150	
Entertainment expenses for customers	750	
Patent royalties paid	1,200	
Legal expenses on acquisition of new factory	250	
		(12,850)
Finance costs		
Bank interest paid		(300)
Net profit		17,710

Salaries include £500 paid to Mrs Pring who works full time in the business.

Compute the adjusted taxable trade profit. You should start with the net profit figure of £17,710 and indicate by the use of zero (0) any items which do not require adjustment.

	£	£
Net profit		17,710
Add: wages and salaries	0	
rent and rates	0	
depreciation	1,500	
impairment of trade receivables	0	
entertainment expenses for customers	750	
patent royalties	0	
legal expenses (capital)	250	
bank interest paid	0	
		2,500
		20,210
Less bank interest received		(860)
Profit adjusted for tax purposes		19,350

3 Pre-trading expenditure

Pre-trading expenditure incurred within the seven years prior to the commencement of trade is allowable if it would have been allowable had the trade already started.

Expenditure incurred before the commencement of trade is deductible, if it is incurred within seven years of the start of trade and it is of a type that would have been deductible had the trade already started. **It is treated as a trading expense incurred on the first day of trading**.

Chapter Roundup

- The badges of trade are used to decide whether or not a trade exists. If one does exist, the accounts profits need to be adjusted in order to establish the taxable profits.

- The net profit in the income statement must be adjusted to find the taxable trading profit.

- Disallowable (ie non-deductible) expenditure must be added back to the net profit in the computation of the taxable trading profit. Any item not deducted wholly and exclusively for trade purposes is disallowable expenditure. Certain other items, such as depreciation, are specifically disallowable.

- Receipts not taxable as trading profit must be deducted from the net profit. For example, rental income and interest received are not taxable as trading profit. The rental income is taxed instead as property business income, whilst the interest is taxed as savings income.

- Amounts not charged in the accounts that are deductible from trading profits must be deducted when computing the taxable trading income. An example is capital allowances.

- Pre-trading expenditure incurred within the seven years prior to the commencement of trade is allowable if it would have been allowable had the trade already started.

Quick Quiz

1. List the traditional badges of trade.

2. What are the remoteness test and the duality test?

3. No adjustment for taxation is required to the accounts for deduction of a trader's salary. TRUE/FALSE?

4. Sid is a sole trader. Included in his most recent income statement are the following deductions:

   £3,000 legal fees for acquiring a new 15-year lease of his business premises.

   £180 car parking fines incurred by Sid whilst on business trips.

   £40 interest for late payment of Sid's previous year's income tax.

   How much must be added back to the net profit figure when calculating the tax adjusted profit figure?

   A £3,180
   B £3,220
   C £220
   D £3,040

5. Which ONE of the following items of expenditure will Leila, a fashion designer, be allowed to deduct in calculating her tax adjusted trading profit?

   A The cost of building a new wall in front of her retail shop

   B The cost of installing air conditioning in her workshop

   C The cost of initial repairs to a recently acquired second-hand office building which was not usable until the repairs were carried out

   D The cost of redecorating her retail shop

6. Which ONE of the following is an allowable expense for a sole trader?

   A Gift of fleece jackets to customers with trade logo costing £60 each
   B A subscription to a local trade association
   C Legal fees in respect of employment contracts
   D A Gift Aid donation

7. Pre-trading roxpenditure is deductible if it is incurred within ____ years of the start of trade and is of a type that would have been deductible if the trade had already started. Fill in the blank.

1   The subject matter
    The frequency of transactions
    Existence of similar trading transactions or interests
    The length of ownership
    The organisation of the activity as a trade
    Supplementary work and marketing
    Method of finance
    A profit motive
    The way in which the goods were acquired

2   Expenditure is not deductible if it is not for trade purposes (the remoteness test) or if it reflects more than one purpose (the duality test).

3   False. The trader's salary must be added back as it is an appropriation of profit.

4   B   All three items are disallowed and must be added back.

5   D   The cost of redecoration is an allowable expense in calculating trading profit. The other expenditure is capital expenditure and so is not allowable.

6   C   Legal fees on employment contracts are an allowable income expense.

7   Pre-trading expenditure is deductible if it is incurred within **seven** years of the start of the trade and is of a type that would have been deductible if the trade had already started.

Now try the questions below from the Exam Question Bank

Number	Level	Marks	Time
Q9	Examination	15	27 mins

Capital allowances

Topic list	Syllabus reference
1 Capital allowances in general	B3(g)
2 Plant and machinery – qualifying expenditure	B3(g)(i)
3 The main pool	B3(g)(ii), (iii), (iv)
4 Special rate pool	B3(g)(iii), (vi)
5 Private use assets	B3(g)(ii), (iv)
6 Motor cars	B3(g)(iii)
7 Short life assets	B3(g)(v)

Introduction

We saw in the last chapter that depreciation cannot be deducted in computing taxable trade profits and that capital allowances are given instead. In this chapter, we look at the rules for calculating capital allowances, starting with plant and machinery.

Our study of plant and machinery falls into three parts. First, we look at what qualifies for allowances: many business assets obtain no allowances at all.

Secondly, we see how to compute the allowances on the main pool and the special rate pool.

Lastly, we look at the special rules for assets with private use, motor cars and assets with short lives.

You may wish to return to this chapter while you are studying Chapter 19 on companies.

Study guide

		Intellectual level
B3	**Income from self-employment**	
(g)	Capital allowances	
(i)	Define plant and machinery for capital allowances purposes.	1
(ii)	Compute writing down allowances, first year allowances and the annual investment allowance.	2
(iii)	Compute capital allowances for motor cars, including motor cars already owned at 6 April 2009 (1 April 2009 for companies)	2
(iv)	Compute balancing allowances and balancing charges.	2
(v)	Recognise the treatment of short life assets.	2
(vi)	Explain the treatment of assets included in the special rate pool.	2

Exam guide

You may have to answer a whole question on capital allowances or a capital allowances computation may be included as a working in a computation of taxable trading profits. The computation may be for either income tax or corporation tax purposes; the principles are basically the same. Look out for private use assets; only restrict the capital allowances if there is private use by **traders**, never restrict capital allowances for private use by **employees**. Also watch out for the length of the period of account; you may need to scale WDAs up (income tax only) or down (income tax or corporation tax).

1 Capital allowances in general

FAST FORWARD

Capital allowances are available to give tax relief for certain capital expenditure.

Capital expenditure is not deducted in computing taxable trade profits, but it *may* attract capital allowances. Capital allowances are treated as a trading expense and are deducted in arriving at taxable trade profits. Balancing charges, effectively negative allowances, are added in arriving at those profits.

Capital expenditure on plant and machinery qualifies for capital allowances. Both unincorporated businesses (sole traders and partnerships) and companies are entitled to capital allowances. For completeness, in this Chapter we will look at the rules for companies alongside those for unincorporated businesses. We will look at companies in more detail later in this Text.

For unincorporated businesses, capital allowances are calculated for periods of account. These are simply the periods for which the trader chooses to make up accounts. For companies, capital allowances are calculated for accounting periods (see later in this Text).

For capital allowances purposes, expenditure is generally deemed to be incurred when the obligation to pay becomes unconditional. This will often be the date of a contract, but if for example payment is due a month after delivery of a machine, it would be the date of delivery. However, amounts due more than four months after the obligation becomes unconditional are deemed to be incurred when they fall due.

2 Plant and machinery – qualifying expenditure

FAST FORWARD

There are various statutory rules on what does or does not qualify as plant.

2.1 Definition of plant and machinery

Capital expenditure on plant and machinery qualifies for capital allowances if the plant or machinery is used for a qualifying activity, such as a trade. 'Plant' is not fully defined by the legislation, although some specific exclusions and inclusions are given. The word 'machinery' may be taken to have its normal everyday meaning.

2.2 The statutory exclusions

2.2.1 Buildings

Expenditure on a building and on any asset which is incorporated in a building or is of a kind normally incorporated into buildings does not qualify as expenditure on plant, but see below for exceptions.

In addition to complete buildings, **the following assets count as 'buildings', and are therefore not plant**.

- Walls, floors, ceilings, doors, gates, shutters, windows and stairs
- Mains services, and systems, of water, electricity and gas
- Waste disposal, sewerage and drainage systems
- Shafts or other structures for lifts etc

Note that some features which are integral to a building, such as ventilation systems and lifts, do qualify as plant. These are discussed later in this chapter.

2.2.2 Structures

Expenditure on structures and on works involving the alteration of land **does not qualify as expenditure on plant**, but see below for exceptions.

A 'structure' is a fixed structure of any kind, other than a building.

2.2.3 Exceptions

Over the years a large body of case law has been built up under which plant and machinery allowances have been given on certain types of expenditure which might be thought to be expenditure on a building or structure. Statute therefore gives a list of various assets which *may* still be plant. These include:

- Any machinery not within any other item in this list
- Electrical (including lighting), cold water, gas and sewerage systems:
  - Provided mainly to meet the particular requirements of the trade, or
  - Provided mainly to serve particular machinery or plant used for the purposes of the trade
- Space or water heating systems and powered systems of ventilation
- Manufacturing and display equipment
- Cookers, washing machines, refrigeration or cooling equipment, sanitary ware and furniture and furnishings
- Lifts etc
- Sound insulation provided mainly to meet the particular requirements of the trade
- Computer, telecommunication and surveillance systems
- Sprinkler equipment, fire alarm and burglar alarm systems
- Partition walls, where movable and intended to be moved
- Decorative assets provided for the enjoyment of the public in the hotel, restaurant or similar trades; advertising hoardings

- Movable buildings intended to be moved in the course of the trade
- Expenditure on altering land for the purpose only of installing machinery or plant

Items falling within the above list of exclusions will only qualify as plant if they fall within the meaning of plant as established by case law. This is discussed below.

2.2.4 Land

Land or an interest in land does not qualify as plant and machinery. For this purpose 'land' excludes buildings, structures and assets which are installed or fixed to land in such a way as to become part of the land for general legal purposes.

2.2.5 Computer software

Capital expenditure on computer software (both programs and data) **normally qualifies as expenditure on plant and machinery.**

2.3 Case law

FAST FORWARD

There are also cases on the definition of plant. To help you to absorb them, try to see the function/setting theme running through them.

Exam focus point

In this chapter we mention the names of cases where it was decided what was or wasn't 'plant'. You are **not** expected to know the names of cases for your examination. We have included them for your information only.

The original case law **definition of plant** (applied in this case to a horse) is **'whatever apparatus is used by a businessman for carrying on his business: not his stock in trade which he buys or makes for sale; but all goods and chattels, fixed or movable, live or dead, which he keeps for permanent employment in the business'** (*Yarmouth v France 1887*).

Subsequent cases have refined the original definition and have largely been concerned with the **distinction between plant actively used in the business (qualifying) and the setting in which the business is carried on (non-qualifying). This is the 'functional' test.** Some of the decisions have now been enacted as part of statute law, but they are still relevant as examples of the principles involved.

A barrister succeeded in his claim for his law library: 'Plant includes a man's tools of his trade. It extends to what he uses day by day in the course of his profession. It is not confined to physical things like the dentist's chair or the architect's table' (*Munby v Furlong 1977*).

Office partitioning was allowed. Because it was movable, it was not regarded as part of the setting in which the business was carried on (*Jarrold v John Good and Sons Ltd 1963*) (actual item now covered by statute).

At a motorway service station, false ceilings contained conduits, ducts and lighting apparatus. **They did not qualify because they did not perform a function in the business. They were merely part of the setting in which the business was conducted** (*Hampton v Fortes Autogrill Ltd 1979*).

Similarly, it has been held that when an attractive floor is provided in a restaurant, the fact that the floor performs the function of making the restaurant attractive to customers is not enough to make it plant. It functions as premises, and the cost therefore does not qualify for capital allowances (*Wimpy International Ltd v Warland 1988*).

Conversely, light fittings, decor and murals can be plant. A company carried on business as hoteliers and operators of licensed premises. The function of the items was the creation of an atmosphere conducive to the comfort and well being of its customers (*CIR v Scottish and Newcastle Breweries Ltd 1982*) (decorative assets used in hotels etc, now covered by statute).

General lighting in a department store is not plant, as it is merely setting. Special display lighting, however, can be plant (*Cole Brothers Ltd v Phillips 1982*).

3 The main pool

FAST FORWARD

With capital allowances computations, the main thing is to get the layout right. Having done that, you will find that the figures tend to drop into place.

3.1 Main pool expenditure

Most expenditure on plant and machinery, including expenditure on cars with CO_2 emissions of 160g/km or less, is put into a pool of expenditure (the main pool) on which capital allowances may be claimed. An addition increases the pool whilst a disposal decreases it.

Exceptionally the following items are not put into the main pool:

(a)   assets dealt with in the special rate pool
(b)   assets with private use by the trader
(c)   short life assets where an election has been made.

These exceptions are dealt with later in this Chapter.

Expenditure on plant and machinery by a person about to begin a trade is treated as incurred on the first day of trading. Assets previously owned by a trader and then brought into the trade (at the start of trading or later) are treated as bought for their market values at the times when they are brought in.

3.2 Annual investment allowance

FAST FORWARD

Businesses are entitled to an Annual Investment Allowance (AIA) of £100,000 for a 12 month period of account.

Businesses can claim an **Annual Investment Allowance (AIA) on the first £100,000 spent each year on plant or machinery**, including assets in the main pool, but not including motor cars. Expenditure on motorcycles does qualify for the AIA.

Where the period of account is more or less than a year, the maximum allowance is proportionately increased or reduced.

After claiming the AIA, the balance of expenditure on main pool assets is transferred to the main pool immediately and is eligible for writing down allowances in the same period.

Exam focus point

The Annual Investment Allowance limit was also £100,000 for the year ended 5 April 2011 (31 March 2011 for companies) and so the examiner has stated that there is no reason why a question could not be set involving a period of account spanning 6 April 2011 (1 April 2011 for companies).

3.3 First year allowance for low emission cars

FAST FORWARD

A first year allowance (FYA) at the rate of 100% is available on low emission cars. The FYA is not pro-rated in short periods of account.

Key term

A low emission car is one which has **CO_2 emissions of 110g/km or less**.

A 100% first year allowance (FYA) is available for expenditure incurred on low emission motor cars. If the FYA is not claimed in full, the balance of expenditure is transferred to the main pool after any writing down allowance has been calculated on the main pool.

The FYA is not reduced pro-rata in a short period of account, unlike the AIA and writing down allowances.

3.4 Writing down allowances

Expenditure on plant and machinery in the main pool qualifies for a WDA at 20% every 12 months.

Key term

A **writing down allowance (WDA)** is given on main pool expenditure **at the rate of 20% a year** (on a reducing balance basis). The WDA is calculated on the tax written down value (TWDV) of pooled plant, after adding the current period's additions and taking out the current period's disposals.

When plant is sold, **proceeds**, **limited to a maximum of the original cost,** are taken out of the pool. Provided that the trade is still being carried on, the pool balance remaining is written down in the future by WDAs, even if there are no assets left.

3.5 Example

Elizabeth has tax written down value on her main pool of plant and machinery of £16,000 on 6 April 2011. In the year to 5 April 2012 she bought a car with CO_2 emissions of 130g/km for £8,000 (no non-business use) and she disposed of plant, which originally cost £4,000, for £6,000.

Calculate the maximum capital allowances claim for the year.

	Main pool £	Allowances £
TWDV b/f	16,000	
Addition (not qualifying for AIA)	8,000	
Less disposal (limited to cost)	(4,000)	
	20,000	
WDA @ 20%	(4,000)	4,000
TWDV c/f	16,000	
Maximum capital allowances claim		4,000

Question

Capital allowances

Julia is a sole trader making up accounts to 5 April each year. At 5 April 2011, the tax written down value on her main pool is £12,500.

In the year to 5 April 2012, Julia bought the following assets:

1 June 2011	Machine	£90,000
12 November 2011	Van	£17,500
10 February 2012	Car for salesman (CO2 emissions 150g/km)	£9,000

She disposed of plant on 15 December 2011 for £12,000 (original cost £16,000).

Calculate the maximum capital allowances claim that Julia can make for the year ended 5 April 2012.

	AIA £	Main pool £	Allowances £
y/e 5 April 2012			
TWDV b/f		12,500	
Additions qualifying for AIA			
1.6.11 Machine	90,000		
12.11.11 Van	17,500		
	107,500		
AIA	(100,000)		100,000
	7,500		
Transfer balance to pool	(7,500)	7,500	
Additions not qualifying for AIA			
10.2.12 Car		9,000	
Disposal			
15.12.11 Plant		(12,000)	
		17,000	
WDA @ 20%		(3,400)	3,400
TWDV c/f		13,600	
Maximum capital allowances			103,400

3.6 Short and long periods of account

WDAs are 20% × number of months/12:

(a) For unincorporated businesses where the period of account is longer or shorter than 12 months

(b) For companies where the accounting period is shorter than 12 months (a company's accounting period for tax purposes is never longer than 12 months), or where the trade concerned started in the accounting period and was therefore carried on for fewer than 12 months. Remember that we will be studying companies in detail later in this Text.

Question   Short period of account

Venus is a sole trader and has made up accounts to 30 April each year. At 30 April 2011, the tax written down value of her main pool was £66,667. She decides to make up her next set of accounts to 31 December 2011.

In the period to 31 December 2011, the following acquisitions were made:

1 May 2011	Plant	£80,000
10 July 2011	Car (CO2 emissions 130 g/km)	£9,000
3 August 2011	Car (CO2 emissions 105 g/km)	£11,000

Venus disposed of plant on 1 November 2011 for £20,000 (original cost £28,000).

Calculate the maximum capital allowances that Venus can claim for the period ending 31 December 2011.

Answer

	AIA £	FYA £	Main pool £	Allowances £
p/e 31 December 2011				
TWDV b/f			66,667	
Additions qualifying for AIA				
1.5.11 Plant	80,000			
AIA £100,000 × 8/12	(66,667)			66,667
	13,333			
Transfer balance to pool	(13,333)		13,333	
Additions qualifying for FYA				
3.8.11 Car (low emission)		11,000		
Less: 100% FYA		(11,000)		11,000
Additions not qualifying for AIA or FYA				
10.7.11 Car			9,000	
Disposals				
1.11.11 Plant			(20,000)	
			69,000	
WDA @ 20% × 8/12			(9,200)	9,200
TWDVs c/f			59,800	
Maximum allowances claim				86,867

Note that the annual investment allowance and the writing down allowance are reduced for the short period of account, but the first year allowance is given in full.

Question

Long period of account

Oscar started trading on 1 July 2010 and made up his first set of accounts to 31 December 2011. He bought the following assets:

10 July 2010	Plant	£130,000
10 October 2010	Car for business use only (CO2 emissions 140g/km)	£11,000
12 February 2011	Plant	£85,000

Calculate the maximum capital allowances claim that Oscar can make for the period ended 31 December 2011. The rates of capital allowances in 2011/12 also applied in 2010/11.

Answer

	AIA £	Main pool £	Allowances £
p/e 31 December 2011			
Additions qualifying for AIA			
10.7.10 Plant	130,000		
12.2.11 Plant	85,000		
	215,000		
AIA £100,000 × 18/12	(150,000)		150,000
	65,000		
Transfer balance to main pool	(65,000)	65,000	
Additions not qualifying for AIA			
1.10.10 Car		11,000	
		76,000	
WDA @ 20% × 18/12		(22,800)	22,800
TWDV c/f		53,200	
Maximum capital allowances			172,800

Note that the annual investment allowance and the writing down allowance are increased for the long period of account.

3.7 Small balance on main pool

A writing down allowance equal to unrelieved expenditure in the main pool can be claimed where this is **£1,000 or less**. If the maximum WDA is claimed, the main pool will then have a nil balance carried forward.

| Question | Small balance on main pool |

Alan has traded for many years, making up accounts to 30 April each year. At 30 April 2011, the tax written down value of his main pool was £15,000. On 1 October 2011, he sold some plant and machinery for £14,200 (original cost £16,000).

Calculate the maximum capital allowances claim that Alan can make for the period ending 30 April 2012.

Answer

	Main pool £	Allowances £
y/e 30 April 2012		
TWDV b/f	15,000	
Disposal	(14,200)	
	800	
WDA (small pool)	(800)	800
TWDV c/f	nil	
Maximum capital allowances		800

Exam focus point

Note the tax planning opportunities available. If plant is bought just before an accounting date, allowances become available as soon as possible. Alternatively, it may be desirable to claim less than the maximum allowances to even out annual taxable profits and avoid a higher rate of tax in later years. However, in the exam you should always claim the maximum available capital allowances unless you are told otherwise.

3.8 Balancing charges and allowances

Balancing charges occur when the disposal value deducted exceeds the balance remaining in the pool. The charge equals the excess and is effectively a negative capital allowance, increasing profits. Most commonly this happens when the trade ceases and the remaining assets are sold. It may also occur, however, whilst the trade is still in progress.

Balancing allowances on the main and special pools of expenditure arise only when the trade ceases. The balancing allowance is equal to the remaining unrelieved expenditure after deducting the disposal value of all the assets. Balancing allowances may also arise on single pool items (see later in this Chapter) whenever those items are disposed of.

3.9 Cessation of trade

For plant and machinery, **when a business ceases to trade, no AIAs, FYAs or WDAs are given in the final period of account** (unincorporated businesses) or accounting period (companies – see later in this Text). Each asset is deemed to be disposed of on the date the trade ceased (usually at the then market value). Additions (if any) in the relevant period are brought in and then the disposal proceeds (limited to cost) are deducted from the balance of qualifying expenditure. If the proceeds exceed the balance then a balancing charge arises. If the balance of qualifying expenditure exceeds the proceeds then a balancing allowance is given.

4 Special rate pool

FAST FORWARD

The special rate pool contains expenditure on thermal insulation, long life assets, features integral to a building and cars with CO_2 emissions over 160g/km. The AIA can be used against such expenditure except cars. The WDA is 10%.

4.1 Operation of the special rate pool

Expenditure on thermal insulation, long life assets, features integral to a building, and cars with CO_2 emissions over 160g/km is not dealt with in the main pool but in a special rate pool.

The Annual Investment Allowance can apply to expenditure on such assets except on cars. The taxpayer can decide how to allocate the AIA. It will be more tax efficient to set the allowance against special rate pool expenditure in priority to main pool expenditure where there is expenditure on assets in both pools in the period. Expenditure in excess of the AIA is added to the special rate pool and will be eligible for writing down allowance in the same period in which the expenditure is incurred.

The writing down allowance for the special rate pool is 10% for a twelve month period. As with the writing down allowance on the main pool, this is adjusted for short and long periods of account.

Where the **tax written down balance of the special rate pool is £1,000 or less**, a writing down allowance can be claimed of up to £1,000. This is in addition to any similar claim in relation to the main pool.

4.2 Long life assets

Key term

Long life assets are assets with an expected working life of 25 years or more.

The **long life asset rules only apply to businesses whose total expenditure on assets with an expected working life of 25 years or more in a chargeable period is more than £100,000.** If the expenditure exceeds £100,000, the whole of the expenditure enters the special rate pool. For this purpose all expenditure incurred under a contract is treated as incurred in the first chargeable period to which that contract relates.

The £100,000 limit is reduced or increased proportionately in the case of a chargeable period of less or more than 12 months.

The following are **not** treated as long life assets:

(a)   **Plant and machinery in dwelling houses, retail shops, showrooms, hotels and offices**
(b)   **Cars**

4.3 Integral features

Features which are integral to a building include the following:

- electrical and lighting systems
- cold water systems
- space or water heating systems
- powered systems of ventilation, cooling or air conditioning
- lifts and escalators

When a building is sold, the vendor and purchaser can make a joint election to determine how the sale proceeds are apportioned between the building and its integral features.

4.4 Example

Lucy has been trading for many years, making up accounts to 5 April each year. The tax written down value of her main pool at 5 April 2011 was £110,000. In the year to 5 April 2012, Lucy had the following expenditure:

10 June 2011	General plant costing £45,000
12 December 2011	Lighting system in shop £20,000
15 January 2012	Car for business use only (CO2 emissions 175 g/km) £25,000
26 January 2012	Delivery van £15,000
4 March 2012	Lifts £90,000

The maximum capital allowances claim that Lucy can make for the year to 5 April 2012 is:

	AIA £	Main pool £	Special rate pool £	Allowances £
y/e 5 April 2012				
TWDV b/f		110,000		
Additions for AIA (best use)				
12.12.11 Lighting	20,000			
4.3.12 Lifts	90,000			
	110,000			
AIA	(100,000)			100,000
	10,000			
Transfer balance to special rate pool	(10,000)		10,000	
Additions not given AIA				
10.6.11 Plant		45,000		
26.1.12 Van		15,000		
Additions not qualifying for AIA				
15.1.12 Car			25,000	
		170,000	35,000	
WDA @ 20%		(34,000)		34,000
WDA @ 10%			(3,500)	3,500
TWDVs c/f		136,000	31,500	
Allowances				137,500

5 Private use assets

An asset which is used privately by a trader is dealt with in a single asset pool and the capital allowances are restricted.

An asset which is used partly for private purposes by a sole trader or a partner is put into its own pool (single asset pool).

Capital allowances are calculated on the full cost. However, only the business use proportion of the allowances is allowed as a deduction from trading profits. This restriction applies to the AIA, FYAs, WDAs, balancing allowances and balancing charges.

An asset with some private use by an employee (not the owner of the business) suffers no such restriction. The employee may be taxed under the benefits code (see earlier in this Text) so the business receives capital allowances on the full cost of the asset.

Exam focus point

Capital allowances on assets with some private use is a common exam topic. Check carefully whether the private use is by the owner of the business or by an employee.

Jacinth has been in business as a sole trader for many years, making up accounts to 31 March. On 1 November 2011 she bought computer equipment for £2,700 which she uses 75% in her business and 25% privately. She has already used the AIA against other expenditure in the year to 31 March 2012.

Calculate the maximum capital allowance that Jacinth can claim in respect to the computer equipment in the year to 31 March 2012.

Answer

	Computer equipment £	Allowances @ 75% £
y/e 31 March 2012		
Acquisition	2,700	
WDA @ 20%	(540)	405
TWDV c/f	2,160	
Maximum capital allowance on computer equipment		405

6 Motor cars

6.1 Motor cars acquired before April 2009

FAST FORWARD

Motor cars acquired before 6 April 2009 (1 April 2009 for companies) which cost more than £12,000 are each dealt with in a single asset pool. The maximum WDA on such cars is £3,000 for a 12 month period.

Each motor car acquired before 6 April 2009 (1 April 2009 for companies) which cost more than £12,000 (sometimes called an 'expensive' car) is dealt with in a single asset pool. This means that a separate record of allowances and WDV is kept for each such car and when it is sold a balancing allowance or charge arises.

Exam focus point

> You will not be expected to deal with allowances on expensive cars before 2011/12: the relevance of the April 2009 date is to alert you to the treatment of brought forward tax written down values on these cars.

Expensive cars are eligible for writing down allowances at 20% regardless of their CO_2 emissions. However, the maximum WDA is £3,000 a year. The limit is £3,000 × months/12 in periods of account which are not 12 months long.

Motor cars acquired before 6 April 2009 which cost £12,000 or less were pooled in the main pool, unless there was private use by a sole trader or partner.

Question

Cars acquired before April 2009

Niall is a sole trader making up accounts to 5 April each year. His business already owns four cars, all acquired before 6 April 2009 and used only for business purposes:

Car 1: This car was acquired for £27,000 and had a tax written down value at 6 April 2011 of £18,000. The car has CO_2 emissions of 150g/km.

Car 2: This car cost £22,000 and had a tax written down value at 6 April 2011 of £13,000. The car has CO_2 emissions of 180g/km.

Car 3: This car cost £18,000 and had a tax written down value at 6 April 2011 of £9,000. The car has CO_2 emissions of 140g/km. It was sold on 10 December 2011 for £7,500.

Car 4: This car cost £9,000. It is included in the main pool which had a total tax written down value at 6 April 2011 of £33,000. The car has CO_2 emissions of 120g/km. It was sold on 10 March 2012 for £6,600.

There were no acquisition and no other disposals of assets in the year ended 5 April 2012.

Calculate the maximum capital allowances that Niall can claim for the year ended 5 April 2012.

Answer

	Main pool	Car 1 £	Car 2 £	Car 3 £	Allowances £
y/e 5 April 2012					
TWDVs b/f	33,000	18,000	13,000	9,000	
Disposals					
10.12.11 Car 3				(7,500)	
Balancing allowance				1,500	1,500
10.3.12 Car 4	(6,600)			—	
	26,400				
WDA @ 20%	(5,280)				5,280
WDA @ 20% (max)		(3,000)			3,000
WDA @ 20%			(2,600)		2,600
TWDVs c/f	21,120	15,000	10,400	—	
Maximum allowances claim					12,380

Notes

1.   The writing down allowance for Car 2 is 20% even though it has CO_2 emissions of 180g/km. This is because it was acquired before 6 April 2009. If it had been acquired on or after 6 April 2009, it would only have been eligible for a writing down allowance of 10% (see further below).

2.   The disposal of Car 4 does not result in a balancing event because it is part of the main pool. Contrast this treatment with the disposal of Car 3 which does lead to a balancing allowance.

A motor car with private use by a sole trader or partner is always dealt with in a single asset pool, regardless of cost. Such cars acquired before 6 April 2009 will be eligible for writing down allowances at 20%, subject to a maximum of £3,000 per year. Only the business use proportion of the allowances is allowed as a deduction from trading profit, but the full allowance is deducted in calculating the car's tax written down value carried forward.

6.2 Motor cars acquired from April 2009

FAST FORWARD

Motor cars acquired from 6 April 2009 (1 April 2009 for companies) are generally dealt with in the special rate pool (cars emitting over 160g/km) or the main pool, unless there is private use by the trader.

As we have already seen, motor cars acquired from 6 April 2009 (1 April 2009 for companies) are categorised in accordance with their CO_2 emissions:

(a)   **Cars emitting over 160g/km**: expenditure is added to the special rate pool,

(b)   **Cars emitting between 111 and 160 g/km**: expenditure is added to the main pool,

(c)   **Cars emitting 110 g/km or less**: expenditure eligible for 100% first year allowance, if allowance not claimed in full, excess added to main pool.

Cars with an element of private use continue to be kept separate from the main and special pools and are dealt with in single asset pools. They are entitled to a WDA of 20% (car with CO_2 emissions between 111 and 160 g/km) or 10% (car with CO_2 emissions over 160 g/km). There is no maximum (£3,000 limit) WDA for such cars.

Question

Capital allowances on private use car

Quodos started to trade on 1 July 2010, making up accounts to 31 December 2010 and each 31 December thereafter. On 1 August 2010 he bought a car for £17,000 with CO_2 emissions of 130 g/km. The private use proportion is 10%. The car was sold in July 2013 for £4,000. Quodos has no other assets which qualify for capital allowances.

Calculate the capital allowances, assuming:

(a)   The car was used by an employee, or

(b)   The car was used by Quodos

and that the capital allowances rates in 2011/12 apply throughout.

Answer

(a)

	Main pool £	Allowances £
1.7.10 – 31.12.10		
Purchase price	17,000	
WDA 20% × 6/12 x £17,000	(1,700)	1,700
	15,300	
1.1.11 – 31.12.11		
WDA 20% x £15,300	(3,060)	3,060
	12,240	
1.1.12 – 31.12.12		
WDA 20% x £12,240	(2,448)	2,448
	9,792	
1.1.13 – 31.12.13		
Proceeds	(4,000)	
	5,792	
WDA 20% x £5,792	(1,158)	1,158
TWDV c/f	4,634	

The private use of the car by the employee has no effect on the capital allowances due to Quodos. The car will be placed in the main pool. No balancing allowance is available on the main pool until trade ceases even though the car has been sold.

(b)

	Car £	Allowances 90% £
1.7.10 – 31.12.10		
Purchase price	17,000	
WDA 20% × 6/12 x £17,000	(1,700)	1,530
	15,300	
1.1.11 – 31.12.11		
WDA 20% x £15,300	(3,060)	2,754
	12,240	
1.1.12 – 31.12.12		
WDA 20% x £12,240	(2,448)	2,203
	9,792	
1.1.13 – 31.12.13		
Proceeds	(4,000)	
Balancing allowance	5,792	5,213

The car is placed in a single asset pool because of the private use by the trader, Quodos. Only 90% of the WDAs and balancing allowance are available as a result of this private use.

6.3 Motor cars: summary table

	Main pool WDA @ 20%	Special rate pool WDA @ 10%	Single asset pool WDA @ 20%	Single asset pool WDA @ 10%
Car acquired before 6.4.09 (1.4.09 for companies)				
Cost less than £12,000, no private use	•			
Cost £12,000 or more, no private use			• max £3,000	
Cost less than £12,000, private use (sole trader or partner only)			•	
Cost £12,000 or more, private use (sole trader or partner only)			• max £3,000	
Car acquired on or after 6.4.09 (1.4.09 for companies)				
CO_2 emissions 111g/km – 160g/km, no private use	•			
CO_2 emissions over 160g/km, no private use		•		
CO_2 emissions 111g/km – 160g/km, private use (sole trader or partner only)			•	
CO_2 emissions over 160g/km, private use (sole trader or partner only)				•

7 Short life assets

FAST FORWARD

Short life asset elections can bring forward the allowances due on an asset.

A trader can elect that specific items of plant, which are expected to have a short working life, be kept separately from the main pool.

Key term

Any asset subject to this election is known as a 'short life asset', and the election is known as a 'de-pooling election'.

The election is irrevocable. For an unincorporated business, the time limit for electing is the 31 January which is 22 months after the end of the tax year in which the period of account of the expenditure ends. (For a company, it is two years after the end of the accounting period of the expenditure.) **Short life asset treatment cannot be claimed for any motor cars, or plant used partly for non-trade purposes.**

The short life asset is kept in a single asset pool. Provided that the short life asset is disposed of **within eight years of the end of the accounting period** in which it was bought (for assets acquired on or after 6 April 2011 (1 April 2011 for companies)), a balancing charge or allowance arises on its disposal.

If the asset is not disposed of within this time period, its tax written down value is added to the main pool at the beginning of the next period of account (accounting period for companies). This will be after allowances have been claimed nine times on the asset; once in the period of acquisition and then each year for the following eight years.

The election should therefore be made for assets likely to be sold for less than their tax written down values within eight years. It should not usually be made for assets likely to be sold within eight years for more than their tax written down values. There is no requirement to show from the outset that the asset will actually have a 'short life', so it is a matter of judgment whether the election should be made.

The relevant time period changed for assets acquired on or after 6 April 2011 (1 April 2011 for companies).

The examiner has stated that a question will not be set involving a short life asset purchased prior to 6 April 2011 (1 April 2011 for companies.

The Annual Investment Allowance can be set against short life assets. The taxpayer can decide how to allocate the AIA. It will be more tax efficient to set the allowance against main pool expenditure in priority to short life asset expenditure.

Question

Short life assets

Caithlin bought a machine for business use on 1 May 2011 for £9,000 and elected for de-pooling. She did not claim the AIA in respect of this asset. Her accounting year end is 30 April.

Calculate the capital allowances due if:

(a)   The asset is scrapped for £300 in August 2019

(b)   The asset is scrapped for £200 in August 2020

and assuming that the capital allowances rates in 2011/12 apply throughout.

Answer

		£
(a)	*Year to 30.4.12*	
	Cost	9,000
	WDA 20%	(1,800)
		7,200
	Year to 30.4.13	
	WDA 20%	(1,440)
		5,760
	Year to 30.4.14	
	WDA 20%	(1,152)
		4,608
	Year to 30.4.15	
	WDA 20%	(922)
		3,686
	Year to 30.4.16	
	WDA 20%	(737)
		2,949
	Year to 30.4.17	
	WDA 20%	(590)
		2,359
	Year to 30.4.18	
	WDA 20%	(472)
		1,887
	Year to 30.4.19	
	WDA 20%	(377)
		1,510
	Year to 30.4.20	
	Disposal proceeds	(300)
	Balancing allowance	1,210

(b) If the asset is still in use at 30 April 2020, WDAs up to 30.4.19 will be as above. In the year to 30.4.20, a WDA can be claimed of 20% × £1,510 = £302. The tax written down value of £1,510 – £302 = £1,208 will be added to the main pool at the beginning of the next period of account. The disposal proceeds of £200 will be deducted from the main pool in that period's capital allowances computation. No balancing allowance will arise and the main pool will continue.

Chapter Roundup

- Capital allowances are available to give tax relief for certain capital expenditure.

- There are various statutory rules on what does or does not qualify as plant.

- There are also cases on the definition of plant. To help you to absorb them, try to see the function/setting theme running through them.

- With capital allowances computations, the main thing is to get the layout right. Having done that, you will find that the figures tend to drop into place.

- Businesses are entitled to an Annual Investment Allowance (AIA) of £100,000 for a 12 month period of account.

- A first year allowance (FYA) at the rate of 100% is available on low emission cars. The FYA is not pro-rated in short periods of account.

- Expenditure on plant and machinery in the main pool qualifies for a WDA at 20% every 12 months.

- The special rate pool contains expenditure on thermal insulation, long life assets, features integral to a building and cars with CO_2 emissions over 160g/km. The AIA can be used against such expenditure except cars. The WDA is 10%.

- An asset which is used privately by a trader is dealt with in a single asset pool and the capital allowances are restricted.

- Motor cars acquired before 6 April 2009 (1 April 2009 for companies) which cost more than £12,000 are each dealt with in a single asset pool. The maximum WDA on such cars is £3,000 for a 12 month period.

- Motor cars acquired from 6 April 2009 (1 April 2009 for companies) are generally dealt with in the special rate pool (cars emitting over 160g/km) or the main pool, unless there is private use by the trader.

- Short life asset elections can bring forward the allowances due on an asset.

Quick Quiz

1   Writing down allowances are pro-rated in a six month period of account. TRUE/FALSE.

2   Lucas makes up accounts for a 15 month period to 30 June 2012. What Annual Investment Allowance is he entitled to?

    A   £25,000
    B   £75,000
    C   £100,000
    D   £125,000

3   Is a first year allowance on a low emission car pro-rated in a six month period of account?

4   When may balancing allowances arise?

5   An asset acquired in August 2011 must be disposed of within ____ years of the end of the accounting period (or period of account) in which it was acquired in order for it to be advantageous to treat it as a short life asset. Fill in the blank.

6   Paula makes up accounts to 5 April each year. She buys a car in August 2011 costing £20,000 for use in her business. Her private use of the car is 30%. The CO_2 emissions of the car are 170g/km.

    What WDA is available on the car for the year ended 5 April 2012?

    A   £1,400
    B   £2,000
    C   £2,800
    D   £4,000

Answers to Quick Quiz

1   True. In a six month period, writing down allowance are pro-rated by multiplying by 6/12.

2   D. £100,000 × 15/12 = £125,000.

3   No. A first year allowance is given in full in a short period of account.

4   Balancing allowances may arise in respect of main or special pool expenditure only when the trade ceases. Balancing allowances may arise on single pool assets whenever those assets are disposed of.

5   An asset acquired in August 2011 must be disposed of within **8** years of the end of the accounting period (or period of account) in which it was acquired in order for it to be advantageous to treat it as a short life asset.

6   A. £20,000 x 10% (CO_2 emissions of the car exceed 160g/km) = £2,000. WDA is £2,000 x 70% = £1,400.

Now try the questions below from the Exam Question Bank

Number	Level	Marks	Time
Q10	Examination	15	27 mins
Q11	Examination	8	14 mins

Assessable trading income

Topic list	Syllabus reference
1 Recognise the basis of assessment	B3(a)
2 Commencement and cessation	B3(e)
3 Change of accounting date	B3(f)(i)-(iii)

Introduction

In the previous two chapters we have seen how to calculate the taxable trading profits after capital allowances. We are now going to look at how these are taxed in the owner's hands.

Businesses do not normally prepare accounts for tax years so we look at the basis of assessment which is the method by which the taxable trading profits of periods of account are allocated to tax years. As well as the normal rules for a continuing business we need special rules for the opening years of a trade, and again in the closing years.

Special rules are also needed if the business changes its accounting date.

In the next chapter we will look at the tax reliefs available should the business make a loss.

Study guide

		Intellectual level
B3	**Income from self-employment**	
(a)	Recognise the basis of assessment for self-employment income.	2
(e)	Compute the assessable profits on commencement and on cessation.	2
(f)	Change of accounting date	
(i)	Recognise the factors that will influence the choice of accounting date.	2
(ii)	State the conditions that must be met for a change of accounting date to be valid.	1
(iii)	Compute the assessable profits on a change of accounting date.	2

Exam guide

You are likely to have to deal with a tax computation for an unincorporated business at some point in the exam. It may be a simple computation for a continuing business, or you may have to deal with a business in its opening or closing years, including computing taxable trading profits and allocating them to tax years. You must be totally familiar with the rules and be able to apply them in the exam.

1 Recognise the basis of assessment

FAST FORWARD

> Basis periods are used to link periods of account to tax years. Broadly, the profits of a 12 month period of account ending in a tax year are taxed in that year (current year basis).

1.1 Basis periods and tax years

A tax year runs from 6 April to 5 April, but most businesses do not have periods of account ending on 5 April. **Thus there must be a link between a period of account of a business and a tax year.** The procedure is to **find a period to act as the basis period for a tax year. The profits for a basis period are taxed in the corresponding tax year**. If a basis period is not identical to a period of account, the profits of periods of account are time-apportioned as required on the assumption that profits accrue evenly over a period of account. We will apportion to the nearest month for exam purposes.

The general rule is that **the basis period is the year of account ending in the tax year**. This is known as the **current year basis of assessment**.

This general rule does not apply in the opening or closing years of a business. This is because in the first few years the business has not normally established a pattern of annual accounts, and very few businesses cease trading on the annual accounting date.

Apart from the first tax year of trade and the last tax year of trade, HMRC will expect to see 12 months of profits showing in the income tax computation each year. As the periods of account may not be 12 months long in the opening and closing years, the current year basis may be impossible to apply, therefore special rules need to be applied to establish which 12 months should be allocated to which tax year.

Special rules are also needed when the trader changes his accounting date.

We will look at these rules in the next sections.

2 Commencement and cessation

FAST FORWARD

In the first tax year of trade actual profits of the tax year are taxed. In the second tax year, the basis period is either the first 12 months, the 12 months to the accounting date ending in year two or the actual profits from April to April. Profits of the twelve months to the accounting date are taxed in year three.

2.1 The first tax year

The first tax year is the year during which the trade commences. For example, if a trade commences on 1 June 2011 the first tax year is 2011/12.

The **basis period for the first tax year runs from the date the trade starts to the next 5 April** (or to the date of cessation if the trade does not last until the end of the tax year).

So continuing the above example a trader commencing in business on 1 June 2011 will be taxed on profits arising form 1 June 2011 to 5 April 2012 in 2011/12, the first tax year.

2.2 The second tax year

(a)   If the accounting date falling in the second tax year is at least 12 months after the start of trading, the basis period is the 12 months to that accounting date.

(b)   If the accounting date falling in the second tax year is less than 12 months after the start of trading, the basis period is the first 12 months of trading.

(c)   If there is no accounting date falling in the second tax year, because the first period of account is a very long one which does not end until a date in the third tax year, the basis period for the second tax year is the year itself (from 6 April to 5 April).

The following flowchart may help you determine the basis period for the second tax year.

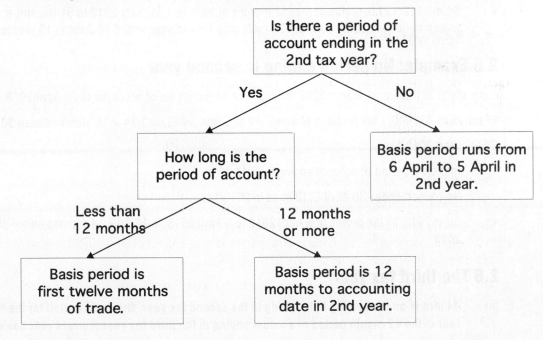

2.3 Example: period of twelve months or more ending in second year

John starts to trade on 1 January 2012 making up accounts to 31 December 2012.

1st tax year: 2011/12 – tax profits 1 January 2012 to 5 April 2012, ie 3/12 × year ended 31 December 2012

2nd tax year: 2012/13

- Is there a period of account ending in 2012/13?

  Yes – Year ended 31 December 2012 ends in 2012/13.

- How long is the period of account?

  12 months or more, ie 12 months (exactly) to 31 December 2012.

- So in 2012/13 tax profits of 12 months to 31 December 2012.

2.4 Example: short period ending in second year

Janet starts to trade on 1 January 2012 making up accounts as follows:

- 6 months to 30 June 2012
- 12 months to 30 June 2013.

1st tax year: 2011/12 – tax profits 1 January 2012 to 5 April 2012, ie 3/6 × 6 months ended 30 June 2012

2nd tax year: 2012/13.

- Is there a period of account ending in 2012/13?

  Yes – period ended 30 June 2012 ends in 2012/13.

- How long is the period of account?

  Less than 12 months.

- So in 2012/13 tax profits of first 12 months of trade ie 1 January 2012 to 31 December 2012, ie 6 month period ended 30 June 2012 profits plus 6/12 of year ended 30 June 2013 profits

2.5 Example: No period ending in second year

Jodie starts to trade on 1 March 2012 making up a 14 month set of accounts to 30 April 2013.

1st tax year: 2011/12 – tax profits 1 March 2012 to 5 April 2012, ie 1/14 × 14 months ended 30 April 2013

2nd tax year: 2012/13

- Is there a period of account ending in 2012/13?

  No (period ended 30 April 2013 ends in 2013/14)

- So in 2012/13 tax profits of 6 April 2012 to 5 April 2013, ie 12/14 × 14 months ended 30 April 2013

2.6 The third tax year

(a) **If there is an accounting date falling in the second tax year, the basis period for the third tax year is the 12 month period of account ending in the third tax year (current year basis).**

(b) If there is no accounting date falling in the second tax year, the basis period for the third tax year is the 12 months to the accounting date falling in the third tax year.

2.7 Example: Accounting date in second year

Wilma starts to trade on 1 October 2011. She made taxable profits of £9,000 for the first 9 months to 30 June 2012 and £30,000 for the year to 30 June 2013.

The taxable profits for the first three tax years are as follows:

Year	Basis period	Working	Taxable profits £
2011/12	1.10.11 – 5.4.12	£9,000 × 6/9	6,000
2012/13	1.10.11 – 30.9.12	£9,000 + £30,000 × 3/12	16,500
2013/14	1.7.12 – 30.6.13		30,000
	(period of account ending in 3rd year)		

2.8 Example: No accounting date in the second year

Thelma starts to trade on 1 March 2012. Her first accounts, covering the 16 months to 30 June 2013 show a profit of £36,000. The taxable profits for the first three tax years are as follows.

Year	Basis period	Working	Taxable profits £
2011/12	1.3.12 – 5.4.12	£36,000 × 1/16	2,250
2012/13	6.4.12 – 5.4.13	£36,000 × 12/16	27,000
2013/14	1.7.12 – 30.6.13	£36,000 × 12/16	27,000
	(12 months to the accounting date in 3rd year)		

2.9 Later tax years

For later tax years, except the year in which the trade ceases, the normal current year basis of assessment applies, ie the basis period is the 12 month period of account ending in the tax year (see above).

Question

Basis periods

Peter commenced trading on 1 September 2007 preparing accounts to 30 April each year with the following results.

Period		Profit £
1.9.07 – 30.4.08		8,000
1.5.08 – 30.4.09		15,000
1.5.09 – 30.4.10		9,000
1.5.10 – 30.4.11		10,500

Show the profits to be taxed in each year from 2007/08 to 2011/12.

Answer

Year	Basis period	Working	Taxable Profits £
2007/08	1.9.07 – 5.4.08	£8,000 × 7/8	7,000
2008/09	1.9.07 – 31.8.08	£8,000 + (£15,000 × 4/12)	13,000
2009/10	1.5.08 – 30.4.09		15,000
2010/11	1.5.09 – 30.4.10		9,000
2011/12	1.5.10 – 30.4.11		10,500

2.10 The final year

FAST FORWARD

On a cessation the basis period runs from the end of the basis period for the previous tax year.

(a) If a trade starts and ceases in the same tax year, the basis period for that year is the whole lifespan of the trade.

(b) If the final year is the second year, the basis period runs from 6 April at the start of the second year to the date of cessation. This rule overrides the rules that normally apply for the second year.

(c) If the final year is the third year or a later year, **the basis period runs from the end of the basis period for the previous year to the date of cessation**. This rule overrides the rules that normally apply in the third and later years.

Question   Ceasing to trade

Harriet, who has been trading since 1998, ceases her trade on 31 March 2012.

Her results for recent years were:

Year ended 31 December	£
2009	10,000
2010	14,000
2011	21,000
Period ended 31 March 2012	4,000

Show the taxable trade profits for the last three tax years of trading.

Answer

Trade ceases in 2011/12.

Year	Basis period	Working	Assessment £
2009/10	Y/e 31.12.09		10,000
2010/11	Y/e 31.12.10		14,000
2011/12	1.1.11 – 31.3.12	Y/e 31.12.11 plus p/e 31.3.12	25,000

2.11 Overlap profits

Key term

Profits which have been taxed more than once are called **overlap profits**.

When a business starts, some profits may be taxed twice because the basis period for the second year includes some or all of the period of trading in the first year or because the basis period for the third year overlaps with that for the second year, or both.

Overlap profits may be deducted on a change of accounting date (see below). Any overlap profits unrelieved when the trade ceases are deducted from the final year's taxable profits. Any deduction of overlap profits may create or increase a loss. The usual loss reliefs (covered later in this Text) are then available.

Exam focus point

A business with a 31 March year end will have no overlap profits as its accounting year coincides with the tax year. A business with a 31 December year end, for example, will have 3 months of overlap profit as its accounting year ends three months before the end of the tax year. Use this rule of thumb to check your calculation of overlap profits.

2.12 Examples: overlap profits

(a) John starts to trade on 1 January 2012 making up accounts to 31 December 2012. Show the overlap period.

Tax year	Basis period
2011/12	1.1.12 – 5.4.12
2012/13	1.1.12 – 31.12.12
2013/14	1.1.13 – 31.12.13

Overlap period: 1.1.12 – 5.4.12 (3 months)

(b) Janet starts to trade on 1 January 2012 making up accounts as follows:

6m to 30 June 2012
12m to 30 June 2013

Show the overlap period.

Tax year	Basis period
2011/12	1.1.12 – 5.4.12
2012/13	1.1.12 – 31.12.12
2013/14	1.7.12 – 30.6.13

Overlap period: 1.1.12 – 5.4.12 plus 1.7.12 – 31.12.12 (9 months)

(c) Jodie starts to trade on 1 March 2012 making up a 14 month set of accounts to 30 April 2013. Show the overlap period.

Tax year	Basis period
2011/12	1.3.12 – 5.4.12
2012/13	6.4.12 – 5.4.13
2013/14	1.5.12 – 30.4.13

Overlap period: 1.5.12 – 5.4.13 (11 months)

Question

Ceasing to trade and overlap profits

Jenny trades from 1 July 2006 to 31 December 2011, with the following results.

Period	Profit £
1.7.06 – 31.8.07	7,000
1.9.07 – 31.8.08	12,000
1.9.08 – 31.8.09	15,000
1.9.09 – 31.8.10	21,000
1.9.10 – 31.8.11	18,000
1.9.11 – 31.12.11	5,600
	78,600

Calculate the taxable trade profits to be taxed from 2006/07 to 2011/12, the overlap profits and state when these overlap profits can be relieved.

The profits to be taxed in each tax year from 2006/07 to 2011/12 and the total of these taxable profits are calculated as follows.

Year	Basis period	Working	Taxable profit £
2006/07	1.7.06 – 5.4.07	£7,000 × 9/14	4,500
2007/08	1.9.06 – 31.8.07	£7,000 × 12/14	6,000
2008/09	1.9.07 – 31.8.08		12,000
2009/10	1.9.08 – 31.8.09		15,000
2010/11	1.9.09 – 31.8.10		21,000
2011/12	1.9.10 – 31.12.11	£(18,000 + 5,600 – 3,500)	20,100
			78,600

The overlap profits are those in the period 1 September 2006 to 5 April 2007, a period of seven months. They are £7,000 × 7/14 = £3,500. Overlap profits are either relieved on a change of accounting date (see below) or are deducted from the final year's taxable profit when the business ceases. In this case the overlap profits are deducted when the business ceases.

Exam focus point

Over the life of the business, the total taxable profits equal the total actual profits.

2.13 The choice of an accounting date

A new trader should consider which accounting date would be best. There are **a number of factors to consider** from the point of view of taxation.

- **If profits are expected to rise, a date early in the tax year** (such as 30 April) will delay the time when rising accounts profits feed through into rising taxable profits, whereas a date late in the tax year (such as 31 March) will accelerate the taxation of rising profits. This is because with an accounting date of 30 April, the taxable profits for each tax year are mainly the profits earned in the previous tax year. With an accounting date of 31 March the taxable profits are almost entirely profits earned in the current year.

- If the accounting date in the second tax year is less than 12 months after the start of trading, the taxable profits for that year will be the profits earned in the first 12 months. If the accounting date is at least 12 months from the start of trading, they will be the profits earned in the 12 months to that date. **Different profits may thus be taxed twice**, and if profits are fluctuating this can make a considerable difference to the taxable profits in the first few years. (See below for the relief given where profits are taxed twice – 'overlap relief'.)

- **The choice of an accounting date affects the profits shown in each set of accounts**, and this may affect the taxable profits.

- **An accounting date of 30 April gives the maximum interval between earning profits and paying the related tax liability.** For example if a trader makes up accounts to 30 April 2012, this falls into the tax year 2012/13 with payments on account being due on 31 January 2013 and 31 July 2013, and a balancing payment due on 31 January 2014 (details of payment of income tax are dealt with later in this Text). If the trader makes up accounts to 31 March 2012, this falls in the tax year 2011/12 and the payments will be due one year earlier (ie on 31 January 2012, 31 July 2012 and 31 January 2013).

- **Knowing profits well in advance of the end of the tax year makes tax planning much easier.** For example, if a trader wants to make personal pension contributions and makes up accounts to 30 April 2012 (2012/13), he can make contributions up to 5 April 2013 based on those relevant earnings. If he makes up accounts to 31 March 2012, he will probably not know the amount of his relevant earnings until after the end of the tax year 2011/12, too late to adjust his pension contributions for 2011/12.

- However, a 31 March or 5 April accounting date means that the application of the basis period rules is more straightforward and there will be no overlap profits. This may be appropriate for small traders.

- With an accounting date of 30 April, the assessment for the year of cessation could be based on up to 23 months of profits. For example, if a trader who has made up accounts to 30 April ceases trading on 31 March 2012 (2011/12), the basis period for 2011/12 will run from 1 May 2010 to 31 March 2012. This could lead to larger than normal trading profits being assessable in the year of cessation. However, this could be avoided by carrying on the trade for another month so that a cessation arises on 30 April 2012 so that the profits from 1 May 2010 to 30 April 2011 are taxable in 2011/12 and those from 1 May 2011 to 30 April 2012 are taxable in 2012/13. Each case must be looked at in relation to all relevant factors, such as other income which the taxpayer may have and loss relief – there is no one rule which applies in all cases.

Question | The choice of an accounting date

Christine starts to trade on 1 December 2009. Her monthly profits are £1,000 for the first seven months, and £2,000 thereafter. Show the taxable profits for the first three tax years with each of the following accounting dates (in all cases starting with a period of account of less than 12 months).

(a) 31 March
(b) 30 April
(c) 31 December

Answer

(a) *31 March*

Period of account	Working	Profits £
1.12.09 – 31.3.10	£1,000 × 4	4,000
1.4.10 – 31.3.11	£1,000 × 3 + £2,000 × 9	21,000
1.4.11 – 31.3.12	£2,000 × 12	24,000

Year	Basis period	Taxable profits £
2009/10	1.12.09 – 5.4.10	4,000
2010/11	1.4.10 – 31.3.11	21,000
2011/12	1.4.11 – 31.3.12	24,000

(b) *30 April*

Period of account	Working	Profits £
1.12.09 – 30.4.10	£1,000 × 5	5,000
1.5.10 – 30.4.11	£1,000 × 2 + £2,000 ×10	22,000

Year	Basis period	Working	Taxable profits £
2009/10	1.12.09 – 5.4.10	£5,000 × 4/5	4,000
2010/11	1.12.09 – 30.11.10	£5,000 + £22,000 × 7/12	17,833
2011/12	1.5.10 – 30.4.11		22,000

(c) *31 December*

Period of account	Working	Profits £
1.12.09 – 31.12.09	£1,000 × 1	1,000
1.1.10 – 31.12.10	£1,000 × 6 + £2,000 × 6	18,000
1.1.11 – 31.12.11	£2,000 × 12	24,000

Year	Basis period	Working	Taxable profits £
2009/10	1.12.09 – 5.4.10	£1,000 + £18,000 × 3/12	5,500
2010/11	1.1.10 – 31.12.10		18,000
2011/12	1.1.11 – 31.12.11		24,000

3 Change of accounting date

FAST FORWARD

On a change of accounting date, special rules may apply for fixing basis periods. Overlap profits may either be created or relieved on a change of accounting date. Overlap profits may be relieved if more than 12 months worth of profits would otherwise be taxed in a year following a change of accounting date. On cessation any remaining overlap profits are relieved.

3.1 Need for special rules

A trader may change the date to which he prepares his annual accounts for a variety of reasons. For example, he may wish to move to a calendar year end or to fit in with seasonal variations of his trade. Special rules normally apply for fixing basis periods when a trader changes his accounting date.

On a change of accounting date, there may be

- One set of accounts covering a period of less than twelve months, or
- One set of accounts covering a period of more than twelve months, or
- Two sets of accounts, or
- No set of accounts

ending in a tax year. In each case, the basis period for the year relates to the new accounting date. We will look at each of the cases in turn.

3.2 One short period of account ending in tax year

When a change of accounting date results in one short period of account ending in a tax year, the basis period for that year is always the 12 months to the new accounting date.

3.3 Example: change of accounting date – short period

Sue prepares accounts to 31 December each year until she changes her accounting date to 30 June by preparing accounts for the six months to 30 June 2011.

There is one short period of account ending during 2011/12. This means the basis period for 2011/12 is the twelve months to 30 June 2011.

Sue's basis period for 2010/11 was the twelve months to 31 December 2010. This means the profits of the six months to 31 December 2010 are overlap profits that have been taxed twice. These overlap profits must be added to any overlap profits that arose when the business began. The total is either relieved when the business ceases or is relieved on a subsequent change of accounting date.

3.4 One long period of account ending in tax year

When a change of accounting date results in one long period of account ending in a tax year, the basis period for that year ends on the new accounting date. It begins immediately after the basis period for the previous year ends. This means the basis period will exceed 12 months.

No overlap profits arise in this situation. However, more than twelve months worth of profits are taxed in one income tax year and to compensate for this, relief is available for brought forward overlap

profits. The overlap relief cannot reduce the number of months worth of profits taxed in the year to below twelve. So, if you have a fourteen month basis period you can give relief for up to two months worth of overlap profits.

3.5 Example: change of accounting date – long period

Zoe started trading on 1 October 2008 and prepared accounts to 30 September until she changed her accounting date by preparing accounts for the fifteen months to 31 December 2011. Her results were as follows

	£
Year to 30 September 2009	24,000
Year to 30 September 2010	48,000
Fifteen months to 31 December 2011	75,000

Profits for the first three tax years of the business are:

	£
2008/09 (1.10.08 – 5.4.09) 6/12 × £24,000	12,000
2009/10 (1.10.08 – 30.9.09)	24,000
2010/11 (1.10.09 – 30.9.10)	48,000

Overlap profits are £12,000. These arose in the six months to 5.4.09.

The change in accounting date results in one long period of account ending during 2011/12 which means the basis period for 2011/12 is the fifteen months to 31 December 2011. Three months worth of the brought forward overlap profits can be relieved.

	£
2011/12 (1.10.10 – 31.12.11)	75,000
Less overlap profits 3/6 × £12,000	(6,000)
	69,000

The unrelieved overlap profits of £6,000 (£12,000 – £6,000) are carried forward for relief either when the business ceases or on a further change of accounting date.

3.6 Two sets of accounts ending in tax year

When a change of accounting date results in two sets of accounts (one 12 month period to the old accounting date and a short period to the new accounting date) ending in a tax year, the basis period for that year is the period to the new accounting date. It begins immediately after the basis period for the previous year ends. This means the basis period will exceed 12 months and will include both sets of accounts ending in the tax year. This situation is dealt with in the same way as a one long period of account ending in the tax year.

 Question   Two periods of account in same tax year

Muriel started in business on 1 October 2001 making up accounts to 31 July. Her overlap profits on commencement were £9,720 which represented 6 months of overlap. In 2011, she decides to change her accounting date to 30 November and makes up accounts for the four month period to 30 November 2011. Profits are as follows:

Basis period	Profits
	£
1.8.09 – 31.7.10	15,000
1.8.10 – 31.7.11	19,600
1.8.11 – 30.11.11	6,750
1.12.11 – 30.11.12	27,300

Show the taxable profits for 2010/11, 2011/12 and 2012/13 and compute the balance of overlap profits carried forward.

The change in accounting date results in two periods of account ending during 2011/12 (12 months to 31.7.11 and 4 months to 30.11.11). The basis period for 2011/12 starts immediately after the end of the accounting period for 2010/11 which means the basis period for 2011/12 is the sixteen months to 30 November 2011. Four months worth of the brought forward overlap profits can be relieved.

		£
2011/12 (1.8.10 – 30.11.11) £(19,600 + 6,750)		26,350
Less overlap profits 4/6 × £9,720		(6,480)
		19,870

The taxable profits are therefore:

Year	Basis period	Taxable profit
		£
2010/11	1.8.09 – 31.7.10	15,000
2011/12	1.8.10 – 30.11.11	19,870
2012/13	1.12.11 – 30.11.12	27,300

The unrelieved overlap profits of £3,240 (£9,720 – £6,480) are carried forward for relief either when the business ceases or on a further change of accounting date.

3.7 No set of accounts ending in tax year

When a change of accounting date results in one long period of account such that there is one tax year where there is no set of accounts ending in that year, the long period of account is treated as being divided into:

- a short period of account up to the new accounting date in the tax year in which there is no actual accounting date, and

- a twelve month period of account.

In the tax year in which there is no actual accounting date, the basis period is then the 12 months to the new accounting date in that tax year. This is dealt with in the same way as a short period of account and so overlap profits will be generated. In the following tax year, the basis period will be the 12 months to the new accounting date.

3.8 Conditions

The above changes in basis period automatically occur if the trader changes his accounting date during the first three tax years of his business.

In other cases **the following conditions must be met before a change in basis periods can occur**:

- The trader must notify HMRC of the change by the 31 January, following the tax year in which the change is made (by 31 January 2013 for a change made during 2011/12.)

- The period of account resulting from the change must not exceed 18 months.

- In general, there must have been no previous change of accounting date in the last 5 tax years. However, a second change can be made within this period if the later change is for genuine commercial reasons. If HMRC do not respond to a notification of a change of accounting date within 60 days of receiving it, the trader can assume that they are satisfied that the reasons for making the change are genuine commercial ones.

If the above conditions are not satisfied because the first period of account ending on the new date exceeds 18 months or the change of accounting date was not notified in time, but the 'five year gap or commercial reasons' condition is satisfied, then the basis period for the year of change is the 12 months to the *old* accounting date in the year of change. The basis period for the next year is then found using rules above as if it were the year of change.

If the 'five year gap or commercial reasons' test is not satisfied, the old accounting date remains in force for tax purposes (with the profits of accounts made up to the new date being time-apportioned as necessary) until there have been five consecutive tax years which were not years of change. The sixth tax year is then treated as the year of change to the new accounting date, and the rules above apply.

Chapter Roundup

- Basis periods are used to link periods of account to tax years. Broadly, the profits of a 12 month period of account ending in a tax year are taxed in that year (current year basis).

- In the first tax year of trade actual profits of the tax year are taxed. In the second tax year, the basis period is either the first 12 months, the 12 months to the accounting date ending in year two or the actual profits from April to April. Profits of the twelve months to the accounting date are taxed in year three.

- On a cessation the basis period runs from the end of the basis period for the previous tax year.

- On a change of accounting date, special rules may apply for fixing basis periods. Overlap profits may either be created or relieved on a change of accounting date. Overlap profits may be relieved if more than 12 months worth of profits would otherwise be taxed in a year following a change of accounting date. On cessation any remaining overlap profits are relieved.

Quick Quiz

1   What is the normal basis of assessment?

2   Isabella started trading on 1 September 2011. She made up her first set of accounts to 31 December 2012. The basis period for the year of commencement is:

    A   1 September 2011 to 31 December 2011
    B   1 September 2011 to 5 April 2012
    C   1 September 2011 to 31 August 2012
    D   1 September 2011 to 31 December 2012

3   Ernie started trading on 1 January 2011. He decided to make up accounts to 31 October each year. His taxable trading profits is as follows:

p/e 31.10.11	£3,000
y/e 31.10.12	£23,760

What are Ernie's overlap profits?

    A   £900
    B   £2,880
    C   £3,960
    D   £4,860

4   Gita ceased trading on 31 March 2012. Her taxable trading profits were:

y/e 31.12.11	£5,600
p/e 31.3.12	£4,500

Gita had £2,300 of unused overlap profits.

What is her taxable trading profit for 2011/12?

    A   £10,100
    B   £7,800
    C   £6,400
    D   £2,200

5   On what two occasions can overlap profits potentially be relieved?

Answers to Quick Quiz

1   The normal basis of assessment is that the profits for a tax year are those of the 12 month accounting period ending in the tax year.

2   B. 1 September 2011 to 5 April 2012 ie the actual tax year.

3   D £4,860

First tax year (2010/11)
Actual basis
Basis period 1.1.11 to 5 4.11

Second tax year (2011/12)
Period of account in 2nd year less than 12 months
Basis period 1.1.11 to 31.12.11

Third tax year (2012/13)
Current year basis
Basis period 1.11.11 to 31.10.12

Overlap profits
Period of overlap 1.1.11 to 5.4.11 and 1.11.11 to 31.12.11

Overlap profits

	£
3/10 × £3,000	900
2/12 × £23,760	3,960
	4,860

4   B £7,800

Last tax year (2011/12) Basis period 1.1.11 to 31.3.12

	£
y/e 31.12.11	5,600
p/e 31.3.12	4,500
	10,100
Less: overlap profits	(2,300)
	7,800

5   On a change of accounting date where a basis period resulting from the change exceeds 12 months or on the cessation of a business.

Now try the questions below from the Exam Question Bank

Number	Level	Marks	Time
Q12	Examination	15	27 mins
Q13	Examination	15	27 mins
Q14	Examination	15	27 mins

Trading losses

Topic list	Syllabus reference
1 Losses	B3(h)
2 Carry forward trade loss relief	B3h(i)
3 Trade transferred to company	B3h(ii)
4 Trade loss relief against general income	B3h(iii)
5 Losses in the early years of a trade	B3h(iv)
6 Terminal trade loss relief	B3h(v)

Introduction

We have seen how to calculate taxable trading profits and how to allocate them to tax years so that they can be slotted into the income tax computation.

Traders sometimes make losses rather than profits. In this chapter we consider the reliefs available for losses. A loss does not in itself lead to getting tax back from HMRC. Relief is obtained by setting a loss against trading profits, against general income or against capital gains (which are covered later in this Text), so that tax need not be paid on them. An important consideration is the choice between different reliefs. The aim is to use a loss to save as much tax as possible, as quickly as possible.

In the next chapter we will see how the rules on trading profits and losses for sole traders are extended to those trading in partnership.

Study guide

		Intellectual level
B3	**Income from self-employment**	
(h)	Relief for trading losses	
h(i)	Understand how trading losses can be carried forward.	2
h(ii)	Explain how trading losses can be carried forward following the incorporation of a business.	2
h(iii)	Understand how trading losses can be claimed against total income and chargeable gains.	2
h(iv)	Explain and compute the relief for trading losses in the early years of a trade.	1
h(v)	Explain and compute terminal loss relief.	1

Exam guide

Losses are likely to be included in one or more questions in the exam. The focus may, however, be on corporation tax losses, and you may not have to deal with trading losses for income tax purposes at all. Alternatively you could have a detailed computational question involving the carry back and carry forward of losses for a sole trader. Ensure you know the rules for ongoing trades and the additional relief in the early years of trading. On a cessation carry forward is only possible if an unincorporated business is incorporated, but terminal loss relief may be due instead. Once you have established the reliefs available look to see which is most beneficial.

1 Losses

> Trading losses may be relieved against future profits of the same trade, against general income and against capital gains.

1.1 Introduction

When computing taxable trade profits, profits may turn out to be negative, meaning a loss has been made in the basis period. **A loss is computed in exactly the same way as a profit**, making the same adjustments to the accounts profit or loss.

If there is a loss in a basis period, the taxable trade profits for the tax year based on that basis period are nil.

This chapter considers how losses are calculated and how a loss-suffering taxpayer can use a loss to reduce his tax liability.

The rules in this chapter apply only to individuals, trading alone or in partnership. Loss reliefs for companies are completely different and are covered later in this Text.

1.2 The computation of the loss

The trade loss for a tax year is the trade loss in the basis period for that tax year.

1.3 Example: computation of trade loss

Here is an example of a trader with a 31 December year end who has been trading for many years.

Period of account		Loss £
Y/e 31.12.2011		9,000
Y/e 31.12.2012		24,000

Tax year	Basis period	Trade loss for the tax year £
2011/12	Y/e 31.12.11	9,000
2012/13	Y/e 31.12.12	24,000

1.4 How loss relief is given

Loss relief is given by deducting the loss from total income to calculate net income. Carry forward loss relief and terminal loss relief can only be set against the trading profits of the same trade. Other loss reliefs may be set against general income (ie any component of total income).

2 Carry forward trade loss relief

Trading losses may be relieved against future profits of the same trade. The relief is against the first available profits of the same trade.

2.1 The relief

A trade loss not relieved in any other way will be **carried forward to set against the first available trade profits of the same trade** in the calculation of net trading income. Losses may be carried forward for any number of years unless they have been entirely used up.

Carry forward trade loss relief is the only trade loss relief which applies to furnished holiday lettings (see earlier in this Text).

2.2 Example: carrying forward losses

Brian has the following results.

Year ending	£
31 December 2009	(6,000)
31 December 2010	5,000
31 December 2011	11,000

Brian's net trading income, assuming that he claims carry forward loss relief only are:

	2009/10 £		2010/11 £		2011/12 £
Trade profits	0		5,000		11,000
Less carry forward loss relief	(0)	(i)	(5,000)	(ii)	(1,000)
Net trading income	0		0		10,000

Loss memorandum		£
Trading loss, y/e 31.12.09		6,000
Less: claim in y/e 31.12.10 (10/11)	(i)	(5,000)
claim in y/e 31.12.11 (balance of loss) (11/12)	(ii)	(1,000)
		0

3 Trade transferred to company

Where a business is transferred to a company, loss relief is available for any remaining unrelieved losses of the unincorporated business against income received from the company.

Although carry forward loss relief is restricted to future profits of the same business, this is extended to cover income received from a company to which the business is transferred.

The amount carried forward is the total unrelieved trading losses of the business.

The set off is against income derived from the company including salary, interest and dividends. Set-off the loss against non-savings income, then against savings income and finally against dividend income.

The consideration for the transfer of the business must be wholly or mainly in the form of shares (at least 80%) which must be retained by the vendor throughout any tax year in which the loss is relieved .

4 Trade loss relief against general income

A trading loss may be set against general income in the year of the loss and/or the preceding year. Personal allowances may be lost as a result of a claim. Once a claim has been made in any year, the remaining loss can be set against net chargeable gains.

4.1 The relief

Instead of carrying a trade loss forward against future trade profits, a claim may be made to relieve it against general income.

4.2 Relieving the loss

Relief is against the income of the tax year in which the loss arose. In addition or instead, relief may be claimed **against the income of the preceding year**.

If there are losses in two successive years, and relief is claimed against the first year's income both for the first year's loss and for the second year's loss, relief is given for the first year's loss before the second year's loss.

A claim for a loss must be made by the 31 January which is 22 months after the end of the tax year of the loss: thus by 31 January 2014 for a loss in 2011/12.

The taxpayer cannot choose the amount of loss to relieve: thus the loss may have to be set against income part of which would have been covered by the personal allowance. However, the taxpayer can choose whether to claim full relief in the current year and then relief in the preceding year for any remaining loss, or the other way round.

Question

Loss relief against general income

Janet has a loss in her period of account ending 31 December 2011 of £26,000. Her other income is £19,000 part time employment income a year, and she wishes to claim loss relief against general income for the year of loss and then for the preceding year. Her trading income in the previous year was £nil. Show her taxable income for each year, and comment on the effectiveness of the loss relief. Assume that tax rates and allowances for 2011/12 have always applied.

The loss-making period ends in 2011/12, so the year of the loss is 2011/12.

	2010/11	2011/12
	£	£
Total income	19,000	19,000
Less loss relief against general income	(7,000)	(19,000)
Net income	12,000	0
Less personal allowance	(7,475)	(7,475)
Taxable income	4,525	0

In 2011/12, £7,475 of the loss has been wasted because that amount of income would have been covered by the personal allowance. If Janet just claims loss relief against general income, there is nothing she can do about this waste of loss relief.

4.3 Capital allowances

The trader may adjust the size of the loss relief claim by not claiming all the capital allowances he is entitled to: a reduced claim will increase the balance carried forward to the next year's capital allowances computation. This may be a useful **tax planning point to preserve the personal allowance or where the effective rate of relief for capital allowances in future periods will be greater than the rate of tax relief for the loss relief**.

Capital allowances and loss relief

Mario is a sole trader making up accounts to 31 December each year. In the year to 31 December 2011, he makes a trading loss, before taking capital allowances into account, of £8,000. Mario has a tax written down value on his main pool at 1 January 2011 of £12,000. He does not make any additions or disposals in the year to 31 December 2011 and does not intend to make any additions or disposals in the year to 31 December 2012.

Mario has gross savings income of £17,000 in 2011/12 and wishes to use trade loss relief against general income in 2011/12 only (ie. without any carry back to 2010/11). He expects to make a trading profit of £30,000 in the year to 31 December 2012.

What advice would you give Mario?

Mario should make a reduced capital allowance claim so that the loss relief claim will preserve his personal allowance in 2011/12.

The maximum capital allowances claim that Mario could make in 2011/12 is £12,000 x 20% = £2,400. He should only claim £(17,000 − 8,000 − 7,475) = £1,525. The tax written down value of the pool at 1 January 2012 will then be £(12,000 − 1,525) = £10,475 on which Mario can claim the maximum allowance at 20% for relief in 2012/13.

4.4 Trading losses relieved against capital gains

Where relief is claimed against general income of a given year, the taxpayer may include **a further claim to set the loss against his chargeable gains for the year** less any allowable capital losses for the same year or for previous years. This amount of net gains is computed ignoring the annual exempt amount (see later in this Text).

The trading loss is first set against general income of the year of the claim, and only any excess loss is set against capital gains. The taxpayer cannot specify the amount to be set against capital gains, so the annual exempt amount may be wasted. We include an example here for completeness. You will study chargeable gains later in this Text and we suggest that you come back to this example at that point.

         Loss relief against income and gains

Sibyl had the following results for 2011/12.

	£
Loss available for relief against general income	27,000
Income	19,500
Capital gains less current year capital losses	15,000
Annual exempt amount for capital gains tax purposes	10,600
Capital losses brought forward	9,000

Show how the loss would be relieved against income and gains.

	£
Income	19,500
Less loss relief against general income	(19,500)
Net income	0
Capital gains	15,000
Less loss relief: lower of £(27,000 – 19,500) = £7,500 (note 1) and £(15,000 – 9,000) = £6,000 (note 2)	(6,000)
	9,000
Less annual exempt amount (restricted)	(9,000)
	0

Notes

1   This equals the loss left after the loss relief claim against general income
2   This equals the gains left after losses b/fwd but ignoring the annual exempt amount.

A trading loss of £(7,500 – 6,000) = £1,500 is carried forward. Sibyl's personal allowance and £(10,600 – 9,000) = £1,600 of her capital gains tax annual exempt amount are wasted. Her capital losses brought forward of £9,000 are carried forward to 2012/13. Although we deducted this £9,000 in working out how much trading loss we were allowed to use in the claim, we do not actually need to use any of the £9,000 as the remaining gain is covered by the annual exempt amount.

4.5 Restrictions on trade loss relief against general income

Relief cannot be claimed against general income unless a business is conducted on a commercial basis with a view to the realisation of profits throughout the basis period for the tax year; this condition applies to all types of business.

There is also a limit on the amount of loss relief that a trader can claim against general income if he is a non-active trader. A non-active trader is one who spends less than 10 hours a week personally engaged in trade activities. The limit is £25,000 per tax year.

This restriction applies also to early years trading loss relief (see later in this Chapter).

4.6 The choice between loss reliefs

It is important for a trader to choose the right loss relief, so as to save tax at the highest possible rate and so as to obtain relief reasonably quickly.

When a trader has a choice between loss reliefs, he should aim to obtain relief both quickly and at the highest possible tax rate. However, do consider that losses relieved against income which would otherwise be covered by the personal allowance are wasted.

Another consideration is that a trading loss cannot be set against the capital gains of a year unless relief is first claimed against general income of the same year. It may be worth making the claim against income and wasting the personal allowance in order to avoid a CGT liability.

Question

The choice between loss reliefs

Felicity's trading results are as follows.

Year ended 30 September	Trading profit/(loss) £
2009	1,900
2010	(21,000)
2011	13,000

Her other income (all non-savings income) is as follows.

	£
2009/10	3,200
2010/11	29,500
2011/12	16,000

Show the most efficient use of Felicity's trading loss. Assume that the personal allowance has been £7,475 throughout.

Answer

Relief could be claimed against general income for 2009/10 and/or 2010/11, with any unused loss being carried forward. Relief in 2009/10 would be against general income of £(1,900 + 3,200) = £5,100, all of which would be covered by the personal allowance anyway, so this claim should not be made.

A claim against general income should be made for 2010/11 as this saves tax quicker than a carry forward claim in 2011/12.

The final results will be as follows:

	2009/10 £	2010/11 £	2011/12 £
Trading income	1,900	0	13,000
Less carry forward loss relief	(0)	(0)	(0)
	1,900	0	13,000
Other income	3,200	29,500	16,000
	5,100	29,500	29,000
Less loss relief against general income	(0)	(21,000)	(0)
Net income	5,100	8,500	29,000
Less personal allowance	(7,475)	(7,475)	(7,475)
Taxable income	0	1,025	21,525

Before recommending loss relief against general income consider whether it will result in the waste of the personal allowance. Such waste is to be avoided if at all possible.

5 Losses in the early years of a trade

5.1 The computation of the loss

Under the rules determining the basis period for the first three tax years of trading, there may be periods where the basis periods overlap. If profits arise in these periods, they are taxed twice but are relieved later (on cessation or on a change of accounting date). However, a loss in an overlap period can only be relieved once. It must not be double counted.

If basis periods overlap, **a loss in the overlap period is treated as a loss for the earlier tax year only.**

5.2 Example: losses in early years

Here is an example of a trader who starts to trade on 1 July 2011 and makes losses in opening periods.

Period of account			Loss £
P/e 31.12.2011			9,000
Y/e 31.12.2012			24,000

Tax year	Basis period	Working	Trade loss for the tax year £
2011/12	1.7.11 – 5.4.12	£9,000 + (£24,000 × 3/12)	15,000
2012/13	1.1.12 – 31.12.12	£24,000 less loss already used in 2011/12 (£24,000 × 3/12 = 6,000)	18,000

5.3 Example: losses and profits in early years

The rule against using losses twice also applies when losses are netted off against profits in the same basis period. Here is an example, with a commencement on 1 July 2011.

Period of account			(Loss)/profit £
1.7.11 – 30.4.12			(10,000)
1.5.12 – 30.4.13			24,000

Tax year	Basis period	Working	Trade (Loss)/Profit £
2011/12	1.7.11 – 5.4.12	£(10,000) × 9/10	(9,000)
2012/13	1.7.11 – 30.6.12	£24,000 × 2/12 + £(10,000) × 1/10	3,000

5.4 Early trade losses relief

FAST FORWARD

In opening years, a special relief involving the carry back of losses against general income is available. Losses arising in the first four tax years of a trade may be set against general income in the three years preceding the loss making year, taking the earliest year first.

Early trade losses relief is available for **trading losses incurred in the first four tax years of a trade.**

Relief is obtained by **setting the allowable loss against general income in the three years preceding the year of loss**, applying the loss to the earliest year first. Thus a loss arising in 2011/12 may be set off against income in 2008/09, 2009/10 and 2010/11 in that order.

A claim for early trade losses relief applies to all three years automatically, provided that the loss is large enough. The taxpayer cannot choose to relieve the loss against just one or two of the years, or to relieve only part of the loss. However, the taxpayer could reduce the size of the loss by not claiming the full capital allowances available to him. This will result in higher capital allowances in future years.

Claims for the relief must be made by the 31 January which is 22 months after the end of the tax year in which the loss is incurred.

Early trade losses relief is an alternative to using trade loss relief against general income or using carry forward loss relief. The advantage of early trade losses relief is that it enables losses to be carried back for three years and so gives relief earlier than the other loss reliefs. Whether that is advantageous or not depends on the particular circumstances of the trader, for example whether the trader has any other income and whether there are different rates of tax in the tax years which might be affected by a particular loss relief claim.

Question | Early trade losses relief

Mr A is employed as a dustman until 1 January 2010. On that date he starts up his own business as a scrap metal merchant, making up his accounts to 30 June each year. His earnings as a dustman are:

	£
2006/07	5,000
2007/08	6,000
2008/09	7,000
2009/10 (nine months)	6,000

His trading results as a scrap metal merchant are:

	Profit/(Loss) £
Six months to 30 June 2010	(3,000)
Year to 30 June 2011	(1,500)
Year to 30 June 2012	(1,200)

Assuming that loss relief is claimed as early as possible, show the net income for each of the years 2006/07 to 2012/13 inclusive.

Answer

Since reliefs are to be claimed as early as possible, early trade loss relief is applied. The losses available for relief are as follows.

	£	£	Years against which relief is available
2009/10 (basis period 1.1.10 – 5.4.10)			
3 months to 5.4.10 £(3,000) × 3/6		(1,500)	2006/07 to 2008/09
2010/11 (basis period 1.1.10 – 31.12.10)			
3 months to 30.6.10			
(omit 1.1.10 – 5.4.10 : overlap) £(3,000) × 3/6	(1,500)		
6 months to 31.12.10 £(1,500) × 6/12	(750)		
		(2,250)	2007/08 to 2009/10
2011/12 (basis period 1.7.10 – 30.6.11)			
6 months to 30.6.11			
(omit 1.7.10 – 31.12.10: overlap) £(1,500) × 6/12		(750)	2008/09 to 2010/11
2012/13 (basis period 1.7.11 – 30.6.12)			
12 months to 30.6.12		(1,200)	2009/10 to 2011/12

The net income is as follows.

		£	£
2006/07			
Original		5,000	
Less 2009/10 loss		(1,500)	
			3,500
2007/08			
Original		6,000	
Less 2010/11 loss		(2,250)	
			3,750
2008/09			
Original		7,000	
Less 2011/12 loss		(750)	
			6,250
2009/10			
Original		6,000	
Less 2012/13 loss		(1,200)	
			4,800

The taxable trade profits for 2009/10 to 2012/13 are zero because there were losses in the basis periods.

6 Terminal trade loss relief

FAST FORWARD

On the cessation of trade, a loss arising in the last 12 months of trading may be set against trade profits of the tax year of cessation and the previous 3 years, taking the latest year first.

6.1 The relief

Trade loss relief against general income will often be insufficient on its own to deal with a loss incurred in the last months of trading. For this reason there is a special relief, **terminal trade loss relief, which allows a loss on cessation to be carried back for relief against taxable trading profits in previous years.**

6.2 Computing the terminal loss

A terminal loss is **the loss of the last 12 months of trading**.

It is built up as follows.

		£
(a)	The actual trade loss for the tax year of cessation (calculated from 6 April to the date of cessation)	X
(b)	The actual trade loss for the period from 12 months before cessation until the end of the penultimate tax year	X
Total terminal trade loss		X

If the result of either (a) or (b) is a profit rather than a loss, it is treated as zero.

Any unrelieved overlap profits are included within (a) above.

If any loss cannot be included in the terminal loss (eg because it is matched with a profit) it can be relieved instead against general income.

6.3 Relieving the terminal loss

The loss is relieved against trade profits only.

Relief is given in the tax year of cessation and the three preceding years, later years first.

Set out below are the results of a business up to its cessation on 30 September 2011.

	Profit/(loss) £
Year to 31 December 2008	2,000
Year to 31 December 2009	400
Year to 31 December 2010	300
Nine months to 30 September 2011	(1,950)

Overlap profits on commencement were £450. These were all unrelieved on cessation.

Show the available terminal loss relief, and suggest an alternative claim if the trader had had other non-savings income of £10,000 in each of 2010/11 and 2011/12. Assume that 2011/12 tax rates and allowances apply to all years.

Answer

The terminal loss comes in the last 12 months, the period 1 October 2010 to 30 September 2011. This period is split as follows.

2010/11   Six months to 5 April 2011
2011/12   Six months to 30 September 2011

The terminal loss is made up as follows.

Unrelieved trading losses		£	£
2011/12			
6 months to 30.9.11	£(1,950) × 6/9		(1,300)
Overlap relief	£(450)		(450)
2010/11			
3 months to 31.12.10	£300 × 3/12	75	
3 months to 5.4.11	£(1,950) × 3/9	(650)	
			(575)
			(2,325)

Taxable trade profits will be as follows.

Year	Basis period	Profits £	Terminal loss relief £	Final taxable Profits £
2008/09	Y/e 31.12.08	2,000	1,625	375
2009/10	Y/e 31.12.09	400	400	0
2010/11	Y/e 31.12.10	300	300	0
2011/12	1.1.11 – 30.9.11	0	0	0
			2,325	

If the trader had had £10,000 of other income in 2010/11 and 2011/12 we could consider loss relief claims against general income for these two years, using the loss of £(1,950 + 450) = £2,400 for 2011/12.

The final results would be as follows. (We could alternatively claim loss relief in 2010/11.)

	2008/09	2009/10	2010/11	2011/12
	£	£	£	£
Trade profits	2,000	400	300	0
Other income	0	0	10,000	10,000
	2,000	400	10,300	10,000
Less loss relief against general income	0	0	0	(2,400)
Net income	2,000	400	10,300	7,600

Another option would be to make a claim against general income for the balance of the loss not relieved as a terminal loss £(2,400 – 2,325) = £75 in either 2010/11 or 2011/12.

However, as there is only taxable income in 2010/11 and 2011/12 the full claim against general income is more tax efficient.

Chapter Roundup

- Trading losses may be relieved against future profits of the same trade, against general income and against capital gains.

- Trading losses may be relieved against future profits of the same trade. The relief is against the first available profits of the same trade.

- Where a business is transferred to a company, loss relief is available for any remaining unrelieved losses of the unincorporated business against income received from the company.

- A trading loss may be set against general income in the year of the loss and/or the preceding year. Personal allowances may be lost as a result of the claim. Once a claim has been made in any year, the remaining loss can be set against net chargeable gains.

- It is important for a trader to choose the right loss relief, so as to save tax at the highest possible rate and so as to obtain relief reasonably quickly.

- In opening years, a special relief involving the carry back of losses against general income is available. Losses arising in the first four tax years of a trade may be set against general income in the three years preceding the loss making year, taking the earliest year first.

- On the cessation of trade, a loss arising in the last 12 months of trading may be set against trade profits of the tax year of cessation and the previous 3 years, taking the latest year first.

Quick Quiz

1   Against what income can trade losses carried forward be set off?

   A   General income
   B   Non-savings income
   C   Any trading income
   D   Trading income from the same trade

2   When a loss is to be relieved against general income, how are losses linked to particular tax years?

3   Against which years' general income may a loss be relieved, for a continuing business which has traded for many years?

4   Maggie has been trading as a decorator for many years. In 2010/11, she made a trading profit of £10,000. She has savings income of £6,000 each year. She makes no capital gains.

   Maggie makes a loss of £(28,000) in 2011/12 and expects to make either a loss or smaller profits in the foreseeable future. How can Maggie obtain loss relief?

5   Joe starts trading on 6 April 2011, having previously been employed for many years. He makes a loss in his first year of trading. Against income of which years can he set the loss under early trade loss relief?

6   Terminal loss relief can be given in the year of _____ and then in the _____ preceding years, _____ years first. Fill in the blanks.

1   D. Against trading income from the same trade.

2   The loss for a tax year is the loss in the basis period for that tax year. However, if basis periods overlap, a loss in the overlap period is a loss of the earlier tax year only.

3   The year in which the loss arose and/or the preceding year.

4   Maggie can make a claim to set the loss against general income of £6,000 in 2011/12. She can also claim loss relief against general income of £(10,000 + 6,000) = £16,000 in 2010/11. The remaining £(28,000 − 6,000 - 16,000) = £6,000 will be carried forward and set against the first available trading profits of her decorating trade.

5   Loss incurred 2011/12: set against general income of 2008/09, 2009/10 and 2010/11 in that order.

6   Terminal loss relief can be given in the year of **cessation** and then in the **three** preceding years, **later** years first.

Now try the question below from the Exam Question Bank

Number	Level	Marks	Time
Q15	Examination	15	27 mins

11

Partnerships and limited liability partnerships

Topic list	Syllabus reference
1 Partnerships	B3(i)(i)-(iii)
2 Loss reliefs	B3(i)(iv)
3 Limited liability partnerships	B3(i)(v)

Introduction

We have covered sole traders, learning how to calculate taxable trading profits after capital allowances and allocate them to tax years and how to deal with losses.

We now see how the Income tax rules for traders are adapted to deal with business partnerships. On the one hand, a partnership is a single trading entity, making profits as a whole. On the other hand, each partner has a personal tax computation, so the profits must be apportioned to the partners. The general approach is to work out the profits of the partnership, then tax each partner as if he were a sole trader running a business equal to his slice of the partnership (for example 25% of the partnership).

This chapter concludes our study of the income tax computation. In the next chapter we will turn our attention to national insurance.

Study guide

		Intellectual level
B3	**Income from self-employment**	
(i)	Partnerships and limited liability partnerships	
(i)(i)	Explain how a partnership is assessed to tax.	2
(i)(ii)	Compute the assessable profits for each partner following a change in the profit sharing ratio.	2
(i)(iii)	Compute the assessable profits for each partner following a change in the membership of the partnership.	2
(i)(iv)	Describe the alternative loss relief claims that are available to partners.	1
(i)(v)	Explain the loss relief restriction that applies to the partners of a limited liability partnership.	1

Exam guide

Although partnerships are an important topic you are not guaranteed to get a question on them in your exam. This does not mean that you can ignore them. As long as you remember to allocate the profits between the partners according to their profit sharing arrangements for the period of account you should be able to cope with any aspect of partnership tax. Remember that each partner is taxed as a sole trader, and you should apply the opening and closing year rules and loss reliefs as appropriate to that partner.

1 Partnerships

FAST FORWARD

A partnership is simply treated as a source of profits and losses for trades being carried on by the individual partners. Divide profits or losses between the partners according to the profit sharing arrangements in the period of account concerned. If any of the partners are entitled to a salary or interest on capital, apportion this first, not forgetting to pro-rate in periods of less than 12 months.

1.1 Introduction

A partnership is a group of individuals who are trading together. They will agree amongst themselves how the business should be run and how profits and losses should be shared. It is not treated as a separate entity for tax purposes (in contrast to a company).

1.2 Basis of assessment

A business partnership is treated like a sole trader for the purposes of computing its profits. Partners' salaries and interest on capital are not deductible expenses and must be added back in computing profits, because they are a form of drawings.

Once the partnership's profits for a period of account have been computed, they are shared between the partners according to the profit sharing arrangements for that period of account.

Question

Allocating profits

Steve and Tanya have been in partnership for many years. For the year ended 31 October 2011, taxable trading profits were £70,000.

Steve is allocated an annual salary of £12,000 and Tanya's salary is £28,000.

The profit sharing ratio is 2:1.

Allocate the trade profit to each partner for the year ended 31 October 2011.

Answer

Allocate the profits for the year ended 31 October 2011.

	Total £	Steve £	Tanya £
Profit	70,000		
Salaries	40,000	12,000	28,000
Balance (2:1)	30,000	20,000	10,000
Total	70,000	32,000	38,000

1.3 Change in profit sharing arrangements

If the profit sharing arrangements change part way through the period of account, the profits, salaries and interest for the period of account must be pro-rated accordingly.

Question

Change in profit sharing arrangements

Sue and Tim have been in partnership for many years. For the year ended 31 December 2011, taxable trading profits were £50,000.

Sue is allocated an annual salary of £10,000 and Tim's salary is £15,000.

The profit sharing ratio was 1:1 until 31 August 2011 when it changed to 1:2 with no provision for salaries.

Allocate the trade profit to each partner for the year ended 31 December 2011.

Answer

Allocate the profits for the year ended 31 December 2011.

	Total £	Sue £	Tim £
Profit	50,000		
1 January – 31 August (8 months)	33,333		
Salaries (8/12 × £10,000/£15,000)	16,667	6,667	10,000
Balance (1:1)	16,666	8,333	8,333
	33,333		
1 September – 31 December (4 months)	16,667		
Salaries	Nil	–	–
Balance (1:2)	16,667	5,556	11,111
	16,667		
Total	50,000	20,556	29,444

Note. Since the profit sharing arrangements changed part way through the period of account, the profits and salaries for the period of account must be pro-rated accordingly.

1.4 The tax positions of individual partners

Each partner is taxed like a sole trader who runs a business which:

- Starts when he joins the partnership
- Finishes when he leaves the partnership

- Has the same periods of account as the partnership (except that a partner who joins or leaves during a period will have a period which starts and/or ends part way through the partnership's period)
- Makes profits or losses equal to the partner's share of the partnership's profits or losses

1.5 Assets owned individually

Where the partners own assets (such as their cars) individually, capital allowances must be calculated in respect of such assets (not forgetting any adjustment for private use). The capital allowances must go into the partnership's tax computation as they must be claimed by the partnership, not by the individual partner.

Question   Partnership with asset owned by individual partner

Gustav and Melanie are in partnership making up accounts to 31 March each year. They share profits in the ratio 3:2. In the year to 31 March 2012, the partnership's trading profit is £60,000. The partnership does not own any assets which qualify for capital allowances but Gustav owns a car (which he acquired in August 2010) which he uses 75% for the business of the partnership. The car has CO_2 emissions of 170 g/km. The car had a tax written down value of £22,000 at 1 April 2011.

Show the trade profits taxable on Gustav and Melanie for 2011/12, assuming that the partnership makes the maximum capital allowances claim.

Answer

	Total £	Gustav £	Melanie £
Partnership profit	60,000		
Less: capital allowance on car £22,000 x 10% x 75%	(1,650)		
Taxable trade profits 2011/12 (3:2)	58,350	35,010	23,340

1.6 Changes in membership

FAST FORWARD

Commencement and cessation rules apply to partners individually when they join or leave.

When a trade continues but partners join or leave (including cases when a sole trader takes in partners or a partnership breaks up leaving only one partner as a sole trader), the special rules for basis periods in opening and closing years do not apply to the people who were carrying on the trade both before and after the change. They carry on using the period of account ending in each tax year as the basis period for the tax year (ie the current year basis). The commencement rules only affect joiners, and the cessation rules only affect leavers.

However, when no-one carries on the trade both before and after the change, as when a partnership transfers its trade to a completely new owner or set of owners, the cessation rules apply to the old owners and the commencement rules apply to the new owners.

1.7 Example: a comprehensive partnership example

Alice and Bertrand start a partnership on 1 July 2008, making up accounts to 31 December each year. On 1 May 2010, Charles joins the partnership. On 1 November 2011, Charles leaves. On 1 January 2012, Deborah joins. The profit sharing arrangements are as follows.

	Alice	Bertrand	Charles	Deborah
1.7.08 – 31.1.09				
Salaries (per annum)	£3,000	£4,500		
Balance	3/5	2/5		
1.2.09 – 30.4.10				

	Alice	Bertrand	Charles	Deborah
Salaries (per annum)	£3,000	£6,000		
Balance	4/5	1/5		
1.5.10 – 31.10.11				
Salaries (per annum)	£2,400	£3,600	£1,800	
Balance	2/5	2/5	1/5	
1.11.11 – 31.12.12				
Salaries (per annum)	£1,500	£2,700		
Balance	3/5	2/5		
1.1.12 onwards				
Salaries (per annum)	£1,500	£2,700		£600
Balance	3/5	1/5		1/5

Profits as adjusted for tax purposes are as follows.

Period	Profit £
1.7.08 – 31.12.08	22,000
1.1.09 – 31.12.09	51,000
1.1.10 – 31.12.10	39,000
1.1.11 – 31.12.11	15,000
1.1.12 – 31.12.12	18,000

When approaching the question, we must first share the trade profits for the periods of account between the partners, remembering to adjust the salaries for periods of less than a year.

	Total £	Alice £	Bertrand £	Charles £	Deborah £
1.7.08 – 31.12.08					
Salaries	3,750	1,500	2,250		
Balance	18,250	10,950	7,300		
Total (P/e 31.12.08)	22,000	12,450	9,550		
1.1.09 – 31.12.09					
January					
Salaries	625	250	375		
Balance	3,625	2,175	1,450		
Total	4,250	2,425	1,825		
February to December					
Salaries	8,250	2,750	5,500		
Balance	38,500	30,800	7,700		
Total	46,750	33,550	13,200		
Total for y/e 31.12.09	51,000	35,975	15,025		
1.1.10 – 31.12.10					
January to April					
Salaries	3,000	1,000	2,000		
Balance	10,000	8,000	2,000		
Total	13,000	9,000	4,000		
May to December					
Salaries	5,200	1,600	2,400	1,200	
Balance	20,800	8,320	8,320	4,160	
Total	26,000	9,920	10,720	5,360	
Total for y/e 31.12.10	39,000	18,920	14,720	5,360	

	Total £	Alice £	Bertrand £	Charles £	Deborah £
1.1.11 – 31.12.11					
January to October					
Salaries	6,500	2,000	3,000	1,500	
Balance	6,000	2,400	2,400	1,200	
Total	12,500	4,400	5,400	2,700	
November and December					
Salaries	700	250	450		
Balance	1,800	1,080	720		
Total	2,500	1,330	1,170		
Total for y/e 31.12.11	15,000	5,730	6,570	2,700	
1.1.12 – 31.12.12					
Salaries	4,800	1,500	2,700		600
Balance	13,200	7,920	2,640		2,640
Total for y/e 31.12.12	18,000	9,420	5,340		3,240

The next stage is to work out the basis periods and hence the taxable trade profits for the partners. All of them are treated as making up accounts to 31 December, but Alice and Bertrand are treated as starting to trade on 1 July 2008, Charles as trading only from 1 May 2010 to 31 October 2011 and Deborah as starting to trade on 1 January 2012. Applying the usual rules gives the following basis periods and taxable profits.

Alice

Year	Basis period	Working	Taxable profits £
2008/09	1.7.08 – 5.4.09	£12,450 + (£35,975 × 3/12)	21,444
2009/10	1.1.09 – 31.12.09		35,975
2010/11	1.1.10 – 31.12.10		18,920
2011/12	1.1.11 – 31.12.11		5,730
2012/13	1.1.12 – 31.12.12		9,420

Note that for 2008/09 we take Alice's total for the year ended 2009 and apportion that, because the partnership's period of account runs from 1 January to 31 December 2009. Alice's profits for 2008/09 are *not* £12,450 + £2,425 + (£33,550 × 2/11) = £20,975.

Alice will have overlap profits for the period 1 January to 5 April 2009 (£35,975 × 3/12 = £8,994) to deduct when she ceases to trade.

Bertrand

Year	Basis period	Working	Taxable profits £
2008/09	1.7.08 – 5.4.09	£9,550 + (£15,025 × 3/12)	13,306
2009/10	1.1.09 – 31.12.09		15,025
2010/11	1.1.10 – 31.12.10		14,720
2011/12	1.1.11 – 31.12.11		6,570
2012/13	1.1.12 – 31.12.12		5,340

Bertrand's overlap profits are £15,025 × 3/12 = £3,756.

Charles

Year	Basis period	Working	Taxable profits £
2010/11	1.5.10 – 5.4.11	£5,360 + (£2,700 × 3/10)	6,170
2011/12	6.4.11 – 31.10.11	£2,700 × 7/10	1,890

Because Charles ceased to trade in his second tax year of trading, his basis period for the second year starts on 6 April and he has no overlap profits.

Deborah

Year	Basis period	Working	Taxable profits £
2011/12	1.1.12 – 5.4.12	£3,240 × 3/12	810
2012/13	1.1.12 – 31.12.12		3,240

Deborah's overlap profits are £3,240 × 3/12 = £810.

Exam focus point

Partners are effectively taxed in the same way as sole traders with just one difference. Before you tax the partner you need to take each set of accounts (as adjusted for tax purposes) and divide the trade profit (or loss) between each partner.

Then carry on as normal for a sole trader – each partner is that sole trader in respect of his trade profits for each accounting period.

2 Loss reliefs

 FAST FORWARD

Partners are individually entitled to loss relief in the same way as sole traders.

2.1 Entitlement to loss relief

Partners are entitled to the same loss reliefs as sole traders. The reliefs are:

(a) **Carry forward against future trading profits**. If the business is transferred to a company this is extended to carry forward against future income from the company.

(b) **Set off against general income of the same and/or preceding year**. This claim can be extended to set off against capital gains.

(c) **For a new partner, losses in the first four tax years of trade can be set off against general income of the three preceding years**. This is so even if the actual trade commenced many years before the partner joined.

(d) **For a ceasing partner, terminal loss relief is available** when he is treated as ceasing to trade. This is so even if the partnership continues to trades after he leaves.

Different partners may claim loss reliefs in different ways.

 Question

Partnership losses

Mary and Natalie have been trading for many years sharing profits equally. On 1 January 2012 Mary retired and Oliver joined the partnership. Natalie and Oliver share profits in the ratio of 2:1. Although the partnership had previously been profitable it made a loss of £24,000 for the year to 31 March 2012. The partnership is expected to be profitable in the future.

Calculate the loss accruing to each partner for 2011/12 and explain what reliefs are available.

We must first share the loss for the period of account between the partners, remembering to adjust the salaries for periods of less than a year.

	Total £	Mary £	Natalie £	Oliver £
y/e 31.3.12				
1.4.11 – 31.12.11				
Total £24,000 × 9/12	(18,000)	(9,000)	(9,000)	
1.1.12 – 31.3.12				
Total £24,000 × 3/12	(6,000)		(4,000)	(2,000)
Total for y/e 31.03.12	(24,000)	(9,000)	(13,000)	(2,000)

Mary

For 2011/12, Mary has a loss of £9,000. She may claim relief against general income of 2011/12 and/or 2010/11 and may extend the claim to capital gains.

Mary has ceased trading and may instead claim terminal loss relief. The terminal loss will be £9,000 (a profit arose in the period 1.1.11 – 31.3.11 which would be treated as zero) and this may be set against her taxable trade profits for 2011/12 (£nil), 2010/11, 2009/10 and 2008/09.

Natalie

For 2011/12, Natalie has a loss of £13,000. She may claim relief against general income of 2011/12 and/or 2010/11 and may extend the claim to capital gains. Any loss remaining unrelieved may be carried forward against future income from the same trade.

Oliver

Oliver's loss for 2011/12 is £2,000. He may claim relief for the loss against general income (and gains) of 2011/12 and/or 2010/11. As he has just started to trade he may claim relief for the loss against general income of 2008/09, 2009/10 and 2010/11. Any loss remaining unrelieved may be carried forward against future income from the same trade.

3 Limited liability partnerships

FAST FORWARD

Limited liability partnerships are taxed on virtually the same basis as normal partnerships except that loss relief is restricted for all partners.

It is possible to form a limited liability partnership. The difference between a limited liability partnership (LLP) and a normal partnership is that **in a LLP the liability of the partners is limited to the capital they contributed.**

The partners of a LLP are taxed on virtually the same basis as the partners of a normal partnership (see above). However, the amount of loss relief that a partner can claim against general income when the claim is against non-partnership income is restricted to the capital he contributed plus his undrawn profit subject to an overall cap of £25,000.

Chapter Roundup

- A partnership is simply treated as a source of profits and losses for trades being carried on by the individual partners. Divide profits or losses between the partners according to the profit sharing arrangements in the period of account concerned. If any of the partners are entitled to a salary or interest on capital, apportion this first, not forgetting to pro-rate in periods of less than 12 months.

- Commencement and cessation rules apply to partners individually when they join or leave.

- Partners are individually entitled to loss relief in the same way as sole traders.

- Limited liability partnerships are taxed on virtually the same basis as normal partnerships except that loss relief is restricted for all partners.

Quick Quiz

1   How are partnership trading profits divided between the individual partners?

2   What loss reliefs are partners entitled to?

3   Janet and John are partners sharing profits 60:40. For the years ended 30 June 2011 and 2012 the partnership made profits of £100,000 and £150,000 respectively. John's taxable trading profits in 2011/12 are:

    A   £30,000
    B   £40,000
    C   £50,000
    D   £60,000

4   Yolanda and Yan are in partnership sharing profits 80:20. For the year ended 31 December 2011 the business makes a loss of £40,000. If Yan decides to use his share of the loss against general income what loss relief(s) can Yolanda claim?

5   Pete and Doug have been partners for many years, sharing profits equally. On 1 January 2011 Dave joins the partnership and it is agreed to share profits 40:40:20. For the year ended 30 June 2011 profits are £100,000.

Doug's share of these profits is:

    A   £42,500
    B   £45,000
    C   £47,500
    D   £50,000

Answers to Quick Quiz

1   Profits are divided in accordance with the profit sharing arrangements that existed during the period of account in which the profits arose.

2   Partners are entitled to the same loss reliefs as sole traders as appropriate.

3   B. £40,000.

    2011/12: ye 30 June 2011

    £100,000 × 40% = £40,000.

4   Yolanda has a choice of loss reliefs:

    Loss relief against general income or carry forward loss relief.

    Her loss relief claim is unaffected by Yan's.5   B. £45,000

	Pete £	Doug £	Dave £
Y/e 30 June 2011			
1.7.10 – 31.12.10			
6m × £100,000			
£50,000 50:50	25,000	25,000	
1.1.11 – 30.6.11			
6m × £100,000			
£50,000 40:40:20	20,000	20,000	10,000
	45,000	45,000	10,000

Now try the questions below from the Exam Question Bank

Number	Level	Marks	Time
Q16	Examination	15	27 mins
Q17	Examination	15	27 mins

12

National insurance contributions

Topic list	Syllabus reference
1 Scope of national insurance contributions (NICs)	F1(a)
2 Class 1 and Class 1A NICs for employed persons	F2(a), (b)
3 Class 2 and Class 4 NICs for self-employed persons	F3(a), (b)

Introduction

In the previous chapters we have covered income tax for employees and for the self-employed.

We look at the national insurance contributions payable under Classes 1 and 1A in respect of employment and under Classes 2 and 4 in respect of self-employment.

In the next chapter we will turn our attention to the taxation of chargeable gains.

Study guide

		Intellectual level
F1	**The scope of national insurance**	
(a)	Describe the scope of national insurance.	1
F2	**Class 1 and Class 1A contributions for employed persons**	
(a)	Compute Class 1 NIC.	2
(b)	Compute Class 1A NIC.	2
F3	**Class 2 and Class 4 contributions for self-employed persons**	
(a)	Compute Class 2 NIC.	2
(b)	Compute Class 4 NIC.	2

Exam guide

You will not find a complete question on national insurance in the F6 exam, but it is likely to form part of a larger question on the taxation of employees or the self-employed. You must be absolutely clear who is liable for which class of contributions; only employers, for example, pay Class 1A.

1 Scope of national insurance contributions (NICs)

Four classes of national insurance contribution (NIC) exist, as set out below.

(a) **Class 1**. This is divided into:

    (i)   **Primary**, paid by employees

    (ii)   **Secondary, Class 1A and Class 1B** paid by employers

(b) **Class 2**. Paid by the self-employed

(c) **Class 3**. Voluntary contributions (paid to maintain rights to certain state benefits)

(d) **Class 4**. Paid by the self-employed

> **Exam focus point**
>
> Class 1B and Class 3 contributions are outside the scope of your syllabus.

The National Insurance Contributions Office (NICO), which is part of HM Revenue and Customs, examines employers' records and procedures to ensure that the correct amounts of NICs are collected.

2 Class 1 and Class 1A NICs for employed persons

2.1 Class 1 NICs

> **FAST FORWARD**
>
> Class 1 NICs are payable by employees and employers on earnings.

Both **employees** and **employers pay NICs** related to the employee's earnings. NICs are not deductible from an employee's gross salary for income tax purposes. However, employers' contributions are deductible trade expenses.

2.1.1 Earnings

'Earnings' broadly comprise gross pay, excluding benefits which cannot be turned into cash by surrender (eg holidays). Earnings also include payments for use of the employee's own car on business over the approved amount of 45p per mile (irrespective of total mileage.) Therefore, where an employer reimburses an employee using his own car for business mileage, the earnings element is the excess of the mileage rate paid over 45 per mile. This applies even where business mileage exceeds 10,000 pa.

Certain payments are exempt. In general the income tax and NIC exemptions mirror one another. For example, payment of personal incidental expenses covered by the £5/£10 a night income tax de minimis exemption are excluded from NIC earnings. Relocation expenses of a type exempt from income tax are also excluded from NIC earnings but without the income tax £8,000 upper limit (although expenses exceeding £8,000 are subject to Class 1A NICs as described below).

An expense with a business purpose is not treated as earnings. For example, if an employee is reimbursed for business travel or for staying in a hotel on the employer's business this is not normally 'earnings'. Again the NIC rules for travel expenses follow the income tax rules.

One commonly met expenses payment is telephone calls. If an employee is reimbursed for his own telephone charges the reimbursed cost of private calls (and all reimbursed rental) is earnings.

In general, non cash vouchers are subject to Class 1 NICs. However, the following are exempt.

- Childcare vouchers up to the amount exempt from income tax (see earlier in this Text)
- Any other voucher which is exempt from income tax

An employer's contribution to an employee's occupational or private registered pension scheme is excluded from the definition of 'earnings'.

2.1.2 Rates of Class 1 NICs

The rates of contribution for 2011/12, and the income bands to which they apply, are set out in the Rates and Allowance Tables in this Text.

Employees pay main primary contributions of 12% of earnings between the primary earnings threshold of £7,225 and the upper earnings limit (UEL) of £42,475 or the equivalent monthly or weekly limit (see below). They also pay additional primary contributions of 2% on earnings above the upper earnings limit.

Employers pay secondary contributions of 13.8% on earnings above the secondary earnings threshold of £7,072 or the equivalent monthly or weekly limit. There is no upper limit.

If an individual has more than one job then NIC is calculated on the earnings from each job separately and independently. However there is an overall annual maximum amount of Class 1 NIC any individual will be due to pay. If the total NIC paid from those different jobs exceeds the maximum that individual can claim a refund of the excess.

2.1.3 Earnings period

NICs are calculated in relation to an earnings period. This is the period to which earnings paid to an employee are deemed to relate. Where earnings are paid at regular intervals, the earnings period will generally be equated with the payment interval, for example a week or a month. An earnings period cannot usually be less than seven days long.

Exam focus point

> In the exam NICs will generally be calculated on an annual basis.

Question   Class 1 contributions

Sally works for Red plc. She is paid £4,000 per month.

Show Sally's primary contributions and the secondary contributions paid by Red plc for 2011/12.

Primary earnings threshold £7,225
Secondary earnings threshold £7,072
Upper earnings limit £42,475
Annual salary £4,000 × 12 = £48,000

Sally

	£
Primary contributions	
£(42,475 – 7,225) = £35,250 × 12% (main)	4,230
£(48,000 – 42,475) = £5,525 × 2% (additional)	110
Total primary contributions	4,340

	£
Red plc	
Secondary contributions	
£(48,000 – 7,072) = £40,928 × 13.8%	5,648

Special rules apply to company directors, regardless of whether they are paid at regular intervals or not. Where a person is a director at the beginning of the tax year, his earnings period is the tax year, even if he ceases to be director during the year. **The annual limits as shown in the Tax Tables apply.**

Question   **Employees and directors**

Bill and Ben work for Weed Ltd. Bill is a monthly paid employee. Ben who is a director of Weed Ltd, is also paid monthly. Each is paid an annual salary of £42,000 in 2011/12 and each also received a bonus of £3,000 in December 2011.

Show the primary and secondary contributions for both Bill and Ben, using a monthly earnings period for Bill.

Answer

Bill
Primary earnings threshold £7,225/12 = £602
Secondary earnings threshold £7,072/12 = £589
Upper earnings limit £42,475/12 = £3,540
Regular monthly earnings £42,000/12 = £3,500

Primary contributions

	£
11 months	
£(3,500 – 602) = £2,898 × 12% × 11 (main only)	3,825
1 month (December)	
£(3,540 – 602) = £2,938 × 12% (main)	353
£(6,500 – 3,540) = £2,960 × 2% (additional)	59
Total primary contributions	4,237

Secondary contributions

	£
11 months	
£(3,500 − 589) = £2,911 × 13.8% × 11	4,419
1 month (December)	
£(3,500 + £3,000 − 589) = £5,911 × 13.8%	816
Total secondary contributions	5,235

Ben

Total earnings £(42,000 + 3,000) = £45,000

Primary contributions

	£
Total earnings exceed UEL	
£(42,475 − 7,225) = £35,250 × 12% (main)	4,230
£(45,000 − 42,475) = £2,525 × 2% (additional)	50
Total primary	4,280

Secondary contributions

	£
£(45,000 − 7,072) = £37,928 × 13.8%	5,234

Because Ben is a director an annual earnings period applies. The effect of this is that increased primary contributions are due.

2.2 Class 1A NICs

FAST FORWARD

Class 1A NICs are payable by employers on benefits provided for employees.

Employers must pay Class 1A NIC at 13.8% in respect of most taxable benefits. Taxable benefits are calculated in accordance with income tax rules. There is no Class 1A in respect of any benefits already treated as earnings for Class 1 purposes (eg non cash vouchers). Tax exempt benefits are not liable to Class 1A NIC.

No contributions are levied when an employee is earning less than £8,500 a year.

Question

Class IA NIC

James has the following benefits for income tax purposes

	£
Company car	5,200
Living accommodation	10,000
Medical insurance	800

Calculate the Class 1A NICs that the employer will have to pay.

Answer

Total benefits are £16,000 (£10,000 + £5,200 + £800)

Class 1A NICs:

13.8% × £16,000 = £2,208

2.3 Miscellaneous points

Class 1 contributions are collected under the PAYE system described earlier in this Text. Class 1A contributions are collected annually in arrears, and are due by 19 July following the tax year.

Class 1 and 1A contributions broadly apply to amounts which are taxable as employment income. They do not apply to dividends paid to directors and employees who are also shareholders in the company.

3 Class 2 and Class 4 NICs for self-employed persons

FAST FORWARD

> The self-employed pay Class 2 and Class 4 NICs. Class 2 NICs are paid at a flat weekly rate. Class 4 NICs are based on the level of the individual's profits.

3.1 Class 2 contributions

The self-employed (sole traders and partners) pay NICs in two ways.

Class 2 contributions are payable at a flat rate. It is possible, however, to be excepted from payment of Class 2 contributions (or to obtain a repayment of contributions already paid) if **annual accounts profits are less than the small earnings exception limit which is £5,315 (2011/12). The Class 2 rate for 2011/12 is £2.50 a week.**

HMRC recommend that Class 2 contributions be paid monthly or six monthly by direct debit. Alternatively payments can be made in response to notices issued by HMRC twice yearly. Whichever method is used, payment for the first six months of Class 2 NICs for the tax year must be received by HMRC no later than 31 January in the tax year, and payment for the remaining six months must be received by HMRC no later than 31 July following the end of the tax year. Payment by direct debit will guarantee that these deadlines are met..

Self-employed people must register with HMRC for Class 2 contributions by 31 January following the end of the tax year in which the business starts. A late notification penalty may be charged (see later in this Text).

3.2 Class 4 contributions

Additionally, **the self-employed pay Class 4 NICs,** based on the level of the individual's taxable business profits.

Main rate Class 4 NICs are calculated by applying a fixed percentage (9% for 2011/12) to the individual's profits between the lower profits limit (£7,225 for 2011/12) and the upper profits limit (£42,475 for 2011/12). Additional rate contributions are 2% (for 2011/12) on profits above that limit.

3.3 Example: Class 4 contributions

If a sole trader had profits of £16,080 for 2011/12 his Class 4 NIC liability would be as follows.

	£
Profits	16,080
Less lower profits limit	(7,225)
	8,855

Class 4 NICs = 9% × £8,855 = £797 (main only)

3.4 Example: additional Class 4 contributions

If an individual's profits are £46,000, additional Class 4 NICs are due on the excess over the upper profits limit. Thus the amount payable in 2011/12 is as follows.

	£
Profits (upper limit)	42,475
Less lower limit	(7,225)
	35,250
Main rate Class 4 NICs 9% × £35,250	3,172
Additional rate Class 4 NICs £(46,000 – 42,475) = £3,525 × 2%	70
	3,242

For Class 4 NIC purposes, profits are the trade profits taxable for income tax purposes, less trading losses.

There is no deduction for personal pension premiums.

Class 4 NICs are collected by HMRC. They are paid at the same time as the associated income tax liability. Interest is charged on overdue contributions. The administration of tax is covered later in this Text.

Chapter Roundup

- Class 1 NICs are payable by employees and employers on earnings.

- Class 1A NICs are payable by employers on benefits provided for employees.

- The self-employed pay Class 2 and Class 4 NICs. Class 2 NICs are paid at a flat weekly rate. Class 4 NICs are based on the level of the individual's profits.

Quick Quiz

1   What national insurance contributions are payable by employers and employees?
2   On what are Class 1A NICs based?
3   Class 2 NICs are paid by an employer. TRUE/FALSE?
4   How are Class 4 NICs calculated?

Answers to Quick Quiz

1   Employees –   Class 1 primary contributions

    Employers –   Class 1 secondary contributions
                  Class 1A contributions

2   Class 1A NICs are based on taxable benefits paid to P11D employees.

3   False. Class 2 contributions are paid by the self-employed.

4   The main rate is a fixed percentage (9% in 2011/12) of an individual's tax profits between an upper profits limit and lower profits limit. The additional rate (2%) applies above the upper profits limit.

Now try the questions below from the Exam Question Bank

Number	Level	Marks	Time
Q18	Examination	10	18 mins
Q19	Examination	15	27 mins

Chargeable gains for individuals

13

Computing chargeable gains

Topic list	Syllabus reference
1 Chargeable persons, disposals and assets	D1(a)-(c)
2 Computing a gain or loss	D2(a)
3 The annual exempt amount	D5(a)
4 Capital losses	D2(c)
5 CGT payable by individuals	D5(a)
6 Transfers between spouses/civil partners	D2(d)
7 Part disposals	D2(e)
8 The damage, loss or destruction of an asset	D2(f)

Introduction

Now that we have completed our study of the income tax and national insurance liabilities we turn our attention to the capital gains tax computation. We deal with individuals in this chapter. Chargeable gains for companies are dealt with later in this Study Text.

We look at the circumstances in which a chargeable gain or allowable loss may arise. Then we look at the detailed calculation of the gain or loss on a disposal of an asset.

We then consider the annual exempt amount and look at the relief for capital losses, including the interaction between capital losses brought forward and the annual exempt amount. This enables us to compute CGT payable by individuals.

Following on from this, we start to identify the different types of disposals you may be presented with in the exam. We look first at part disposals. If only part of an asset has been disposed of we need to know how to allocate the cost between the part disposed of and the part retained.

Finally, for this chapter we consider the damage or destruction of an asset and the receipt of compensation or insurance proceeds, and look at the reliefs available where the proceeds are applied in restoring or replacing the asset.

In the following chapters we look at further rules, including those for disposals of shares, and various CGT reliefs that may be available.

Study guide

		Intellectual level
D1	**The scope of the taxation of capital gains**	
(a)	Describe the scope of capital gains tax.	2
(b)	Explain how the residence and ordinary residence of an individual is determined.	2
(c)	List those assets which are exempt.	1
D2	**The basic principles of computing gains and losses**	
(a)	Compute capital gains for both individuals and companies.	2
(c)	Explain the treatment of capital losses for both individuals and companies.	1
(d)	Explain the treatment of transfers between a husband and wife or between a couple in a civil partnership.	2
(e)	Compute the amount of allowable expenditure for a part disposal.	2
(f)	Explain the treatment where an asset is damaged, lost or destroyed, and the implications of receiving insurance proceeds and reinvesting such proceeds.	2
D5	**The computation of capital gains tax payable by individuals**	
(a)	Compute the amount of capital gains tax payable.	2

Exam guide

Question 3 of the exam will always be a 15 mark question focusing on chargeable gains. The examiner has stated there may also be a small element of chargeable gains included in questions other than Question 3. You are almost certain to have to prepare a detailed capital gains computation, whether for an individual or company. Learn the basic layout, so that slotting in the figures becomes automatic. Then in the exam you will be able to turn your attention to the particular points raised in the question. The A/(A+B) formula for part disposals must be learnt. The rules for damage or destruction of an asset are less likely to be examined in detail, but try to remember the objective of the reliefs available where the proceeds are used for restoration or replacement and they will seem more straightforward.

1 Chargeable persons, disposals and assets

FAST FORWARD

A gain is chargeable if there is a chargeable disposal of a chargeable asset by a chargeable person.

Key term

For a chargeable gain to arise there must be:

- A **chargeable person**; and
- A **chargeable disposal**; and
- A **chargeable asset**

otherwise no charge to tax occurs.

1.1 Chargeable persons

FAST FORWARD

Capital gains are chargeable on individuals and companies.

The following are chargeable persons.

- Individuals
- Companies

We will look at the taxation of chargeable gains on companies later in this Text. Note that individuals pay capital gains tax (CGT) on capital gains, whilst companies bring chargeable gains into their corporation tax computation and pay corporation tax on them.

1.2 Chargeable disposals

The following are chargeable disposals.

- **Sales of assets or parts of assets**
- **Gifts of assets or parts of assets**
- **The loss or destruction of assets**

A chargeable disposal occurs on the date of the contract (where there is one, whether written or oral), or the date of a conditional contract becoming unconditional. This may differ from the date of transfer of the asset. However, when a capital sum is received for example on the loss or destruction of an asset, the disposal takes place on the day the sum is received.

Where a disposal involves an acquisition by someone else, the date of acquisition for that person is the same as the date of disposal.

Transfers of assets on death are exempt disposals.

1.3 Chargeable assets

All forms of property, wherever in the world they are situated, are chargeable assets unless they are specifically designated as exempt (see further below).

1.4 Overseas aspects of CGT

FAST FORWARD

CGT applies primarily to persons resident or ordinarily resident in the UK.

Individuals are liable to CGT on the disposal of assets situated anywhere in the world if for any part of the tax year in which the disposal occurs they are resident or ordinarily resident in the UK. By concession, when a person first becomes resident in the UK, he is normally charged to CGT only on those gains which arise after his arrival provided he has not been resident or ordinarily resident in the UK for four out of the last seven years.

Residence and ordinary residence are defined for CGT in the same way as for income tax (see Sections 1.2 and 1.3 in Chapter 2).

Exam focus point

The computation of capital gains arising on overseas assets is outside the scope of your syllabus.

1.5 Exempt assets

The following are exempt assets.

- **Motor vehicles** suitable for private use
- **National Savings and Investments certificates** and **premium bonds**
- **Gilt-edged securities (treasury stock)**
- **Qualifying corporate bonds (QCBs)**
- **Certain chattels**

- **Investments held in individual savings accounts**
- Foreign currency for private use
- Decorations for bravery where awarded, not purchased
- Damages for personal or professional injury
- Debts (except debts on a security)

If an asset is an exempt asset any gain is not chargeable and any loss is not allowable.

<table>
<tr><td>**Exam focus point**</td><td>In the exam, if you think that an asset is exempt just state this – don't waste time working out a gain or loss.</td></tr>
</table>

2 Computing a gain or loss

A gain or loss is computed by taking the proceeds and deducting the cost. Incidental costs of acquisition and disposal are deducted together with any enhancement expenditure reflected in the state and nature of the asset at the date of disposal.

2.1 Basic calculation

A gain (or an allowable loss) is generally calculated as follows.

	£
Disposal consideration	45,000
Less incidental costs of disposal	(400)
Net proceeds	44,600
Less allowable costs	(21,000)
Gain	23,600

Usually the disposal consideration is the proceeds of sale of the asset, but a disposal is deemed to take place at market value:

- **Where the disposal is not a bargain at arm's length**
- **Where the disposal is made for a consideration which cannot be valued**
- **Where the disposal is by way of a gift.**

Special valuation rules apply for shares (see later in this Text).

Incidental costs of disposal may include:

- Valuation fees
- Estate agency fees
- Advertising costs
- Legal costs.

Allowable costs include:

- The original cost of acquisition
- Incidental costs of acquisition
- Capital expenditure incurred in enhancing the asset.

Enhancement expenditure is capital expenditure which enhances the value of the asset and is reflected in the state or nature of the asset at the time of disposal, or expenditure incurred in establishing, preserving or defending title to, or a right over, the asset. Excluded from this category are:

- Costs of repairs and maintenance
- Costs of insurance
- Any expenditure deductible from trading profits
- Any expenditure met by public funds (for example council grants).

Question

Joanne bought a piece of land as an investment for £20,000. The legal costs of purchase were £250. Joanne spent £2,000 on installing drainage pipes on the land which enhanced its value.

Joanne sold the land on 12 December 2011 for £35,000. She incurred estate agency fees of £700 and legal costs of £500 on the sale.

Calculate Joanne's gain on sale.

Answer

		£
Proceeds of sale		35,000
Less costs of disposal £(700 + 500)		(1,200)
		33,800
Less costs of acquisition £(20,000 + 250)		(20,250)
costs of enhancement		(2,000)
Gain		11,550

3 The annual exempt amount

FAST FORWARD

An individual is entitled to an annual exempt amount for each tax year.

There is an annual exempt amount for each tax year. For each individual for 2011/12 it is £10,600.

The annual exempt amount is deducted from the **chargeable gains** for the year after the deductions of losses and other reliefs. The resulting amount is the individual's **taxable gains**.

An individual who has gains taxable at more than one rate of tax may deduct the annual exempt amount for that year in the way that produces the lowest possible tax charge.

4 Capital losses

FAST FORWARD

Losses are set off against gains of the same year and any excess carried forward. Brought forward losses are only set off to reduce net gains down to the amount of the annual exempt amount.

4.1 Allowable losses of the same year

Allowable capital losses arising in a tax year are deducted from gains arising in the same tax year.

An individual who has gains taxable at more than one rate of tax may deduct any allowable losses in the way that produces the lowest possible tax charge.

Any loss which cannot be set off is carried forward to set against future gains. Losses must be used as soon as possible (but see below).

4.2 Allowable losses brought forward

Allowable losses brought forward are only set off to reduce net current year gains to the annual exempt amount. No set-off is made if net chargeable gains for the current year do not exceed the annual exempt amount.

Net current year gains are current year gains less current year allowable losses. Note that if a claim is made to set trading losses against capital gains in any tax year (as we saw earlier in this Text),they will be set off before capital losses brought forward. Unlike capital losses brought forward, trading losses cannot be restricted to preserve the annual exempt amount.

4.3 Example: the use of losses

(a) George has gains for 2011/12 of £11,000 and allowable losses of £6,000. As the losses are *current year losses* they must be fully relieved against the £11,000 of gains to produce net gains of £5,000 despite the fact that net gains are below the annual exempt amount.

(b) Bob has gains of £14,500 for 2011/12 and allowable losses brought forward of £6,000. Bob restricts his loss relief to £3,900 so as to leave net gains of £(14,500 – 3,900) = £10,600, which will be exactly covered by his annual exempt amount for 2011/12. The remaining £2,100 of losses will be carried forward to 2012/13.

(c) Tom has gains of £10,000 for 2011/12 and losses brought forward from 2010/11 of £4,000. He will leapfrog 2011/12 and carry forward all of his losses to 2012/13. His gains of £10,000 are covered by his annual exempt amount for 2011/12.

5 CGT payable by individuals

FAST FORWARD

Capital gains tax is usually payable at the rate of 18% or 28% depending on the individual's taxable income.

Taxable gains are usually chargeable to capital gains tax at the rate of 18% or 28% depending on the individual's taxable income.

To work out which rate applies, follow these rules:

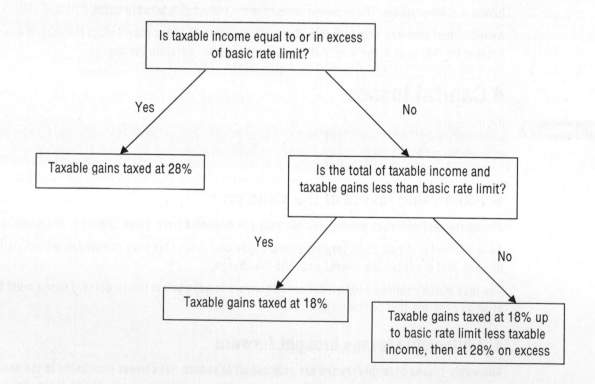

Remember that that basic rate band limit will usually be £35,000 for 2011/12 but the limit will be increased by the gross amount of gift aid donations and personal pension contributions.

Question

Mo has taxable income of £25,000 in 2011/12. He made personal pension contributions of £200 (net) per month during 2011/12. In December 2011, he makes a chargeable gain of £28,500. The gain does not qualify for entrepreneurs' relief.

Calculate the CGT payable by Mo for 2011/12.

Answer

	£
Chargeable gain	28,500
Less: annual exempt amount	(10,600)
Taxable gain	17,900
Taxable income	25,000
Taxable gains	17,900
Total of taxable income and taxable gains	42,900
Basic rate limit	35,000
Add: personal pension contributions £(200 x 12) = £2,400 x 100/80	3,000
Increased basic rate limit	38,000
CGT	
£(38,000 – 25,000) = £13,000 @ 18%	2,340
£(42,900 – 38,000) = £4,900 @ 28%	1,372
Total CGT payable	3,712

There is also a special 10% rate of tax for gains on which the taxpayer claims entrepreneurs' relief. We will look at this situation later in this Text when we deal with entrepreneurs' relief.

6 Transfers between spouses/civil partners

FAST FORWARD

Disposals between spouses or members of a civil partnership are made on a no gain no loss basis and do not give rise to a chargeable gain or allowable loss.

Spouses and civil partners are taxed as separate individuals. Each has his own annual exempt amount. Losses of one spouse or civil partner cannot be set against gains of the other spouse or civil partner.

Disposals between spouses or civil partners living together give rise to no gain no loss, whatever actual price (if any) was charged by the transferor. **This means that there is no chargeable gain or allowable loss, and the transferee takes over the transferor's cost.** This is not the same as the disposal being exempt from CGT.

Question

Harry bought an asset for £150,000. He gave it to his wife Margaret when it was worth £350,000 on 10 May 2011. Margaret sold it on 27 August 2011 for £400,000.

Calculate any chargeable gains arising to Harry and Margaret.

The disposal from Harry to Margaret is a no gain no loss disposal. Harry has no chargeable gain, and the cost for Margaret is Harry's original cost.

The gain on the sale by Margaret is:

	£
Proceeds of sale	400,000
Less cost	(150,000)
Gain	250,000

7 Part disposals

On a part disposal, the cost must be apportioned between the part disposed of and the part retained.

The disposal of part of a chargeable asset is a chargeable event. The chargeable gain (or allowable loss) is computed by deducting a fraction of the original cost of the whole asset from the disposal value. The balance of the cost is carried forward until the eventual disposal of the remaining part of the asset.

Exam formula

The fraction is:

$$\text{Cost} \times \frac{A}{A+B} = \frac{\text{value of the part disposed of}}{\text{value of the part disposed of} + \text{market value of the remainder}}$$

In this fraction, A is the proceeds *before* deducting incidental costs of disposal.

The part disposal fraction should not be applied indiscriminately. Any expenditure incurred wholly in respect of a particular part of an asset should be treated as an allowable deduction in full for that part and not apportioned. An example of this is incidental selling expenses, which are wholly attributable to the part disposed of.

Question   Part disposal

Mr Heal owns a 4 hectare plot of land which originally cost him £150,000. He sold one hectare in July 2011 for £60,000. The incidental costs of sales were £3,000. The market value of the 3 hectares remaining is estimated to be £180,000. What is the gain on the sale of the one hectare?

Answer

The amount of the cost attributable to the part sold is

$$\frac{60,000}{60,000+180,000} \times £150,000 = £37,500$$

	£
Proceeds	60,000
Less: disposal cost	(3,000)
Net proceed of sale	57,000
Less cost (see above)	(37,500)
Gain	19,500

8 The damage, loss or destruction of an asset

The gain which would otherwise arise on the receipt of insurance proceeds may, subject to certain conditions, be deferred.

8.1 Destruction or loss of an asset

If an asset is destroyed any compensation or insurance monies received will normally be brought into an ordinary CGT disposal computation as proceeds.

If all the proceeds are applied for the replacement of the asset within 12 months, any gain can be deducted from the cost of the replacement asset. The replacement asset can be any type of asset as long as it falls within the charge to CGT.

If only part of the proceeds are used, the gain immediately chargeable can be limited to the amount not used. The rest of the gain is then deducted from the cost of the replacement.

Question   Asset destroyed

Fiona bought an asset for £25,000. It was destroyed in July 2011. Insurance proceeds were £34,000, and Fiona spent £30,500 on a replacement asset in January 2012. Compute the gain immediately chargeable and the base cost of the new asset.

Answer

	£
Proceeds	34,000
Less cost	(25,000)
Gain	9,000
Gain immediately chargeable £(34,000 – 30,500)	(3,500)
Deduction from base cost	5,500

The base cost of the new asset is £(30,500 – 5,500) = £25,000.

8.2 Damage to an asset

If an asset is damaged then the receipt of any compensation or insurance monies received will normally be treated as a part disposal.

If all the proceeds are applied in restoring the asset the taxpayer can elect to disregard the part disposal. The proceeds will instead be deducted from the cost of the asset.

Question   Asset damaged

Frank bought an investment property for £100,000 in May 2011. It was damaged two and a half months later. Insurance proceeds of £20,000 were received in November 2011, and Frank spent a total of £25,000 on restoring the property. Prior to restoration the property was worth £120,000. Compute the chargeable gain immediately chargeable, if any, and the base cost of the restored property assuming Frank elects for there to be no part disposal.

How would your answer differ if no election were made?

As the proceeds have been applied in restoring the property Frank has elected to disregard the part disposal.

The base cost of the restored property is £(100,000 − 20,000 + 25,000) = £105,000.

If no election were made, the receipt of the proceeds would be a part disposal in November 2011:

	£
Proceeds	20,000
Less cost £100,000 × 20,000/(20,000 + 120,000)	(14,286)
Gain	5,714

The base cost of the restored asset is £(100,000 − 14,286 + 25,000) = £110,714.

Assuming this is Frank's only disposal in the tax year, the gain is covered by the annual exempt amount. It may therefore be preferable not to make the election.

Chapter Roundup

- A gain is chargeable if there is a chargeable disposal of a chargeable asset by a chargeable person.

- Capital gains are chargeable on individuals and companies.

- CGT applies primarily to persons resident or ordinarily resident in the UK.

- A gain or loss is computed by taking the proceeds and deducting the cost. Incidental costs of acquisition and disposal are deducted together with any enhancement expenditure reflected in the state and nature of the asset at the date of disposal.

- An individual is entitled to an annual exempt amount for each tax year.

- Losses are set off against gains of the same year and any excess carried forward. Brought forward losses are only set off to reduce net gains down to the amount of the annual exempt amount.

- Capital gains tax is usually payable at the rate of 18% or 28% depending on the individual's taxable income.

- Disposals between spouses or members of a civil partnership are made on a no gain no loss basis and do not give rise to a chargeable gain or allowable loss.

- On a part disposal, the cost must be apportioned between the part disposed of and the part retained.

- The gain which would otherwise arise on the receipt of insurance proceeds may, subject to certain conditions, be deferred.

Quick Quiz

1   Give some examples of chargeable disposals.

2   On what assets does a UK resident pay CGT?

3   What is enhancement expenditure?

4   To what extent must allowable losses be set against chargeable gains?

5   At what rate or rates do individuals pay CGT on gains which do not qualify for entrepreneurs' relief?

6   10 acres of land are sold for £15,000 out of 25 acres. Original cost for the 25 acres was £9,000. Costs of sale are £2,000. Rest of land valued at £30,000. What is the total amount deductible from proceeds?

   A   £2,000
   B   £2,872
   C   £5,000
   D   £5,600

7   Emma drops and destroys a vase. She receives compensation for £2,000 from her insurance company. How can she avoid a charge to CGT arising?

1   The following are chargeable disposals

    - Sales of assets or parts of assets
    - Gifts of assets or parts of assets
    - Receipts of capital sums following the loss or destruction of an asset

2   All assets, whether situated in the UK or abroad, unless specifically exempt.

3   Enhancement expenditure is capital expenditure enhancing the value of the asset and reflected in the state/nature of the asset at disposal, or expenditure incurred in establishing, preserving or defending title to asset.

4   Current year losses must be set off against gains in full, even if this reduces net gains below the annual exempt amount. Losses brought forward are set off to bring down gains to the level of the annual exempt amount.

5   Individuals pay CGT at the rate of 18% or 28% depending on their taxable income.

6   C. $\dfrac{15,000}{15,000 + 30,000} \times £9,000 = £3,000 + £2,000$ (costs of disposal) = £5,000

7   Emma can avoid a charge to CGT on receipt of the compensation by investing at least £2,000 in a replacement asset within 12 months.

Now try the questions below from the Exam Question Bank

Number	Level	Marks	Time
Q20	Introductory	10	18 mins

14

Chattels and the principal private residence exemption

Topic list	Syllabus reference
1 Chattels	D3(a), (b)
2 Wasting assets	D3(a), (c)
3 Private residences	D3(d)-(f)

Introduction

In the previous chapter we have considered the basic rules for the capital gains computation and the calculation of CGT payable by an individual, together with the rules for part disposals and assets damaged or destroyed.

We now turn our attention to specific assets, starting with chattels. Where there is a disposal of low value assets, the chattels rules may apply to restrict the gain or allowable loss. The gain may even be exempt in certain circumstances. We look at the detailed rules.

The highest value item that an individual is likely to sell is his home. We look at the rules to see when the gain may be wholly or partly exempt.

In the next chapter we will consider the reliefs specifically available on business assets, and later we will turn our attention to the special rules for shares.

Study guide

		Intellectual level
D3	**Gains and losses on the disposal of movable and immovable property**	
(a)	Identify when chattels and wasting assets are exempt.	1
(b)	Compute the chargeable gain when a chattel is disposed of.	2
(c)	Calculate the chargeable gain when a wasting asset is disposed of.	2
(d)	Compute the exemption when a principal private residence is disposed of.	2
(e)	Calculate the chargeable gain when a principal private residence has been used for business purposes.	2
(f)	Identify the amount of letting relief available when a principal private residence has been let out.	2

Exam guide

As at least 15% of the marks for the exam will be for capital gains, you are quite likely to come across a question on either chattels or the reliefs available on the disposal of a principal private residence.

With chattels always look for the exemption for wasting chattels, a restriction of the gain if proceeds exceed £6,000, or a restriction of loss relief if proceeds are less than £6,000. The rules for chattels apply to companies as well as individuals, but watch out for assets on which capital allowances have been given.

On the disposal of a principal private residence if there has been any non-occupation or business use make a schedule of the relevant dates before you start to calculate the gain in case it turns out to be wholly exempt.

1 Chattels

1.1 What is a chattel?

Key term

> A **chattel** is tangible moveable property.
>
> A **wasting asset** is an asset with an estimated remaining useful life of 50 years or less.

Plant and machinery, whose predictable useful life is always deemed to be less than 50 years, is an example of a wasting chattel (unless it is immoveable, in which case it will be wasting but not a chattel). Machinery includes, in addition to its ordinary meaning, motor vehicles (unless exempt as cars), railway and traction engines, engine-powered boats and clocks.

1.2 Wasting chattels

FAST FORWARD

Gains on most wasting chattels are exempt and losses are not allowable.

Wasting chattels are exempt (so that there are no chargeable gains and no allowable losses).

There is one exception to this: assets used for the purpose of a trade, profession or vocation in respect of which capital allowances have been or could have been claimed. This means that items of plant and machinery used in a trade are not exempt merely on the ground that they are wasting. However, cars are always exempt.

1.3 Gains on non-wasting chattels

When a non-wasting chattel is sold for less than £6,000, any gain is exempt. There is marginal relief for gains where sale proceeds exceed £6,000.

If a chattel is not exempt under the wasting chattels rule, any gain arising on its disposal will still be exempt if the asset is sold for gross proceeds of £6,000 or less, even if capital allowances were claimed on it.

If sale proceeds exceed £6,000, any gain is limited to a maximum of 5/3 × (gross proceeds – £6,000).

Question
Chattels: gains

Adam purchased a Chippendale chair for £1,800. On 10 October 2011 he sold the chair at auction for £6,300 (which was net of the auctioneer's 10% commission). What is the gain?

Answer

	£
Proceeds (£6,300 × 100/90)	7,000
Less incidental costs of sale	(700)
Net proceeds	6,300
Less cost	(1,800)
Gain	4,500

The maximum gain is 5/3 × £(7,000 – 6,000) = £1,667

The chargeable gain is the lower of £4,500 and £1,667, so it is £1,667.

1.4 Losses on non-wasting chattels

A loss on the sale of a non-wasting chattel is restricted where proceeds are less than £6,000.

Where a chattel which is not exempt under the wasting chattels rule is sold for less than £6,000 and a loss arises, the allowable loss is restricted by assuming that the chattel was sold for gross proceeds of £6,000. This rule cannot turn a loss into a gain, only reduce the loss, perhaps to zero.

Question
Chattels: losses

Eve purchased a rare first edition for £8,000 which she sold in October 2011 at auction for £2,700 (which was net of 10% commission). Compute the gain or loss.

Answer

	£
Proceeds (assumed)	6,000
Less incidental costs of disposal (£2,700 × 10/90)	(300)
	5,700
Less cost	(8,000)
Allowable loss	(2,300)

1.5 Chattels and capital allowances

The CGT rules are modified for assets eligible for capital allowances.

The wasting chattels exemption does not apply to chattels on which capital allowances have been claimed or could have been claimed. The chattels rules based on £6,000 do apply.

Where a chattel on which capital allowances have been obtained is sold at a loss, the allowable cost for chargeable gains purposes is reduced by the lower of the loss and the net amount of allowances given (taking into account any balancing allowances or charges). The result is no gain and no loss. This is because relief for the loss has already been given through the capital allowances computation.

If the chattel is sold at a gain the cost is not adjusted for capital allowances. This is because the capital allowances will have been repaid through the balancing charge.

2 Wasting assets

When a wasting asset is disposed of its cost must be depreciated over its estimated useful life.

2.1 Introduction

A wasting asset is one which has an estimated remaining useful life of 50 years or less and whose original value will depreciate over time. Examples of such assets are copyrights and registered designs.

2.2 The computation

The normal capital gains computation is amended to reflect the anticipated depreciation over the life of the asset.

The cost is written down on a straight line basis, and it is this depreciated cost which is deducted in the computation.

Thus if a taxpayer acquires a wasting asset with a remaining life of 40 years and disposes of it after 15 years, so that 25 years of useful life remain, only 25/40 of the cost is deducted in the computation.

Any enhancement expenditure must be separately depreciated.

2.3 Example: wasting asset

Harry bought a copyright on 1 July 2007 for £20,000. The copyright is due to expire in July 2027. He sold it on 1 July 2011 for £22,000.

Harry's gain is:

	£
Proceeds of sale	22,000
Less depreciated cost £20,000 × 16/20	(16,000)
Gain	6,000

2.4 Capital allowances

If capital allowances have been given on a wasting asset its cost is not depreciated over time.

3 Private residences

There is an exemption for gains on principal private residences, but the exemption may be restricted because of periods of non-occupation or because of business use.

3.1 General principles

A gain arising on the sale of **an individual's only or main private residence** (sometimes called **his principal private residence or PPR**) **is exempt from CGT**. The exemption covers total grounds, including the house, of up to half a hectare. The total grounds can exceed half a hectare if the house is large enough to warrant it, but if not, the gain on the excess grounds is taxable.

For the exemption to be available the taxpayer must have occupied the property as a residence rather than just as temporary accommodation.

3.2 Occupation

The gain is wholly exempt where the owner has occupied the whole of the residence throughout his period of ownership. Where occupation has been for only part of the period, the proportion of the gain exempted is

$$\text{Total gain} \times \frac{\text{Period of occupation}}{\text{Total period of ownership}}$$

The **last 36 months of ownership are always** treated as **a period of occupation**, if at some time the residence has been the taxpayer's main residence, even if within those last 36 months the taxpayer also has another house which is his actual principal private residence.

Where a loss arises and all, or a proportion of, any gain would have been exempt, all or the same proportion of the loss is not allowable.

3.3 Deemed occupation

The **period of occupation is also deemed to include certain periods of absence, provided the individual had no other exempt residence at the time and the period of absence was at some time both preceded and followed by a period of actual occupation.** The last 36 months rule (see above) takes precedence over this rule.

These periods of **deemed occupation** are:

(a) **Any period** (or periods taken together) of absence, **for any reason**, **up to three years**, and

(b) **Any periods** during which the owner was **required by his employment** (ie employed taxpayer) **to live abroad**, and

(c) **Any period** (or periods taken together) **up to four years** during which the owner was **required to live elsewhere due to his work** (ie both employed and self employed taxpayer) so that he could not occupy his private residence.

It does not matter if the residence is let during the absence.

Exempt periods of absence must normally be preceded and followed by periods of actual occupation. An extra-statutory concession relaxes this where an individual who has been required to work abroad or elsewhere (ie (b) and (c) above) is unable to resume residence in his home because the terms of his employment require him to work elsewhere.

Question

Mr A purchased a house on 1 April 1986 for £88,200. He lived in the house until 30 June 1986. He then worked abroad for two years before returning to the UK to live in the house again on 1 July 1988. He stayed in the house until 31 December 2004 before retiring and moving out to live with friends in Spain until the house was sold on 31 December 2011 for £150,000.

Calculate the gain arising.

Answer

	£
Proceeds	150,000
Less cost	(88,200)
Gain before PPR exemption	61,800
Less PPR exemption (working)	
$\dfrac{261}{309} \times £61,800$	(52,200)
Gain	9,600

Working

Exempt and chargeable periods

Period	Total months	Exempt months	Chargeable Months
(i) April 1986 – June 1986 (occupied)	3	3	0
(ii) July 1986 – June 1988 (working abroad)	24	24	0
(iii) July 1988 – December 2004 (occupied)	198	198	0
(iv) January 2005 – December 2008 (see below)	48	0	48
(v) January 2009 – December 2011 (last 36 months)	36	36	0
	309	261	48

No part of the period from January 2005 to December 2008 can be covered by the exemption for three years of absence for any reason because it is not followed at any time by actual occupation.

Exam focus point

To help you to answer questions such as that above it is useful to draw up a table showing the period of ownership, exempt months (actual/deemed occupation) and chargeable months (non-occupation) similar to that in the working.

3.4 Business use

Where part of a residence is used exclusively for business purposes throughout the period of ownership, the gain attributable to use of that part is taxable. The 'last 36 months always exempt' rule does not apply to that part.

Question

Mr Smail purchased a property for £35,000 on 31 May 2005 and began operating a dental practice from that date in one quarter of the house. He closed the dental practice on 31 December 2011, selling the house on that date for £130,000.

Compute the gain arising.

Answer

	£
Proceeds	130,000
Less: cost	(35,000)
Gain before PPR exemption	95,000
Less PPR exemption 0.75 × £95,000	(71,250)
Gain	23,750

Exemption is lost on one quarter throughout the period of ownership (including the last 36 months) because of the use of that fraction for business purposes.

If part of a residence was used for business purposes for only part of the period of ownership, the gain is apportioned between chargeable and exempt parts. If the business part was *at some time* used as part of the residence, the gain apportioned to that part *will* qualify for the last 36 months exemption.

3.5 Letting relief

The principal private residence exemption is extended to any gain accruing while the property is let, up to a certain limit. The two main circumstances in which the letting exemption applies are:

(a) When the owner is absent and lets the property, where the absence is not a deemed period of occupation.

(b) When the owner lets part of the property while still occupying the rest of it. The absence from the let part cannot be a deemed period of occupation, because the owner has another residence (the rest of the property). However, the let part will qualify for the last 36 months exemption *if* the let part has *at some time* been part of the only or main residence.

In both cases the letting must be for residential use. **The extra exemption is restricted to the lowest of:**

(a) The amount of the total **gain** which is already **exempt under the PPR provisions**

(b) The gain accruing during the letting period (the **letting part of the gain**)

(c) **£40,000** (maximum)

Letting relief cannot convert a gain into an allowable loss.

If a lodger lives as a member of the owner's family, sharing their living accommodation and eating with them, the **whole** property is regarded as the owner's main residence.

Question

Mr Ovett purchased a house in Truro on 5 October 1997 and sold it on 5 April 2012 making a gain of £290,000.

On 5 January 1999 he had been sent to work in Edinburgh, and he did not return to his own house until 6 July 2008. The property was let out during his absence, and he lived in a flat provided for him by his employer. What is the gain arising?

Answer

		£
Gain before PPR exemption		290,000
Less PPR exemption (working)		
£290,000 × 144/174		(240,000)
		50,000

Less letting exemption: Lowest of:

(a) gain exempt under PPR rules: £240,000

(b) gain attributable to letting: $£290,000 \times \dfrac{30}{174} = £50,000$

		£
(c) £40,000 (maximum)		(40,000)
Gain		10,000

Working

Period	Notes	Total ownership months	Exempt months	Chargeable Months
5.10.97 – 4.1.99	Actual occupation	15	15	0
5.1.99 – 4.1.03	4 years absence working in the UK	48	48	0
5.1.03 – 4.1.06	3 year of absence for any reason	36	36	0
5.1.06 – 5.7.08	Absent – let	30	0	30
6.7.08 – 5.4.12	Occupied (includes last 36 months)	45	45	0
		174	144	30

Question

Letting relief (2)

Miss Coe purchased a house on 31 March 1997 for £90,000. She sold it on 31 August 2011 for £340,000. In 2000 the house was redecorated and Miss Coe began to live on the top floor renting out the balance of the house (constituting 60% of the total house) to tenants between 1 January 2001 and 31 December 2010. On 2 January 2011 Miss Coe put the whole house on the market but continued to live only on the top floor until the house was sold. What is the gain arising?

Answer

	£
Proceeds	340,000
Less: cost	(90,000)
Gain before PPR exemption	250,000
Less PPR exemption (working)	
$£250,000 \times \dfrac{117.8}{173}$	(170,231)
	79,769

Less letting exemption: Lowest of:

(a) gain exempt under PPR rules: £170,231

(b) gain attributable to letting: $£250,000 \times \dfrac{55.2}{173} = £79,769$

	£
(c) £40,000 (maximum)	(40,000)
Gain	39,769

Working

Period	Notes	Total ownership months	Exempt months	Chargeable months
1.4.97 – 31.12.00	100% of house occupied	45	45	0
1.1.01 – 31.8.08	40% of house occupied	92	36.8	
	60% of house let			55.2
1.9.08 – 31.8.11	Last 36 months treated as 100% of house occupied	36	36	0
		173	117.8	55.2

Note. The gain on the 40% of the house always occupied by Miss Coe is fully covered by PPR relief. The other 60% of the house has not always been occupied by Miss Coe and thus any gain on this part of the house is taxable where it relates to periods of time when Miss Coe was not actually (or deemed to be) living in it.

Even if Miss Coe reoccupied all floors prior to the sale, she cannot claim exemption for part of the period of letting under the '3 year absence for any reason' rule since during this time she has a main residence which qualifies for relief (ie the rest of the house). However, she can claim exemption for the whole of the house for the last 36 months since the let part was part of her only residence prior to the letting.

Chapter Roundup

- Gains on most wasting chattels are exempt and losses are not allowable.

- When a non-wasting chattel is sold for less than £6,000, any gain is exempt. There is marginal relief for gains where sale proceeds exceed £6,000.

- A loss on the sale of a non-wasting chattel is restricted where proceeds are less than £6,000.

- The CGT rules are modified for assets eligible for capital allowances.

- When a wasting asset is disposed of its cost must be depreciated over its estimated useful life.

- There is an exemption for gains on principal private residences, but the exemption may be restricted because of periods of non-occupation or because of business use.

Quick Quiz

1 How are gains on non-wasting chattels sold for more than £6,000 restricted?
2 How are losses on non-wasting chattels sold for less than £6,000 restricted?
3 For what periods may an individual be deemed to occupy his principal private residence?
4 The maximum letting exemption is

    A   £30,000
    B   £40,000
    C   £60,000
    D   £80,000

Answers to Quick Quiz

1   Gain restricted to 5/3 × (gross proceeds − £6,000)

2   Allowable loss restricted by deeming proceeds to be £6,000

3   Periods of deemed occupation are:

    - last 36 months of ownership, and

    - any period of absence up to three years, and

    - any period during which the owner was required by his employment to work abroad, and

    - any period up to four years during which the owner was required to live elsewhere due to his work (employed or self employed) or that he could not occupy his private residence.

4   B. £40,000.

Now try the questions below from the Exam Question Bank

Number	Level	Marks	Time
Q21	Examination	10	18 mins

15

Business reliefs

Topic list	Syllabus reference
1 Entrepreneurs' relief	D6(a)
2 The replacement of business assets (rollover relief)	D6(b)
3 Gift relief (holdover relief)	D6(c)
4 Incorporation relief	D6(d)

Introduction

Having discussed the general rules for capital gains we now turn our attention to specific reliefs for businesses.

Entrepreneurs' relief is a very important relief. It applies on the sale of a business and certain trading company shares. It reduces the rate of tax payable from 18% or 28% to 10% on all or part of the chargeable gains arising on such disposals.

Another important relief is rollover relief, which enables a gain on the disposal of a business asset to be rolled over if a new asset is purchased for business use. This enables the payment of tax to be deferred until the business has actually retained the proceeds of sale uninvested so that it can meet the liability. This is the only relief that is available to both individuals and companies.

Next we consider the relief for gifts of business assets. This relief allows an entrepreneur to give away his business during his lifetime and pass any gains to the donee.

The final relief, incorporation relief, enables an individual to transfer his sole trade or partnership business into a company without crystallising a tax charge. The gain is deferred until the eventual disposal of the shares in the company.

In the next chapter we will cover the computation of capital gains on the disposal of shares.

Study guide

		Intellectual level
D6	**The use of exemptions and reliefs in deferring and minimising tax liabilities arising on the disposal of capital assets**	
(a)	Explain and apply entrepreneurs' relief as it applies to individuals.	2
(b)	Explain and apply rollover relief as it applies to individuals and companies.	2
(c)	Explain and apply holdover relief for the gift of business assets.	2
(d)	Explain and apply the incorporation relief that is available upon the transfer of a business to a company.	2

Exam guide

Capital gains form at least 15% of your exam, and may be found in the context of corporation tax or CGT. Rollover relief may be met in either context, and as it is an extremely important relief for all businesses it is likely to be examined. If you are required to compute a gain on a business asset look out for the purchase of a new asset, but carefully check the date and cost of the acquisition. Do not be caught out by the purchase of an investment property. The relief for gifts of assets is only available to individuals, and effectively passes the gain to the donee. Entrepreneurs' relief is only available to individuals but is a particularly valuable relief as it reduces the rate of capital gains tax to 10%. Incorporation relief is again only available to individuals. It defers gains made by an unincorporated trader into shares received when that business is incorporated. The relief is automatic but can be disclaimed.

1 Entrepreneurs' relief

FAST FORWARD

> Entrepreneurs' relief applies on the disposal of a business and certain trading company shares. Gains on assets qualifying for the relief are taxed at 10%.

1.1 Conditions for entrepreneurs' relief

Entrepreneurs' relief is available where there is a **material disposal of business assets**.

A **material disposal** of **business assets** is:

- a disposal of the **whole or part of a business** which has been **owned by the individual** throughout the period of **one year** ending with the date of the disposal

- a disposal of **one or more assets in use for the purposes of a business at** the time at which the business **ceases to be carried on** provided that:

  - the business was owned by the individual throughout **the period of one year** ending with the date on which the business ceases to be carried on; **and**

  - the date of cessation is within **three years** ending with the date of the disposal.

- a disposal of **shares or securities of a company where** the company is the individual's **personal company**; the company is either a **trading company** or the **holding company of a trading group**; the individual is an **officer or employee** of the company (or a group company) and these conditions are met either:

  - throughout the period of **one year** ending with the date of the disposal; **or**

  - throughout the period of **one year** ending with the date on which the company (or group) **ceases to be a trading company (or trading group)** and that date is within the period of **three years** ending with the date of the disposal.

For the first category to apply, there has be a **disposal of the whole or part of the business as a going concern**, not just a disposal of individual assets. A business includes one carried on as a partnership of which the individual is a partner. The business must be a **trade, profession or vocation** conducted on a **commercial basis with a view to the realisation of profits**. Note that gains on all business assets on such a disposal are eligible for entrepreneurs' relief, provided the business has been owned for more than a year. This is the case regardless of how long the assets themselves have been owned.

In relation to the third category, a **personal company** in relation to an individual is one where:

- the individual holds **at least 5% of the ordinary share capital**; and

- the individual can exercise **at least 5% of the voting rights in the company** by virtue of that holding of shares.

For both the first and second category, relief is only available on **relevant business assets**. These are assets **used for the purposes of the business** and **cannot include shares and securities** or **assets held as investments**.

1.2 The operation of the relief

Where there is a material disposal of business assets which results in both gains and losses, losses are netted off against gains to give a single chargeable gain on the disposal of the business assets.

The rate of tax on this chargeable gain is 10%.

An individual may use losses on assets not qualifying for entrepreneurs' relief and the annual exempt amount in the most beneficial way. This means that these amounts should **first be set against gains which do not qualify for entrepreneurs' relief** in order to save tax at either 18% or 28% rather than at 10%.

The chargeable gain qualifying for entrepreneurs' relief is treated as the lowest part of the amount on which an individual is chargeable to capital gains tax. This means chargeable gains qualifying for entrepreneurs' relief will use up any unused basic rate band before those gains that do not qualify for the relief. Although this does not affect the tax on the gain qualifying for entrepreneurs' relief (which is always at 10%), it may have an effect on the rate of tax on other taxable gains.

1.3 Example

Simon sells his business, all the assets of which qualify for entrepreneurs' relief, in September 2011. The chargeable gain arising is £10,000.

Simon also made a chargeable gain of £24,500 in December 2011 on an asset which did not qualify for entrepreneurs' relief.

Simon has taxable income of £18,000 in 2011/12.

The CGT payable for 2011/12 is calculated as follows:

	Gains £	CGT £
Gain qualifying for entrepreneurs' relief		
Taxable gain	10,000	
CGT @ 10%		1,000
Gain not qualifying for entrepreneur's relief		
Gain	24,500	
Less: annual exempt amount (best use)	(10,600)	
Taxable gain	13,900	
CGT on £(35,000 – 18,000 – 10,000)		
= 7,000 @ 18%		1,260
CGT on £(13,900 – 7,000) = 6,900 @ 28%		1,932
CGT 2011/12		4,192

Note that the £10,000 gain qualifying for entrepreneurs' relief is deducted from the basic rate limit for the purposes of computing the rate of tax on the gain not qualifying for entrepreneurs' relief.

1.4 Lifetime limit

There is a limit of £10 million of gains on which entrepreneurs' relief can be claimed. **This is a lifetime amount applicable to disposals made on or after 6 April 2008.** The £10 million limit applies when computing entrepreneurs' relief for disposals made on or after 6 April 2011. There were lower previous limits for disposals in earlier tax years but you will not be expected to deal with these.

Question	Limit on entrepreneurs' relief

Maureen sells a shareholding, which qualifies for entrepreneurs' relief, in January 2012, realising a gain of £9,300,000. Maureen had already made a claim for entrepreneurs' relief in 2010/11 in respect of gains totalling £900,000. Maureen also makes an allowable loss of £(20,000) in 2011/12 on an asset not qualifying for entrepreneur's relief. Her taxable income for 2011/12 is £200,000.

Calculate the CGT payable by Maureen for 2011/12.

Answer

	Gains £	CGT £
Gain qualifying for entrepreneurs' relief		
£(10,000,000 – 900,000)	9,100,000	
CGT @ 10% on £9,100,000		910,000
Gain not qualifying for entrepreneurs' relief		
£(9,300,000 – 9,100,000)	200,000	
Less: allowable loss (best use)	(20,000)	
Net gain	180,000	
Less: annual exempt amount (best use)	(10,600)	
Taxable gain	169,400	
CGT @ 28% on £169,400		47,432
Total CGT due		957,432

1.5 Claim

An individual must claim entrepreneurs' relief: it is not automatic. The claim deadline is the first anniversary of 31 January following the end of the tax year of disposal. For a 2011/12 disposal, the taxpayer must claim by 31 January 2014.

2 The replacement of business assets (rollover relief)

Rollover relief is available to all businesses that reinvest in qualifying assets in the period commencing one year before and ending 36 months after the disposal concerned.

2.1 Conditions

A gain may be 'rolled over' (deferred) where the proceeds received on the disposal of a business asset are spent on a replacement business asset. This is **rollover relief**. A claim cannot specify that only part of a gain is to be rolled over.

All the following conditions must be met.

(a) **The old asset sold and the new asset bought are both used only in the trade** or trades carried on **by the person claiming rollover relief**. Where part of a building is in non-trade use for all or a substantial part of the period of ownership, the building (and the land on which it stands) is treated as two separate assets, the trade part (qualifying) and the non-trade part (non-qualifying). This split cannot be made for other assets.

(b) **The old asset and the new asset both fall within one** (but not necessarily the same one) **of the following classes.**

    (i) Land and buildings (including parts of buildings) occupied as well as used only for the purpose of the trade

    (ii) Fixed (that is, immovable) plant and machinery

    (iii) Goodwill.

(c) **Reinvestment of the proceeds received on the disposal of the old asset** takes place in a period beginning one year before and ending three years after the date of the disposal.

(d) **The new asset is brought into use in the trade on its acquisition** (not necessarily immediately, but not after any significant and unnecessary delay).

The new asset can be used in a different trade from the old asset.

A claim for relief must be made within four years of the end of the tax year in which the disposal of the old asset is made.

2.2 Operation of relief

FAST FORWARD

A rolled over gain is deducted from the base cost of the replacement asset acquired.

Deferral is obtained by deducting the chargeable gain from the cost of the new asset. For full relief, the whole of the proceeds must be reinvested. Where only part is reinvested, a gain equal to the amount not reinvested or the full gain, if lower, will be chargeable to tax immediately.

The new asset will have a base cost for chargeable gains purposes of its purchase price less the gain rolled over.

 Question   **Rollover relief**

A freehold factory was purchased by Zoë for business use in August 2002. It was sold in December 2011 for £70,000, giving rise to a gain of £17,950. A replacement factory was purchased in June 2012 for £60,000. Compute the base cost of the replacement factory, taking into account any possible rollover of the gain from the disposal in December 2011.

Answer

	£
Gain	17,950
Less: rollover relief (balancing figure)	(7,950)
Chargeable gain: amount not reinvested £(70,000 – 60,000)	10,000
Cost of new factory	60,000
Less rolled over gain	(7,950)
Base cost of new factory	52,050

2.3 Non-business use

Where the old asset has not been used in the trade for a fraction of its period of ownership, the amount of the gain that can be rolled over is reduced by the same fraction. When considering proceeds not reinvested the restriction on rollover relief is based on the proportion of proceeds relating to the part of the asset used in the trade or the proportion relating to the period of trade use.

Exam focus point

Look out for both the old and the new asset having some non-business use. You must compare the proceeds of the business use proportion with the amount reinvested in the business use portion of the new asset.

Question   Assets with non-business use

John bought a factory for £150,000 on 11 January 2007, for use in his business. From 11 January 2008, he let the factory out for a period of two years. He then used the factory for his own business again, until he sold it on 10 July 2011 for £225,000. On 13 January 2012, he purchased another factory for use in his business. This second factory cost £100,000.

Calculate the chargeable gain on the sale of the first factory and the base cost of the second factory.

Answer

Gain on first factory

	Non business £	Business £
Proceeds of sale (24:30) (W1)	100,000	125,000
Less: cost (24:30)	(66,667)	(83,333)
Gain	33,333	41,667
Less: rollover relief		(16,667)
Chargeable gain (W2)	33,333	25,000

Base cost of second factory

	£
Cost	100,000
Less gain rolled over	(16,667)
Base cost c/f	83,333

Workings

1   *Use of factory*

Total ownership period:

11.1.07 – 10.07.11 = 54 months

Attributable to non business use:

11.1.08 – 10.1.10 = 24 months

Attributable to business use (balance: 54m – 24m) = 30 months

2   *Proceeds not reinvested*

	£
Proceeds of business element	125,000
Less: cost of new factory	(100,000)
Not reinvested	25,000

2.4 Depreciating assets

When the replacement asset is a depreciating asset, the gain on the old asset is 'frozen' rather than rolled over.

Where the replacement asset is a depreciating asset, the gain is not rolled over by reducing the cost of the replacement asset. Rather it is deferred until it crystallises on the earliest of:

(a)   The disposal of the replacement asset.

(b)   The date the replacement asset ceases to be used in the trade (but the gain does not crystallise on the taxpayer's death).

(c)   Ten years after the acquisition of the replacement asset (maximum).

Key term

An asset is a **depreciating asset** if it is, or within the next ten years will become, a wasting asset. Thus, any asset with an expected life of 60 years or less is covered by this definition. Plant and machinery is always treated as depreciating.

Question   Gain deferred into depreciating asset

Norma bought a freehold shop for use in her business in June 2010 for £125,000. She sold it for £140,000 on 1 August 2011. On 10 July 2011, Norma bought some fixed plant and machinery to use in her business, costing £150,000. She then sells the plant and machinery for £167,000 on 19 November 2013. Show Norma's gains in relation to these transactions.

Answer

Gain deferred

	£
Proceeds of shop	140,000
Less cost	(125,000)
Gain	15,000

This gain is deferred in relation to the purchase of the plant and machinery as all the proceeds have been reinvested.

Sale of plant and machinery

	£
Proceeds	167,000
Less cost	(150,000)
Gain	17,000

Total gain chargeable on sale (gain on plant and machinery plus deferred gain)
£(15,000 + 17,000) = £32,000

Where a gain on disposal is deferred against a replacement depreciating asset it is possible to transfer the deferred gain to a non-depreciating asset provided the non-depreciating asset is bought before the deferred gain has crystallised.

3 Gift relief (holdover relief)

FAST FORWARD

Gift relief can be claimed on gifts of business assets.

3.1 The relief

If an individual gives away a qualifying asset, the transferor and the transferee can jointly claim within four years of the end of the tax year of the transfer, that the transferor's gain be reduced to nil. The transferee is then deemed to acquire the asset for market value at the date of transfer less the transferor's deferred gain.

If a disposal involves actual consideration rather than being an outright gift, but is still not a bargain made at arm's length (so that the proceeds are deemed to be the market value of the asset), this is known as a sale at undervalue. **Any excess of actual consideration over actual cost) is chargeable immediately and only the balance of the gain is deferred.** The amount chargeable immediately is limited to the full gain.

Exam focus point

> The asset need only be a business asset in the hands of the donor. It is immaterial if the donee does not use it for business purposes.

3.2 Qualifying assets

Gift relief can be claimed on gifts or sales at undervalue on transfers of **business assets**. The definition of a business asset for gift relief is **not** the same as for entrepreneurs' relief.

Business assets are:

(a)   Assets used in a trade, profession or vocation carried on:

    (1)   by the donor

    (2)   by the donor's personal company (ie one where the individual holds at least 5% of the voting rights).

If the asset was used for the purposes of the trade, profession or vocation for only part of its period of ownership, the gain to be held over is the gain otherwise eligible × period of such use/total period of ownership.

If the asset was a building or structure only partly used for trade, professional or vocational purposes, only the **part of the gain attributable to the part so used is eligible for gift relief.**

(b)   **Shares and securities in trading companies**

    (1)   the shares or securities are **not listed on a recognised stock exchange** (but they may be on the AIM); or

    (2)   if the donor is an individual, the company concerned is his **personal company** (defined as above);

If the company has chargeable non-business assets at the time of the gift, and (2) applied at any time in the last 12 months, **the gain to be held over is:**

Exam formula

$$\text{Gain} \times \frac{\text{the value of the chargeable business assets (CBA)}}{\text{the value of the chargeable assets (CA)}}$$

Question

On 6 December 2011 Angelo sold to his son Michael a freehold shop valued at £200,000 for £50,000, and claimed gift relief. Angelo had originally purchased the shop from which he had run his business for £30,000. Michael continued to run a business from the shop premises but decided to sell the shop in May 2013 for £195,000. Compute any chargeable gains arising. Assume the rules of CGT in 2011/12 continue to apply in May 2013.

Answer

(a) *Angelo's CGT position (2011/12)*

	£
Proceeds (market value)	200,000
Less cost	(30,000)
Gain	170,000
Less gain deferred (balance)	(150,000)
Chargeable gain £(50,000 – 30,000)	20,000

(b) *Michael's CGT position (2013/14)*

	£
Proceeds	195,000
Less cost £(200,000 – 150,000)	(50,000)
Gain	145,000

Question

Morris gifts shares in his personal company to his son Minor realising a gain of £100,000. The company balance sheet at the date of the gift shows:

	£
Freehold factory and offices	150,000
Leasehold warehouse	80,000
Investments	120,000
Other net assets	200,000
	550,000

You are required to show the gain qualifying for hold-over relief and the chargeable gain.

Answer

Gain qualifying for hold-over relief:

$$£100,000 \times \frac{\text{Chargeable business assets (CBA)}}{\text{Chargeable assets (CA)}} = £100,000 \times \frac{150+80}{150+80+120}$$

$$= £100,000 \times \frac{230}{350}$$

$$= \underline{£65,714}$$

The gain which is not held-over is £100,000 – £65,714 = £34,286

4 Incorporation relief

A gain arising on the incorporation of a business is automatically deferred into the base cost of the shares acquired by incorporation relief. However, an individual can elect for the relief not to apply.

If a person transfers his business to a company this is a disposal of the business assets for CGT purposes and he realises net chargeable gains (chargeable gains less allowable losses) on those assets. It is, however, clearly undesirable to discourage individuals from incorporating their businesses and so relief is available.

The relief (incorporation relief) is automatic (so no claim need be made). All, or some, of the gains are held over if all the following conditions are met.

(a) **The business is transferred as a going concern**
(b) **All its assets (other than cash) are transferred**
(c) **The consideration is wholly or partly in shares.**

Exam formula

> **The amount held over is found by applying the fraction:**
>
> $$\text{Gain} \times \frac{\text{Value of shares received from the company}}{\text{Total value of consideration from the company}}$$

This amount is then deducted from the base cost of the shares received. The company is deemed to acquire assets transferred at their market values.

An individual can elect not to receive incorporation relief. He might do this, for example, in order to claim entrepreneurs' relief instead.

Question

Incorporation relief

Mr P transferred his business to a company in July 2011, realising a gain of £24,000 on the only business asset transferred (a factory). The consideration comprised cash of £15,000 and shares at a market value of £75,000.

(a) What is the chargeable gain on the transfer?
(b) What is the base cost of the shares for any future disposal?

Answer

(a)

	£
Gain	24,000
Less held over $\dfrac{75,000}{15,000+75,000} \times £24,000$	(20,000)
Gain	4,000

(b)

	£
Market value	75,000
Less gain held over	(20,000)
Base cost of shares	55,000

Chapter Roundup

- Entrepreneurs' relief applies on the disposal of a business and certain trading company shares. Gains on assets qualifying for the relief are taxed at 10%.

- Rollover relief is available to all businesses that reinvest in qualifying assets in the period commencing one year before and ending 36 months after the disposal concerned.

- A rolled over gain is deducted from the base cost of the replacement asset acquired.

- When the replacement asset is a depreciating asset, the gain on the old asset is 'frozen' rather than rolled over.

- Gift relief can be claimed on gifts of business assets.

- A gain arising on the incorporation of a business is automatically deferred into the base cost of the shares acquired by incorporation relief. However, an individual can elect for the relief not to apply.

Quick Quiz

1   Patrick has been running a trading business for five years. In 2011/12 he sold the business to Andrew realising gains of £75,000. Patrick has already used his annual exempt amount for 2011/12 against other gains. He had not made any previous claim for entrepreneurs' relief. What is Patrick's CGT liability?

2   Alice sells a factory for £500,000 realising a gain of £100,000. She acquires a factory two months later for £480,000. How much rollover relief is available?

 A £20,000
 B £60,000
 C £80,000
 D £100,000

3   What deferral relief is available when a business asset is replaced with a depreciating business asset?

4   Which disposals of shares qualify for gift relief?

5   List the conditions for deferring gains on the incorporation of a business.

Answers to Quick Quiz

1   CGT @ 10% on £75,000   £7,500

2   C. Amount not reinvested £(500,000 – 480,000) = £20,000. Rollover relief £(100,000 – 20,000) = £80,000.

3   The gain is frozen on the acquisition of a depreciating asset until the earliest of: disposal of that asset; the date the asset is no longer used in the trade; 10 years after the acquisition of replacement asset.

4   Shares which qualify for gift relief are those in trading companies

    • which are not listed on a recognised stock exchange, or
    • which are in the individual's personal company ie the individual holds at least 5% of the voting rights

5   The conditions for incorporation relief are:

    • the business is transferred as a going concern
    • all of its assets (other than cash) are transferred
    • the consideration is wholly or partly in shares

Now try the question below from the Exam Question Bank

Number	Level	Marks	Time
Q22	Examination	14	25 mins
Q23	Introductory	5	9 mins
Q24	Introductory	10	18 mins
Q45	Examination	25	45 mins

Question 45 has been analysed to give you guidance on how to answer exam questions.

16

Shares and securities

Topic list	Syllabus reference
1 Valuing quoted shares	D4(a)
2 The matching rules for individuals	D4(b)
3 The share pool	D4(c)
4 Bonus and rights issues	D4(d)
5 Reorganisations and takeovers	D4(d)
6 Gilts and qualifying corporate bonds	D4(e)

Introduction

We have now covered most aspects of the capital gains computation apart from shares and securities.

Shares and securities need special rules because an individual may hold several shares or securities in the same company, bought at different times for different prices but otherwise identical. We need to identify the shares which are disposed to compute the gain or loss.

We also discuss bonus and rights issues, takeovers and reorganisations.

In the next chapter we will conclude our study of personal taxation by considering administration.

Study guide

		Intellectual level
D4	**Gains and losses on the disposal of shares and securities**	
(a)	Calculate the value of quoted shares where they are disposed of by way of a gift.	2
(b)	Explain and apply the identification rules as they apply to individuals including the same day, and thirty day matching rules.	2
(c)	Explain the pooling provisions.	2
(d)	Explain the treatment of bonus issues, rights issues, takeovers and reorganisations.	2
(e)	Explain the exemption available for gilt-edged securities and qualifying corporate bonds.	1

Exam guide

Shares and securities are likely to form at least part of a question on capital gains. You must learn the identification rules as they are crucial in calculating the gain correctly. The identification rules for companies are covered later in this Text. Takeovers and reorganisations are important; remember to apportion the cost across the new holding.

1 Valuing quoted shares

FAST FORWARD

Quoted shares are valued at the lower of the 'quarter-up' value and the average of the highest and lowest marked bargains.

Where quoted shares are disposed of by way of a gift, the market value of these shares is needed as 'proceeds' in order to calculate the chargeable gain or allowable loss.

Quoted shares and securities are valued using prices in The Stock Exchange Daily Official List, taking the lower of:

- the 'quarter-up' value: lower quoted price + $\frac{1}{4}$ × (higher quoted price – lower quoted price)
- the average of the highest and lowest marked bargains (ignoring bargains marked at special prices)

Question

CGT value of shares

Shares in A plc are quoted at 100-110p. The highest and lowest marked bargains were 99p and 110p. What would be the market value for CGT purposes?

Answer

The value will be the lower of:

(a) $100 + \frac{1}{4} \times (110 - 100) = 102.5$;

(b) $\dfrac{110 + 99}{2} = 104.5$.

The market value for CGT purposes will therefore be 102.5p per share.

2 The matching rules for individuals

There are special rules for matching shares sold with shares purchased. Disposals are matched first with shares acquired on the same day, then within the following 30 days and finally with the share pool.

Quoted and unquoted shares and securities present special problems when attempting to compute gains or losses on disposal. For instance, suppose that an individual buys some quoted shares in X plc as follows.

Date	Number of shares	Cost £
5 May 1983	220	150
17 August 2011	100	375

On 15 August 2011, he sells 120 of the shares for £1,450. To determine the chargeable gain, we need to be able to work out which shares out of the two original holdings were actually sold.

We therefore need **matching rules**. These **allow us to decide which shares have been sold and so work out what the allowable cost on disposal should be.**

At any one time, we will only be concerned with shares or securities of the same class in the same company. If an individual owns both ordinary shares and preference shares in X plc, we will deal with the two classes of share entirely separately, because they are distinguishable.

Below 'shares' refers to both shares and securities.

For individuals, share disposals are matched with acquisitions in the following order.

(a)   **Same day acquisitions.**

(b)   **Acquisitions within the following 30 days** (known as the 'bed and breakfast rule') if more than one acquisition, use a 'first in, first out' (FIFO) basis.

(c)   **Any shares in the share pool (see below).**

The 'bed and breakfast' rule stops shares being sold to crystallise a capital gain or loss, usually to use the annual exempt amount, and then being repurchased a day or so later. Without the rule a gain or loss would arise on the sale, since it would be 'matched' to the original acquisition.

Exam focus point

Learn the 'matching rules' because a crucial first step to getting a shares question right is to correctly match the shares sold to the original shares purchased.

3 The share pool

3.1 Composition of pool

We treat any shares acquired (other than those acquired on the same day or within the next 30 days) as a 'pool' which grows as new shares are acquired and shrinks as they are sold.

In making computations which use the share pool, we must keep track of:

(a)   The **number** of shares
(b)   The **cost** of the shares

3.2 Disposals from the share pool

In the case of a disposal the cost attributable to the shares disposed of are deducted from the amounts within the share pool. The proportion of the cost to take out of the pool should be computed using the A/(A + B) fraction that is used for any other part disposal. However, we are not usually given the value of the remaining shares (B in the fraction). We just use numbers of shares.

Question

In August 2005 Oliver acquired 4,000 shares in Twist plc at a cost of £10,000. Oliver sold 3,000 shares on 10 July 2011 for £17,000. Compute the gain and the value of the share pool following the disposal.

Answer

The gain is computed as follows:

	£
Proceeds	17,000
Less cost (working)	(7,500)
Gain	9,500

Working – share pool

	No of shares	Cost £
Acquisition – August 2005	4,000	10,000
Disposal – July 2011	(3,000)	
Cost $\dfrac{3,000}{4,000} \times £10,000$		(7,500)
	1,000	2,500

Question

Anita acquired shares in Kent Ltd as follows:

1 July 1995   1,000 shares for £2,000

11 April 2000 2,500 shares for £7,500

17 July 2011   400 shares for £1,680

10 August 2011   500 shares for £2,000

Anita sold 4,000 shares for £16,400 on 17 July 2011.

Calculate Anita's net gain on sale.

Answer

First match the disposal with the acquisition on the same day:

	£
Proceeds $\dfrac{400}{4,000} \times £16,400$	1,640
Less: cost	(1,680)
Loss	(40)

Next match the disposal with the acquisition in the next thirty days:

	£
Proceeds $\dfrac{500}{4,000} \times £16,400$	2,050
Less: cost	(2,000)
Gain	50

Finally, match the disposal with the shares in the share pool:

		£
Proceeds $\dfrac{3,100}{4,000} \times £16,400$		12,710
Less: cost (working)		(8,414)
Gain		4,296
Net gain £(50 + 4,296 – 40)		4,306

Working

	No. of shares	Cost
		£
1.7.95 Acquisition	1,000	2,000
11.4.00 Acquisition	2,500	7,500
	3,500	9,500
17.7.11 Disposal	(3,100)	(8,414)
c/f	400	1,086

4 Bonus and rights issues

 Bonus shares are shares acquired at no cost. Rights issue shares are acquired for payment.

4.1 Bonus issues

Bonus shares are shares issued by a company in proportion to each shareholder's existing holding. For example, a shareholder may have 1,000 shares. If the company makes a 2 shares for each 1 share held bonus issue (called a '2 for 1 bonus issue'), the shareholder will receive 2 bonus shares for each 1 share held. So the shareholder will end up with 1,000 original shares and 2,000 bonus shares making 3,000 shares in total.

When a company issues bonus shares all that happens is that the size of the original holding is increased. Since bonus shares are issued at no cost there is no need to adjust the original cost.

4.2 Rights issues

In a rights issue the company offers shareholders rights issue shares in proportion to their existing shareholdings.

The difference between a bonus issue and a rights issue is that in a rights issue the new shares are paid for by the shareholder and this results in an adjustment to the original cost.

 Question   **Rights issue**

Simon had the following transactions in S Ltd.

1.10.96	Bought 10,000 shares for £15,000
1.2.09	Took up rights issue 1 for 2 at £2.75 per share
14.10.11	Sold 2,000 shares for £6,000

Compute the gain arising in October 2011.

Share pool

	Number	Cost
		£
1.10.96 Acquisition	10,000	15,000
1.2.09 Rights issue	5,000	13,750
	15,000	28,750
14.10.11 Sale	(2,000)	(3,833)
c/f	13,000	24,917

Gain

	£
Proceeds	6,000
Less cost	(3,833)
Gain	2,167

5 Reorganisations and takeovers

 FAST FORWARD

The costs of the original holding are allocated to the new holdings pro rata to their values on a takeover or reorganisation.

5.1 Reorganisations

A reorganisation takes place where new shares or a mixture of new shares and debentures are issued in exchange for the original shareholdings. The new shares take the place of the old shares. The problem is how to apportion the original cost between the different types of capital issued on the reorganisation.

If the new shares and securities are quoted, then the cost is apportioned by reference to the market values of the new types of capital on the first day of quotation after the reorganisation.

 Question   *Reorganisations*

An original quoted shareholding of 3,000 shares is held in a share pool with a cost of £13,250.

In 2011 there is a reorganisation whereby each ordinary share is exchanged for two 'A' ordinary shares (quoted at £2 each) and one preference share (quoted at £1 each). Show how the original cost will be apportioned.

Answer

Share pool

	New holding	MV	Cost
		£	£
Ords 2 new shares	6,000	12,000	10,600 (W)
Prefs 1 new shares	3,000	3,000	2,650 (W)
Total		15,000	13,250

Working

$^{12}/_{15} \times £13,250$ = cost of ordinary shares

$^{3}/_{15} \times £13,250$ = cost of preference shares

5.2 Takeovers

A chargeable gain does not arise on a 'paper for paper' takeover. The cost of the original holding is passed on to the new holding which takes the place of the original holding. **If part of the takeover consideration is cash then a gain must be computed**: the normal part disposal rules will apply.

The takeover rules apply where the company issuing the new shares ends up with **more than 25%** of the ordinary share capital of the old company or the majority of the voting power in the old company, or the company issuing the new shares makes a general offer to shareholders in the other company which is initially made subject to a condition which, if satisfied, would give the first company control of the second company.

The exchange must take place for bona fide commercial reasons and does not have as its main purpose, or one of its main purposes, the avoidance of CGT or corporation tax.

Question   Takeover

Mr Le Bon held 20,000 £1 shares in Duran plc out of a total number of issued shares of one million. They were bought in 2002 for £2 each. In 2011 the board of Duran plc agreed to a takeover bid by Spandau plc under which shareholders in Duran plc received three ordinary Spandau plc shares plus one preference share for every four shares held in Duran plc. Immediately following the takeover, the ordinary shares in Spandau plc were quoted at £5 each and the preferences shares at 90p. Show the base costs of the ordinary shares and the preference shares.

Answer

The total value due to Mr Le Bon on the takeover is as follows.

		£
Ordinary	20,000 × 3/4 × £5	75,000
Preference	20,000 × 1/4 × 90p	4,500
		79,500

The base costs are therefore:

	£
Ordinary shares: 75,000/79,500 × 20,000 × £2	37,736
Preference shares: 4,500/79,500 × 20,000 × £2	2,264
	40,000

6 Gilts and qualifying corporate bonds

FAST FORWARD

> Gilts and Qualifying corporate bonds held by individuals are exempt from CGT. You should never waste time computing gains and losses on them.

Key term

> **Gilts are UK Government securities issued by HM Treasury** as shown on the Treasury list. You may assume that the list includes all issues of Treasury Loan, Treasury Stock, Exchequer Loan, Exchequer Stock and War Loan.

Disposals of gilt edged securities (gilts) and qualifying corporate bonds by individuals are exempt from CGT.

A **qualifying corporate bond (QCB)** is a security (whether or not secured on assets) which:

(a)   represents a **'normal commercial loan'**. This excludes any bonds which are convertible into shares (although bonds convertible into other bonds which would be QCBs are not excluded), or which carry the right to excessive interest or interest which depends on the results of the issuer's business;

(b)   is **expressed in sterling** and for which no provision is made for conversion into or redemption in another currency;

(c)   was **acquired** by the person now disposing of it **after 13 March 1984**; and

(d)   does not have a redemption value which depends on a published index of share prices on a stock exchange.

Permanent interest bearing shares issued by building societies which meet condition (b) above are also QCBs.

Chapter Roundup

- Quoted shares are valued at the lower of the 'quarter-up' value and the average of the highest and lowest marked bargains.

- There are special rules for matching shares sold with shares purchased. Disposals are matched first with acquisitions on the same day, then within the following 30 days and finally with the share pool.

- Bonus shares are shares acquired at no cost. Rights issue shares are acquired for payment.

- The costs of the original holding are allocated to the new holdings pro rata to their values on a takeover or reorganisation.

- Gilts and Qualifying corporate bonds held by individuals are exempt from CGT. You should never waste time computing gains and losses on them.

Quick Quiz

1 In what order are acquisitions of shares matched with disposals for individuals?

2 In July 1995 an individual acquired 1,000 shares. He acquired 1,000 more shares on each of 15 January 2005 and 15 January 2012 in X plc. He sells 2,500 shares on 10 January 2012. How are the shares matched on sale?

3 Sharon acquired 10,000 shares in Z plc in 1986. She takes up a 1 for 2 rights offer in May 2011. How many shares does Sharon have in her share pool after the rights offer?

4 What is a qualifying corporate bond?

Answers to Quick Quiz

1   The matching of shares sold is in the following order.

    (a)   Same day acquisitions.

    (b)   Acquisitions within the following 30 days.

    (c)   Shares in the share pool.

2   January 2012 1,000 shares (following 30 days)
    Share pool 1,500 shares

3   10,000 + 5,000 = 15,000 shares

4   A qualifying corporate bond is a security which:

- represents a normal commercial loan
- is expressed in sterling
- was acquired after 13 March 1984
- is not redeemable in relation to share prices on a stock exchange

Now try the questions below from the Exam Question Bank

Number	Level	Marks	Time
Q25	Examination	10	18 mins

Tax administration for individuals

17

Self assessment and payment of tax by individuals

Topic list	Syllabus reference
1 The self assessment system	H1(a)
2 Tax returns and keeping records	H2(a), (e)
3 Self-assessment and claims	H2(a)
4 Payments of income tax and capital gains tax	H2(b), (c)
5 Revenue powers	H3(a), (b)
6 Penalties	H4(a), (b)
7 Appeals	H4(b)

Introduction

In the earlier chapters we have learned how to calculate an individual's liability to income tax, capital gains tax and national insurance.

In this chapter we see how individuals (including partners) must 'self assess' their liability to income tax, capital gains tax and Class 4 NICs.

In the remaining chapters we will consider the other taxes within the syllabus: inheritance tax, corporation tax and VAT.

Study guide

		Intellectual level
H1	**The systems for self-assessment and the making of returns**	
(a)	Explain and apply the features of the self assessment system as it applies to individuals.	2
H2	**The time limits for the submission of information, claims and payment of tax, including payments on account**	
(a)	Recognise the time limits that apply to the filing of returns and the making of claims.	2
(b)	Recognise the due dates for the payment of tax under the self-assessment system.	2
(c)	Compute payments on account and balancing payments/repayments for individuals.	2
(e)	List the information and records that taxpayers need to retain for tax purposes.	1
H3	**The procedures relating to compliance checks, appeals and disputes**	
(a)	Explain the circumstances in which HM Revenue & Customs can make a compliance check into a self assessment tax return.	2
(b)	Explain the procedures for dealing with appeals and disputes.	1
H4	**Penalties for non-compliance**	
(a)	Calculate late payment interest.	2
(b)	State the penalties that can be charged.	2

Exam guide

Question 1 of the exam will always be on income tax and question 3 on CGT. Either of these could include a part on the self assessment system, be it the filing of a return, the payment of tax or compliance checks by HMRC, or it could be included in questions 4 or 5. Your knowledge should include the penalties used to enforce the self assessment system.

1 The self assessment system

This section relates to your PER requirement:
19   Evaluate and compute taxes payable

1.1 Introduction

The self assessment system relies upon the taxpayer completing and filing a tax return and paying the tax due. The system is enforced by a system of penalties for failure to comply within the set time limits, and by interest for late payment of tax.

Many taxpayers have very simple affairs: receiving a salary under deduction of tax through PAYE, with a small amount of investment income which can be dealt with through the PAYE code. These individuals will not normally have to complete a tax return. Self-employed taxpayers, company directors and individuals with complicated affairs will have to complete a tax return.

Individuals within the self assessment system are required to complete and file a return every year unless HMRC recognise that their affairs have become sufficiently straightforward for no return to be required.

Conversely, individuals whose affairs become more complicated so that they are likely to owe tax must notify HMRC that they should be brought within the self assessment system.

1.2 Notification of liability to income tax and CGT

FAST FORWARD

Individuals who do not receive a tax return must notify their chargeability to income tax or CGT.

Individuals who are chargeable to income tax or CGT for any tax year and who have not received a notice to file a return are required to give notice of chargeability to an Officer of the Revenue and Customs within six months from the end of the year ie by 5 October 2012 for 2011/12.

A person who has no chargeable gains and who is not liable to higher rate tax does not have to give notice of chargeability if all his income:

(a)   Is taken into account under PAYE
(b)   Is from a source of income not subject to tax under a self-assessment
(c)   Has had (or is treated as having had) income tax deducted at source, or
(d)   Is UK dividends.

A penalty may be imposed for late notification (see later in this Chapter).

2 Tax returns and keeping records

FAST FORWARD

Tax returns must usually be filed by 31 October (paper) or 31 January (electronic) following the end of the tax year.

2.1 Tax returns

The tax return comprises a basic six-page return form, **together with supplementary pages for particular sources of income.** Taxpayers are sent a return and a number of supplementary pages depending on their known sources of income, together with a Tax Return Guide and various notes relating to the supplementary pages. Taxpayers with new sources of income may have to ask for further supplementary pages. Taxpayers with simple tax returns may be asked to complete a short four- page tax return. If a return for the previous year was filed electronically the taxpayer may be sent a notice to file a return, rather than the official HMRC form.

Partnerships must file a separate return which includes a Partnership Statement showing the firm's profits, losses, proceeds from the sale of assets, tax suffered, tax credits, charges on income and the division of all these amounts between partners.

A partnership return must include a declaration of the name and tax reference of each partner, as well as the usual declaration that the return is correct and complete to the best of the signatory's knowledge. Each partner must then include his share of partnership profits on his personal tax return.

2.2 Time limit for submission of tax returns

Key term

The **latest filing date** for a personal tax return for a tax year (Year 1) is:

- **31 October** in the next tax year (Year 2), for a **non-electronic return** (eg a paper return).
- **31 January** in Year 2, for an **electronic return** (eg made via the internet).

There are **two exceptions to this general rule**.

The **first exception applies if the notice to file a tax return is issued by HMRC to the taxpayer after 31 July in Year 2, but on or before 31 October in Year 2**. In this case, the **latest filing date is**:

- **the end of 3 months following the notice, for a non-electronic return.**
- **31 January in Year 2, for an electronic return.**

The second exception applies **if the notice to file the tax return is issued to the taxpayer after 31 October in Year 2**. In this case, **the latest filing date is the end of 3 months following the notice**.

Question | Submission of tax returns

Advise each of the following clients of the latest filing date for her personal tax return for 2011/12 if the return is:

(a) non-electronic; or
(b) electronic.

Norma Notice to file tax return issued by HMRC on 6 April 2012
Melanie Notice to file tax return issued by HMRC on 10 August 2012
Olga Notice to file tax return issued by HMRC on 12 December 2012

Answer

	Non-electronic	Electronic
Norma	31 October 2012	31 January 2013
Melanie	9 November 2012	31 January 2013
Olga	11 March 2013	11 March 2012

A partnership return may be filed as a non-electronic return or an electronic return. **The general rule and the exceptions to the general rule for personal returns apply also to partnership returns**.

2.3 Keeping records

All taxpayers must retain all records required to enable them to make and deliver a correct tax return.

Records must be retained until the later of:

(a) (I) **5 years after the 31 January following the tax year where the taxpayer is in business** (as a sole trader or partner or letting property). Note that this applies to all of the records, not only the business records, or

(ii) 1 year after the 31 January following the tax year otherwise, or

(b) Provided notice to deliver a return is given before the date in (a):

(i) **The time after which a compliance check by HMRC into the return can no longer be commenced, or**

(ii) **The date any such compliance check has been completed.**

HMRC can specify a shorter time limit for keeping records where the records are bulky and the information they contain can be provided in another way.

Where a person receives a notice to deliver a tax return after the normal record keeping period has expired, he must keep all records in his possession at that time until no compliance issues can be raised in respect of the return or until such a check has been completed.

Taxpayers can keep 'information', rather than 'records', but must show that they have prepared a complete and correct tax return. The information must also be able to be provided in a legible form on request. Records can be kept in electronic format.

HMRC can inspect 'in-year' records, ie *before* a return is submitted, if they believe it is reasonably required to check a tax position.

3 Self-assessment and claims

FAST FORWARD If a paper return is filed the taxpayer can ask HMRC to compute the tax due. Electronic returns have tax calculated automatically.

3.1 Self-assessment

Key term

A self-assessment is a calculation of the amount of taxable income and gains after deducting reliefs and allowances, a calculation of income tax and CGT payable after taking into account tax deducted at source and tax credits on dividends.

If the taxpayer is filing a **paper return (other than a Short Tax Return), he may make the tax calculation on his return or ask HMRC to do so on his behalf.**

If the taxpayer wishes HMRC to make the calculation for Year 1, a paper return must be filed:

- on or before 31 October in Year 2 or,
- if the notice to file the tax return is issued after 31 August in Year 2, within 2 months of the notice.

If the taxpayer is filing an **electronic return, the calculation of tax liability is made automatically when the return is made online**.

3.2 Amending the self-assessment

The taxpayer may amend his return (including the tax calculation) for Year 1 within twelve months after the filing date. For this purpose the filing date means:

- 31 January of Year 2; or
- where the notice to file a return was issued after 31 October in Year 2, the last day of the three month period starting with the issue.

A return may be amended by the taxpayer at a time when a compliance check is in progress into the return. The amendment does not restrict the scope of a compliance check into the return but may be taken into account in that check. If the amendment made during a compliance check is the amount of tax payable, the amendment does not take effect while the check is in progress.

A return may be amended by HMRC to correct any obvious error or omission in the return (such as errors of principle and arithmetical mistakes) or anything else that an officer has reason to believe is incorrect in the light of information available. The correction must be usually be made within nine months after the day on which the return was actually filed. The taxpayer can object to the correction but must do so within 30 days of receiving notice of it.

3.3 Claims

All claims and elections which can be made in a tax return must be made in this manner if a return has been issued. A claim for any relief, allowance or repayment of tax must be quantified at the time it is made.

In general, the time limit for making a claim is 4 years from the end of tax year. Where different time limits apply these have been mentioned throughout this Text.

3.4 Recovery of overpaid tax

If a taxpayer discovers that he has overpaid tax, for example because he has made an error in his tax return, he can make a claim to have the overpaid tax repaid to him. The claim must be made within four years of the end of the tax year to which the overpayment relates.

4 Payment of income tax and capital gains tax

FAST FORWARD

> Two payments on account and a final balancing payment of income tax and Class 4 NICs are due. All capital gains tax is due on 31 January following the end of the tax year.

4.1 Payments on account and final payment

4.1.1 Introduction

The self-assessment system may result in the taxpayer making three payments of income tax and Class 4 NICs.

Date	Payment
31 January in the tax year	1st payment on account
31 July after the tax year	2nd payment on account
31 January after the tax year	Final payment to settle the remaining liability

HMRC issue payslips/demand notes in a credit card type 'Statement of Account' format, but there is no statutory obligation for it to do so and **the onus is on the taxpayer to pay the correct amount of tax on the due date.**

4.1.2 Payments on account

Key term

> **Payments on account** are usually required where the income tax and Class 4 NICs due in the previous year exceeded the amount of income tax deducted at source; this excess is known as **'the relevant amount'**. Income tax deducted at source includes tax deducted at source on interest, PAYE deductions and tax credits on dividends.

The payments on account are each equal to 50% of the relevant amount for the previous year.

Exam focus point

> Payments on account of CGT are never required.

 Question   Payments on account

Sue is a self employed writer who paid tax for 2011/12 as follows:

	£
Total amount of income tax charged	9,200
This included: Tax deducted on savings income	3,200
She also paid: Class 4 NIC	1,900
Capital gains tax	4,800

How much are the payments on account for 2012/13 and by what dates are they due?

	£
Income tax:	
Total income tax charged for 2011/12	9,200
Less tax deducted for 2011/12	(3,200)
	6,000
Class 4 NIC	1,900
'Relevant amount'	7,900
Payments on account for 2012/13:	
31 January 2013 £7,900 × 50%	3,950
31 July 2013 £7,900 × 50%	3,950

There is no requirement to make payments on account of capital gains tax.

Payments on account are not required if the relevant amount falls below a de minimis limit of £1,000. Also, payments on account are not required from taxpayers who paid 80% or more of their tax liability for the previous year through PAYE or other deduction at source arrangements.

4.1.3 Reducing payments on account

Payments on account are normally fixed by reference to the previous year's tax liability but if a taxpayer expects his liability to be lower than this **he may claim to reduce his payments on account to:**

(a) **A stated amount, or**
(b) **Nil.**

The claim must state the reason why he believes his tax liability will be lower, or nil.

If the taxpayer's eventual liability is higher than he estimated he will have reduced the payments on account too far. Although the payments on account will not be adjusted, the taxpayer will suffer an interest charge on late payment.

A penalty of the difference between the reduced payment on account and the correct payment on account may be levied if the reduction was claimed fraudulently or negligently.

4.1.4 Balancing payment

The balance of any income tax and Class 4 NICs together with all CGT due for a year, is normally payable on or before the 31 January following the year.

Question   Payment of tax

Giles made payments on account for 2011/12 of £6,500 each on 31 January 2012 and 31 July 2012, based on his 2010/11 liability. He then calculates his total income tax and Class 4 NIC liability for 2011/12 at £18,000 of which £2,750 was deducted at source. In addition he calculated that his CGT liability for disposals in 2011/12 is £5,120.

What is the final payment due for 2011/12?

Answer

Income tax and Class 4 NIC: £18,000 – £2,750 – £6,500 – £6,500 = £2,250. CGT = £5,120.

Final payment due on 31 January 2013 for 2011/12 £2,250 + £5,120 = £7,370

In one case the due date for the final payment is later than 31 January following the end of the year. **If a taxpayer has notified chargeability by 5 October but the notice to file a tax return is not issued before 31 October, then the due date for the payment is three months after the issue of the notice.**

Tax charged in an amended self-assessment is usually payable on the later of:

(a) The normal due date, generally 31 January following the end of the tax year, and

(b) The day following 30 days after the making of the revised self-assessment.

Tax charged on a discovery assessment (see below) is due thirty days after the issue of the assessment.

4.2 Penalty for late payment of tax

FAST FORWARD

A penalty is chargeable where tax is paid after the due date based on the amount of unpaid tax. Up to 15% of that amount is payable where the tax is more than 12 months late.

A penalty is chargeable where tax is paid after the penalty date. The penalty date is 30 days after the due date for the tax. Therefore no penalty arises if the tax is paid within 30 days of the due date.

The penalty chargeable is:

Date of payment	Penalty
Not more than 5 months after the penalty date	5% of tax which is unpaid at the penalty date.
More than 5 months after the penalty date but not more than 11 months after the penalty date	5% of tax which is unpaid at the end of the 5 month period. This is in addition to the 5% penalty above.
More than 11 months after the penalty date	5% of tax which is unpaid at the end of the 11 month period. This is in addition to the two 5% penalties above.

Penalties for late payment of tax apply to:

(a) **Balancing payments of income tax and Class 4 NICs and any CGT under self-assessment or a determination**

(b) Tax due on the amendment of a self-assessment

(c) Tax due on a discovery assessment

Penalties for late payment do not apply to late payments on account.

4.3 Interest on late paid tax

Interest is chargeable on late payment of both payments on account and balancing payments. In both cases interest runs from the due date until the day before the actual date of payment.

Exam focus point

You will be given the rate of interest to use in the exam.

Interest is charged from 31 January following the tax year (or the normal due date for the balancing payment, in the rare event that this is later), even if this is before the due date for payment on:

(a) Tax payable following an amendment to a self-assessment
(b) Tax payable in a discovery assessment, and
(c) Tax postponed under an appeal, which becomes payable.

Since a determination (see below) is treated as if it were a self-assessment, interest runs from 31 January following the tax year.

If a taxpayer claims to reduce his payments on account and there is still a final payment to be made, interest is normally charged on the payments on account as if each of those payments had been the lower of:

(a)   the reduced amount, plus 50% of the final income tax liability; and

(b)   the amount which would have been payable had no claim for reduction been made.

Question

Herbert's payments on account for 2011/12 based on his income tax liability for 2010/11 were £4,500 each. However when he submitted his 2010/11 income tax return in January 2012 he made a claim to reduce the payments on account for 2011/12 to £3,500 each. The first payment on account was made on 29 January 2012 and the second on 12 August 2012.

Herbert filed his 2011/12 tax return in December 2012. The return showed that his tax liabilities for 2011/12 (before deducting payments on account) were income tax and Class 4 NIC: £10,000, capital gains tax: £2,500. Herbert paid the balance of tax due of £5,500 on 19 February 2013.

For what periods and in respect of what amounts will Herbert be charged interest?

Answer

Herbert made an excessive claim to reduce his payments on account, and will therefore be charged interest on the reduction. The payments on account should have been £4,500 each based on the original 2010/11 liability (not £5,000 each based on the 2011/12 liability). Interest will be charged as follows:

(a)   First payment on account

(i)   On £3,500 – nil – paid on time

(ii)   On £1,000 from due date of 31 January 2012 to day before payment, 18 February 2013

(b)   Second payment on account

(i)   On £3,500 from due date of 31 July 2012 to day before payment, 11 August 2012

(ii)   On £1,000 from due date of 31 July 2012 to day before payment, 18 February 2013

(c)   Balancing payment and capital gains tax.

(i)   On £3,500 from due date of 31 January 2013 to day before payment, 18 February 2013

Where interest has been charged on late payments on account but the final balancing settlement for the year produces a repayment, all or part of the original interest is repaid.

4.4 Repayment of tax and repayment supplement

Tax is repaid when claimed unless a greater payment of tax is due in the following 30 days, in which case it is set-off against that payment.

Interest is paid on overpayments of:

(a)   Payments on account

(b)   Final payments of income tax and Class 4 NICs and CGT, including tax deducted at source or tax credits on dividends, and

(c)   Penalties.

Repayment supplement runs from the original date of payment (even if this was prior to the due date), until the day before the date the repayment is made. Income tax deducted at source and tax credits are treated as if they were paid on the 31 January following the tax year concerned.

Repayment supplement paid to individuals is tax free.

5 Revenue powers

5.1 Compliance checks on returns

FAST FORWARD HMRC can carry out compliance checks on tax returns. Strict procedural rules govern compliance checks.

5.1.1 Starting a compliance check

An officer of the Revenue and Customs has a limited period within which to commence a compliance check on a return or amendment. **The officer must give written notice of his intention by:**

(a) **The first anniversary of the actual filing date (if the return was delivered on or before the due filing date), or**

(b) **If the return is filed after the due filing date, the quarter day following the first anniversary of the actual filing date. The quarter days are 31 January, 30 April, 31 July and 31 October.**

If the taxpayer amended the return after the due filing date, the compliance check 'window' extends to the quarter day following the first anniversary of the date the amendment was filed. Where the compliance check was not started within the limit which would have applied had no amendment been filed, the check is restricted to matters contained in the amendment.

The officer does not have to have, or give, any reason for starting a compliance check. In particular the taxpayer will not be advised whether he has been selected at random for an audit. Compliance checks may be full checks, or may be limited to 'aspect' checks.

5.1.2 During the compliance check

In the course of the compliance check **the officer may require the taxpayer to produce documents, accounts or any other information required. The taxpayer can appeal to the Tax Tribunal against such a requirement.**

During the course of a compliance check, an officer may amend a self assessment if it appears that insufficient tax has been charged and an immediate amendment is necessary to prevent a loss to the Crown. This might apply if, for example, there is a possibility that the taxpayer will emigrate.

If a return is under a compliance check HMRC may postpone any repayment due as shown in the return until the check is complete. HMRC have discretion to make a provisional repayment but there is no facility to appeal if the repayment is withheld.

At any time during the course of a compliance check, the taxpayer may apply to the Tax Tribunal to require the officer to notify the taxpayer within a specified period that the checks are complete, unless the officer can demonstrate that he has reasonable grounds for continuing the compliance check.

5.1.3 Finishing a compliance check

An officer must issue a notice that the compliance check is complete, state his conclusions and amend the self-assessment, partnership statement or claim accordingly.

If the taxpayer is not satisfied with the officer's amendment he may, within 30 days, appeal to the Tax Tribunal.

Once a compliance check is complete the officer cannot make further checks. HMRC may, in limited circumstances, raise a discovery assessment if they believe that there has been a loss of tax (see below).

5.2 Determinations

If notice has been served on a taxpayer to submit a return but the return is not submitted by the due filing date, an officer of HMRC may make a determination of the amounts liable to income tax and CGT and of the tax due. Such a determination must be made to the best of the officer's information and belief, and is then treated as if it were a self-assessment. This enables the officer to seek payment of tax, including payments on account for the following year and to charge interest.

A determination must be made within four year following the end of the relevant tax year.

5.3 Discovery assessments

If an officer of HMRC discovers that profits have been omitted from assessment, that any assessment has become insufficient, or that any relief given is, or has become excessive, an assessment may be raised to recover the tax lost.

If the tax lost results from an error in the taxpayer's return but the return was made in accordance with prevailing practice at the time, no discovery assessment may be made.

A discovery assessment may only be raised where a return has been made if:

(a) There has been **careless or deliberate understatement** by the taxpayer or his agent, or

(b) At the time that compliance checks on the return were completed, or could no longer be made, the officer **did not have information** to make him aware of the loss of tax.

Information is treated as available to an officer if it is contained in the taxpayer's return or claim for the year or either of the two preceding years, or it has been provided as a result of a compliance check covering those years, or it has been specifically provided.

The time limit for raising a discovery assessment is 4 years from the end of the tax year but this is extended to 6 years if there has been careless understatement and 20 years if there has been deliberate understatement. The taxpayer may appeal against a discovery assessment within 30 days of issue.

5.4 Information and inspection powers

HMRC have powers to request documents from taxpayers and third parties. HMRC also has powers to inspect business premises.

5.4.1 Information powers

HMRC has one set of information and inspection powers covering income tax, capital gains tax, corporation tax, VAT and PAYE to ensure taxpayers comply with their obligations, pay the right amount of tax at the right time and claim the correct reliefs and allowances.

HMRC usually informally requests information and documents from taxpayers in connection with their tax affairs. If, however, a taxpayer does not co-operate fully, **HMRC can use its statutory powers to request information and documents** from taxpayers and third parties via a written 'information notice'. HMRC can request both statutory records and supplementary information, such as appointment diaries, notes of board meetings, correspondence and contracts.

HMRC can only issue a taxpayer notice if the information and documents requested are 'reasonably required' for the purpose of checking the taxpayer's tax position. A taxpayer notice may be issued either with or without the approval of the Tax Tribunal.

An information notice issued to a third party must be issued with the agreement of the taxpayer or the approval of the Tax Tribunal, unless the information relates only to the taxpayer's statutory VAT records. The taxpayer to whom the notice relates must receive a summary of the reasons for the third party notice unless the Tax Tribunal believes it would prejudice the assessment or collection of tax.

Tax advisers and auditors cannot be asked to provide information connected with their functions. For example, a tax adviser does not have to provide access to his working papers used in the preparation of the taxpayer's return. In addition, HMRC cannot ask a tax adviser to provide communications between himself and either the taxpayer or his other advisers. This 'professional privilege' does not apply in certain situations, for example, to explanatory material provided to a client in relation to a document already supplied to HMRC.

The taxpayer or third party must provide the information or document requested by the information notice within such period as is reasonably specified within the notice.

The recipient of an information notice has a right of appeal against an information notice unless the Tax Tribunal has approved the issue of the notice.

5.4.2 Inspection powers

An authorised officer of HMRC can enter the business premises of a taxpayer whose liability is being checked and inspect the premises and the business assets and business documents that are on the premises. The power does not extend to any part of the premises used solely as a dwelling. If an information notice has been issued, the documents required in that notice can be inspected at the same time. The inspection must be reasonably required for the purposes of checking the taxpayer's tax position.

HMRC will usually agree a time for the inspection with the taxpayer. However, an authorised HMRC officer can carry out the inspection at 'any reasonable time' if either:

(a)   The taxpayer receives at least seven days' written notice, or
(b)   The inspection is carried out by, or with the approval of, an authorised HMRC officer.

There is no right of appeal against an inspection notice.

6 Penalties

6.1 Penalties for errors

FAST FORWARD

> There is a common penalty regime for errors in tax returns, including income tax, NICs, corporation tax and VAT. Penalties range from 30% to 100% of the Potential Lost Revenue. Penalties may be reduced.

A common penalty regime for errors in tax returns for income tax, national insurance contributions, corporation tax and value added tax.

A penalty may be imposed where **a taxpayer makes an inaccurate return** if he has:

* been **careless** because he has not taken reasonable care in making the return or discovers the error later but does not take reasonable steps to inform HMRC; or

* made a **deliberate error** but **does not make arrangements to conceal it**; or

* made a **deliberate error** and **has attempted to conceal it** eg by submitting false evidence in support of an inaccurate figure.

Note that **an error which is made where the taxpayer has taken reasonable care** in making the return and which he **does not discover later, does not result in a penalty**.

In order for a penalty to be charged, the **inaccurate return must result in**:

* **an understatement of the taxpayer's tax liability**; or
* **a false or increased loss for the taxpayer**; or
* **a false or increased repayment of tax to the taxpayer**.

If a return contains more than one error, a penalty can be charged for each error.

The rules also extend to **errors in claims for allowances and reliefs** and in **accounts submitted in relation to a tax liability**.

Penalties for error also apply where **HMRC has issued an assessment estimating a person's liability** where:

* **a return has been issued to that person and has not been returned**, or
* the taxpayer was **required to deliver a return to HMRC but has not delivered it**.

The taxpayer will be charged a penalty where

* the **assessment understates the taxpayer's liability** to income tax, capital gains tax, corporation tax or VAT, and

* **the taxpayer fails to take reasonable steps within 30 days of the date of the assessment** to tell HMRC that there is an under-assessment.

The amount of **the penalty for error is based on the Potential Lost Revenue (PLR)** to HMRC as a result of the error. For example, if there is an understatement of tax, this understatement will be the PLR.

The maximum amount of the penalty for error depends on the type of error:

Type of error	Maximum penalty payable
Careless	30% of PLR
Deliberate not concealed	70% of PLR
Deliberate and concealed	100% of PLR

Question **Penalty for error**

Alex is a sole trader. He files his tax return for 2011/12 on 10 January 2013. The return shows his trading income to be £60,000. In fact, due to carelessness, his trading income should have been stated to be £68,000. State the maximum penalty that could be charged by HMRC on Alex for his error.

Answer

The Potential Lost Revenue as a result of Alex's error is:

£(68,000 – 60,000) = £8,000 x [40% (income tax) + 2% (NICs)]   £3,360

Alex's error is careless so the maximum penalty for error is:

£3,360 x 30%   £1,008

A **penalty for error may be reduced if the taxpayer tells HMRC about the error – this is called a disclosure**. The reduction depends on the **circumstances of** the disclosure and the **help that the taxpayer gives to HMRC in relation to the disclosure**.

An **unprompted disclosure is one made at a time when the taxpayer has no reason to believe HMRC has discovered, or is about to discover, the error**. Otherwise, the disclosure will be a **prompted disclosure**. The **minimum penalties** that can be imposed are as follows:

Type of error	Unprompted	Prompted
Careless	0% of PLR	15% of PLR
Deliberate not concealed	20% of PLR	35% of PLR
Deliberate and concealed	30% of PLR	50% of PLR

Question **Reduction of penalty**

Sue is a sole trader. She files her tax return for 2010/11 on 31 January 2012. The return shows a loss for the year of £(80,000). In fact, Sue has deliberately increased this loss by £(12,000) and has submitted false figures in support of her claim. HMRC initiate a review into Sue's return and in reply Sue then makes a disclosure of the error. Sue is a higher rate taxpayer due to her substantial investment income and she has made a claim to set the loss against general income in 2010/11.

State the maximum and minimum penalties that could be charged by HMRC on Sue for her error.

The potential lost revenue as a result of Sue's error is:

£12,000 x 40%   £4,800

Sue's error is deliberate and concealed so the maximum penalty for error is:

£4,800 x 100%   £4,800

Sue has made a prompted disclosure so the minimum penalty for error is:

£4,800 x 50%   £2,400

The help that the taxpayer gives to HMRC relates to when, how and to what extent the taxpayer:

- **tells HMRC about the error,** making full disclosure and explaining how the error was made;
- **gives reasonable help** to HMRC to enable it **to quantify the error**; and
- **allows access to business and other records** and other relevant documents.

A taxpayer can appeal to the First Tier Tax Tribunal against:

- the **penalty being charged;**
- the **amount of the penalty**.

6.2 Penalties for late notification of chargeability

FAST FORWARD

A common penalty regime also applies to late notification of chargeability.

A common penalty regime also applies to certain taxes for failures to notify chargeability to, or liability to register for, tax that result in a loss of tax. The taxes affected include income tax, NICs, PAYE, CGT, corporation tax and VAT. Penalties are behaviour related, increasing for more serious failures, and are based on the 'potential lost revenue'.

The minimum and maximum penalties as percentages of PLR are as follows:

Behaviour	Maximum penalty	Minimum penalty with unprompted disclosure		Minimum penalty with prompted disclosure	
Deliberate and concealed	100%	30%		50%	
Deliberate but not concealed	70%	20%		35%	
		>12m	<12m	>12m	<12m
Careless	30%	10%	0%	20%	10%

Note that there is no zero penalty for reasonable care (as there is for penalties for errors on returns – see above), although the penalty may be reduced to 0% if the failure is rectified within 12 months through unprompted disclosure. The penalties may also be reduced at HMRC's discretion in 'special circumstances'. However, inability to pay the penalty is not a 'special circumstance'.

The same penalties apply for failure to notify HMRC of a new taxable activity.

Where the taxpayer's failure is not classed as deliberate, there is no penalty if he can show he has a 'reasonable excuse'. Reasonable excuse does not include having insufficient money to pay the penalty. Taxpayers have a right of appeal against penalty decisions to the First Tier Tribunal.

6.3 Penalties for late filing of tax return

FAST FORWARD

A penalty can be charged for late filing of a tax return based on how late the return is and how much tax is payable.

An individual is liable to a penalty where a tax return is filed after the due filing date. The penalty date is the date on which the return will be overdue (ie the date after the due filing date).

The initial penalty for late filing of the return is £100.

If the failure continues after the end of the period of 3 months starting with the penalty date, HMRC may give the individual notice specifying that a daily penalty of £10 is payable for a maximum of 90 days. The daily penalty runs from a date specified in the notice which may be earlier than the date of the notice but cannot be earlier than the end of the 3 month period.

If the failure continues after the end of the period of 6 months starting with the penalty date, a further penalty is payable. This penalty is the greater of:

- **5% of the tax liability** which would have been shown in the return; and
- **£300.**

If the failure continues after the end of the period of 12 months starting with the penalty date, a further penalty is payable. This penalty is determined in accordance with the taxpayer's conduct in withholding information which would enable or assist HMRC in assessing the taxpayer's liability to tax. **The penalty is computed as follows:**

Type of conduct	Penalty
Deliberate and concealed	Greater of: • 100% of tax liability which would have been shown on return; and • £300
Deliberate not concealed	Greater of: • 70% of tax liability which would have been shown on return; and • £300
Any other case (eg careless)	Greater of: • 5% of tax liability which would have been shown on return; and • £300

6.4 Penalty for late payment of tax

This penalty was dealt with in Section 4.2 earlier in this Chapter.

6.5 Penalty for failure to keep records

The maximum penalty for each failure to keep and retain records is £3,000 per tax year/accounting period. This penalty can be reduced by HMRC.

7 Appeals

 FAST FORWARD

Disputes between taxpayers and HMRC can be dealt with by an HMRC internal review or by a Tribunal hearing.

7.1 Internal reviews

For direct taxes, appeals must first be made to HMRC, which will assign a 'caseworker'.

For indirect taxes, appeals must be sent directly to the Tax Tribunal, although the taxpayer can continue to correspond with his caseworker where, for example, there is new information.

At this stage the taxpayer may be offered, or may ask for, an **'internal review'**, which will be made by an objective HMRC review officer not previously connected with the case. This is a less costly and more effective way to resolve disputes informally, without the need for a Tribunal hearing. An appeal to the Tax Tribunal cannot be made until any review has ended.

The taxpayer must either accept the review offer, or notify an appeal to the Tax Tribunal within 30 days of being offered the review, otherwise the appeal will be treated as settled.

HMRC must usually carry out the review within 45 days, or any longer time as agreed with the taxpayer. The review officer may decide to uphold, vary or withdraw decisions.

After the review conclusion is notified, **the taxpayer has 30 days to appeal to the Tax Tribunal.**

7.2 Tribunal hearings

If there is no internal review, or the taxpayer is unhappy with the result of an internal review, the case may be heard by the Tax Tribunal. The person wishing to make an appeal (the appellant) must send a notice of appeal to the Tax Tribunal. The Tax Tribunal must then give notice of the appeal to the respondent (normally HMRC).

The Tax Tribunal is made up of two 'tiers':

(a) A First Tier Tribunal and
(b) An Upper Tribunal.

The case will be allocated to one of four case **'tracks':**

(a) **Complex cases**, which the Tribunal considers will require lengthy or complex evidence or a lengthy hearing, or involve a complex or important principle or issue, or involves a large amount of money. Such cases will usually be heard by the Upper Tribunal,

(b) **Standard cases, heard by the First Tier Tribunal**, which have detailed case management and are subject to a more formal procedure than basic cases,

(c) **Basic cases, also heard by the First Tier Tribunal**, which will usually be disposed of after a hearing, with minimal exchange of documents before the hearing, and

(d) **Paper cases, dealt with by the First Tier Tribunal**, which applies to straightforward matters such as fixed filing penalties and will usually be dealt with in writing, without a hearing.

A decision of the First Tier Tribunal may be appealed to the Upper Tribunal.

Decisions of the Upper Tribunal are binding on the Tribunals and any affected public authorities. A decision of the Upper Tribunal may be appealed to the Court of Appeal.

Chapter Roundup

- Individuals who do not receive a tax return must notify their chargeability to income tax or CGT.

- Tax returns must usually be filed by 31 October (paper) or 31 January (electronic) following the end of the tax year.

- If a paper return is filed the taxpayer can ask HMRC to compute the tax due. Electronic returns have tax calculated automatically.

- Two payments on account and a final balancing payment of income tax and Class 4 NICs are due. All capital gains tax is due on 31 January following the end of the tax year.

- A penalty is chargeable where tax is paid after the due date based on the amount of unpaid tax. Up to 15% of that amount is payable where the tax is more than 12 months late.

- HMRC carry out compliance checks on tax returns. Strict procedural rules govern these.

- HMRC have powers to request documents from taxpayers and third parties. HMRC also has powers to inspect business premises.

- There is a common penalty regime for errors in tax returns, including income tax, NICs, corporation tax and VAT. Penalties range from 30% to 100% of the Potential Lost Revenue. Penalties may be reduced.

- A common penalty regime also applies to late notification of chargeability.

- A penalty can be charged for late filing of a tax return based on how late the return is and how much tax is payable.

- Disputes between taxpayers and HMRC can be dealt with by an HMRC internal review or by a Tribunal hearing.

Quick Quiz

1   A taxpayer who has not received a tax return must give notice of his chargeability to capital gains tax due in 2011/12 by_____. Fill in the blank.

2   By when must a taxpayer normally file a paper tax return for 2011/12?

    A   31 October 2012
    B   31 December 2012
    C   31 January 2013
    D   5 April 2013

3   What are the normal payment dates for income tax?

4   What penalty is due in respect of income tax payments on account that are paid two months after the due date?

5   What is the maximum penalty for failure to keep records?

6   Which body hears tax appeals?

Answers to Quick Quiz

1. A taxpayer who has not received a tax return must give notice to his chargeability to capital gains tax due in 2011/12 by **5 October 2012**.

2. A. 31 October 2012.

3. Two payments on account of income tax are due on 31 January in the tax year and on 31 July following. A final balancing payment is due on 31 January following the tax year.

4. None. The penalty for late paid tax does not apply to late payment of payments on account.

5. £3,000

6. The Tax Tribunal which consists of the First Tier Tribunal and the Upper Tribunal.

Now try the question below from the Exam Question Bank

Number	Level	Marks	Time
Q26	Introductory	8	15 mins
Q27	Examination	25	45 mins

Inheritance tax

18

Inheritance tax: scope and transfers of value

Topic list	Syllabus reference
1 The scope of inheritance tax	E1
2 Computing transfers of value	E2
3 Calculation of tax on lifetime transfers	E3(a),(b)
4 Calculation of tax on death estate	E3(c)
5 Transfer of unused nil rate band	E3(d)
6 Exemptions	E4
7 Payment of inheritance tax	E5

Introduction

In this chapter we introduce Inheritance tax (IHT). IHT is primarily a tax on wealth left on death. It also applies to gifts within seven years of death and to certain lifetime transfers of wealth.

The tax is different from income tax and CGT, where the basic question is: how much has the taxpayer made? With IHT, the basic question is, how much has been given away? We tax the amount which the taxpayer has transferred - the amount by which he is worse off. If the taxpayer pays IHT on a lifetime gift, he is worse off by the amount of the gift plus the tax due, and we have to take that into account. Some transfers are, however, exempt from IHT.

We will see that the first £325,000 of transfers is taxed at 0% (the 'nil rate band'), and is therefore effectively tax-free. To stop people from avoiding IHT by, for example, giving away £1,625,000 in five lots of £325,000, we need to look back seven years every time a transfer is made to decide how much of the nil rate band is available to set against the current transfer.

Next, we will see how to bring together all of a deceased person's assets at death, and compute the tax on the estate. Finally, we look at the administration and payment of IHT.

In the next chapter we will start our study of corporation tax.

Study guide

		Intellectual level
E1	**The scope of inheritance tax**	
(a)	Describe the scope of inheritance tax:	2
(b)	Identify and explain the persons chargeable	2
E2	**The basic principles of computing transfers of value**	
(a)	State, explain and apply the meaning of transfers of value, chargeable transfer and potentially exempt transfer	2
(b)	Demonstrate the diminution in value principle	2
(c)	Demonstrate the seven year accumulation principle taking into account changes in the level of the nil rate band	2
E3	**The liabilities arising on chargeable lifetime transfers and on the death of an individual**	
(a)	Understand the tax implications of chargeable lifetime transfers and compute the relevant liabilities	2
(b)	Understand the tax implications of transfers within seven years of death and compute the relevant liabilities	2
(c)	Compute the tax liability on a death estate	2
(d)	Understand and apply the transfer of any unused nil rate band between spouses	2
E4	**The use of exemptions in deferring and minimising inheritance tax liabilities**	
(a)	Understand and apply the following exemptions:	2
(i)	small gifts exemption	
(ii)	annual exemption	
(iii)	normal expenditure out of income	
(iv)	gifts in consideration of marriage	
(v)	gifts between spouses	
E5	**Payment of inheritance tax**	
(a)	Identify who is responsible for the payment of inheritance tax	2
(b)	Advise on the due date for payment of inheritance tax	2

Exam guide

Inheritance tax (IHT) could be examined in either of questions four or five for a maximum of 15 marks. You will need to know when IHT is charged: transfers of value (basically gifts) and chargeable persons. The concepts of potentially exempt transfers (PETs), chargeable lifetime transfers (CLTs) and the seven year accumulation principle are all fundamental to an understanding of IHT. Once you have worked out the amount of a transfer of value, you need to be able to work out the IHT liability on it. This could be payable during the donor's lifetime and/or on death for a lifetime transfer and on death for a death estate. There are a number of exemptions which may be used to reduce IHT liability such as gifts between spouses/civil partners. Finally, you need to have an understanding of how IHT is paid and who pays it.

1 The scope of inheritance tax

IHT is a tax on gifts made by individuals to other individuals or trustees.

Inheritance tax is a tax on gifts or '**transfers of value**' made by **chargeable persons**. This generally involves a transaction as a result of which wealth is transferred by one individual to another, either directly or via a trust.

1.1 Chargeable persons

Individuals are chargeable persons for inheritance tax.

Spouses and civil partners are taxed separately under inheritance tax although there is an exemption for transfers between the couple (dealt with later in this Chapter).

1.2 The scope of the charge

The general principle is that all transfers of value of assets made by individuals, whether during lifetime or on death, are within the charge to IHT.

2 Computing transfers of value

IHT applies to lifetime transfers of value and transfers of value made on death.

2.1 Introduction

There are **two main chargeable occasions** for inheritance tax:

(a) transfers of value made in the lifetime of the donor (**lifetime transfers**), and
(b) transfers of value made on death, for example when property is left in a Will (**death estate**).

An example of a transfer of value is a **gift by an individual** to **another individual.**

Another example of a transfers of value is a **gift by an individual** to **trustees. A trust is a legal structure where one person (the settlor) gives property to one or more people (the trustees) to be held for the benefit of one or more people (the beneficiaries).**

2.2 Transfers of value

2.2.1 What is a transfer of value?

IHT cannot arise unless there is a transfer of value.

A transfer of value is any gratuitous disposition (eg a gift) made by a person which results in his being worse off, that is, he suffers a diminution (ie reduction) in the value of his estate. An individual's estate is basically all the assets which he owns.

Exam focus point

The examiner has stated that, as far as Paper F6 is concerned, the terms 'transfer' and 'gift' can be taken to mean the same thing and that a transfer of value will always be a gift of assets.

2.2.2 Gratuitous intent

Transfers where there is no gratuitous intent are not chargeable to IHT. An example would be selling a painting for £1,000 at auction which later turns out to be worth £100,000 or other poor business deals. The transfer must have been made at arm's length between unconnected persons if it is to be treated as one where there is no gratuitous intent.

2.2.3 Diminution in value

In many cases the diminution in value of the donor's estate will be the same as the increase in the value of the donee's estate, for example if there is a cash gift or the gift of a house. However, sometimes the two will not be the same. Typically this is the situation where unquoted shares are gifted.

The measure of the transfer for inheritance tax purposes is always the loss to the donor (the diminution in value of his estate), not the amount gained by the donee.

2.2.4 Example

Audrey holds 5,100 of the shares in an unquoted company which has an issued share capital of 10,000 shares. Currently Audrey's majority holding is valued at £15 per share.

Audrey wishes to give 200 shares to her son, Brian. However, the shares are worth only £2.50 each to Brian, since Brian will have only a small minority holding in the company. After the gift Audrey will hold 4,900 shares and these will be worth £10 each. The value per share to Audrey will fall from £15 to £10 per share since she will lose control of the company.

The diminution in value of Audrey 's estate is £27,500, as follows.

	£
Before the gift: 5,100 shares × £15	76,500
After the gift: 4,900 shares × £10	(49,000)
Diminution in value	27,500

Brian has only been given shares with a market value of 200 × £2.50 = £500. Remember, a gift is also a deemed disposal at market value for CGT purposes and it is this value that will be used in any CGT computation. IHT, however, uses the principle of diminution in value which can, as in this case, give a much greater value than the value of the asset transferred.

2.3 Chargeable transfers and potentially exempt transfers

Inheritance tax is chargeable on a **chargeable transfer**. This is any transfer of value which is not an exempt transfer (see later in this Text).

Key terms

> A potentially exempt transfer (**PET**) is a **lifetime transfer (**other than an exempt transfer**) made by an individual to another individual**. Any other lifetime transfer by an individual (eg a gift to trustees) which is not an exempt transfer is a chargeable lifetime transfer (CLT).

A **potentially exempt transfer (PET)** is exempt from IHT when made and will remain exempt if the donor survives for at least seven years from making the gift. If the donor dies within seven years of making the PET, the transfer will become chargeable to IHT.

A **chargeable lifetime transfer (CLT)** is immediately chargeable to IHT when made.

On death, an individual is treated as if he had made a transfer of value of the property comprised in his estate immediately before death. This is a **chargeable transfer** to the extent that it is not covered by an exemption.

3 Calculation of tax on lifetime transfers

> This section relates to your PER requirement:
> 19   Evaluate and compute taxes payable

 The tax on a chargeable transfer is calculated with reference to chargeable transfers in the previous seven years.

There are two aspects of the calculation of tax on lifetime transfers:

(a) lifetime tax on CLTs, and

(b) additional death tax on CLTs and death tax on PETs, in both cases where the donor dies within seven years of making the transfer.

You should always calculate the lifetime tax on any CLTs first, then move on to calculate the death tax on all CLTs and PETs made within seven years of death.

3.1 Lifetime tax

IHT is charged on what a donor loses. If the donor pays the IHT on a lifetime gift he loses both the asset given away and the money with which he paid the tax due on it. Grossing up is required.

3.1.1 Donee pays tax

Lifetime inheritance tax on lifetime transfers is chargeable at two rates of tax: a 0% rate (the 'nil rate') and 20%. The nil rate is chargeable where accumulated transfers do not exceed the nil rate band limit. The excess is chargeable at 20%.

When a CLT is made and the donee (ie the trustees) pays the lifetime tax, follow these steps to work out the lifetime IHT on it:

Step 1 Look back seven years from the date of the transfer to see if any other CLTs have been made. If so, these transfers use up the nil rate band available for the current transfer. This is called **seven year accumulation**. Work out the value of any nil rate band still available.

Step 2 Compute the gross value of the CLT. You may be given this in the question or you may have to work out the diminution of value or deduct exemptions (such as the annual exemption described later in this Chapter).

Step 3 Any part of the CLT covered by the nil rate band is taxed at 0%. Any part of the CLT not covered by the nil rate band is charged at 20%.

The nil band and the lifetime rate will be given in the rates and allowances section of the exam paper. Where nil rate bands are required for previous years, these will be given in the question.

Question   Donee pays the lifetime tax

Eric makes a gift of £330,000 to a trust on 10 July 2011. There are no exemptions available (we will deal with exemptions later in this Text). The trustees agree to pay the tax due.

Calculate the lifetime tax payable by the trustees if Eric has made:

(a) a lifetime chargeable transfer of value of £100,000 in August 2003

(b) a lifetime chargeable transfer of value of £100,000 in August 2004

(c) a lifetime chargeable transfer of value of £350,000 in August 2004.

Answer

(a) **Step 1** No lifetime transfers in seven years before 10 July 2011 (transfers after 10 July 2004). Nil rate band of £325,000 available.

Step 2 Value of CLT is £330,000

Step 3

	IHT £
£325,000 × 0%	0
£5,000 × 20%	1,000
£330,000	1,000

(b) **Step 1** Lifetime transfer of value of £100,000 in seven years before 10 July 2011 (transfers after 10 July 2004). Nil rate band of £(325,000 – 100,000) = £225,000 available.

Step 2 Value of CLT is £330,000.

Step 3

	IHT £
£225,000 × 0%	0
£105,000 × 20%	21,000
£330,000	21,000

(c) **Step 1** Lifetime transfer of value of £350,000 in seven years before 10 July 2011 (transfers after 10 July 2004). No nil rate band available as all covered by previous transfer.

Step 2 Value of CLT is £330,000.

Step 3

	IHT £
£330,000 @ 20%	66,000

3.1.2 Donor pays tax

Where IHT is payable on a CLT, the **primary liability to pay tax is on the donor,** although the donor may agree with the donee (as in the above example) that the donee is to pay the tax instead.

If the donor pays the lifetime IHT due on a CLT, the total reduction in value of his estate is the transfer of value plus the IHT due on it. The transfer is therefore a net transfer and must be grossed up in order to find the gross value of the transfer. **We do this by working out the tax as follows.**

Formula to learn

> Chargeable amount (ie not covered by nil band) × $\dfrac{20\,(\text{rate of tax})}{80\,(100\,\text{minus the rate of tax})}$

When a CLT is made and the donor pays the lifetime tax, follow these steps to work out the lifetime IHT on it:

Step 1 Look back seven years from the date of the transfer to see if any other CLTs have been made. If so, these transfers use up the nil rate band available for the current transfer. Work out the value of any nil rate band still available.

Step 2 Compute the net value of the CLT. You may be given this in the question or may have to work out the diminution of value or deduct exemptions (such as the annual exemption discussed later in this Chapter).

Step 3 Any part of the CLT covered by the nil rate band is taxed at 0%. Any part of the CLT not covered by the nil rate band is taxed at 20/80.

Step 4 Work out the gross transfer by adding the net transfer and the tax together. You can check your figure by working out the tax on the gross transfer.

Question

James makes a gift of £330,000 to a trust on 10 July 2011. No exemptions are available. James will pay the tax due.

Calculate the lifetime tax payable, if James has made:

(a) a lifetime chargeable transfer of value of £100,000 in August 2003
(b) a lifetime chargeable transfer of value of £100,000 in August 2004
(c) a lifetime chargeable transfer of value of £350,000 in August 2004.

Answer

(a) **Step 1** No lifetime transfers in seven years before 10 July 2011 (transfers after 10 July 2004). Nil rate band of £325,000 available.

Step 2 Net value of CLT is £330,000

Step 3

	IHT £
£325,000 × 0%	0
£5,000 × 20/80	1,250
£330,000	1,250

Step 4 Gross transfer is £(330,000 + 1,250) = £331,250.

Check: Tax on the gross transfer would be:

	IHT £
£325,000 × 0%	0
£6,250 × 20%	1,250
£331,250	1,250

(b) **Step 1** Lifetime transfer of value of £100,000 in seven years before 10 July 2011 (transfers after 10 July 2004). Nil rate band of £(325,000 − 100,000) = £225,000 available.

Step 2 Net value of CLT is £330,000.

Step 3

	IHT £
£225,000 × 0%	0
£105,000 × 20/80	26,250
£330,000	26,250

Step 4 Gross transfer is £(330,000 + 26,250) = £356,250.

Check: Tax on the gross transfer would be:

	IHT £
£225,000 × 0%	0
£131,250 × 20%	26,250
£356,250	26,250

(c) **Step 1** Lifetime transfer of value of £350,000 in seven years before 10 July 2011 (transfers after 10 July 2004). No nil rate band available as all covered by previous transfer.

Step 2 Net value of CLT is £330,000.

Step 3

	IHT £
£330,000 × 20/80	82,500

Step 4 Gross transfer is £(330,000 + 82,500) = £412,500.

Check: Tax on the gross transfer would be:

	IHT £
£412,500 × 20%	82,500

3.2 Death tax on chargeable lifetime transfers

Death tax is chargeable on chargeable lifetime transfers if the donor dies within seven years of making the transfer. Taper relief reduces the death tax if the donor survives between three and seven years.

Death inheritance tax on lifetime transfers is chargeable if the donor dies within seven years of making the lifetime transfer. It is chargeable at two rates: 0% and 40%. The nil rate is chargeable where accumulated transfers do not exceed the nil rate band limit at the date of death. The excess is chargeable at 40%.

The longer the donor survives after making a gift, the lower the death tax. This is because taper relief applies to lower the amount of death tax payable as follows:

Years before death	% reduction
Over 3 but less than 4 years	20
Over 4 but less than 5 years	40
Over 5 but less than 6 years	60
Over 6 but less than 7 years	80

Exam focus point

> The taper relief table will be given in the tax rates and allowances section of the examination paper.

Death tax on a lifetime transfer is **always** payable by the donee, so grossing up is not relevant.

Follow these steps to work out the death tax on a CLT:

Step 1 Look back seven years from the **date of the transfer** to see if any other chargeable transfers were made. If so, these transfers use up the nil rate band available for the current transfer. Work out the value of any nil rate band remaining.

Step 2 Compute the value of the CLT. This is the gross value of the transfer that you worked out for computing lifetime tax.

Step 3 Any part of the CLT covered by the nil rate band is taxed at 0%. Any part of the CLT not covered by the nil rate band is charged at 40%.

Step 4 Reduce the death tax by taper relief (if applicable).

Step 5 Deduct any lifetime tax paid. The death tax may be reduced to nil, but there is **no repayment of lifetime tax.**

Question | Lifetime tax and death tax on CLTs

Trevor makes a gross chargeable transfer of value of £195,000 in December 2001. He then makes a gift to a trust of shares worth £200,000 on 15 November 2007. The trustees pay the lifetime tax due. There are no exemptions available. The nil rate band in 2007/2008 was £300,000.

Trevor dies in February 2012. The shares held by the trustees were then worth £500,000.

Compute:

(a)   the lifetime tax payable by the trustees on the lifetime transfer in November 2007, and

(b)   the death tax (if any) payable on the lifetime transfer in November 2007.

Answer

Lifetime tax

Step 1   Lifetime transfer of value of £195,000 in seven years before 15 November 2007 (transfers after 15 November 2000). Nil rate band of £(300,000 − 195,000) = £105,000 available.

Step 2   Value of CLT is £200,000.

Step 3

	IHT
	£
£105,000 × 0%	0
£ 95,000 × 20%	19,000
£200,000	19,000

Death tax

Step 1   Lifetime transfer of value of £195,000 in seven years before 15 November 2007 (transfers after 15 November 2000). Nil rate band of £(325,000 − 195,000) = £130,000 available.

Step 2   Value of CLT is £200,000. Note that the value of the transfer does not change even though the shares are worth £500,000 at the date of the donor's death.

Step 3

	IHT
	£
£ 130,000 × 0%	0
£ 70,000 × 40%	28,000
£200,000	28,000

Step 4   Transfer over 4 but less than 5 years before death

	£
Death tax	28,000
Less: taper relief @ 40%	(11,200)
Death tax left in charge	16,800

Step 5   Tax due £(16,800 − 19,000) (no repayment of lifetime tax) | 0

3.3 Death tax on potentially exempt transfers

Death tax is chargeable on a potentially exempt transfers if the donor dies within seven years of making the transfer. Taper relief reduces the death tax if the donor survives between three and seven years. Grossing up is never required on PET because the death tax is payable by the donee.

If the donor dies within seven years of making a PET it will become chargeable to death tax in the same way as a CLT. There will be no lifetime tax paid, so Step 5 above will not apply.

We will now work through an example where there is both a PET and a CLT.

Exam focus point

Calculate lifetime tax on CLTs first. Then move on to death tax, working through all CLTs and PETs in chronological order. Remember: on death, PETs become chargeable so must be taken into account when calculating the death tax on later CLTs.

Question
Lifetime tax and death tax on CLTs and PETs

Louise gave £340,000 to her son on 1 February 2008. There were no exemptions available. This was the first transfer that Louise had made.

On 10 October 2011, Louise gave £370,000 to a trust. The trustees paid the lifetime IHT due. There were no exemptions available.

On 11 January 2012, Louise died.

Compute:

(a) the lifetime tax payable by the trustees on the lifetime transfer made in 2011,
(b) the death tax payable on the lifetime transfer made in 2008, and
(c) the death tax payable on the lifetime transfer made in 2011.

Answer

(a) Lifetime tax – 2011 CLT

Step 1 There are no chargeable lifetime transfers in the seven years before 10 October 2011 because the 2008 transfer is a PET and therefore exempt during Louise's lifetime. Nil rate band of £325,000 available.

Step 2 Value of CLT £370,000

Step 3

	IHT £
£325,000 × 0%	0
£ 45,000 × 20%	9,000
£370,000	9,000

(b) Death tax – 2008 PET becomes chargeable

Step 1 No lifetime transfers of value in seven years before 1 February 2008 (transfers after 1 February 2001). Nil rate band of £325,000 available.

Step 2 Value of PET £340,000

Step 3

	IHT £
£325,000 × 0%	0
£ 15,000 × 40%	6,000
£340,000	6,000

Step 4   Transfer over 3 but less than 4 years before death

	£
Death tax	6,000
Less: taper relief @ 20%	(1,200)
Death tax due	4,800

(c)   Death tax – 2011 CLT additional tax

Step 1   Lifetime transfer of value of £340,000 in seven years before 10 October 2011 (transfers after 10 October 2004). Note that as the PET becomes chargeable on death, its value is now included in calculating the death tax on the CLT. No nil rate band available.

Step 2   Value of CLT is £370,000 as before

Step 3

	IHT
	£
£370,000 @ 40%	148,000

Step 4   Transfer within 3 years before death so no taper relief.

Step 5   Tax due £(148,000 – 9,000)   139,000

3.4 Advantages of making lifetime transfers

There are a number of inheritance tax advantages of making lifetime transfers:

(a)   **If the donor makes a potentially exempt transfer and survives 7 years, he has reduced his estate for IHT but the transfer is exempt.** No inheritance tax is payable on the transfer and it does not form part of the seven year cumulation for later transfers.

(b)   **If the donor makes a chargeable lifetime transfer and survives 7 years, he has reduced his estate for IHT and the only inheritance tax payable is that on the lifetime transfer at lifetime rates.** However, note that the chargeable lifetime transfer remains in cumulation and affects the calculation of tax on transfers made in the seven years after it.

(c)   If the donor does not survive 7 years, IHT is payable on lifetime transfers at death rates at the date of death but **taper relief reduces the death tax if the donor survives between 3 and 7 years**.

(d)   **The values of lifetime transfers cannot exceed the transfer of value when made.** Therefore, **it is good tax planning to give away assets which are likely to increase in value such as land and shares.**

However, there is one situation where **it may not be advantageous for the donor to make a lifetime transfer** in terms of overall tax liability. This is where a **gift of an asset would result in a large chargeable gain (either immediately chargeable or deferred under gift relief)**. In this case, it may be better for the donor to retain the asset until death as there is a tax-free uplift in value on death for capital gains tax purposes so that the donee will receive the asset at market value at the date of the donor's death. This is particularly relevant if the donor is unlikely to survive 3 years from the date of a lifetime gift and so death rates without the benefit of taper relief would apply to a lifetime transfer.

4 Calculation of tax on death estate

When someone dies, we must bring together all their assets to find the value of their death estate and then charge inheritance tax on it to the extent that it is not exempt, taking account of transfers made in the seven years before death.

4.1 Death estate

4.1.1 What is in the death estate?

An individual's death estate consists of all the property he owned immediately before death (such as land and buildings, shares and other investments, cars and cash) **less debts and funeral expenses.**

The death estate also includes anything received as a result of death, for example the proceeds of a life assurance policy which pays out on the individual's death. The value of the policy immediately before the death is not relevant.

Exam focus point

> The specific rules for valuation of assets are not in the syllabus. Values will be provided in the question where relevant.

4.1.2 Debts and funeral expenses

The rules on debts are as follows.

(a) **Only debts incurred by the deceased in good faith and for full consideration may be deducted.** For example, gaming debts are not deductible.

(b) **Debts incurred by the deceased but payable after the death may be deducted** but the amount should be discounted because of the future date of payment.

(c) **Rent and similar amounts which accrue day by day should be accrued up to the date of death.**

(d) **Taxes to the date of death are deductible** as they are a liability imposed by law.

(e) **If a debt is charged on a specific property it is deductible primarily from that property.** For example, a mortgage secured on a house is deductible from the value of that house.

This does not include endowment mortgages as these are repaid upon death by the life assurance element of the mortgage.

Repayment mortgages and interest-only mortgages are deductible (although there may be separate life assurance policies which become payable at death and which will effectively cancel out the mortgage).

Reasonable funeral expenses may also be deducted:

(a) What is reasonable depends on the deceased's condition in life.
(b) Reasonable costs of mourning for the family are allowed.
(c) **The cost of a tombstone is deductible.**

Question

The death estate

Zack died on 19 June 2011. His estate consisted of the following.

10,000 shares in A plc valued at £8,525

8,000 shares in B plc valued at £9,280

Freehold property valued at £150,000 subject to a repayment mortgage of £45,000

His debts were as follows:

Electricity bill £150

Income tax due £300

Funeral expenses (all reasonable) incurred, including a tombstone, amounted to £2,000

Calculate Zack's death estate for IHT purposes.

	£	£
A plc shares		8,525
B plc shares		9,280
Freehold property	150,000	
Less mortgage	(45,000)	
		105,000
Gross estate		122,805
Less debts and funeral expenses		
electricity bill	150	
income tax	300	
funeral expenses	2,000	
		(2,450)
Death estate		120,355

4.2 Computing death tax on the death estate

Inheritance tax on the death estate is chargeable at two rates: 0% and 40%. The nil rate is chargeable where accumulated transfers do not exceed the nil rate band limit. The excess is chargeable at 40%.

In order to calculate the tax on the death estate, use the following steps:

Step 1 Look back seven years from the date of death to see if any CLTs or PETs which have become chargeable have been made. If so, these transfers use up the nil rate band available for the death estate. Work out the value of any nil rate band still available.

Step 2 Compute the value of the death estate.

Step 3 Any part of the death estate covered by the nil rate band is taxed at 0%. Any part of the death estate not covered by the nil rate band is charged at 40%.

Question

Tax on death estate

Laura dies on 1 August 2011, leaving a death estate valued at £400,000. No exemptions were available. Laura had made a gift of £165,000 to her sister on 11 September 2010. No exemptions were available.

Compute the tax payable on Laura's death estate.

Answer

Death tax

Note. There is no death tax on the September 2010 PET which becomes chargeable as a result of Laura's death, as it is within the nil rate band at her death. However, it will use up part of the nil rate band, as shown below.

Step 1 Lifetime transfer of value of £165,000 in seven years before 1 August 2011 (transfers after 1 August 2004). Nil rate band of £(325,000 – 165,000) = £160,000 available.

Step 2 Value of death estate is £400,000.

Step 3

	IHT £
£160,000 × 0%	0
£240,000 × 40%	96,000
£400,000	96,000

5 Transfer of unused nil rate band

If one spouse or civil partner does not use up the whole nil rate band on death, the excess may be transferred to the surviving spouse/civil partner.

5.1 How the transfer of unused nil rate band works

If:

- **an individual ("A") dies; and**
- **A had a spouse or civil partner ("B") who died before A; and**
- **A and B were married or in a civil partnership immediately before B's death; and**
- **B had unused nil rate band (wholly or in part) on death;**

then **a claim may be made to increase the nil rate band maximum at the date of A's death by B's unused nil-rate band in order to calculate the IHT on A's death.**

The revised nil rate band will apply to the calculation of additional death tax on CLTs made by A, PETs made by A and death tax on A's death estate.

5.2 Example

Robert and Claudia were married for many years until the death of Robert on 10 April 2011. In his will, Robert left his death estate valued at £100,000 to his sister. He had made no lifetime transfers.

Claudia died on 12 January 2012 leaving a death estate worth £850,000 to her brother. Claudia had made a chargeable lifetime transfer of £50,000 in 2009.

The inheritance tax payable on the death of Claudia, assuming that a claim is made to transfer Robert's unused nil rate band, is calculated as follows:

Step 1   (a)   Lifetime transfer of value of £50,000 in seven years before 12 January 2012 (transfers after 12 January 2005).

(b)   Nil rate band at Claudia's death is £325,000. Nil rate band is increased by claim to transfer Robert's unused nil rate band at death £(325,000 − 100,000) = £225,000. The maximum nil rate band at Claudia's death is therefore £(325,000 + 225,000) = £550,000 and the available nil rate band for working out the tax on her estate is £(550,000 − 50,000) = £500,000.

Step 2   Value of Claudia's death estate is £850,000.

Step 3

	IHT
	£
£500,000 x 0%	0
£350,000 x 40%	140,000
£850,000	140,000

5.3 Changes in nil rate band between deaths of spouses/civil partners

If the nil rate band increases between the death of B and the death of A, the amount of B's unused nil rate band must be scaled up so that it represents the same proportion of the nil rate band at A's death as it did at B's death.

For example, if the nil rate band at B's death was £300,000 and B had an unused nil rate band of £90,000, the unused proportion in percentage terms is therefore 90,000/300,000 × 100 = 30%. If A dies when the nil rate band has increased to £325,000, B's unused nil rate band is £325,000 × 30% = £97,500 and this amount is transferred to increase the nil rate band maximum available on A's death.

The increase in the nil rate band maximum cannot exceed the nil rate band maximum at the date of A's death eg if the nil rate band is £325,000, the increase cannot exceed £325,000, giving a total of £650,000.

Jenna and Rebecca were civil partners until the death of Jenna on 19 August 2007.

Jenna made no lifetime transfers. Her death estate was £240,000 and she left it to her mother. The nil rate band at Jenna's death was £300,000.

Rebecca died on 24 February 2012. Her death estate was £550,000 and she left her entire estate to her brother. She had made no lifetime transfers.

Calculate the inheritance tax payable on the death of Rebecca, assuming that any beneficial claims are made.

Answer

Step 1   (a)   No lifetime transfers of value in seven years before 24 February 2012.

           (b)   Nil rate band at Rebecca's death is £325,000. Nil rate band is increased by claim to transfer Jenna's unused nil rate band at death. Unused proportion was £(300,000 – 240,000) = 60,000/300,000 × 100 = 20%. The adjusted unused proportion is therefore £325,000 x 20% = £65,000. The maximum nil rate band at Rebecca's death is therefore £(325,000 + 65,000) = £390,000 and this is also the available nil rate band for her estate.

Step 2   Value of Rebecca's death estate is £550,000.

Step 3

	IHT
	£
£390,000 x 0%	0
£160,000 x 40%	64,000
£550,000	64,000

5.4 Claim to transfer unused nil rate band

The claim to transfer the unused nil rate band is usually made by the personal representatives of A. The time limit for the claim is two years from the end of the month of A's death (or the period of three months after the personal representatives start to act, if later) or such longer period as an officer of HMRC may allow in a particular case.

If the personal representatives do not make a claim, a claim can be made by any other person liable to tax chargeable on A's death within such later period as an officer of HMRC may allow in a particular case.

6 Exemptions

Exemptions may apply to make transfers or parts of transfers non chargeable. Some exemptions only apply on lifetime transfers (annual, normal expenditure out of income, marriage/civil partnership), but the spouse/civil partner exemption applies on both life and death transfers.

This section relates to your PER requirement:
20   Assist with tax planning

6.1 Introduction

There are various exemptions available to eliminate or reduce the chargeable amount of a lifetime transfer or property passing on an individual's death.

The lifetime exemptions apply to PETs as well as to CLTs. Only the balance of such gifts after the lifetime exemptions have been taken into account is then potentially exempt.

6.2 Exemptions applying to lifetime transfers only

6.2.1 The small gifts exemptions

Outright gifts to individuals totalling £250 or less per donee in any one tax year are exempt. If gifts total more than £250 the whole amount is chargeable. A donor can give up to £250 each year to each of as many donees as he wishes. The small gifts exemption cannot apply to gifts into trusts.

6.2.2 The annual exemption (AE)

The first £3,000 of value transferred in a tax year is exempt from IHT. The annual exemption is used only after all other exemptions (such as for transfers to spouses/civil partners (see below)). If several gifts are made in a year, the £3,000 exemption is applied to earlier gifts before later gifts. The annual exemption is used up by PETs as well as CLTs, even though the PETs might never become chargeable.

Exam focus point

> Where CLTs and PETS made in the same year the CLTs should be made first to use any available annual exemptions. If used up against the PETs the exemption(s) will be wasted if the PET never becomes chargeable.

Any unused portion of the annual exemption is carried forward for one year only. Only use it the following year *after* that year's own annual exemption has been used.

Question

Annual exemptions

Frank has no unused annual exemption brought forward at 6 April 2010.

On 1 August 2010 he makes a transfer of £600 to his son Peter.
On 1 September 2010 he makes a transfer of £2,000 to his nephew Quentin.
On 1 July 2011 he makes a transfer of £3,300 to a trust for his grandchildren.
On 1 June 2012 he makes a transfer of £5,000 to his friend Rowan.

Show the application of the annual exemptions.

Answer

	£
2010/11	
1.8.10 Gift to Peter	600
Less AE 2010/11	(600)
	0

	£
1.9.10 Gift to Quentin	2,000
Less AE 2010/11	(2,000)
	0

The unused annual exemption carried forward is £3,000 – £600 – £2,000 = £400.

2011/12	£	£
1.7.11 Gift to trust		3,300
Less: AE 2011/12	3,000	
AE 2010/11 b/f	300	
		(3,300)
		0

The unused annual exemption carried forward is zero because the 2011/12 exemption must be used before the 2010/11 exemption brought forward. The balance of £100 of the 2010/11 exemption is lost, because it cannot be carried forward for more than one year.

2012/13	£
1.6.12 Gift to Rowan	5,000
Less AE 2012/13	(3,000)
	2,000

6.2.3 Normal expenditure out of income

Inheritance tax is a tax on transfers of capital, not income. A transfer of value is exempt if:

(a)   It is made as part of the normal expenditure of the donor
(b)   Taking one year with another, it was made out of income, and
(c)   It leaves the donor with sufficient income to maintain his usual standard of living.

As well as covering such things as regular presents **this exemption can cover regular payments out of income such as a grandchild's school fees or the payment of life assurance premiums on a policy for someone else.**

6.2.4 Gifts in consideration of marriage/civil partnership

Gifts in consideration of marriage/civil partnership are exempt up to:

(a)   **£5,000 if from a parent of a party to the marriage/civil partnership**
(b)   **£2,500 if from a remoter ancestor or from one of the parties to the marriage/civil partnership**
(c)   **£1,000 if from any other person.**

The limits apply to gifts from any one donor for any one marriage/civil partnership. The exemption is available only if the marriage/civil partnership actually takes place.

6.3 Exemption applying to both lifetime transfers and transfers on death

6.3.1 Transfers between spouses/civil partners

Any transfers of value between spouses/civil partners are exempt. The exemption covers lifetime gifts between them and property passing under a will or on intestacy.

Question	Exemptions

Dale made a gift of £153,000 to her son on 17 October 2007 on the son's marriage. Dale gave £100,000 to her spouse on 1 January 2011. Dale gave £70,000 to her daughter on 11 May 2011. The only other gifts Dale made were birthday and Christmas presents of £100 each to her grandchildren.

Show what exemptions are available in respect of these transfers.

17 October 2007

	£
Gift to Dale's son	153,000
Less: ME	(5,000)
AE 2007/08	(3,000)
AE 2006/07 b/f	(3,000)
PET	142,000

1 January 2011

	£
Gift to Dale's spouse	100,000
Less spouse exemption	(100,000)
	0

11 May 2011

	£
Gift to Dale's daughter	70,000
Less: AE 2011/12	(3,000)
AE 2010/11 b/f	(3,000)
PET	64,000

The gifts to the grandchildren are covered by the small gifts exemption.

7 Payment of IHT

7.1 Liability for IHT

FAST FORWARD

> The liability to pay IHT depends on the type of transfer and whether it was made in lifetime or on death.

The donor is primarily liable for the tax due on chargeable lifetime transfers. However the donee (ie the trustees) may agree to pay the tax out of the trust assets.

On death, liability for payment is as follows.

(a) **Tax on the death estate is paid by the deceased's personal representatives (PRs)** out of estate assets.

(b) **Tax on a PET that has become chargeable is paid by donee.**

(c) **Additional liabilities on a CLT is paid by the donee.**

7.2 Due dates

(a) **For chargeable lifetime transfers the due date is the later of:**

(i) **30 April just after the end of the tax year of the transfer.**

(ii) **Six months after the end of the month of the transfer.**

(b) **Tax arising on the death estate: the due date is six months from the end of the month of death.** However, if the personal representatives **submit an account of the death estate** within the six month period, they must **pay the IHT due on the death estate on the submission of the account.**

(c) **Tax arising on death in respect of PETs and CLTs: the due date for additional tax is six months from the end of the month of death.**

Question

Lisa gave some shares to a trust on 10 July 2007. She gave a house to her daughter on 12 December 2009. Lisa died on 17 May 2011 leaving her death estate to her son.

For each of these transfers of value, state who is liable to pay any inheritance tax due and the due date for payment.

Answer

10 July 2007

Chargeable lifetime transfer.

Lifetime tax payable by Lisa (unless trustees agree to pay tax), due later of 30 April 2008 and 31 January 2008 ie 30 April 2008

Death tax payable by trustees, due 30 November 2011.

12 December 2009

Death tax payable by daughter, due 30 November 2011

17 May 2011

Death tax payable by personal representatives out of death estate, due on earlier of submission of account and 30 November 2011.

Chapter Roundup

- IHT is a tax on gifts made by individuals to other individuals or trustees.

- IHT applies to lifetime transfers of value and transfers of value made on death.

- The tax on a chargeable transfer is calculated with reference to chargeable transfers in the previous seven years.

- IHT is charged on what a donor loses. If the donor pays the IHT on a lifetime gift he loses both the asset given away and the money with which he paid the tax due on it. Grossing up is required.

- Death tax is chargeable on chargeable lifetime transfers if the donor dies within seven years of making the transfer. Taper relief reduces the death tax if the donor survives between three and seven years.

- Death tax is chargeable on a potentially exempt transfers if the donor dies within seven years of making the transfer. Taper relief reduces the death tax if the donor survives between three and seven years. Grossing up is never required on a PET because the death tax is payable by the donee.

- When someone dies, we must bring together all their assets to find the value of their death estate and then charge inheritance tax on it to the extent that it is not exempt, taking account of transfers made in the seven years before death.

- If one spouse or civil partner does not use up the whole nil rate band on death, the excess may be transferred to the surviving spouse/civil partner.

- Exemptions may apply to make transfers or parts of transfers non chargeable. Some exemptions only apply on lifetime transfers (annual, normal expenditure out of income, marriage/civil partnership), but the spouse/civil partner exemption applies on both life and death transfers.

- The liability to pay IHT depends on the type of transfer and whether it was made in lifetime or on death.

Quick Quiz

1   What is a transfer of value?

2   What type of transfer by an individual is a potentially exempt transfers?

3   Why must some lifetime transfers be grossed up?

4   What is taper relief?

5   Greg dies leaving the following debts:

    (a)   Grocery bill
    (b)   HM Revenue and Customs – income tax to death
    (c)   Mortgage on house
    (d)   Gambling debt

    Which are deductible against his death estate and why?

6   Mark and Hilary had been married for many years. Mark died on 11 May 2011 leaving his estate to Hilary. He had made a chargeable lifetime transfer of £160,000 in July 2008. If Hilary dies in February 2012, what is the maximum nil rate band on her death?

7   To what extent may unused annual exemption be carried forward?

8   Don gives some money to his daughter on her marriage. What marriage exemption is applicable?

9   When is lifetime inheritance tax on a chargeable lifetime transfer due for payment?

1   A transfer of value is any gratuitous disposition by a person resulting in a diminution of the value of his estate.

2   A potentially exempt transfer is a lifetime transfer made by an individual to another individual.

3   Where the donor pays the lifetime tax due it must be grossed up to calculate the total reduction in value of the estate.

4   Taper relief reduces death tax where a transfer is made between three and seven years before death.

5   (a)   grocery bill – deductible as incurred for full consideration
    (b)   income tax to death – deductible as imposed by law
    (c)   mortgage – deductible, will be set against value of house primarily
    (d)   gambling debt – not allowable as executor be liable for misuse of estate assets if paid

6   Hilary's nil rate band is £325,000. Mark's unused nil rate band is £(325,000 – 160,000) = £165,000. The nil rate band maximum on Hilary's death is therefore £490,000.

7   An unused annual exemption can be carried forward one tax year.

8   The marriage exemption for a gift to the donor's child is £5,000.

9   The due date for lifetime tax on a chargeable lifetime transfer is the later of:

    (a)   30 April just after the end of the tax year of the transfer, and
    (b)   6 months after the end of the month of transfer

Now try the questions below from the Exam Question Bank

Number	Level	Marks	Time
Q28	Introductory	15	27 mins
Q29	Introductory	15	27 mins

Corporation tax

Computing taxable total profits

19

Topic list	Syllabus reference
1 The scope of corporation tax	C1(a)-(c)
2 Taxable total profits	C2(k)
3 Trading income	C2(a)-(c)
4 Property business income	C2(d)
5 Loan relationships (interest income)	C2(e)
6 Miscellaneous income	C2(k)
7 Gift aid donations	C2(f)
8 Long periods of account	C2(k)

Introduction

Now that we have completed our study of personal tax we turn our attention to corporation tax, ie the tax that a company must pay on its profits.

First we consider the scope of corporation tax and we see that a company must pay tax for an 'accounting period' which may be different from its period of account.

We then learn how to calculate taxable total profits. This involves first calculating total profits by adding together income from different sources, such as trading income, interest and property income, and capital gains, and then deducting trading and property losses and gift aid donations. You have learnt the general rules for calculating income in your earlier studies, but here we see where there are special rules for companies.

In the next chapter you will learn how to compute the corporation tax liability on taxable total profits.

Study guide

		Intellectual level
C1	**The scope of corporation tax**	
(a)	Define the terms 'period of account', 'accounting period', and 'financial year'.	1
(b)	Recognise when an accounting period starts and when an accounting period finishes.	1
(c)	Explain how the residence of a company is determined.	2
C2	**Taxable total profits**	
(a)	Recognise the expenditure that is allowable in calculating the tax-adjusted trading profit.	2
(b)	Explain how relief can be obtained for pre-trading expenditure.	1
(c)	Compute capital allowances (as for income tax).	2
(d)	Compute property business profits.	2
(e)	Explain the treatment of interest paid and received under the loan relationship rules.	1
(f)	Explain the treatment of gift aid donations.	2
(k)	Compute taxable trading profits.	2

Exam guide

Question 2 in the exam will focus on corporation tax. Corporation tax may also feature in other questions (apart from question 1 on income tax). When dealing with a corporation tax question you must first be able to identify the accounting period(s) involved; watch out for long periods of account. You must also be able to calculate taxable total profits; learn the standard layout so that you can easily slot in figures from your workings.

1 The scope of corporation tax

FAST FORWARD

Companies pay corporation tax on their taxable total profits.

1.1 Companies

Companies must pay corporation tax on their **taxable total profits** for each **accounting period**. We look at the meaning of these terms below.

Key term

A 'company' is any corporate body (limited or unlimited) or unincorporated association, eg sports club.

1.2 Accounting periods

FAST FORWARD

An accounting period cannot exceed 12 months in length so a long period of account must be split into two accounting periods. The first accounting period is always twelve months in length.

Corporation tax is chargeable in respect of accounting periods. It is important to understand the difference between an accounting period and a period of account.

| Key term | A **period of account** is any period for which a company prepares accounts; usually this will be 12 months in length but it may be longer or shorter than this. |

| Key term | An **accounting period** is the period for which corporation tax is charged and cannot exceed 12 months. Special rules determine when an accounting period starts and ends. |

An accounting period starts when a company starts to trade, or otherwise becomes liable to corporation tax, or immediately after the previous accounting period finishes. An accounting period finishes on the earliest of:

- 12 months after its start
- the end of the company's period of account
- the commencement of the company's winding up
- the company's ceasing to be resident in the UK
- the company's ceasing to be liable to corporation tax

If a company has a period of account exceeding 12 months (a long period), it is split into two accounting periods: the first 12 months and the remainder. For example, if a company prepares accounts for the sixteen months to 30 April 2011, the two accounting periods for which the company will pay corporation tax will be the twelve months to 31 December 2010 and the four months to 30 April 2011.

1.3 Financial year

FAST FORWARD

Tax rates are set for financial years.

The rates of corporation tax are fixed for financial years.

| Key term | **A financial year runs from 1 April to the following 31 March and is identified by the calendar year in which it begins.** For example, the year ended 31 March 2012 is the Financial year 2011 (FY 2011). This should not be confused with a tax year, which runs from 6 April to the following 5 April. |

1.4 Residence of companies

FAST FORWARD

A company is UK resident if it is incorporated in the UK or if it is incorporated abroad and its central management and control are exercised in the UK.

A company incorporated in the UK is resident in the UK. A company incorporated abroad is resident in the UK if its central management and control are exercised here. Central management and control are usually treated as exercised where the board of directors meet.

Question   Residence of a company

Supraville SARL is a company incorporated in France. It has its head office in London where the board of directors meet monthly. It trades throughout the European Union.

Is Supraville SARL resident in the UK?

Answer

Yes, Supraville SARL is resident in the UK.

The central management and control of Supraville SARL is in London (ie the UK) where the board of directors meet.

2 Taxable total profits

FAST FORWARD

Taxable total profits comprises the company's income and chargeable gains (total profits) less some losses and gift aid donations. It does not include dividends received from other companies.

This section relates to your PER requirement:
19   Evaluate and compute taxes payable

2.1 Proforma computation

FAST FORWARD

Income includes trading income, property income, income from non-trading loan relationships (interest) and miscellaneous income.

A company may have both income and gains. As a general rule income arises from receipts which are expected to recur regularly (such as the profits from a trade) whereas chargeable gains arise on the sale of capital assets which have been owned for several years (such as the sale of a factory used in the trade).

A company may receive income from various sources. All income received must be classified according to the nature of the income as different computational rules apply to different types of income. The main types of income for a company are:

- Profits of a trade
- Profits of a property business
- Investment income
- Miscellaneous income

The computation of chargeable gains for a company is dealt with later in this Text. At the moment, you will be given a figure for chargeable gains in order to compute taxable total profits. We also deal with losses in detail later in this Text so, at the moment, you just need to know that some losses are given tax relief by being deducted from total profits.

A company's taxable total profits are arrived at by aggregating its various sources of income and its chargeable gains and then deducting losses and gift aid donations. Here is a pro forma computation.

	£
Trading profits	X
Investment income	X
Foreign income	X
Miscellaneous income	X
Property business profits	X
Chargeable gains	X
Total profits	X
Less losses deductible from total profits	(X)
Less gift aid donations	(X)
Taxable total profits for an accounting period	X

Exam focus point

It would be of great help in the exam if you could learn the above proforma. When answering a corporation tax question you could immediately reproduce the proforma and insert the appropriate numbers as you are given the information in the question.

Dividends received from other companies (UK resident and non-UK resident), for the purposes of the F6 exam, are usually exempt and so not included in taxable trading profits.

3 Trading income

3.1 Adjustment of profits

FAST FORWARD

The adjustment of profits computation for companies broadly follows that for computing business profits subject to income tax. There are, however, some minor differences.

The trading income of companies is derived from the profit before taxation figure in the income statement, just as for individuals, adjusted as follows.

	£	£
Profit before taxation		X
Add expenditure not allowed for taxation purposes		X
		X
Less: income not taxable as trading income	X	
expenditure not charged in the accounts but allowable for the purposes of taxation	X	
capital allowances	X	
		(X)
Profit adjusted for tax purposes		X

Exam focus point

An examination question requiring adjustment to profit will direct you to start the adjustment with the profit before taxation of £XXXX and deal with all the items listed indicating with a zero (0) any items which do not require adjustment. Marks will not be given for relevant items unless this approach is used. Therefore students who attempt to rewrite the income statement will be penalised.

The adjustment of profits computation for companies broadly follows that for computing business profits subject to income tax. There are, however, some minor differences. There is no disallowance for 'private use' for companies; instead the director or employee will be taxed on the benefit received.

Gift aid donations are added back in the calculation of adjusted profit. They are treated instead as a deduction from total profits.

Investment income including rents is deducted from profit before taxation in arriving at trading income but brought in again further down in the computation (see below).

Exam focus point

When adjusting profits as supplied in an income statement confusion can arise as regards whether figures are net or gross. Properly drawn up company accounts should normally include all income gross. However, some examination questions include items 'net'. Read the question carefully.

3.2 Pre-trading expenditure

Pre-trading expenditure incurred by the company within the 7 years before trade commences is treated as an allowable expense incurred on the first day of trading provided it would have been allowable had the company been trading when the expense was actually incurred.

3.3 Capital allowances

The calculation of capital allowances follows income tax principles.

For companies, however, there is never any reduction of allowances to take account of any private use of an asset. The director or employee suffers a taxable benefit instead. As shown above capital allowances must be deducted in arriving at taxable trading income.

A company's accounting period can never exceed 12 months. If the period of account is longer than 12 months it is **divided into two**; one for the first 12 months and one for the balance. **The capital allowances computation must be carried out for each period separately.**

The calculation of trading income should be undertaken as a first step to the calculation of taxable total profits. However, it is important to realise that these are two distinct aspects when calculating a company's liability to corporation tax and you should not attempt to present them in one calculation.

4 Property business income

Rental income is deducted in arriving at trading income but brought in again further down in the computation as property business income.

The calculation of property business income follows income tax principles. The income tax rules for property businesses were set out earlier in this Text. In summary all UK rental activities are treated as a single source of income calculated in the same way as trading income.

However **interest paid by a company on a loan to buy or improve property is not a property business expense.** The **loan relationship rules apply** instead (see below).

5 Loan relationships (interest income)

5.1 General principle

If a company borrows or lends money, including issuing or investing in debentures or buying gilts, it has a loan relationship. This can be a creditor relationship (where the company lends or invests money) **or a debtor relationship** (where the company borrows money or issues securities).

5.2 Treatment of trading loan relationships

If the company is a party to a **loan relationship for trade purposes, any debits – ie interest paid or other debt costs – charged through its accounts are allowed as a trading expense** and are therefore deductible in computing trading income.

Similarly **if any credits – ie interest income or other debt returns – arise on a trading loan these are treated as a trading receipt and are taxable as trading income.** This is not likely to arise unless the trade is one of money lending.

5.3 Treatment of non-trading loan relationships

If a loan relationship is not one to which the company is a party for trade purposes any debits or credits must be pooled. A net credit on the pool is chargeable as interest income.

Interest charged on underpaid tax is allowable and interest received on overpaid tax is assessable under the rules for non-trading loan relationships.

You will not be expected to deal with net deficits (ie losses) on non-trading loan relationships in your exam.

5.4 Accounting methods

Debits and credits must be brought into account using the UK generally accepted accounting practice (GAAP) or using the International Accounting Standards (IAS). This will usually be the **accruals basis**.

5.5 Incidental costs of loan finance

Under the loan relationship rules expenses ('debits') are allowed if incurred directly:

(a)   to bring a loan relationship into existence
(b)   entering into or giving effect to any related transactions
(c)   making payment under a loan relationship or related transactions or
(d)   taking steps to ensure the receipt of payments under the loan relationship or related transaction.

A related transaction means 'any disposal or acquisition (in whole or in part) of rights or liabilities under the relationship, including any arising from a security issue in relation to the money debt in question'.

The above categories of incidental costs are also allowable even if the company does not enter into the loan relationship (ie abortive costs). Costs directly incurred in varying the terms of a loan relationship are also allowed.

5.6 Other matters

It is not only the interest costs of borrowing that are allowable or taxable. The capital costs are treated similarly. Thus if a company issues a loan at a discount and repays it eventually at par, the capital cost is usually allowed on redemption (if the accruals basis is adopted).

6 Miscellaneous income

Patent royalties received which do not relate to the trade are taxed as miscellaneous income. Patent royalties which relate to the trade are included in trading income normally on an accruals basis.

7 Gift aid donations

FAST FORWARD

Gift aid donations are paid gross by a company and deducted from total profits when computing taxable total profits.

Gift aid donations are deductible from total profits when computing taxable total profits.

Almost all donations of money to charity can be made under the **gift aid scheme** whether they are one off donations or are regular donations. **Gift aid donations are paid gross**.

Donations to local charities which are incurred wholly and exclusively for the purposes of a trade are deducted in the calculation of the tax adjusted trading profits.

8 Long periods of account

FAST FORWARD

Long periods of account are split into two accounting periods: the first 12 months and the remainder.

As we saw above, if a company has a long period of account exceeding 12 months, it is split into two accounting periods: the first 12 months and the remainder.

Where the period of account differs from the corporation tax accounting periods, profits are **allocated to the relevant periods** as follows:

- **Trading income** before capital allowances and **property income** are apportioned on a **time basis**.
- **Capital allowances** and balancing charges are **calculated for each accounting period.**
- **Other income is allocated to the period to which it relates** (eg interest accrued). Miscellaneous income, however, is apportioned on a time basis.
- **Chargeable gains and losses** are allocated to the **period in which they are realised.**
- **Gift aid donations** are deducted in the accounting **period in which they are paid.**

Question

Xenon Ltd makes up an 18 month set of accounts to 30 September 2012 with the following results.

	£
Trading income (no capital allowances claimed)	180,000
Interest income	
18 months @ £500 accruing per month	9,000
Capital gain (1 August 2012 disposal)	250,000
Less: Gift aid donation (paid 31 March 2012)	(50,000)
	389,000

What are the taxable total profits for each of the accounting periods based on the above accounts?

Answer

The 18 month period of account is divided into:

Year ending 31 March 2012
6 months to 30 September 2012

Results are allocated:

	Y/e 31.3.12	6m to 30.9.12
	£	£
Trading income 12:6	120,000	60,000
Interest income		
12 × £500	6,000	
6 × £500		3,000
Capital gain (1.8.12)		250,000
Total profits	126,000	313,000
Less: Gift aid donation (31.3.12)	(50,000)	
Taxable total profits	76,000	313,000

Chapter Roundup

- Companies pay corporation tax on their taxable total profits.

- An accounting period cannot exceed 12 months in length so a long period of account must be split into two accounting periods. The first accounting period is always twelve months in length.

- Tax rates are set for financial years.

- A company is UK resident if it is incorporated in the UK or if it is incorporated abroad and its central management and control are exercised in the UK.

- Taxable total profits comprises the company's income and chargeable gains (total profits) less some losses and gift aid donations. It does not include dividends received from other companies.

- Income includes trading income, property income, income from non-trading loan relationships (interest) and miscellaneous income.

- The adjustment of profits computation for companies broadly follows that for computing business profits subject to income tax. There are, however, some minor differences.

- Gift aid donations are paid gross by a company and deducted from total profits when computing taxable total profits.

- Long periods of account are split into two accounting periods: the first 12 months and the remainder.

Quick Quiz

1   When does an accounting period end?

2   What is the difference between a period of account and an accounting period?

3   Should interest paid on a trading loan be adjusted in the trading income computation?

4   How is trading income (before capital allowances) of a long period of account divided between accounting periods?

   A   On a receipts basis
   B   On an accruals basis
   C   On a time basis
   D   On any basis the company chooses

Answers to Quick Quiz

1　An accounting period ends on the earliest of:

(a)　12 months after its start
(b)　the end of the company's period of account
(c)　the commencement of the company's winding up
(d)　the company ceasing to be resident in the UK
(e)　the company ceasing to be liable to corporation tax

2　A period of account is the period for which a company prepares accounts. An accounting period is the period for which corporation tax is charged. If a company prepares annual accounts the two will coincide.

3　Interest paid on a trading loan should not be adjusted in the trading income computation as it is an allowable expense, computed on the accruals basis.

4　C. Trading income (before capital allowances) is apportioned on a time basis.

Now try the question below from the Exam Question Bank

Number	Level	Marks	Time
Q30	Examination	15	27 mins

Computing the corporation tax liability

Topic list	Syllabus reference
1 Charge to corporation tax	C3(a)-(c)
2 Associated companies	C3(a), C4(a)

Introduction

In the previous chapter you learnt how to identify a company's accounting period and how to compute the taxable total profits for that accounting period.

In this chapter you will learn how to compute the corporation tax liability on those profits.

In the next chapter we will deal with chargeable gains for companies.

Study guide

		Intellectual level
C3	**The comprehensive computation of corporation tax liability**	
(a)	Compute the corporation tax liability and apply marginal relief.	2
(b)	Explain the implications of receiving franked investment income.	2
(c)	Explain how exemptions and reliefs can defer or minimise corporation tax liabilities.	2
C4	**The effect of a group corporate structure for corporation tax purposes**	
(a)	Define an associated company and recognise the effect of being an associated company for corporation tax purposes.	2

Exam guide

Question 2 of the exam will always be on corporation tax and corporation tax may also be part of questions 3, 4 or 5. Computing the corporation tax is usually an integral part of at least one question, and you must be sure that you understand the rules for marginal relief. Note in particular the consequences of short accounting periods and of having associated companies. It will be crucial for you to know the marginal rate of corporation tax for a company when you are dealing with loss relief and group relief later in your studies.

1 Charge to corporation tax

This section relates to your PER requirement:
19   Evaluate and compute taxes payable

1.1 Augmented profits

A company pays corporation tax on its taxable total profits, but the rate of tax depends on augmented profits. Augmented profits are taxable total profits plus franked investment income (FII).

Although we tax taxable total profits, another figure needs to be calculated, called augmented profits, to determine the rate of corporation tax to apply to taxable total profits.

Augmented profits means taxable total profits plus the grossed-up amount of dividends received from other companies (UK and non-UK). The exception to this rule is any dividends received from a company which is a 51% or more subsidiary of the receiving company or from a company of which the recipient company is a 51% or more subsidiary of the paying company: these dividends ('group dividends') are completely ignored for corporation tax purposes.

The grossed-up amount of dividends is the dividend received multiplied by 100/90. You may see the grossed up amount of dividend received referred to as **franked investment income (FII)**.

Exam focus point

> Be careful to charge corporation tax on taxable total profits, not on augmented profits.

1.2 The main rate

The rates of corporation tax are fixed for financial years. The main rate of corporation tax is 26% for FY 2011 and was 28% for FY 2010 and FY 2009. The main rate applies to taxable total profits of companies with augmented profits of £1,500,000 or more (for all relevant FYs). So a company with taxable total profits of £2 million in FY 2011, will pay £520,000 corporation tax.

1.3 The small profits rate

Companies may be taxed at the small profits rate or obtain marginal relief, depending on their augmented profits.

The small profits rate of corporation tax is 20% for FY 2011 and was 21% for FY 2010 and FY 2009. The small profits rate applies to the taxable total profits of UK resident companies whose augmented profits are not more than £300,000 (for all relevant FYs).

Question

The small profits rate

B Ltd had the following results for the year ended 31 March 2012.

	£
Trading profits	42,000
Dividend received 1 May 2011	9,000

Compute the corporation tax payable.

Answer

	£
Trading profits/Taxable total profits	42,000
Dividend plus tax credit £9,000 × 100/90	10,000
Augmented profits (less than £300,000 limit)	52,000
Corporation tax payable	
£42,000 × 20%	£8,400

1.4 Marginal relief

Marginal relief applies where the augmented profits of an accounting period of a UK resident company are over £300,000 but under £1,500,000.

We first calculate the corporation tax at the main rate and then deduct:

Standard fraction × (U − A) × N/A

where U = upper limit (£1,500,000 for all relevant FYs)
     A = augmented profits
     N = taxable total profits

The standard fraction is 3/200 for FY 2011 and was 7/400 for FY 2010 and FY 2009.

This information is given in the rates and allowances section of the exam paper.

Question

Lenox Ltd has the following results for the year ended 31 March 2012.

	£
Taxable total profits	296,000
Dividend received 1 December 2011	12,600

Calculate the corporation tax liability.

Answer

	£
Taxable total profits	296,000
Dividend plus tax credit £12,600 × 100/90	14,000
Augmented profits	310,000

Augmented profits are above £300,000 but below £1,500,000, so marginal relief applies.

	£
Corporation tax on taxable total profits £296,000 × 26%	76,960
Less marginal relief	
£(1,500,000 – 310,000) × 296,000/310,000 × 3/200	(17,044)
	59,916

FAST FORWARD

> The marginal rate of corporation tax between the small profits limits is 27.5% for FY 2011. The marginal rate of tax is an effective rate; it is never actually used in working out corporation tax.

In exam questions you often need to be aware that there is a **marginal rate of 27.5%** which applies to any taxable total profits that lie in between the small profits limits.

This is calculated as follows:

	£				£
Upper limit	1,500,000	@	26%		390,000
Lower limit	(300,000)	@	20%		(60,000)
Difference	1,200,000				330,000

$$\frac{330,000}{1,200,000} = 27.5\%$$

Effectively the band of profits (here £1,200,000) falling between the upper and lower limits are taxed at a rate of 27.5%.

The marginal rate in FY 2010 and FY 2009 was 29.75%.

1.5 Example: effective marginal rate of tax

A Ltd has taxable total profits of £350,000 for the year ended 31 March 2012. Its corporation tax liability is

	£
£350,000 × 26%	91,000
Less marginal relief	
£(1,500,000 – 350,000) × 3/200	(17,250)
	73,750

This is the same as calculating tax at 20% × £300,000 + 27.5% × £50,000 = £60,000 + £13,750 = £73,750.

Consequently tax is charged at an effective rate of 27.5% on taxable total profits that exceed the small profits lower limit.

Note that although there is an effective corporation tax charge of 27.5%, this rate of tax is never used in actually calculating corporation tax. The rate is just an effective marginal rate that you must be aware of. It will be particularly important when considering loss relief and group relief (see later in this Text).

1.6 Accounting period in more than one Financial Year

An accounting period **may fall within more than one Financial Year. If the rates and limits for corporation tax are the same in both Financial Years, tax can be computed for the accounting period as if it fell within one Financial Yea**r.

However, **if the rates and/or limits for corporation tax are different in the Financial Years, taxable total profits and augmented are time apportioned between the Financial Years**.

1.7 Example: accounting period in more than one Financial Year

Wentworth Ltd makes up its accounts to 31 December each year. For the year to 31 December 2011, it has taxable total profits of £174,000. It receives a dividend of £5,400 on 1 December 2011.

The corporation tax payable by Wentworth Ltd is calculated as follows.

	£
Taxable total profits	174,000
Dividend plus tax credit £5,400 × 100/90	6,000
Augmented profits	180,000
Small companies rate applies for both FY 2010 and FY2011	

	£
FY 2010 (1.1.11 to 31.3.11 – 3 months)	
£174,000 × 3/12 = 43,500 × 21%	9,135
FY 2011 (1.4.11 to 31.12.11 – 9 months)	
£174,000 × 9/12 = 130,500 × 20%	26,100
Corporation tax liability for year to 31 December 2011	35,235

Question   Accounting period in more than one financial year

Elliot Ltd has the following results for the year to 30 September 2011.

	£
Taxable total profits	360,000
Dividend received 15 July 2011	8,100

Calculate the corporation tax payable by Elliot Ltd.

Answer

	£
Taxable total profits	360,000
Add: FII £8,100 × 100/90	9,000
Augmented profits	369,000
Marginal relief applies for both FY 2010 and FY2011	

FY 2010 (1.10.10 to 31.3.11 – 6 months)
£360,000 × 6/12 = 180,000 × 28%   50,400

Less: marginal relief £(1,500,000 – 369,000) × $\dfrac{360,000}{369,000}$ × 7/400 × 6/12   (9,655)

FY 2011(1.4.11 to 30.9.11 – 6 months)
£360,000 × 6/12 = 180,000 × 26%   46,800

Less: marginal relief £(1,500,000 – 369,000) × $\dfrac{360,000}{369,000}$ × 3/200 × 6/12   (8,276)

Corporation tax liability for year to 30 September 2011   79,269

1.8 Short accounting periods

FAST FORWARD

The upper and lower limits which are used to be determine tax rates are pro-rated on a time basis if an accounting period lasts for less than 12 months.

Question
Short accounting period

Ink Ltd prepared accounts for the six months to 31 March 2012. Taxable total profits for the period were £200,000. No dividends were received. Calculate the corporation tax payable for the period.

Answer

Upper limit £1,500,000 × 6/12 = £750,000

Lower limit £300,000 × 6/12 = £150,000

As augmented profits fall between the limits, marginal relief applies.

     £

Corporation tax (FY 11)
£200,000 × 26%   52,000
Less marginal relief
    3/200 × (£750,000 – £200,000)   (8,250)
Corporation tax   43,750

1.9 Long periods of account

Remember that an accounting period cannot be more than 12 months long. If the period of account exceeds 12 months it must be split into two accounting periods, the first of 12 months and the second of the balance.

Exam focus point

If you have to deal with a long period of account remember to pro-rate the upper and lower limits on a time basis for the second (short) accounting period.

Question

Xenon Ltd (in the previous chapter) made up an 18 month set of accounts to 30 September 2012.

The 18 month period of account is divided into:

Year ending 31 March 2012
6 months to 30 September 2012

Results were allocated:

	Y/e 31.3.12 £	6m to 30.9.12 £
Trading profits 12:6	120,000	60,000
Property income	6,000	3,000
Capital gain (1.8.12)		250,000
Less: Gift aid donation (31.3.12)	(50,000)	
Taxable total profits	76,000	313,000

Assuming Xenon Ltd received FII of £27,000 on 31 August 2012, calculate the corporation tax payable for each accounting period. Assume that the corporation tax rates in FY12 are the same as in FY11.

Answer

	Y/e 31.3.12 £	6m to 30.9.12 £
Taxable total profits	76,000	313,000
FII	0	27,000
Augmented profits	76,000	340,000
Small profits lower limit	300,000	150,000
Small profits upper limit	1,500,000	750,000
	Small company	Marginal relief
	Y/e 31.3.12 £	6m to 30.9.12 £
Corporation tax payable		
£76,000 × 20%	15,200	
£313,000 × 26%		81,380
Less marginal relief £(750,000 – 340,000) × 313,000/340,000 × 3/200		(5,662)
		75,718
Total corporation tax payable £(15,200 + 75,718)		90,918

2 Associated companies

FAST FORWARD

> The upper and lower limits which are used to determine tax rates are divided by the total number of associated companies. Broadly, associated companies are worldwide trading companies under common control.

2.1 What is an associated company?

Key term

The expression **'associated companies'** in tax has no connection with financial accounting. For tax purposes a company is associated with another company if either controls the other or if both are under the control of the same person or persons (individuals, partnerships or companies). Whether such a company is UK resident or not is irrelevant. Control is given by holding over 50% of the share capital or the voting power or being entitled to over 50% of the distributable income or of the net assets in a winding up.

2.2 Effects of associated companies

If a company has one or more 'associated companies', then the profit limits for small profits rate purposes are divided by the number of associated companies + 1 (for the company itself).

Companies which have only been associated for part of an accounting period are deemed to have been associated for the whole period for the purpose of determining the profit limits.

2.3 Exception

An associated company is ignored for these purposes if it has not carried on any trade or business at any time in the accounting period (or the part of the period during which it was associated) ie it is 'dormant'.

Question — Associated companies

For the year to 31 March 2012 a company with two other associated companies had taxable total profits of £200,000 and no dividends paid or received. Compute the corporation tax payable.

Answer

(a)   Reduction in the lower limit for small profits rate

Divide by number of associated companies + 1 = 3

£300,000 ÷ 3 = £100,000

(b)   Reduction in the upper limit for small profits rate

£1,500,000 ÷ 3 = £500,000

(c)   Augmented profits = £200,000

As augmented profits fall between the lower and upper limits for small profits rate purposes, the main rate less marginal relief applies:

(d)   Corporation tax

	£
£200,000 × 26%	52,000
Less marginal relief £(500,000 – 200,000) × 3/200	(4,500)
Corporation tax	47,500

2.4 Associated companies and short accounting periods

If a company has associated companies and also a short accounting period, first reduce the upper and lower limits for the associated companies and then prorate them for the short accounting period.

2.5 Example: small profits limits

Alpha plc, a company with one subsidiary, prepares accounts for the 9 months to 31 December 2011.

The small profits limit will be multiplied by ½ as there is one associated company, and by 9/12 as the accounting period is only 9 months long.

The small profits lower limit will be £300,000 × ½ × 9/12 = £112,500

The small profits upper limit will be £1,500,000 × ½ × 9/12 = £562,500

Chapter Roundup

- A company pays corporation tax on its taxable total profits, but the rate of tax depends on augmented profits. Augmented profits are taxable total profits plus franked investment income (FII).

- Companies may be taxed at the main rate, the small profits rate or obtain marginal relief, depending on their augmented profits.

- The marginal rate of corporation tax between the small profits limits is 27.5% for FY 2011. The marginal tax rate is an effective rate; it is never actually used in working out corporation tax.

- The upper and lower limits which are used to be determine tax rates are pro-rated on a time basis if an accounting period lasts for less than 12 months.

- The upper and lower limits which are used to determine tax rates are divided by the total number of associated companies. Broadly, associated companies are worldwide trading companies under common control.

Quick Quiz

1 Companies are entitled to the small profits rate of corporation tax if they have augmented profits of up to £_____. Fill in the blank.

2 What is the marginal relief formula?

3 What is an associated company?

4 What effect do associated companies have on the corporation tax computation?

Answers to Quick Quiz

1   Companies are entitled to the small profits rate of corporation tax if they have augmented profits of up to **£300,000**.

2   Standard fraction × (U – A) × N/A

where:

U = upper limit
A = augmented profits
N = taxable total profits

3   A company is associated with another company if either controls the other or if both are under the control of the same person or persons (individuals, partnerships or companies).

4   If a company has associated companies the small profits lower and upper limits are divided by the number of associated companies + 1.

Now try the question below from the Exam Question Bank			
Number	**Level**	**Marks**	**Time**
Q31	Introductory	15	27 mins
Q32	Examination	10	18 mins

Chargeable gains for companies

Topic list	Syllabus reference
1 Corporation tax on chargeable gains	C2(k)
2 Indexation allowance	D2(b)
3 Disposal of shares by companies	D4(b)–(d)
4 Relief for replacement of business assets (rollover relief)	D6(b)

Introduction

We studied chargeable gains for individuals earlier in this Text. In this chapter, we will consider the treatment of chargeable gains for companies.

Companies pay corporation tax on their chargeable gains, rather than capital gains tax. The computation of gains for companies is slightly more complicated than for individuals because companies are entitled to indexation allowance.

We also consider the matching rules for companies which dispose of shares in other companies. Again, these rules are slightly more complicated than for individuals.

Finally, we look at how the relief for replacement of business assets applies to companies.

In the next chapters we will deal with losses, groups and overseas matters.

Study guide

		Intellectual level
C2	**Taxable total profits**	
(k)	Compute taxable total profits	2
D2	**The basic principles of computing gains and losses**	
(b)	Calculate the indexation allowance available to companies	2
D4	**Gains and losses on the disposal of shares and securities**	
(b)	Explain and apply the identification rules as they apply to companies including the same day and nine-day matching rules	2
(c)	Explain the pooling provisions	2
(d)	Explain the treatment of bonus issues, rights issues, takeovers and reorganisations	2
D6	**The uses of exemptions and reliefs in deferring and minimising tax liabilities arising on the disposal of capital assets**	
(b)	Explain and apply rollover relief as it applies to companies	2

Exam guide

Question 3 of the exam will always be a 15 mark question on capital gains. This may be a question about the gains of a company so it is important that you can deal with the aspects covered in this chapter. There may also be an element of gains in relation to companies in Question 2.

1 Corporation tax on chargeable gains

FAST FORWARD

Chargeable gains for companies are computed in broadly the same way as for individuals, but indexation allowance applies and there is no annual exempt amount.

Companies do not pay capital gains tax. Instead their chargeable gains are included in the calculation of taxable total profits.

A company's capital gains or allowable losses are computed in a similar way to individuals but with a few major differences:

- There is relief for inflation called the indexation allowance
- **No annual exempt amount** is available
- Different matching rules for shares apply if the shareholder is a company.

2 Indexation allowance

FAST FORWARD

The indexation allowance gives relief for the inflation element of a gain.

The purpose of having an indexation allowance is to remove the inflation element of a gain from taxation.

Companies are entitled to indexation allowance from the date of acquisition until the date of disposal of an asset. It is based on the movement in the Retail Price Index (RPI) between those two dates.

For example, if J Ltd bought a painting on 2 January 1987 and sold it on 19 November 2011 the indexation allowance is available from January 1987 until November 2011.

The indexation factor is:

$$\frac{\text{RPI for month of disposal} - \text{RPI for month of acquisition}}{\text{RPI for month of acquisition}}$$

The calculation is expressed as a decimal and is rounded to three decimal places.

Indexation allowance is available on the allowable cost of the asset from the **date of acquisition** (including incidental costs of acquisition). It is also available on **enhancement expenditure from the month in which such expenditure becomes due and payable. Indexation allowance is not available on the costs of disposal.**

Question

The indexation allowance

An asset is acquired by a company on 15 February 1983 (RPI = 83.0) at a cost of £5,000. Enhancement expenditure of £2,000 is incurred on 10 April 1984 (RPI = 88.6). The asset is sold for £25,500 on 20 December 2011 (RPI =236.7). Incidental costs of sale are £500. Calculate the chargeable gain arising.

Answer

The indexation allowance is available until December 2011 and is computed as follows.

	£
$\frac{236.7 - 83.0}{83.0} = 1.852 \times £5,000$	9,260
$\frac{236.7 - 88.6}{88.6} = 1.672 \times £2,000$	3,344
	12,604

The computation of the chargeable gain is as follows.

	£
Proceeds	25,500
Less incidental costs of sale	(500)
Net proceeds	25,000
Less allowable costs £(5,000 + 2,000)	(7,000)
Unindexed gain	18,000
Less indexation allowance (see above)	(12,604)
Indexed gain	5,396

Indexation allowance cannot create or increase an allowable loss. If there is a gain before the indexation allowance, the allowance can reduce that gain to zero but no further. If there is a loss before the indexation allowance, there is no indexation allowance.

If the indexation allowance calculation gives a negative figure, treat the indexation as nil: do not add to the unindexed gain.

3 Disposal of shares by companies

There are special rules for matching shares sold by a company with shares purchased. Disposals are matched with acquisitions on the same day, the previous nine days and the FA 1985 share pool.

3.1 The matching rules

We have discussed the share matching rules for individuals earlier in this Text. We also need special rules for companies.

For companies the matching of shares sold is in the following order.

(a)   Shares acquired on the **same day**

(b)   Shares acquired in the **previous nine days**, if more than one acquisition on a "first in, first out" (FIFO) basis

(c)   Shares from the **FA 1985 pool**

The composition of the FA 1985 pool in relation to companies which are shareholders is explained below.

Exam focus point

Learn the 'matching rules' because a crucial first step to getting a shares question right is to correctly match the shares sold to the original shares purchased.

3.2 Example: share matching rules for companies

Nor Ltd acquired the following shares in Last plc:

Date of acquisition	No of shares
9.11.02	15,000
15.12.04	15,000
11.7.11	5,000
15.7.11	5,000

Nor Ltd disposed of 20,000 of the shares on 15 July 2011.

We match the shares as follows:

(a)   Acquisition on same day: 5,000 shares acquired 15 July 2011.

(b)   Acquisitions in previous 9 days: 5,000 shares acquired 11 July 2011.

(c)   FA 1985 share pool: 10,000 shares out of 30,000 shares in FA 1985 share pool (9.11.02 and 15.12.04).

3.3 The FA 1985 share pool

Exam focus point

The examiner has stated that a detailed question will not be set on the pooling provisions. However, work through the examples below as you are expected to understand how the pool works.

The FA 1985 pool comprises the following shares of the same class in the same company.

- **Shares held by a company on 1 April 1985 and acquired by that company on or after 1 April 1982.**

- **Shares acquired by that company on or after 1 April 1985.**

We must keep track of:

(a)   the **number** of shares

(b)   the **cost** of the shares ignoring indexation

(c)   the **indexed cost** of the shares

The first step in constructing the FA 1985 share pool is to calculate the value of the pool at 1 April 1985 by indexing the cost of each acquisition before that date up to April 1985.

3.4 Example: the FA 1985 pool

Oliver Ltd bought 1,000 shares in Judith plc for £2,750 in August 1984 and another 1,000 for £3,250 in December 1984. RPIs are August 1984 = 89.9, December 1984 = 90.9 and April 1985 = 94.8. The FA 1985 pool at 1 April 1985 is as follows.

	No of shares	Cost £	Indexed Cost £
August 1984 (a)	1,000	2,750	2,750
December 1984 (b)	1,000	3,250	3,250
	2,000	6,000	6,000

Indexation allowance

$$\frac{94.8-89.9}{89.9} = 0.055 \times £2,750 \qquad\qquad 151$$

$$\frac{94.8-90.9}{90.9} = 0.043 \times £3,250 \qquad\qquad 140$$

Indexed cost of the pool at 1 April 1985 — 6,291

Disposals and acquisitions of shares which affect the indexed value of the FA 1985 pool are termed **'operative events'. Prior to reflecting each such operative event within the FA 1985 share pool, a further indexation allowance (an 'indexed rise') must be computed up to the date of the operative event concerned from the date of the last such operative event** (or from the later of the first acquisition and April 1985 if the operative event in question is the first one).

Indexation calculations within the FA 1985 pool (after its April 1985 value has been calculated) **are not rounded to three decimal places**. This is because rounding errors would accumulate and have a serious effect after several operative events.

If there are several operative events between 1 April 1985 and the date of a disposal, the indexation procedure described above will have to be performed several times over.

Question   Value of FA 1985 pool

Following on from the above example, assume that Oliver Ltd acquired 2,000 more shares on 10 July 1986 at a cost of £4,000. Recalculate the value of the FA 1985 pool on 10 July 1986 following the acquisition. Assume the RPI in July 1986 = 97.5.

Answer

	No of shares	Cost £	Indexed cost £
Value at 1.4.85 b/f	2,000	6,000	6,291
Indexed rise $\frac{97.5-94.8}{94.8} \times £6,291$			179
	2,000	6,000	6,470
Acquisition	2,000	4,000	4,000
Value at 10.7.86	4,000	10,000	10,470

In the case of a disposal, following the calculation of the indexed rise to the date of disposal, the cost and the indexed cost attributable to the shares disposed of are deducted from the amounts within the FA 1985 pool. The proportions of the cost and indexed cost to take out of the pool should be computed by using the proportion of cost that the shares disposed of bear to the total number of shares held.

The indexation allowance is the indexed cost taken out of the pool minus the cost taken out. As usual, the indexation allowance cannot create or increase a loss.

Disposals from the FA 1985 pool

Question

Continuing the above exercise, suppose that Oliver Ltd sold 3,000 shares on 10 July 2011 for £22,000. Compute the gain, and the value of the FA 1985 pool following the disposal. Assume RPI July 2011 = 234.9.

Answer

	No of shares	Cost £	Indexed cost £
Value at 10.7.86	4,000	10,000	10,470
Indexed rise			
$\dfrac{234.9 - 97.5}{97.5} \times £10,470$			14,755
	4,000	10,000	25,225
Disposal	(3,000)		
Cost and indexed cost $\dfrac{3,000}{4,000} \times £10,000$ and £25,225		(7,500)	(18,919)
Value at 10.7.11	1,000	2,500	6,306

The gain is computed as follows:

	£
Proceeds	22,000
Less cost	(7,500)
Unindexed gain	14,500
Less indexation allowance £(18,919 − 7,500)	(11,419)
Indexed gain	3,081

3.5 Bonus and rights issues

When **bonus issue shares are issued**, all that happens is that **the size of the original holding is increased**. Since **bonus issue shares are issued at no cost** there is **no need to adjust the original cost** and there is **no operative event for the FA 1985 pool** (so no indexation allowance needs to be calculated).

When **rights issue shares are issued**, the **size of the original holding is increased** in the same way as for a bonus issue. So if the original shareholding was part of the FA 1985 pool, the rights issue shares are added to that pool. This might be important for the matching rules if a shareholding containing the rights issue shares is sold shortly after the rights issue.

However, in the case of a rights issue, the **new shares are paid for and this results in an adjustment to the original cost**. For the purpose of **calculating the indexation allowance, expenditure on a rights issue is taken as being incurred on the date of the issue** and not the date of the original holding.

3.6 Example: bonus and rights issue

S Ltd bought 10,000 shares in T plc in May 2000 (RPI = 170.7) at a cost of £45,000.

There was a 2 for 1 bonus issue in October 2002.

There was a 1 for 3 rights issue in June 2006 (RPI = 198.5) at a cost of £4 per share. S Ltd took up all of its rights entitlement.

S Ltd sold 20,000 shares in T plc for £120,000 in January 2012 (RPI = 237.0).

FA 1985 share pool

		No. of shares	Cost £	Indexed cost £
5.00	Acquisition	10,000	45,000	45,000
10.02	Bonus 2:1	20,000		
		30,000		
6.06	Indexed rise			
	$\dfrac{198.5-170.7}{170.7}$ x £45,000			7,329
	Rights 1:3	10,000	40,000	40,000
		40,000	85,000	92,329
1.12	Index rise			
	$\dfrac{237.0-198.5}{198.5}$ x £92,329			17,908
				110,237
	Disposal	(20,000)	(42,500)	(55,119)
c/f		20,000	42,500	55,118

The gain is:

	£
Proceeds	120,000
Less: cost	(42,500)
Unindexed gain	77,500
Less: indexation allowance £(55,119 – 42,500)	(12,619)
Indexed gain	64,881

3.7 Reorganisations and takeovers

The rules on reorganisation and takeovers apply in a similar way for company shareholders as they do for individuals.

In the case of a **reorganisation**, the new shares or securities take the place of the original shares. The original cost and the indexed cost of the original shares is apportioned between the different types of capital issued on the reorganisation.

Where there is a takeover of shares which qualifies for the 'paper for paper' treatment, the cost and indexed cost of the original holding is passed onto the new holding which take the place of the original holding.

Question   Takeover

J Ltd acquired 20,000 shares in G Ltd in August 1990 (RPI = 128.1) at a cost of £40,000. It acquired a further 5,000 shares in December 2006 (RPI = 202.7) at a cost of £30,000.

In March 2012, G Ltd was taken over by K plc and J Ltd received one ordinary share and two preference shares in K plc for each one share held in G Ltd. Immediately following the takeover, the ordinary shares in K plc were worth £4 per share and the preference shares in K plc were worth £1 per share.

Show the cost and indexed cost of the ordinary shares and the preference shares.

G Ltd FA 1985 share pool

		No. of shares	Cost £	Indexed cost £
8.90	Acquisition	20,000	40,000	40,000
12.06	Indexed rise			
	$\dfrac{202.7 - 128.1}{128.1} \times £40,000$			23,294
	Acquisition	5,000	30,000	30,000
Pool at takeover		25,000	70,000	93,294

Note that the takeover is not an operative event because the pool of cost is not increased or decreased and so it is not necessary to calculate an indexed rise.

Apportionment of cost/indexed cost to K plc shares

	No. of shares	MV £	Cost £	Indexed cost £
Ords × 1	25,000	100,000	46,667	62,196
Prefs × 2	50,000	50,000	23,333	31,098
Totals		150,000	70,000	93,294

On a disposal of shares in K plc, indexation allowance will be calculated from December 2006.

4 Relief for replacement of business assets (rollover relief)

FAST FORWARD

> Rollover relief for replacement of business assets is available to companies to defer gains arising on the disposal of business assets.

4.1 Conditions for relief

As for individuals, **a gain may be deferred by a company where the proceeds on the disposal of a business asset are spent on a replacement business asset under rollover relief.**

The conditions for the relief to apply to company disposals are:

(a)   The old assets sold and the new asset bought are both used only in the trade of the company (apportionment into business and non-business parts available for buildings).

(b)   The old asset and the new asset both fall within one (but not necessarily the same one) of the following classes.

    (i)   **Land and buildings** (including parts of buildings) occupied as well as used only for the purposes of the trade

    (ii)   Fixed plant and machinery

(c)   Reinvestment of the proceeds received on the disposal of the old asset takes place in a period beginning one year before and ending three years after the date of the disposal.

(d)   The new asset is brought into use in the trade on its acquisition.

Note that goodwill is not a qualifying asset for the purposes of corporation tax.

A claim for relief must be made within four years of the end of the accounting period in which the disposal of the old asset is made.

4.2 Operation of relief

Deferral is obtained by deducting the indexed gain from the cost of the new asset. For full relief, the whole of the proceeds must be reinvested. If only part is reinvested, a gain equal to the amount not invested, or the full gain, if lower, will be chargeable to tax immediately.

The new asset will have a base cost for chargeable gains purposes of its purchase price less the gain rollover over.

Question	Rollover relief

D Ltd acquired a factory in April 2000 (RPI = 170.1) at a cost of £120,000. It used the factory in its trade throughout the period of its ownership.

In August 2011 (RPI = 235.4), D Ltd sold the factory for £210,000. In November 2011, it acquired another factory at a cost of £180,000.

Calculate the gain chargeable on the sale of the first factory and the base cost of the second factory.

Answer

Chargeable gain on sale of first factory

	£
Proceeds	210,000
Less: cost	(120,000)
Unindexed gain	90,000
$\dfrac{235.4 - 170.1}{170.1} = 0.384 \times £120,000$	(46,080)
Indexed gain	43,920
Less: rollover relief (balancing figure)	(13,920)
Chargeable gain: amount not reinvested £(210,000 – 180,000)	30,000

Base cost of second factory

	£
Cost of second factory	180,000
Less: rolled over gain	(13,920)
Base cost	166,080

4.3 Depreciating assets

The relief for investment into depreciating assets works in the same way for companies as it does for individuals.

The indexed gain is calculated on the old asset and is deferred until the gain crystallises on the earliest of:

(a) The disposal of the replacement asset
(b) The date the replacement asset ceases to be used in the trade
(c) Ten years after the acquisition of the replacement asset.

Chapter Roundup

- Chargeable gains for companies are computed in broadly the same way as for individuals, but indexation allowance applies and there is no annual exempt amount.

- The indexation allowance gives relief for the inflation element of a gain.

- There are special rules for matching shares sold by a company with shares purchased. Disposals are matched with acquisitions on the same day, the previous nine days and the FA 1985 share pool.

- Rollover relief for replacement of business assets is available to companies to defer gains arising on the disposal of business assets.

Quick Quiz

1   A company is entitled to an annual exempt amount against its chargeable gains. TRUE/FALSE?

2   Indexation allowance runs from the date of _____ to date of _____. Fill in the blanks.

3   What are the share matching rules for company shareholders?

4   H Ltd sells a warehouse for £400,000. The warehouse cost £220,000 and the indexation allowance available is £40,000. The company acquires another warehouse ten months later for £375,000. What is the amount of rollover relief?

Answers to Quick Quiz

1   FALSE. A company is not entitled to an annual exempt amount against its chargeable gains.

2   Indexation allowance runs from the date of **acquisition** to date of **disposal**.

3   The matching rules for shares disposed of by a company shareholder are:

    (a)   Shares acquired on the same day

    (b)   Shares acquired in the previous nine days

    (c)   Shares from the FA 1985 pool

4   The gain on the sale of first warehouse is:

	£
Proceeds	400,000
Less: cost	(220,000)
Unindexed gain	180,000
Less: indexation allowance	(40,000)
Indexed gain	140,000
Less: rollover relief (balancing figure)	(115,000)
Chargeable gain: amount not reinvested £(400,000 – 375,000)	25,000

Now try the questions below from the Exam Question Bank

Number	Level	Marks	Time
Q33	Introductory	5	9 mins
Q34	Examination	15	27 mins

Losses

Topic list	Syllabus reference
1 Trading losses - overview	C2
2 Carry forward trade loss relief	C2(g)
3 Trade loss relief against total profits	C2(h)
4 Choosing loss reliefs and other planning points	C2(i)
5 Other losses	C2(j), D2(c)

Introduction

In the previous three chapters we have seen how a company calculates its taxable total profits and the corporation tax payable.

We now look at how a company may obtain relief for losses. An important factor in deciding what relief to claim is the marginal rate of tax, which may be 20%, 26% or 27.5% as seen earlier.

In the next chapter we will look at groups, and in particular how losses can be relieved by group relief.

Study guide

		Intellectual level
C2	**Taxable total profits**	
(g)	Understand how trading losses can be carried forward.	2
(h)	Understand how trading losses can be claimed against income of the current or previous accounting periods.	2
(i)	Recognise the factors that will influence the choice of loss relief claim.	2
(j)	Explain how relief for a property business loss is given.	1

Exam guide

Losses could form part of question 2 on corporation tax in the exam, they may also be included in questions 3, 4 or 5, or they may not be examined at all. If they do appear, they may be a significant part of the question. Dealing with losses involves a methodical approach: first establish what loss is available for relief, second identify the different reliefs available, and third evaluate the options. Do check the question for specific instructions; you may be told that loss relief should be taken as early as possible.

1 Trading losses – overview

FAST FORWARD

> Trading losses may be relieved by deduction from current total profits, from total profits of earlier periods or from future trading income.

In summary, the following reliefs are available for trading losses incurred by a company.

(a) Claim to deduct the loss from current total profits
(b) Claim to deduct the loss from earlier total profits
(c) Make no claim and automatically carry forward the loss to be deducted from future trading profits of the same trade

These **reliefs may be used in combination**. The options open to the company are:

(a) Do nothing, so that the loss is automatically carried forward against future trading profits

(b) Claim to deduct the loss from current total profits, then automatically carry forward any remaining unrelieved loss to be deducted future trading profits

(c) Claim to deduct the loss from current total profits, then claim to carry any unused loss back and deduct from earlier total profits, and then automatically carry any remaining unrelieved loss forward to be deducted from future trading profits.

The reliefs are explained in further detail below.

Remember that total profits is income and gains before the deduction of gift aid donations. This may lead to gift aid donations becoming unrelieved.

2 Carry forward trade loss relief

FAST FORWARD

> Trading losses carried forward can only be deducted from future trading profits arising from the same trade.

A company must deduct a trading loss which is carried forward against trading profits from the same trade in future accounting periods (unless it has been otherwise relieved by making a claim to deduct it from total profits). **Relief is against the first available profits.**

Question

A Ltd has the following results for the three years to 31 March 2012.

	Year ended		
	31.3.10	31.3.11	31.3.12
	£	£	£
Trading profit/(loss)	(8,550)	3,000	6,000
Property income	0	1,000	1,000
Gift aid donation	300	1,400	1,700

Calculate the taxable total profits for all three years showing any losses available to carry forward at 1 April 2012.

Answer

	Year ended		
	31.3.10	31.3.11	31.3.12
	£	£	£
Trading profits	0	3,000	6,000
Less: carry forward loss relief		(3,000)	(5,550)
	0	0	450
Property income	0	1,000	1,000
Total profits	0	1,000	1,450
Less: Gift aid donation	0	(1,000)	(1,450)
Taxable total profits	0	0	0
Unrelieved gift aid donation	300	400	250

Note that the trading loss carried forward is deducted from the trading profit in future years. It cannot be deducted from the property income.

The gift aid donations become unrelieved.

Loss memorandum

	£
Loss for y/e 31.3.10	8,550
Less used y/e 31.3.11	(3,000)
Loss carried forward at 1.4.11	5,550
Less used y/e 31.3.12	(5,550)
Loss carried forward at 1.4.12	0

3 Trade loss relief against total profits

Loss relief by deduction from total profits is given before gift aid donations and so gift aid donations may become unrelieved.

3.1 Current year relief

A company may claim to deduct a trading loss incurred in an accounting period from total profits. This may make gift aid donations unrelieved because such donations are deducted from total profits after this loss relief to compute taxable total profits.

3.2 Carry back relief

FAST FORWARD Loss relief by deduction from total profits may be given by deduction from current period profits and from the previous 12 months.

Such a loss may then be carried back and deducted from total profits of an accounting period falling wholly or partly within the 12 months of the start of the period in which the loss was incurred. Again, this may cause gift aid donations to be unrelieved.

FAST FORARD A claim for current period loss relief can be made without a claim for carry back. However, if a loss is to be carried back, a claim for current period relief must have been made first.

Any possible loss relief claim for the period of the loss must be made before any excess loss can be carried back to a previous period.

Any carry back is to more recent periods before earlier periods. Relief for earlier losses is given before relief for later losses.

Any loss remaining unrelieved after any loss relief claims against total profits is automatically carried forward to be deducted from future profits of the same trade.

Question   Loss relief against total profits

Helix Ltd has the following results.

	Y/e 30.11.10	y/e 30.11.11
		£
Trading profit/(loss)	22,500	(19,500)
Bank interest received	500	500
Chargeable gains	0	4,000
Gift Aid donation	250	250

Show the taxable total profits for both years affected assuming that loss relief by deduction from total profits is claimed.

Answer

The loss of the year to 30 November 2011 is relieved by deduction from current year total profits and from total profits of the previous 12 months.

	y/e 30.11.10	y/e 30.11.11
	£	£
Trading profit	22,500	0
Investment income	500	500
Chargeable gains	0	4,000
Total profits	23,000	4,500
Less current period loss relief	0	(4,500)
	23,000	0
Less carry back loss relief	(15,000)	(0)
	8,000	0
Less gift aid donation	(250)	0
Taxable total profits	7,750	0
Unrelieved gift aid donation		250

Loss memorandum

Loss incurred in y/e 30.11.11	19,500
Less used: y/e 30.11.11	(4,500)
y/e 30.11.10	(15,000)
Loss available to carry forward	0

If a period falls partly outside the prior 12 months, loss relief is limited to the proportion of the period's profits (before gift aid donations) equal to the proportion of the period which falls within the 12 months.

Question   Short accounting period and loss relief

Tallis Ltd had the following results for the three accounting periods to 31 December 2011.

	Y/e 30.9.10	3 months to 31.12.10	Y/e 31.12.11
	£	£	£
Trading profit (loss)	20,000	12,000	(39,000)
Building society interest received	1,000	400	1,800
Gift aid donations	600	500	0

Show the taxable total profits for all years. Assume loss relief is claimed by deduction from total profits where possible.

Answer

	Y/e 30.9.10	3 months to 31.12.10	Y/e 31.12.11
	£	£	£
Trading profit	20,000	12,000	0
Interest income	1,000	400	1,800
Total profits	21,000	12,400	1,800
Less current period loss relief			(1,800)
	21,000	12,400	0
Less carry back loss relief	(15,750)	(12,400)	
	5,250	0	0
Less gift aid donations	(600)		0
Taxable total profits	4,650	0	0
Unrelieved gift aid donations	0	500	0

Loss memorandum	£
Loss incurred in y/e 31.12.11	39,000
Less used y/e 31.12.11	(1,800)
Less used p/e 31.12.10	(12,400)
Less used y/e 30.9.10 £21,000 x 9/12 (max)	(15,750)
C/f	9,050

Notes

1   The loss can be carried back to set against total profits of the previous 12 months. This means total profits in the y/e 30.9.10 must be time apportioned by multiplying by 9/12.

2   Losses remaining after the loss relief claims against total profits are carried forward to set against future trading profits.

3.3 Claims

A claim for relief by deduction from current or earlier period total profits must be made within two years of the end of the accounting period in which the loss arose. Any claim must be for the *whole* loss (to the extent that profits are available to relieve it). The loss can however be reduced by not claiming full capital allowances, so that higher capital allowances are given (on higher tax written down values) in future years (see later in this chapter).

3.4 Interaction with losses brought forward

A trading loss carried back is relieved after any trading losses brought forward have been offset.

Question   Losses carried forward and back

Chile Ltd has the following results.

| | Year ended | | |
	30.11.10	30.11.11	30.11.12
	£	£	£
Trading profit/(loss)	21,000	(20,000)	40,000
Bank interest received	1,000	1,500	500
Chargeable gains	0	2,000	0
Gift Aid donations	500	500	500

Chile Ltd had a trading loss of £16,000 carried forward at 1 December 2009.

Show the taxable trading profits for all the years affected assuming that loss relief by deduction from total profits is claimed.

Answer

The loss of the year to 30 November 2011 is relieved by deduction from current year total profits and from total profits of the previous twelve months. The trading loss brought forward at 1 December 2009 is relieved in the year ended 30 November 2010 before the loss brought back.

| | Year ended | | |
	30.11.10	30.11.11	30.11.12
	£	£	£
Trading profit	21,000	0	40,000
Less carry forward loss relief	(16,000)	0	(10,500)
	5,000	0	29,500
Interest income	1,000	1,500	500
Chargeable gains	0	2,000	0
Total profits	6,000	3,500	30,000
Less current period loss relief	0	(3,500)	0
	6,000	0	30,000
Less carry back loss relief	(6,000)	0	0
	0	0	30,000
Less gift aid donation	0	0	(500)
Taxable total profits	0	0	29,500
Unrelieved gift aid donations	500	500	

	£
Loss memorandum (1)	
Loss brought forward at 1 December 2009	16,000
Less used y/e 30.11.10	(16,000)
	0

	Year ended		
	30.11.10	30.11.11	30.11.12
	£	£	£
Loss memorandum (2)			£
Loss incurred in y/e 30.11.11			20,000
Less used: y/e 30.11.11			(3,500)
y/e 30.11.10			(6,000)
			10,500
Less used: y/e 30.11.12			(10,500)
C/f			Nil

3.5 Terminal trade loss relief

FAST FORWARD

Trading losses in the last 12 months of trading can be carried back and deducted from total profits of the previous 3 years.

For trading losses incurred in the twelve months up to the cessation of trade the carry back period is extended from twelve months to three years, later years first.

Question
Terminal losses

Brazil Ltd had the following results for the accounting periods up to the cessation of trade on 30 September 2011.

	Y/e 30.9.08	Y/e 30.9.09	Y/e 30.9.10	Y/e 30.9.11
	£	£	£	£
Trading profits	60,000	40,000	15,000	(180,000)
Gains	0	10,000	0	6,000
Property income	12,000	12,000	12,000	12,000

You are required to show how the losses are relieved assuming the maximum use is made of loss relief by deduction from total profits.

Answer

	Y/e 30.9.08	Y/e 30.9.09	Y/e 30.9.10	Y/e 30.9.11
	£	£	£	£
Trading profits	60,000	40,000	15,000	0
Property income	12,000	12,000	12,000	12,000
Gains	0	10,000	0	6,000
Total profits	72,000	62,000	27,000	18,000
Less current period loss relief				(18,000)
				0
Less carry back loss relief	(72,000)	(62,000)	(27,000)	
Taxable total profits	0	0	0	0

	Y/e 30.9.08 £	Y/e 30.9.09 £	Y/e 30.9.10 £	Y/e 30.9.11 £
Loss memorandum				
Loss in y/e 30.9.11				180,000
Less used y/e 30.9.11				(18,000)
Loss of y/e 30.9.11 available for 3 year carry back				162,000
Less used y/e 30.9.10				(27,000)
				135,000
Less used y/e 30.9.09				(62,000)
				73,000
Less used y/e 30.9.08				(72,000)
Loss remaining unrelieved				1,000

4 Choosing loss reliefs and other planning points

When selecting a loss relief, first consider the rate at which relief is obtained and, secondly, the timing of the relief.

This section relates to your PER requirement:

20   Assist with tax planning

4.1 Making the choice

Several alternative loss reliefs may be available. In making a choice consider:

- **The rate at which relief will be obtained:**

    - 26% at the main rate for FY 2011 (28% for FY 2010 and FY 2009)
    - 20% at the small profits rate (21% for FY 2010 and FY 2009)
    - 27.5% if the marginal relief applies (29.75% for FY 2010 and FY 2009)

    We previously outlined how the 27.5% marginal rate is calculated. Remember it is just a marginal rate of tax; it is never actually used in computing a company's corporation tax.

- **How quickly relief will be obtained**: loss relief against total profits is quicker than carry forward loss relief.

- **The extent to which relief for gift aid donations might be lost.**

Exam focus point

When choosing between loss relief claims **always** consider the rate of tax 'saved' by the loss first.

If in the current period the loss 'saves' 20% tax but if carried forward saves 26% tax then a carry forward is the better choice (even though the timing of loss relief is later).

If the tax saved now is 26% and in the future is the same (26%) **then** consider timing (in this example a current claim is better timing wise).

So, first – rate of tax saved, second – timing.

Question

M Ltd has had the following results.

	Year ended 31 March			
	2009	2010	2011	2012
	£	£	£	£
Trading profit/(loss)	2,000	(1,000,000)	200,000	138,000
Chargeable gains	35,000	750,000	0	0
Gift aid donations paid	30,000	20,000	20,000	20,000

Recommend appropriate loss relief claims, and compute the corporation tax for all years based on your recommendations. Assume that future years' profits will be similar to those of the year ended 31 March 2012 and the small profits rate of corporation tax in FY12 and later years will be the same as in FY11.

Answer

A loss relief against total profits claim for the year ended 31 March 2010 will save tax partly in the marginal relief band and partly at the small profits rate. It will waste the gift aid donation of £20,000.

Taxable total profits in the previous year is £7,000 (£35,000 + £2,000 – £30,000) and falls in the small profits band. Carry back would waste gift aid donations of £30,000 and would use £37,000 of loss to save tax on £7,000.

If no current period loss relief claim is made, £200,000 of the loss will save tax at the small profits rate in the year ended 31 March 2011, with £20,000 of gift aid donations being wasted. The remaining £800,000 of the loss, would be carried forward to the year ended 31 March 2012 and later years to save tax at the small profits rate which is assumed to be 20%.

To conclude, a loss relief claim by deduction from total profits should be made for the year of the loss but not in the previous year. £20,000 of gift aid donations would be wasted in the current year, but much of the loss would save tax at the marginal rate and relief would be obtained quickly. Carrying the loss back would save tax at 21% but £30,000 of gift aid donations would become unrelieved. Therefore it would be more advantageous to carry the loss forward to where it will also save tax at the assumed small profits rate of 20%.

The final computations are as follows.

	Year ended 31 March			
	2009	2010	2011	2012
	£	£	£	£
Trading income	2,000	0	200,000	138,000
Less carry forward loss relief	0	0	(200,000)	(50,000)
	2,000	0	0	88,000
Chargeable gains	35,000	750,000	0	0
Total profits	37,000	750,000	0	88,000
Less current period loss relief	0	(750,000)	0	0
	37,000	0	0	88,000
Less gift aid donations	(30,000)	0	0	(20,000)
Taxable total profits	7,000	0	0	68,000

	Year ended 31 March			
	2009	2010	2011	2012
	£	£	£	£
CT at 21/20%	1,470	0	0	13,600
Unrelieved gift aid donations	0	20,000	20,000	0

4.2 Other tax planning points

A company must normally claim capital allowances on its tax return. A company with losses should consider claiming less than the maximum amount of capital allowances available. This will result in a higher tax written down value to carry forward and therefore higher capital allowances in future years.

Reducing capital allowances in the current period reduces the loss available for relief against total profits. As this relief, if claimed, must be claimed for all of a loss available, a reduced capital allowance claim could be advantageous where all of a loss would be relieved at a lower tax rate in the current (or previous) period than the effective rate of relief for capital allowances will be in future periods.

5 Other losses

5.1 Capital losses

Capital losses can only be set against capital gains in the current or future accounting periods.

Capital losses can only be set against capital gains in the same or future accounting periods, never against income. Capital losses must be set against the first available gains and cannot be carried back.

5.2 Property business losses

Property business losses are set off first against total profits in the current period and then carried forward against future total profits.

Property business losses are first deducted from the company's total profits of the current accounting period. Any excess is then:

(a) **carried forward to the next accounting period** and treated as a loss made by the company in that period, or

(b) available for surrender as **group relief** (see later in this Text).

Chapter Roundup

- Trading losses may be relieved by deduction from current total profits, from total profits of earlier periods or from future trading income.

- Trading losses carried forward can only be deducted from future trading profits arising from the same trade.

- Loss relief by deduction from total profits is given before gift aid donations and so gift aid donations may become unrelieved.

- Loss relief by deduction from total profits may be given by deduction from current period profits and from profits of the previous 12 months.

- A claim for current period loss relief can be made without a claim for carry back relief. However, if a loss is to be carried back, a claim for current period relief must have been made first.

- Trading losses in the last 12 months of trading can be carried back and deducted from total profits of the previous 3 years.

- When selecting a loss relief, first consider the rate at which relief is obtained and, secondly, the timing of the relief.

- Capital losses can only be set against capital gains in the current or future accounting periods.

- Property business losses are set off first against total profits in the current period and then carried forward against future total profits.

Quick Quiz

1   Against what profits may trading losses carried forward be set?

    A   Against all trading profits
    B   Against total profits
    C   Against profits from the same trade
    D   Against trading profits and gains

2   To what extent may losses be carried back?

3   Why might a company make a reduced capital allowances claim?

1 C. Against profits from the same trade.

2 A loss may be carried back and set against total profits of the previous 12 months. The loss carried back is the trading loss left unrelieved after a claim to deduct the loss from total profits of the loss making accounting period has been made. A loss arising on the final 12 months of trading can be carried back and deducted from profits arising in the previous 36 months.

3 Reducing capital allowances in the current accounting period reduces the loss available for relief by deduction from total profits. Such a loss relief claim means that all of the available loss is utilised. Reducing capital allowances reduces the size of the available loss.

Now try the question below from the Exam Question Bank

Number	Level	Marks	Time
Q35	Examination	15	27 mins

23

Groups

Introduction

In the previous chapters in this section we have covered corporation tax on single companies, including the reliefs for losses.

In this chapter we consider the extent to which tax law recognises group relationships between companies. Companies in a group are still separate entities with their own tax liabilities, but tax law recognises the close relationship between group companies. They can, if they meet certain conditions, share their losses and also pass assets between each other without chargeable gains.

In the next chapter we consider overseas aspects of corporation tax.

Study guide

		Intellectual level
C4	**The effect of a group corporate structure for corporation tax purposes**	
(a)	Define an associated company and recognise the effect of being an associated company for corporation tax purposes.	2
(b)	Define a 75% group, and recognise the reliefs that are available to members of such a group.	2
(c)	Define a 75% capital gains group, and recognise the reliefs that are available to members of such a group.	2
C5	**The use of exemptions and reliefs in deferring and minimising corporation tax liabilities**	

Exam guide

Groups may feature in your examination as part of question 2, which will always be on corporation tax, or in questions 4 or 5. Your first step in dealing with any group question must be to establish the relationship between the companies and identify what group or groups exist. You may find it helpful to draw a diagram. You must be aware that 75% groups and capital gains groups do not always coincide. The next steps will be to identify the amounts eligible for relief and to work out your strategy for maximising tax relief. Always look out for companies receiving marginal relief; they will have the highest marginal tax rate of 27.5%.

1 Types of group

A group exists for taxation purposes where one company is a subsidiary of another. The percentage shareholding involved determines the taxation consequences of the fact that there is a group.

The three examinable types of relationship for tax purposes are:

- **Associated companies** (see earlier in this text)
- **75% subsidiaries**
- **Groups for chargeable gains purposes** (capital gains groups)

2 Group relief

FAST FORWARD

Within a 75% group, current period trading losses, excess property business losses and excess gift aid donations can be surrendered between UK companies. Profits and losses of corresponding accounting periods must be matched up. Group relief is available where the existence of a group is established through companies resident anywhere in the world.

2.1 Group relief provisions

The group relief provisions enable companies within a 75% group to transfer trading losses to other companies within the group, in order to set these against taxable total profits and reduce the group's overall corporation tax liability.

2.2 Definition of a 75% group

For one company to be a **75% subsidiary** of another, the holding company must have:

* At least 75% of the ordinary share capital of the subsidiary
* A right to at least 75% of the distributable income of the subsidiary, and
* A right to at least 75% of the net assets of the subsidiary were it to be wound up.

Two companies are members of a 75% group where one is a 75% subsidiary of the other, or both are 75% subsidiaries of a third company.

Two companies are in a 75% group only if there is a 75% effective interest. Thus an 80% subsidiary (T) of an 80% subsidiary (S) is not in a 75% group with the holding company (H), because the effective interest is only 80% × 80% = 64%. However, S and T are in a 75% group and can claim group relief from each other. S *cannot* claim group relief from T and pass it on to H; it can only claim group relief for its own use.

A 75% group may include non-UK resident companies. **However, losses may generally only be surrendered between UK resident companies**.

Relief for trading losses incurred by an overseas subsidiary is not examinable in your paper.

Illustration of a 75% group:

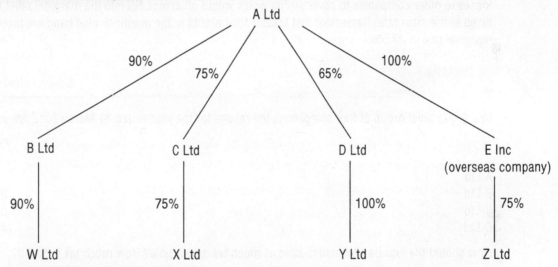

The companies in the 75% group are:

A Ltd
B Ltd
W Ltd (81% effective holding by A)
C Ltd
E Inc
Z Ltd (75% effective holding by A)

In addition C Ltd and X Ltd and also D Ltd and Y Ltd form their own separate mini-75% groups.

Note that a 75% group may also be called a 'group relief' group.

2.3 The relief

A surrendering company can surrender any amount of its trading loss but a claimant company can only claim an amount up to its available taxable total profits. The best option is normally to surrender losses to set against taxable total profits of the company suffering the highest marginal rate of tax.

2.3.1 Transfer of loss

A company which has made a loss (the surrendering company) may transfer its loss to another member of the 75% group (the claimant company).

2.3.2 The claimant company

A **claimant company** is assumed to use its own current year losses or losses brought forward in working out the taxable total profits against which it may claim group relief, even if it does not in fact claim relief for current losses against total profits.

Furthermore, **group relief is against taxable total profits after all other reliefs for the current period (for example gift aid donations) or brought forward from earlier periods**.

Group relief is given before relief for any amounts carried back from later periods.

2.3.3 The surrendering company

A surrendering company may group relieve a trading loss before setting it against its own total profits for the period of the loss, and may specify any amount to be surrendered.

This is **important** for **tax planning as it enables the surrendering company to leave taxable total profits in its own computation to be charged to corporation tax at the small profits rate**, while surrendering its losses to other companies to cover profits which would otherwise fall into the marginal relief band or be taxed at the main rate. Remember that taxable total profits in the marginal relief band are taxed at the marginal rate of 27.5%.

Question
Group relief of losses

In a group relief group of four companies, the results for the year ended 31 March 2012 are as follows.

	Profit/(loss) £
A Ltd	52,000
B Ltd	212,500
C Ltd	1,000,000
D Ltd	(400,000)

How should the loss be allocated to save as much tax as possible? How much tax is saved?

Answer

The upper and lower limits for marginal relief are £1,500,000/4 = £375,000 and £300,000/4 = £75,000 respectively.

	A Ltd £	B Ltd £	C Ltd £
Taxable total profits before group relief	52,000	212,500	1,000,000
Less group relief (note)	0	(137,500)	(262,500)
Taxable total profits after group relief	52,000	75,000	737,500
Tax saved			
£137,500 × 27.5%		37,813	
£262,500 × 26%			68,250
Total £(37,813 + 68,250) = £106,063			

Note. We wish to save the most tax possible for the group.

Since A Ltd is in the small profits band, any loss given to it will save tax at the small profits rate of 20%.

B Ltd is in the marginal relief band. Therefore, any loss given to B saves the effective marginal rate of 27.5% until the profits fall to £75,000 (the marginal relief lower limit). After this only 20% is saved.

C Ltd is in the main rate band of 26% until profits fall to £375,000 (the marginal relief upper limit).

So to conclude it is best to give B Ltd £137,500 of loss and save 27.5% tax on the profits in the marginal relief band. The balance of the loss is then given to C Ltd to save 26% tax.

2.4 Losses eligible for relief

A company may surrender to other group companies trading losses, excess property income losses and excess gift aid donations. Gift aid donations and property income losses can only be group relieved to the extent that they exceed total profits before taking account of any losses of the current period or brought forward or back from other accounting periods. Excess gift aid donations must be surrendered before excess property income losses.

Only current period losses are available for group relief.

2.5 Corresponding accounting periods

Surrendered losses must be set against taxable total profits of a corresponding accounting period. If the accounting periods of a surrendering company and a claimant company are not the same this means that both the profits and losses must be apportioned so that only the results of the period of overlap may be set off. Apportionment is on a time basis. However, in the period when a company joins or leaves a group, an alternative method may be used if the result given by time-apportionment would be unjust or unreasonable.

Question   Corresponding accounting periods

	£
S Ltd incurs a trading loss for the year to 30 September 2011	(150,000)
H Ltd makes taxable total profits:	
for the year to 31 December 2010	200,000
for the year to 31 December 2011	100,000

What group relief can H Ltd claim from S Ltd?

Answer

H Ltd can claim group relief as follows.

	£
For the year ended 31 December 2010 taxable total profits of the corresponding accounting period (1.10.10 – 31.12.10) are £200,000 × 3/12	50,000
Losses of the corresponding accounting period are £150,000 × 3/12	37,500
A claim for £37,500 of group relief may be made against H Ltd's taxable total profits for the year ended 31 December 2010.	
For the year ended 31 December 2011 taxable total profits of the corresponding accounting period (1.1.11 – 30.9.11) are £100,000 × 9/12	75,000
Losses of the corresponding accounting period are £150,000 × 9/12	112,500
A claim for £75,000 of group relief may be made against H Ltd's taxable total profits for the year ended 31 December 2011.	

If a claimant company claims relief for losses surrendered by more than one company, the total relief that may be claimed for a period that overlaps is limited to the proportion of the claimant's taxable total profits attributable to that period. Similarly, if a company surrenders losses to more than one claimant, the total losses that may be surrendered in a period that overlaps is limited to the proportion of the surrendering company's losses attributable to that period.

2.6 Claims

A claim for group relief is normally made on the claimant company's tax return. It is ineffective unless a notice of consent is also given by the surrendering company.

Groupwide claims/surrenders can be made as one person can act for two or more companies at once.

Any payment by the claimant company for group relief, up to the amount of the loss surrendered, is ignored for all corporation tax purposes.

2.7 Tax planning for group relief

This section relates to your PER requirement:
20   Assist with tax planning

This section outlines some tax planning points to bear in mind when dealing with a group.

Group relief should first be given in this order:

1st   To companies in the marginal relief band paying **27.5%** tax (FY 2011) (but only **sufficient loss to bring taxable total profits down to the lower limit**)

2nd   To companies paying the main rate of tax at **26%** (FY 2011)

3rd   To companies paying the small profits rate at **20%** (FY 2011)

Similarly, a company should make a claim to use a loss itself rather than surrender the loss to other group companies if the claim against its own total profits would lead to a tax saving at a higher rate.

Companies with profits may benefit by reducing their claims for capital allowances in a particular year. This may leave sufficient profits to take advantage of group relief which may only be available for the current year. The amount on which writing-down allowances can be claimed in later years is increased accordingly.

3 Capital gains group

A capital gains group consists of the top company plus companies in which the top company has a 50% effective interest, provided there is a 75% holding at each level. Within a capital gains group, assets are transferred at no gain and no loss.

3.1 Definition

Companies are in a capital gains group if:

(a)   At each level, there is a 75% holding, and
(b)   The top company has an effective interest of over 50% in the group companies.

If A holds 75% of B, B holds 75% of C and C holds 75% of D, then A, B and C are in such a group, but D is outside the group because A's interest in D is only 75% × 75% × 75% = 42.1875%. Furthermore, D is not in a group with C, because the group must include the top company (A).

The definition of a capital gains group is wider than a that of a 75% group as only a effective 50% interest is needed compared to a 75% interest. However a company can only be in one capital gains group although it may be a member of more than one 75% group.

Illustration of a capital gains group:

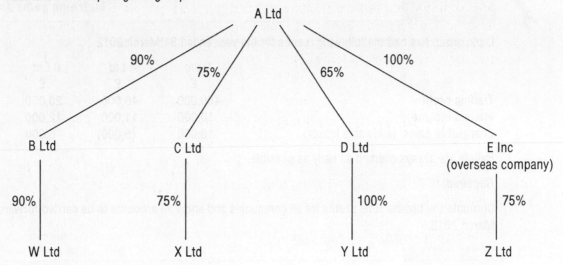

The companies in a group for capital gains purposes are:

A Ltd
B Ltd
W Ltd
C Ltd
X Ltd (75% subsidiary of 75% subsidiary, effective interest over 50%)
E Inc
Z Ltd

There is a separate capital gains group of D Ltd and Y Ltd.

3.2 Intra-group transfers

Companies in a capital gains group make intra-group transfers of chargeable assets without a chargeable gain or an allowable loss arising. No election is needed, as this relief is compulsory. The assets are deemed to be transferred at such a price as will give the transferor no gain and no loss. (ie cost plus indexation allowance up to the date of transfer)

3.3 Matching group gains and losses

Gains and losses can be matched within a group. This can be done by electing that all or part of any gain or loss is treated as transferred between group companies.

This section relates to your PER requirement:
20   Assist with tax planning

Two members of a capital gains group can elect to transfer a chargeable gain or allowable loss, or any part of a gain or loss, between them. This election must be made within two years of the end of the accounting period in which the gain or loss accrues in the company which is making the transfer.

Only current year losses can be transferred, not brought forward losses.

From a tax planning point of view, elections(s) should be made to match gains and losses and ensure that net taxable gains arise in the company subject to the lowest rate of corporation tax.

D plc group has had the following results for the year ended 31 March 2012.

	D plc £	A Ltd £	B Ltd £	C Ltd £
Trading profit	400,000	46,000	20,000	220,000
Interest income	10,000	11,000	12,000	14,000
Chargeable gains/ (allowable losses)	18,000	(5,000)	6,000	(2,000)

Reliefs are always claimed as early as possible.

Required

Compute the taxable total profits for all companies and show all amounts to be carried forward at 31 March 2012.

Answer

Year ended 31.3.12

	D plc £	A Ltd £	B Ltd £	C Ltd £
Trading profit	400,000	46,000	20,000	220,000
Interest income	10,000	11,000	12,000	14,000
Income	410,000	57,000	32,000	234,000

There are 4 companies in the group.

Upper limit   1,500,000/4 = £375,000
Lower limit   300,000/4 = £75,000

D plc is paying tax at the main rate of 26%.

A Ltd and B Ltd are paying tax at the small profits rate of 20%.

C Ltd is paying CT at a marginal rate of 27.5%.

Since the election can be used to transfer all or part of any of the gains, the simplest way to achieve the optimum result is to identify where the resultant net gains should be taxed:

A Ltd up to the lower limit capacity = £75,000 − £57,000 = £18,000 of gains

B Ltd up to the lower limit capacity = £75,000 − £32,000 = £43,000 of gains

One way of achieving this would be to:

(a)   elect that D plc's gain is transferred to A Ltd offsetting A Ltd's loss, and

(b)   elect that C plc's loss is transferred to B Ltd offsetting B Ltd's gain.

The total profits are:

	D plc £	A Ltd £	B Ltd £	C Ltd £
Income	410,000	57,000	32,000	234,000
Capital Gain				
(18,000 − 5,000)/(6,000 − 2,000)		13,000	4,000	
Taxable total profits	410,000	70,000	36,000	234,000

Note that there are other alternatives: all the gains and losses could have been transferred to A Ltd, so that the total net gains of £17,000 resulted in A Ltd having taxable total profits of £74,000.

3.4 Rollover relief

Rollover relief is available in a capital gains group.

If a member of a capital gains group disposes of an asset eligible for capital gains rollover relief it may treat all of the group companies as a single unit for the purpose of claiming such relief. Acquisitions by other group members within the qualifying period of one year before the disposal to three years afterwards may therefore **be matched with the disposal**. However, both the disposing company and the acquiring company must make the claim. If an asset is transferred at no gain and no loss between group members, that transfer does not count as the acquisition of an asset for rollover or holdover relief purpose.

Exam focus point

Try to remember the following summary – it will be of great help in the exam.

Parent Co **controls** over 50% of subsidiary

- associated companies for upper and lower limits

Parent Co **owns** 75% or more of subsidiary (directly and effectively)

- surrender trading losses, excess property business losses, excess gift aid donations to companies with some taxable total profits for same time period

Parent Co **owns** 75% or more of subsidiary and subsidiary owns 75% or more of its subsidiaries

- transfer assets between companies automatically at no gain/no loss
- capital gains and losses can be matched between group member companies
- all companies treated as one for rollover relief purposes.

Chapter Roundup

- Within a 75% group, current period trading losses, excess property business losses and excess gift aid donations can be surrendered between UK companies. Profits and losses of corresponding accounting periods must be matched up. Group relief is available where the existence of a group is established through companies resident anywhere in the world.

- A surrendering company can surrender any amount of its trading loss but a claimant company can only claim an amount up to its available profits. The best option is normally to surrender losses to set against taxable total profits of the company suffering the highest marginal rate of tax.

- A capital gains group consists of the top company plus companies in which the top company has a 50% effective interest, provided there is a 75% holding at each level. Within a capital gains group, assets are transferred at no gain and no loss.

- Gains and losses can be matched within a group. This can be done by electing that all or part of any gain or loss is treated as transferred between group companies.

- Rollover relief is available in a capital gains group.

Quick Quiz

1 List the types of losses which may be group relieved.
2 When may assets be transferred intra-group at no gain and no loss?
3 How can capital gains and losses within a group be matched with each other?

Answers to Quick Quiz

1   Trading losses, excess property business losses and excess gift aid donations.

2   No gain no loss asset transfers are mandatory between companies in a capital gains group.

3   Two members of a gains group can elect that all or part of a gain or loss is transferred between them within two years of the end of the accounting period in which the gain or loss accrued. This election allows the group to match its gains and losses in one company.

Now try the questions below from the Exam Question Bank

Number	Level	Marks	Time
Q36	Examination	15	27 mins
Q37	Examination	15	27 mins

Corporation tax

Overseas matters for companies

Topic list	Syllabus reference
1 Branch or subsidiary abroad	C4(d)
2 Double taxation relief (DTR)	C4(e)
3 Transfer pricing	C4(f)

Introduction

In the previous chapter we considered group relationships. We now turn our attention to UK companies trading abroad. We see how relief may be given for overseas taxes suffered and how the transfer pricing legislation applies.

We will conclude our corporation tax studies in the next chapter by considering the administration of corporation tax.

Study guide

		Intellectual level
C4	**The effect of a group corporate structure for corporation tax purposes**	
(d)	Compare the UK tax treatment of an overseas branch to an overseas subsidiary.	2
(e)	Calculate double taxation relief.	2
(f)	Explain the basic principles of the transfer pricing rules.	2

Exam guide

Overseas aspects of corporation tax may be tested in question 2, ie as part of a larger question or in question 4 or question 5. Questions dealing with DTR need a methodical approach: first calculate the taxable foreign income and the amount of foreign tax available for relief, next compute the UK corporation tax payable, allocating it between UK income and foreign income, and finally apply DTR, which will be the lower of the foreign tax paid and the UK corporation tax payable. The transfer pricing rules are designed to stop profits being shifted abroad; the concept is straightforward – the UK profits must be increased by the shifted profits.

1 Branch or subsidiary abroad

FAST FORWARD

> A UK resident company intending to do business abroad must choose between an overseas branch and an overseas subsidiary. A branch may be useful if losses are expected in the early years. If a subsidiary is chosen, the rules on trading at artificial prices must be considered.

1.1 Taxation of foreign income and gains

A UK resident company is subject to corporation tax on its worldwide profits. It is also (unlike a non-resident company) entitled to the small profits rate of tax and to marginal relief.

If a UK resident company makes investments abroad or has a foreign branch, it will be liable to corporation tax on the income made, the taxable amount being the gross amount, ie before the deduction of any foreign taxes.

A UK resident company may receive dividends from an overseas subsidiary. All dividends received by a UK resident company from a non-UK resident company are exempt from corporation tax for the purposes of the F6 examination. However, such dividends may still affect the calculation of corporation tax. This is because franked investment income includes all dividends received by a company (other than group income), whether received from a UK company or a foreign company.

1.2 Taxation of foreign branches and foreign subsidiaries

An overseas branch of a UK company is effectively an extension of the UK trade, and 100% of the branch profits are assessed to UK corporation tax. Whether or not profits are remitted to the UK is irrelevant.

Exam focus point

New rules are being introduced which will enable a company to elect to treat the profits of an overseas branch as being exempt from corporation tax. However, these rules will only be applicable for accounting periods starting on or after the date that Finance Act 2011 receives Royal Assent. Therefore the examiner has stated that these rules will **not be examined** in the June and December 2012 examinations.

Question

T Ltd is a UK company with an overseas branch. The results of T Ltd for the year ended 31 March 2012 are as follows:

	Total £	UK £	Branch £
Tax adjusted profits	1,000,000	800,000	200,000

The overseas branch is subject to tax overseas at the rate of 22%. Calculate the UK tax liability.

Answer

The corporation tax liability of T Ltd for the year ended 31 March 2012 is as follows.

	£
UK trading profit	800,000
Overseas trading profit	200,000
Trading profits/ Taxable total profits	1,000,000
Corporation tax at 26%	260,000
Marginal relief 3/200 (1,500,000 – 1,000,000)	(7,500)
	252,500
Double taxation relief (see below)	(44,000)
	208,500

(1) Double taxation relief is calculated as £44,000 (200,000 at 22%) being the amount of overseas tax paid.

(2) This is lower than the UK corporation tax on the branch profits of £50,500 (252,500 × 200,000/1,000,000). The UK corporation tax rate is 25.25%.

Note. Double tax relief is covered in more detail in Section 2.

It is important to appreciate the difference between operating overseas through a branch and operating overseas through a subsidiary.

(1) Relief is usually available in the UK for trading losses if incurred by an overseas branch but usually no UK relief is available for trading losses incurred by an overseas subsidiary.

(2) UK capital allowances will be available in respect of plant and machinery purchased by an overseas branch.

(3) An overseas subsidiary will be an associated company, and so the small profits lower and upper limits will be reduced. This may increase the rate of UK corporation tax.

2 Double taxation relief (DTR)

A company may be subject to overseas taxes as well as to UK corporation tax on the same profits. Double taxation relief is available in respect of the foreign tax suffered.

2.1 Types of DTR

In the UK, relief for foreign tax suffered by a company is available in three ways:

(a) Treaty relief

Under a treaty entered into between the UK and the overseas country, a treaty may exempt certain profits from taxation in one of the countries involved, thus completely avoiding double taxation.

More usually treaties provide for credit to be given for tax suffered in one of the countries against the tax liability in the other.

(b) **Unilateral credit relief**

Where no treaty relief is available, unilateral relief may be available in the UK giving credit for the foreign tax against the UK tax.

(c) **Unilateral expense relief**

Not examined in your syllabus.

2.2 Credit relief

Double tax relief (DTR) is the lower of:
- the UK tax on a source of income
- the overseas tax on that income source.

Relief is available for overseas tax suffered on branch profits, up to the amount of the UK corporation tax (at the company's average rate) attributable to that income. The gross income, including the overseas tax, is included in taxable total profits.

Question   Unilateral credit relief

AS plc has UK trading income of £2,000,000 and received £80,000 from a foreign branch for the year to 31 March 2012. The branch income was paid net of 20% overseas tax. Show that the branch profits are £100,000 and compute the corporation tax payable.

Answer

	Total £	UK £	Overseas £
Trading income			
UK trading profits	2,000,000	2,000,000	
Branch profits	100,000		100,000
Taxable total profits	2,100,000	2,000,000	100,000
Corporation tax at 26%	546,000	520,000	26,000
Less DTR: lower of:			
(a) overseas tax: £20,000; or			
(b) UK tax on branch income: £28,000	(20,000)		(20,000)
	526,000	520,000	6,000

Working: Branch profits

£80,000 × 100/(100 − 20) = £100,000.

2.3 Allocation of losses and gift aid donations

Gift aid donations and losses should initially be set against UK income. They should subsequently be set against the overseas income source that suffers the lowest rate of overseas tax.

One further factor affects the computation of UK tax on overseas income against which credit for overseas tax may be claimed. This is the allocation of gift aid donations and losses relieved against total profits.

A company may allocate its gift aid donations and losses relieved against total profits in whatever manner it likes for the purpose of computing double taxation relief. It should set the maximum amount

against any UK profits, thereby maximising the corporation tax attributable to the foreign profits and hence maximising the double taxation relief available.

If a company has several sources of overseas profits, then gift aid donations and losses should be allocated first to UK profits, and then to overseas sources which have suffered the **lowest** rates of overseas taxation.

Losses relieved by carry forward must in any case be set against the first available profits of the trade which gave rise to the loss.

A company with a choice of loss reliefs should consider the effect of its choice on double taxation relief. For example, a claim against total profits might lead to there being no UK tax liability, or a very small liability, so that foreign tax would go unrelieved. Carry forward loss relief against future trading profits might avoid this problem and still leave very little UK tax to pay for the period of the loss.

Question	Allocation of gift aid

Kairo plc is a UK resident company with five UK resident subsidiaries and two overseas branches, one in Atlantis and one in Utopia. The company produced the following results for the year to 31 March 2012.

	£
UK trading profits	10,000
Profits from overseas branch in Atlantis (before overseas tax of £8,000)	40,000
Profits from overseas branch in Utopia (before overseas tax of £110,000)	250,000
Gift aid donations	(15,000)

Compute the UK corporation tax liability.

Answer

KAIRO PLC – CORPORATION TAX – YEAR TO 31 MARCH 2012

	Total £	UK £	Atlantis £	Utopia £
Total profits	300,000	10,000	40,000	250,000
Less Gift aid donations (W)	(15,000)	(10,000)	(5,000)	
Taxable total profits	285,000	Nil	35,000	250,000
Corporation tax @ 26% (N)	74,100	–	9,100	65,000
Less DTR (W)	(73,000)	–	(8,000)	(65,000)
Corporation tax	1,100	–	1,100	–

Note

The main rate of corporation tax applies, since the upper limit for marginal relief (£1,500,000 ÷ 6 = £250,000) is exceeded.

Working
The DTR is the lower of:

Atlantis: UK tax £9,100;
           Overseas tax £8,000 (Rate of overseas tax = 20%), ie £8,000

Utopia: UK tax £65,000;
           Overseas tax £110,000 (Rate of overseas tax = 44%), ie £65,000

Note. The Atlantis branch profits suffer the lower rate of overseas tax so the gift aid donations remaining after offset against the UK income are allocated against the Atlantis branch income in preference to the Utopia branch income.

3 Transfer pricing

The transfer pricing legislation restricts the freedom of a company to buy and sell goods at whatever price it wishes between associated persons. A profit on such a transfer must be computed as though the transfer had been made at an arm's length price. The transfer pricing legislation does not apply to transactions between two UK resident persons unless they are large enterprises.

Companies under common control could structure their transactions in such a way that they can shift profit (or losses) from one company to another.

For example consider a company which wishes to sell goods valued at £20,000 to an independent third party.

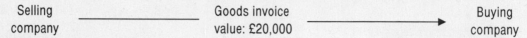

In this case all the profit on the sale arises to the selling company. Alternatively the sale could be rearranged:

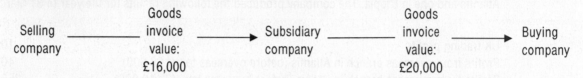

In this case £4,000 of the profit has been diverted to the subsidiary.

This technique could be used to direct profits to a company which will pay less tax on those profits.

This is a 'tax advantage' and there is **anti avoidance legislation** which **requires the profit to be computed as if the transactions had been carried out at arm's length and not at the prices actually used.**

The transfer pricing rules apply to transactions between two persons if either:

(a)   one person directly or indirectly participates in the management, control or capital of the other; or

(b)   a third party directly or indirectly participates in the management, control or capital of both.

<table>
<tr><td>**Exam focus point**</td><td>You will only be expected to deal with situations where profits are being shifted to an overseas company in your exam.</td></tr>
</table>

Companies must self-assess their liability to tax under the transfer pricing rules and pay any corporation tax due. A statutory procedure exists for advance pricing arrangements (APAs) whereby a company can agree in advance that its transfer pricing policy is acceptable to HMRC – ie not requiring a self-assessment adjustment. The APA facility is voluntary but companies may feel the need to use the facility as it provides necessary advance confirmation that their approach to transfer pricing in their self-assessment is acceptable.

Chapter Roundup

- A UK resident company intending to do business abroad must choose between an overseas branch and an overseas subsidiary. A branch may be useful if losses are expected in the early years. If a subsidiary is chosen, the rules on trading at artificial prices must be considered.

- Double tax relief is the lower of:
  - the UK tax on a source of income
  - the overseas tax on that income source.

- Gift aid donations and losses should initially be set against UK income. They should subsequently be set against the overseas income source that suffers the lowest rate of overseas tax.

- The transfer pricing legislation restricts the freedom of a company to buy and sell goods at whatever price it wishes between associated persons. A profit on such a transfer must be computed as though the transfer had been made at an arm's length price. The transfer pricing legislation does not apply to transactions between UK resident persons unless they are large enterprises.

Quick Quiz

1   A UK company is planning to set up a new operation in Australia that will initially be loss making. It should set up as a branch of the UK company rather than as a subsidiary. TRUE/FALSE?

2   How best should gift aid donations be allocated in computing credit relief for foreign tax?

   A   Against UK profits first
   B   Against profits generally
   C   Against overseas profits first
   D   Against UK and overseas profits in proportion

3   What measures are included in tax legislation against the use of artificial transfer prices?

1   True. If losses are expected to arise then a branch operation is best since relief is usually available for losses of a foreign branch.

2   A. Gift aid donations should be set firstly against any UK profits, then against overseas income sources suffering the lowest rates of overseas taxation before those suffering at higher rates.

3   Although a company may buy and sell goods at any price it wishes, the transfer pricing anti-avoidance legislation requires profit to be computed as if the transactions had been carried out at arm's length, in certain circumstances.

Now try the question below from the Exam Question Bank

Number	Level	Marks	Time
Q38	Examination	10	18 mins

Self assessment and payment of tax by companies

Topic list	Syllabus reference
1 Corporation tax self assessment	H1(b)
2 Returns, records and claims	H2(a),(e)
3 Compliance checks, appeals and disputes	H3(a),(b)
4 Payment of corporation tax and interest	H2(b),(d), H4(a)
5 Penalties	H4(b)

Introduction

We now complete our corporation tax studies by looking at the self assessment system for corporation tax, under which companies must file returns and pay the tax due.

In the following chapters we will turn our attention to VAT, which applies to both incorporated and unincorporated businesses.

Study guide

		Intellectual level
H1	**The systems for self-assessment and the making of returns**	
(b)	Explain and apply the features of the self assessment system as it applies to companies, including the use of iXBRL.	2
H2	**The time limits for the submission of information, claims and payment of tax, including payments on account**	
(a)	Recognise the time limits that apply to the filing of returns and the making of claims.	2
(b)	Recognise the due dates for the payment of tax under the self-assessment system.	2
(d)	Explain how large companies are required to account for corporation tax on a quarterly basis.	2
(e)	List the information and records that taxpayers need to retain for tax purposes.	1
H3	**The procedures relating to compliance checks, appeals and disputes**	
(a)	Explain the circumstances in which HM Revenue & Customs can make a compliance check into a self assessment tax return.	2
(b)	Explain the procedures for dealing with appeals and disputes.	1
H4	**Penalties for non-compliance**	
(a)	Calculate late payment interest.	2
(b)	State the penalties that can be charged.	2

Exam guide

Although question 2 of the exam will always be on corporation tax it will not necessarily include any of the administrative procedures of the self assessment system. They could, however, feature in either question 4 or 5. It is unlikely, but not impossible, that you will be tested on the administrative rules for companies and individuals in the same paper.

1 Corporation tax self assessment

FAST FORWARD

A company that does not receive a notice requiring a return to be filed must, if it is chargeable to tax, notify HMRC within twelve months of the end of the accounting period.

1.1 Introduction

This section relates to your PER requirement:
19   Evaluate and compute taxes payable

The self assessment system relies upon the company completing and filing a tax return and paying the tax due. The system is enforced by a system of penalties for failure to comply within the set time limits, and by interest for late payment of tax.

Dormant companies and companies which have not yet started to trade may not be required to complete tax returns. Such companies have a duty to notify HMRC when they should be brought within the self assessment system.

1.2 Notification of first accounting period

A company must notify HMRC of the beginning of its first accounting period (ie usually when it starts to trade) and the beginning of any subsequent period that does not immediately follow the end of a previous accounting period. The notice must be in the prescribed form and submitted within three months of the relevant date.

1.3 Notification of chargeability

A company that does not receive a notice requiring a return to be filed must, if it is chargeable to tax, **notify HMRC within twelve months of the end of the accounting period.**

2 Returns, records and claims

A company must, in general, file a tax return within twelve months of the end of an accounting period.

2.1 Returns

A company's tax return must be filed electronically and must include a self assessment of any tax payable. Limited companies are also required to file electronically a copy of their accounts. Where a return is filed after 1 April 2011 in respect of an accounting period ending after 31 March 2010, the filing of accounts must be done in inLine eXtensIble Business Reporting Language (iXBRL).

iXBRL is a standard for reporting business information in an electronic form which uses tags that can be read by computers. HMRC supplies software which can be used by small companies with simple accounts. This software automatically produces accounts and tax computations in the correct format. Other companies can use:

(a) other software that automatically produces iXBRL accounts and computations; or
(b) a tagging service which will apply the appropriate tags to accounts and computations; or
(c) software that enables the appropriate tags to be added to accounts and computations.

The tags used are contained in dictionaries known as taxonomies, with different taxonomies for different purposes. The tagging of tax computations is based on the corporation tax computational taxonomy, which includes over 1,200 relevant tags.

An obligation to file a return arises only when the company receives a notice requiring a return. A return is required for each accounting period ending during or at the end of the period specified in the notice requiring a return. A company also has to file a return for certain other periods which are not accounting periods (eg for a period when the company is dormant).

A notice to file a return may also require other information, accounts and reports. For a UK resident company the requirement to deliver accounts normally extends only to the accounts required under the Companies Act.

A return is due on or before the filing date. This is normally the later of:

(a) **12 months after the end of the period to which the return relates;**
(b) **three months from the date on which the notice requiring the return was made.**

The relevant period of account is that in which the accounting period to which the return relates ends.

2.2 Amending a return

A company may amend a return within twelve months of the filing date.

HMRC may amend a return to correct obvious errors, or anything else that an officer has reason to believe is incorrect in the light of information available, within nine months of the day the return was filed, or if the correction is to an amended return, within nine months of the filing of an amendment. The company may amend its return so as to reject the correction. If the time limit for amendments has expired, the company may reject the correction by giving notice within three months.

2.3 Records

Companies must keep records until the latest of:

(a)   **six years from the end of the accounting period;**
(b)   **the date any compliance checks are completed;**
(c)   **the date after which a compliance check may not be commenced.**

All business records and accounts, including contracts and receipts, must be kept or information showing that the company has prepared a complete and correct tax return.

If a return is demanded more than six years after the end of the accounting period, any records or information which the company still has must be kept until the later of the end of a compliance check and the expiry of the right to start an one.

2.4 Claims

Wherever possible claims must be made on a tax return or on an amendment to it and must be quantified at the time the return is made.

If a company believes that it has paid excessive tax, for example as a result of an error in its tax return, a claim may be made within four years from the end of the accounting period. An appeal against a decision on such a claim must be made within 30 days. A claim may not be made if the return was made in accordance with a generally accepted practice which prevailed at the time.

Other claims must be made by four years after the end of the accounting period, unless a different time limit is specified.

If HMRC amend a self assessment or issue a discovery assessment then the company has a further period to make, vary or withdraw a claim (unless the claim is irrevocable) even if this is outside the normal time limit. The period is one year from the end of the accounting period in which the amendment or assessment was made, or one year from the end of the accounting period in which the compliance check was complete if the amendment is the result of a compliance check. The relief is limited where there has been fraudulent or negligent conduct by the company or its agent.

3 Compliance checks, appeals and disputes

FAST FORWARD

HMRC can carry out compliance checks on returns.

3.1 Compliance checks

3.1.1 Starting a compliance check

A return or an amendment need not be accepted at face value by HMRC. **They may do a compliance check on it, provided that they first give written notice that they are going to do this.** The notice must be given by a year after the later of:

(a)   Where the return is filed by the due filing date, the due filing date (most group companies) or the actual filing date (other companies)

(b)   Where the return is filed late, the 31 January, 30 April, 31 July or 31 October next following the actual date of delivery of the return or amendment.

Only one compliance check may be made in respect of any one return or amendment.

3.1.2 During a compliance check

If notice of a compliance check has been given, HMRC may demand that the company **produce documents** for inspection and copying. However, documents relating to an appeal need not be produced and the company may appeal against a notice requiring documents to be produced.

HMRC may amend a self assessment at any time during a compliance check if they believe there might otherwise be a loss of tax. The company may appeal against such an amendment within 30 days. The company may itself make amendments during a compliance check under the normal rules for amendments. No effect will be given to such amendments during the compliance check but they may be taken into account in the compliance check.

3.1.3 completing a compliance check

An compliance check ends when HMRC give notice that it has been completed and notify what they believe to be the correct amount of tax payable. Before that time, the company may ask the Tribunal to order HMRC to notify the completion of its compliance check by a specified date. Such a direction will be given unless HMRC can demonstrate that they have reasonable grounds for continuing the compliance check.

Compliance checks relating to a company are closed by the issuing of a closure notice in the same way as for income tax compliance checks.

3.2 Determinations

If a return is not delivered by the filing date, HMRC may issue a determination of the tax payable within the four years from the filing date. This is treated as a self assessment and there is no appeal against it. However, it is automatically replaced by any self assessment made by the company by the later of four years from the filing date and 12 months from the determination.

3.3 Discovery assessments

If HMRC believe that not enough tax has been assessed for an accounting period they can make a discovery assessment to collect the extra tax. However, when a tax return has been delivered this power is limited as outlined below.

No discovery assessment can be made on account of an error or mistake as to the basis on which the tax liability ought to be computed, if the basis generally prevailing at the time when the return was made was applied.

A discovery assessment can only be made if either:

(a)   the loss of tax is due to **deliberate or careless understatement** by the company or by someone acting on its behalf; or

(b)   **HMRC could not reasonably be expected to have been aware of the loss of tax, given the information so far supplied to them,** when their right to start a compliance check expired or when they notified the company that a compliance check was complete. The information supplied must be sufficiently detailed to draw HMRC's attention to contentious matters such as the use of a valuation or estimate.

The time limit for raising a discovery assessment is four years from the end of the accounting period but this is extended to 6 years if there has been careless understatement and 20 years if there has been deliberate understatement. The company may appeal against a discovery assessment within 30 days of issue.

3.4 Appeals

The procedure for HMRC internal reviews and appeals relating to individuals, discussed earlier in this Text, also applies to companies.

4 Payment of corporation tax and interest

FAST FORWARD

In general, corporation tax is due nine months and one day after the end of an accounting period but large companies must pay their corporation tax in four quarterly instalments.

4.1 Payment dates –companies not paying tax at main rate

Corporation tax is due for payment by companies which do not pay tax at the main rate, **nine months and one day after the end of the accounting period**. For example, if a company has an accounting period ending on 31 December 2011, the corporation tax for the period is payable on 1 October 2012.

4.2 Payment dates –companies paying tax at main rate ('large' companies)

Large companies must pay their corporation tax in instalments. Broadly, a large company is any company that pays corporation tax at the main rate.

Instalments are due on the 14th day of the month, starting in the seventh month of the accounting period. Provided that the accounting period is twelve months long subsequent instalments are due in the tenth month during the accounting period and in the first and fourth months after the end of the accounting period.

If an accounting period is less than twelve months long subsequent instalments are due at three monthly intervals but with the final payment being due in the fourth month of the next accounting period.

4.3 Example: quarterly instalments

X Ltd is a large company with a 31 December accounting year end. Instalments of corporation tax will be due to be paid by X Ltd on:

- 14 July and 14 October in the accounting period;
- 14 January and 14 April after the accounting period ends

Thus for the year ended 31 December 2011 instalment payments are due on 14 July 2011, 14 October 2011, 14 January 2012 and 14 April 2012.

4.4 Calculating the instalments

Instalments are based on the estimated corporation tax liability for the current period (not the previous period). **A company is required to estimate its corporation tax liability before the end of the accounting period, and must revise its estimate each quarter.** It is extremely important for companies to forecast their tax liabilities accurately. Large companies whose directors are poor at estimating may find their companies incurring significant interest charges.

The amount of each instalment is computed by:

(a) **working out 3 × CT/n** where CT is the amount of the estimated corporation tax liability payable in instalments for the period and n is the number of months in the period

(b) **allocating the smaller of that amount and the total estimated corporation tax liability to the first instalment**

(c) **repeating the process for later instalments until the amount allocated is equal to the corporation tax liability.**

If the company has an accounting period of 12 months, there will be four instalments and each instalment will be 25% of the estimated amount due.

The position is slightly more complicated if the company has an accounting period of less than 12 months, as is shown in the following question.

Question

A large company has a corporation tax liability of £880,000 for the eight month period to 30 September 2011. Accounts had previously always been prepared to 31 January. Show when the corporation tax liability is due for payment.

Answer

£880,000 must be paid in instalments.

The amount of each instalment is $3 \times \dfrac{£880,000}{8} = £330,000$

The due dates are:

	£
14 August 2011	330,000
14 November 2011	330,000
14 January 2012	220,000 (balance)

Companies can have instalments repaid if they later conclude the instalments ought not to have been paid.

4.5 Exceptions

A company is not required to pay instalments in the first year that it is 'large', unless its augmented profits exceed £10 million. The £10 million limit is reduced proportionately if there are associated companies. For this purpose only, a company will be regarded as an associated company where it was an associated company on the last day of the previous accounting period. (This differs from the normal approach in CT where being an associated company for any part of the AP affects the thresholds of both companies for the whole of the AP).

Any company whose liability does not exceed £10,000 need not pay by instalments.

4.6 Interest on late or overpaid tax

Interest runs from the due date on over/underpaid instalments. The position is looked at cumulatively after the due date for each instalment. HMRC calculate the interest position after the company submits its corporation tax return.

Companies which do not pay by instalments are charged interest if they pay their corporation tax after the due date, and will receive interest if they overpay their tax or pay it early.

Interest paid/received on late payments or over payments of corporation tax is dealt with as investment income as interest paid/received on a non-trading loan relationship. For the purpose of the 2012 exam papers, the assumed rate of interest on underpaid tax is 3.0% and the assumed rate of interest on overpaid tax is 0.5%.

5 Penalties

FAST FORWARD

> Penalties may be levied for failure to notify the first accounting period, failure to notify chargeability, the late filing of returns, failure to keep records, failure to produce documents during a compliance check and errors in returns.

5.1 Notification of first accounting period

Failure to notify, and provide information about, the first accounting period can mean a penalty of £300 plus £60 per day the information is outstanding, and a penalty of up to £3,000 for fraudulently or negligently giving incorrect information.

5.2 Notification of chargeability

The common penalty regime for late notification of chargeability discussed earlier in this Text in relation to individuals also applies to companies.

5.3 Late filing penalties

There is a £100 penalty for a failure to submit a return on time, rising to £200 if the delay exceeds three months. These penalties become £500 and £1,000 respectively when a return was late (or never submitted) for each of the preceding two accounting periods.

An additional tax geared penalty is applied if a return is more than six months late. The penalty is 10% of the tax unpaid six months after the return was due if the total delay is up to 12 months, and 20% of that tax if the return is over 12 months late.

There is a tax geared penalty for a fraudulent or negligent return and for failing to correct an innocent error without unreasonable delay. The maximum penalty is equal to the tax that would have been lost had the return been accepted as correct. HMRC can mitigate this penalty. If a company is liable to more than one tax geared penalty, the total penalty is limited to the maximum single penalty that could be charged.

5.4 Failure to keep records

Failure to keep records can lead to a **penalty of up to £3,000** for each accounting period affected.

5.5 Failure to produce documents during a compliance check

If HMRC demand documents, but the company does not produce them, there is a **penalty of £300**. There may also be a **daily penalty of up to £60**, which applies for each day from the day after the imposition of the £300 penalty until the documents are produced.

5.6 Errors in returns

The common penalty regime for making errors in tax returns discussed earlier in this Text applies for corporation tax.

- A company that does not receive a notice requiring a return to be filed must, if it is chargeable to tax, notify HMRC within twelve months of the end of the accounting period.

- A company must, in general, file a CT600 tax return within twelve months of the end of an accounting period.

- HMRC can carry out compliance checks on returns.

- In general, corporation tax is due nine months and one day after the end of an accounting period, but large companies must pay their corporation tax in four quarterly instalments.

- Penalties may be levied for failure to notify the first accounting period, failure to notify chargeability, the late filing of returns, failure to keep records, failure to produce documents during a compliance check and errors in returns.

Quick Quiz

1   When must HMRC give notice to a non-group company that it is going to start a compliance check if the return was filed by the due filing date?

2   Companies that pay corporation tax at the _____ rate must pay quarterly instalments of their corporation tax liability. Fill in the blank.

3   State the due dates for the payment of quarterly instalments of corporation tax for a 12 month accounting period.

4   What is the maximum penalty if a company fails to keep records?

A   £1,000
B   £2,000
C   £3,000
D   £4,000

Answers to Quick Quiz

1   Notice must be given by one year after the actual filing date.

2   Companies that pay corporation tax at the **main** rate.

3   14th day of:

   (a)   7th month in AP
   (b)   10th month in AP
   (c)   1st month after AP ends
   (d)   4th month after AP ends

4   C. £3,000 for each accounting period affected.

Now try the questions below from the Exam Question Bank

Number	Level	Marks	Time
Q39	Introductory	5	9 mins
Q44	Examination	25	45 mins

Q44 has been analysed to give you guidance on how to answer exam questions.

Value added tax

An introduction to VAT

Topic list	Syllabus reference
1 The scope of VAT	G1(a)
2 Zero-rated and exempt supplies	G1(b)
3 Registration	G2(a),(b),(e)
4 Deregistration	G2(d)
5 Pre-registration input tax	G2(c)
6 Accounting for and administering VAT	G3(a)
7 The tax point	G3(b)
8 The valuation of supplies	G3(d)
9 The deduction of input tax	G3(e)
10 Relief for impairment losses (bad debts)	G3(f)

Introduction

The final topic in our studies is value added tax (VAT). We cover VAT in this and the next chapter.

VAT is a tax on turnover rather than on profits. As the name suggests, it is charged on the value added. The VAT is collected bit by bit along the chain of manufacturer, wholesaler, retailer, until it finally hits the consumer who does not add value, but uses up the goods.

In this chapter we look at the scope of VAT and then consider when a business must, or may, be registered for VAT. We also look at administration and accounting. VAT is a tax with simple computations but many detailed rules to ensure its enforcement. You may find it easier to absorb the detail if you ask yourself, in relation to each rule, exactly how it helps to enforce the tax.

Next we look at the rules regarding the deduction of input tax.

In the following chapter we will conclude our study of VAT and the F6 syllabus.

Study guide

		Intellectual level
G1	**The scope of value added tax (VAT)**	
(a)	Describe the scope of VAT.	2
(b)	List the principal zero-rated and exempt supplies.	1
G2	**The VAT registration requirements**	
(a)	Recognise the circumstances in which a person must register for VAT.	2
(b)	Explain the advantages of voluntary VAT registration.	2
(c)	Explain the circumstances in which pre-registration input VAT can be recovered.	2
(d)	Explain how and when a person can deregister for VAT.	1
(e)	Explain the conditions that must be met for two or more companies to be treated as a group for VAT purposes, and the consequences of being so treated.	1
G3	**The computation of VAT liabilities**	
(a)	Explain how VAT is accounted for and administered.	2
(b)	Recognise the tax point when goods or services are supplied.	2
(d)	Explain and apply the principles regarding the valuation of supplies.	2
(e)	Recognise the circumstances in which input VAT is non-deductible.	2
(f)	Compute the relief that is available for impairment losses on trade debts.	2

Exam guide

There will always be at least 10% of the marks in the exam on VAT. Although this will usually be in question 1 or 2 there may be a separate question on VAT. The registration requirements are often examined; make sure that you know the difference between the historical test and the future test, and the dates by which HMRC must be notified and registration takes effect. Do not overlook pre-registration input VAT. You may be required to calculate the VAT due for a return period; watch out for non deductible input tax and check the dates if there are impairment losses.

1 The scope of VAT

FAST FORWARD

> VAT is charged on turnover at each stage in a production process, but in such a way that the burden is borne by the final consumer.

1.1 The nature of VAT

VAT is a tax on turnover, not on profits. The basic principle is that the VAT should be borne by the final consumer. Registered traders may deduct the tax which they suffer on supplies to them (input tax) from the tax which they charge to their customers (output tax) at the time this is paid to HMRC. Thus, at each stage of the manufacturing or service process, the net VAT paid is on the value added at that stage.

1.2 Example: the VAT charge

A forester sells wood to a furniture maker for £100 plus VAT. The furniture maker uses this wood to make a table and sells the table to a shop for £150 plus VAT. The shop then sells the table to the final consumer for £300 plus VAT of 20%. VAT will be accounted for to HMRC as follows.

	Cost £	Input tax 20% £	Net sale price £	Output tax 20% £	Payable to HMRC £
Forester	0	0	100	20.00	20.00
Furniture maker	100	20.00	150	30.00	10.00
Shop	150	30.00	300	60.00	30.00
					60.00

Because the traders involved account to HMRC for VAT charged less VAT suffered, their profits for income tax or corporation tax purposes are based on sales and purchases net of VAT.

1.3 Taxable supplies

FAST FORWARD

VAT is chargeable on taxable supplies made by a taxable person in the course or furtherance of any business carried on by him. Supplies may be of goods or services.

Key term

A **taxable supply** is a supply of goods or services made in the UK, other than an exempt supply.

A taxable supply is either standard-rated or zero-rated. The standard rate is 20%.

Certain supplies, which fall within the classification of standard rate supplies, are charged at a reduced rate of 5%. An example is the supply of domestic fuel.

Zero-rated supplies are taxable at 0%. A taxable supplier whose outputs are zero-rated but whose inputs are standard-rated will obtain repayments of the VAT paid on purchases.

An exempt supply is not chargeable to VAT. A person making exempt supplies is unable to recover VAT on inputs. The exempt supplier thus has to shoulder the burden of VAT. Of course, he may increase his prices to pass on the charge, but he cannot issue a VAT invoice which would enable a taxable customer to obtain a credit for VAT, since no VAT is chargeable on his supplies.

1.4 Example: standard-rated, zero-rated and exempt supplies

Here are figures for three traders, the first with standard-rated outputs, the second with zero-rated outputs and the third with exempt outputs. All their inputs are standard-rated. The standard rate is 20%.

	Standard-rated £	Zero-rated £	Exempt £
Inputs	20,000	20,000	20,000
VAT	4,000	4,000	4,000
	24,000	24,000	24,000
Outputs	30,000	30,000	30,000
VAT	6,000	0	0
	36,000	30,000	30,000
Pay/(reclaim)	2,000	(4,000)	0
Net profit	10,000	10,000	6,000

VAT legislation lists zero-rated, reduced rate and exempt supplies. There is no list of standard-rated supplies.

We look at the main categories of zero-rated and exempt supplies later in this chapter.

1.5 Supplies of goods

Goods are supplied if exclusive ownership of the goods passes to another person.

The following are treated as supplies of goods.

- The supply of any form of power, heat, refrigeration or ventilation, or of water
- The grant, assignment or surrender of a major interest (the freehold or a lease for over 21 years) in land
- Taking goods permanently out of the business for the non-business use of a taxable person or for other private purposes including the supply of goods by an employer to an employee for his private use
- Transfers under an agreement contemplating a transfer of ownership, such as a hire purchase agreement

Gifts of goods are normally treated as sales at cost (so VAT is due). **However, business gifts are not supplies of goods if**:

(a) **The total cost of gifts made to the same person does not exceed £50 in any 12 month period**. If the £50 limit is exceeded, output tax will be due in full on the total of gifts made. Once the limit has been exceeded a new £50 limit and new 12 month period begins.

(b) **The gift is a sample** (unlimited number of samples allowed).

1.6 Supplies of services

Apart from a few specific exceptions, **any supply which is not a supply of goods and which is done for a consideration is a supply of services**. A consideration is any form of payment in money or in kind, including anything which is itself a supply.

A supply of services also takes place if:

- Goods are lent to someone for use outside the business
- Goods are hired to someone
- Services bought for business purposes are used for private purposes

The European Court of Justice has ruled that restaurants supply services rather than goods.

1.7 Taxable persons

The term 'person' includes **individuals, partnerships** (which are treated as single entities, ignoring the individual partners) and **companies. If a person is in business making taxable supplies, then the value of these supplies is called the taxable turnover. If a person's taxable turnover exceeds certain limits then he is a taxable person and should be registered for VAT** (see later in this Text).

2 Zero-rated and exempt supplies

 FAST FORWARD

Some supplies are taxable (either standard-rated, reduced-rate or zero-rated). Others are exempt.

2.1 Types of supply

We have seen that a trader may make standard rated, reduced-rate, zero-rated or exempt supplies.

If a trader makes a supply we need to categorise that supply for VAT as follows:

Step 1 Consider the zero-rated list to see if it is zero-rated. If not:

Step 2 Consider the exempt list to see if it is exempt. If not:

Step 3 Consider the reduced rate list to see if the reduced rate of VAT applies. If not:

Step 4 The supply is standard rated.

2.2 Zero-rated supplies

The following are items on the **zero-rated list**.

(a) Human and animal food

(b) Sewerage services and water

(c) Printed matter used for reading (eg books, newspapers)

(d) Construction work on new homes or the sale of the freehold of new homes by builders

(e) Transport of goods and passengers

(f) Drugs and medicines on prescription or provided in private hospitals

(g) Clothing and footwear for young children and certain protective clothing eg motor cyclists' crash helmets

2.3 Exempt supplies

The following are items on the **exempt** list.

(a) Financial services

(b) Insurance

(c) Postal services provided by the Post Office

(d) Betting and gaming

(e) Certain education and vocational training

(f) Health services

(g) Burial and cremation services

(h) Sale of freeholds of buildings (other than commercial buildings less than 3 years old) and leaseholds of land and buildings.

2.4 Exceptions to the general rule

The zero-rated, exempt and reduced rate lists outline general categories of goods or services which are either zero-rated or exempt or charged at a rate of 5%. However, the VAT legislation then goes into great detail to outline exceptions to the general rule.

For example the zero-rated list states human food is zero-rated. However, the legislation then states that food supplied in the course of catering (eg restaurant meals, hot takeaways) is not zero-rated. Luxury items of food (eg crisps, peanuts, chocolate covered biscuits) are also not zero-rated.

In the exempt list we are told that financial services are exempt. However the legislation then goes on to state that credit management and processing services are not exempt. Investment advice is also not exempt.

Land and buildings is a complex topic. Broadly, sales of new homes are zero-rated, sales of new commercial buildings are standard rated and most other transactions are exempt.

Thus great care must be taken when categorising goods or services as zero-rated, exempt or standard-rated. It is not as straightforward as it may first appear.

3 Registration

FAST FORWARD

A trader becomes liable to register for VAT if the value of taxable supplies in any past period up to 12 months exceeds £73,000 or if there are reasonable grounds for believing that the value of the taxable supplies will exceed £73,000 in the next 30 days alone. A trader may also register voluntarily.

3.1 Compulsory registration

3.1.1 Historical test

At the end of every month a trader must calculate his cumulative turnover of taxable supplies for the previous 12 months to date. **The trader becomes liable to register for VAT if the value of his cumulative taxable supplies** (excluding VAT) **exceeds £73,000**. The person is required to notify HMRC within 30 days of the end of the month in which the £73,000 limit is exceeded. HMRC will then register the person with effect from the end of the month following the month in which the £73,000 was exceeded, or from an earlier date if they and the trader agree.

Registration under this rule is not required if HMRC are satisfied that the value of the trader's taxable supplies (excluding VAT) in the year then starting will not exceed £71,000.

Question   VAT registration

Fred started to trade cutlery on 1 January 2011. Sales (excluding VAT) were £6,750 a month for the first nine months and £7,700 a month thereafter. From what date should Fred be registered for VAT?

Answer

	£	
Sales to 31 October 2011	68,450	
Sales to 30 November 2011	76,150	(exceeds £73,000)

Fred must notify his liability to register by 30 December 2011 (not 31 December) and will be registered from 1 January 2012 or from an agreed earlier date.

3.1.2 Future test

A person is also liable to register **at any time** (not necessarily at the end of the month) if there are reasonable grounds for believing that his taxable supplies (excluding VAT) in the following 30 days will exceed £73,000. Only taxable turnover of that 30 day period is considered **not** cumulative turnover. HMRC must be notified by the end of the 30 day period and registration will be with effect from the beginning of that period.

Exam focus point

> Be sure you know the difference between the historic and future tests.

Question   Future test

Constant Ltd started to trade on 1 February 2011 with sales of goods as follows

	VAT status	£ per month
Goods A	standard-rated	5,000
Goods B	zero-rated	2,000

On 1 June 2011 Constant Ltd signed a contract to provide £40,000 of Goods A and £30,000 of Goods B to Unicorn plc by 25 June 2011. This is in addition to normal sales.

From which date should Constant Ltd be registered for VAT?

Answer

Goods A and B are taxable supplies.

Cumulative turnover at end of May 2011 is £28,000.

Cumulative turnover at end of June 2011 is £105,000.

But on 1 June 2011 the company signed a contract and hence 'knew' that within the next 30 days it would supply £77,000 of taxable supplies – this meets the future test conditions. Therefore the company needs to notify HMRC of their need to register within 30 days of 1 June 2011, ie by 30 June 2011.

HMRC will then register the company from 1 June 2011.

The historic test is met at the end of June 2011 (this would require notification by 30 July 2011 and registration by 1 August 2011).

However when a trader satisfies both tests HMRC will use the test that gives the earlier registration date.

In this case the future test gives the earliest date, 1 June 2011.

3.1.3 Other registration issues

When determining the value of a person's taxable supplies for the purposes of registration, supplies of goods and services that are *capital assets* of the business are to be disregarded, except for non zero-rated taxable supplies of interests in land.

When a person is liable to register in respect of a past period, it is his responsibility to pay VAT. If he is unable to collect it from those to whom he made taxable supplies, the VAT burden will fall on him. A person must start keeping VAT records and charging VAT to customers as soon as it is known that he is required to register. However, VAT should not be shown separately on any invoices until the registration number is known. The invoice should show the VAT inclusive price and customers should be informed that VAT invoices will be forwarded once the registration number is known. Formal VAT invoices should then be sent to such customers within 30 days of receiving the registration number.

Notification of liability to register must be made on form VAT 1. This can be downloaded from the HMRC website, can be requested by telephone, or an application to register can be made online through the website. Simply writing to, or telephoning, a local VAT office is not enough. On registration the VAT office will send the trader a certificate of registration. This shows the VAT registration number, the date of registration, the end of the first VAT period and the length of the VAT periods.

If a trader makes a supply before becoming liable to register, but gets paid after registration, VAT is not due on that supply.

3.2 Voluntary registration

A person may decide to become registered even though his taxable turnover falls below the registration limit. Unless a person is registered he cannot recover the input tax he pays on purchases.

Voluntary registration is advantageous where a person wishes to recover input tax on purchases, but charging VAT may make the supply less competitive if customers are not VAT registered and the trader may have to absorb the VAT output tax thus reducing his profit.

Therefore, consideration needs to be given to the situation of the customer. For example, consider a trader who has one input during the period which cost £1,000 plus £200 VAT at 20%; he works on the input which becomes his sole output for the year and he decides to make a profit of £1,000.

(a)   If he is not registered he will charge £2,200 and his customer will obtain no relief for any VAT.

(b)   If he is registered he will charge £2,000 plus VAT of £400. His customer will have input tax of £400 which he will be able to recover if he, too, is registered.

If the customer is a non-taxable person he will prefer (a) as the cost to him is £2,200. If he is taxable he will prefer (b) as the net cost is £2,000. Thus, a decision whether or not to register voluntarily may depend upon the status of customers.

The decision to register may also depend on the image of the business the trader wishes to project (registration may give the impression of a substantial business). The **administrative burden of registration** should also be considered.

3.3 Group registration

Two or more companies under common control can register as a group for VAT purposes. A single VAT return and payment are then made by a representative member for a VAT period but all members of the group are jointly and severally liable for VAT due. There is no need to account for VAT on supplies between group members.

Two or more companies under common control may apply for group registration.

The **effects and advantages of group registration** are as follows.

- Each VAT group must appoint a representative member which must **account for the group's output tax and input tax, completing one VAT return and paying VAT on behalf of the group. Thus this simplifies VAT accounting, saving administrative costs,** and allows payments and repayments of VAT to be netted off. However, a**ll members of the group are jointly and severally liable for any VAT due from the representative member**

- **Any supply of goods or services by a member of the group to another member of the group is, in general, disregarded for VAT purposes,** reducing the VAT accounting required

- Any other supply of goods or services by or to a group member is in general treated as a supply by or to the representative member

- Any VAT payable on the import of goods by a group member is payable by the representative member.

Two or more companies are eligible to be treated as members of a group provided each of them is either established in the UK or has a fixed establishment in the UK, and:

- **One of them controls each of the others, or**
- **One person** (which could be an individual or a holding company) **controls all of them**, or
- **Two or more persons carrying on a business in partnership control all of them.**

An application to create, terminate, add to or remove a company from a VAT group may be made at any time.

It is not necessary for each company, which meets the requirements, to join a particular VAT group. It may be beneficial, for example, in the case of a company making largely zero-rated supplies (and so receiving VAT repayments) to remain outside the group and benefit from cash flow repayments from completing monthly VAT returns (see later in this Text).

Note that various limits, such as those for special schemes of accounting for VAT (cash and annual accounting schemes – see the next Chapter), will apply to the VAT group as a whole rather than on an individual company basis.

4 Deregistration

A trader may deregister voluntarily if he expects the value of his taxable supplies in the following one year period will not exceed £71,000. Alternatively, a trader who no longer makes taxable supplies may be compulsorily deregistered.

4.1 Voluntary deregistration

A person is eligible for voluntary deregistration if HMRC are satisfied that the value of his taxable supplies (net of VAT and excluding supplies of capital assets) in the following one year period will not exceed £71,000. However, voluntary deregistration will not be allowed if the reason for the expected fall in value of taxable supplies is the cessation of taxable supplies or the suspension of taxable supplies for a period of 30 days or more in that following year.

HMRC will cancel a person's registration from the date the request is made or from an agreed later date.

4.2 Compulsory deregistration

A trader may be compulsorily deregistered if HMRC are satisfied that he is no longer making nor intending to make taxable supplies. Failure to notify a requirement to deregister within 30 days may lead to a penalty. Compulsory deregistration may also lead to HMRC reclaiming input tax which has been wrongly recovered by the trader since the date on which he should have deregistered.

4.3 The consequences of deregistration

FAST FORWARD

> VAT is chargeable on all goods and services on hand at the date of deregistration.

On deregistration, VAT is chargeable on all stocks and capital assets in a business on which input tax was claimed, since the registered trader is in effect making a taxable supply to himself as a newly unregistered trader. If the VAT chargeable does not exceed £1,000, it need not be paid.

4.4 Transfer of a going concern

FAST FORWARD

> The transfer of a business as a going concern is outside the scope of VAT.

There is no VAT charge if a business (or a separately viable part of it) is sold as a going concern to another taxable person (or a person who immediately becomes a taxable person as a result of the transfer). Such a sale is outside the scope of VAT.

If a transfer of a going concern (TOGC) is from a VAT registered trader to a new owner who is not VAT registered then it is possible to apply to transfer the registration number of the previous owner to the new owner. This would also transfer to the new owner the responsibility for the past VAT history of the old business. So, if the previous owner had committed any VAT misdemeanours the liability for those would transfer to the new owner of the business. As a result of this it may not be wise to apply to transfer the VAT registration number between old and new owners unless of course, it is a situation where there is a very close connection between the two.

If the VAT registration number is not transferred then the new owners do not have any responsibility for the VAT affairs of the previous owner of the business. This is probably a safer way to structure the transfer of a business.

5 Pre-registration input tax

5.1 Introduction

VAT incurred before registration can be treated as input tax and recovered from HMRC subject to certain conditions.

5.2 Pre-registration goods

If the claim is for input tax suffered on goods purchased prior to registration then the following conditions must be satisfied.

(a) The **goods were acquired for the purpose of the business** which either was carried on or was to be carried on by him at the time of supply.

(b) The **goods have not been supplied onwards or consumed before the date of registration** (although they may have been used to make other goods which are still held).

(c) The **VAT must have been incurred in the four years prior to the date of registration**.

5.3 Pre-registration services

If the claim is for input tax suffered on the supply of services prior to registration then the following conditions must be satisfied.

(a) The **services were supplied for the purposes of a business** which either was carried on or was to be carried on by him at the time of supply.

(b) **The services were supplied within the six months prior to the date of registration.**

Input tax attributable to supplies made before registration is not deductible even if the input tax concerned is treated as having been incurred after registration.

6 Accounting for and administering VAT

6.1 Administration

FAST FORWARD

> VAT is administered by HMRC. Appeals are heard by the Tax Tribunal.

6.1.1 Introduction

The administration of VAT is dealt with by HM Revenue and Customs (HMRC).

Local offices are responsible for the local administration of VAT and for providing advice to registered persons whose principal place of business is in their area. They are controlled by regional collectors.

From time to time a registered person will be visited by staff from a local office (a control visit) to ensure that the law is understood and is being applied properly. If a trader disagrees with any decision as to the application of VAT given by HMRC he can ask his local office to reconsider the decision. It is not necessary to appeal formally while a case is being reviewed in this way. Where an appeal can be settled by agreement, a written settlement has the same force as a decision by the Revenue and Customs Prosecution Office.

6.1.2 Assessments

HMRC may issue assessments of VAT due to the best of their judgement if they believe that a trader has failed to make returns or if they believe those returns to be incorrect or incomplete. The time limit for making assessments is normally four years after the end of a VAT period, but this is extended to 20 years in the case of fraud, dishonest conduct, certain registration irregularities and the unauthorised issue of VAT invoices.

HMRC sometimes write to traders, setting out their calculations, before issuing assessments. The traders can then query the calculations.

6.1.3 Appeals

A trader may appeal to the Tax Tribunal in the same way as an appeal may be made for income tax and corporation tax (see earlier in this Study Text). VAT returns and payments shown thereon must have been made before an appeal can be heard.

6.2 VAT periods

> VAT is accounted for on regular returns – most are submitted electronically. Extensive records must be kept.

The VAT period (also known as the tax period) is the period covered by a VAT return. It is usually three calendar months. The return shows the total input and output tax for the tax period and the general rule is that the return must be **submitted, along with any VAT due, within one month of the end of the VAT period**.

HMRC allocate VAT periods according to the class of trade carried on (ending in June, September, December and March; July, October, January and April; or August, November, February and May), to spread the flow of VAT returns evenly over the year. When applying for registration a trader can ask for VAT periods which fit in with his own accounting year. It is also possible to have VAT periods to cover accounting systems not based on calendar months.

A registered person whose input tax will regularly exceed his output tax can elect for a one month VAT period, but will have to balance the inconvenience of making 12 returns a year against the advantage of obtaining more rapid repayments of VAT.

Certain small businesses may submit an annual VAT return (see later in this Text).

6.3 Electronic filing

All VAT registered businesses with an annual VAT exclusive turnover of £100,000 or more and all newly VAT registered businesses (whatever their turnover) must submit their VAT returns online and make payments electronically.

Businesses which file and pay VAT electronically automatically receive a seven-day extension to the usual one month time limit. For example, a business which has a VAT quarter ending 31 March 2012 would normally have to submit its VAT return and pay the VAT due by 30 April 2012. Under electronic filing, this date moves to 7 May 2012.

6.4 Substantial traders

If a trader does not make monthly returns, and the total VAT liability over 12 months to the end of a VAT period exceeds £2,300,000 (from 4 January 2011), he must make payments on account of each quarter's VAT liability during the quarter. Payments are due a month before the end of the quarter and at the end of the quarter, with the final payment due one month after the end of the quarter. Payments must be made electronically.

For a trader who exceeds the £2,300,000 limit in the 12 months to 30 September, 31 October or 30 November, the amount of each of the two payments on account is 1/24 of the total VAT liability of those 12 months. The obligation to pay on account starts with the first VAT period starting *after* 31 March.

6.5 Refunds of VAT

There is a four year time limit on the right to reclaim overpaid VAT. This time limit does not apply to input tax which a business could not have reclaimed earlier because the supplier only recently invoiced the VAT, even though it related to a purchase made some time ago. Nor does it apply to overpaid VAT penalties.

If a taxpayer has overpaid VAT and has overclaimed input tax by reason of the same mistake, HMRC can set off any tax, penalty, interest or surcharge due to them against any repayment due to the taxpayer and repay only the net amount. In such cases the normal four year time limit for recovering VAT, penalties, interest, etc by assessment does not apply.

HMRC can refuse to make any repayment which would unjustly enrich the claimant. They can also refuse a repayment of VAT where all or part of the tax has, for practical purposes, been borne by a person other than the taxpayer (eg by a customer of the taxpayer) except to the extent that the taxpayer can show loss or damage to any of his businesses as a result of mistaken assumptions about VAT.

7 The tax point

FAST FORWARD

> The tax point is the deemed date of supply. The basic tax point is the date on which goods are removed or made available to the customer, or the date on which services are completed. If a VAT invoice is issued or payment is received before the basic tax point, the earlier of these dates becomes the actual tax point. If the earlier date rule does not apply, and the VAT invoice is issued within 14 days of the basic tax point, the invoice date becomes the actual tax point.

7.1 The basic tax point

The tax point of each supply is the deemed date of supply. The basic tax point is the date on which the goods are removed or made available to the customer, or the date on which services are completed.

The tax point determines the VAT period in which output tax must be accounted for and credit for input tax will be allowed. The tax point also determines which rate applies if the rate of VAT or a VAT category changes (for example when a supply ceases to be zero-rated and becomes standard-rated).

7.2 The actual tax point

If a VAT invoice is issued or payment is received before the basic tax point, the earlier of these dates automatically becomes the tax point. If the earlier date rule does not apply and if the VAT invoice is issued within 14 days after the basic tax point, the invoice date becomes the tax point (although the trader can elect to use the basic tax point for all his supplies if he wishes). This 14 day period may be extended to accommodate, for example, monthly invoicing; the tax point is then the VAT invoice date or the end of the month, whichever is applied consistently.

Question

Tax point

Julia sells a sculpture to the value of £1,000 net of VAT. She receives a payment on account of £250 plus VAT on 25 April 2012. The sculpture is delivered on 28 May 2012. Julia's VAT return period is to 30 April 2012. She issues an invoice on 4 June 2012.

Outline the tax point(s) and amount(s) due.

Answer

A separate tax point arises in respect of the £250 deposit and the £750 balance payable.

Julia should account for VAT as follows.

(a)   Deposit

25 April 2012: tax at 20% × £250 = £50. This is accounted for in her VAT return to 30 April 2012. The charge arises on 25 April 2012 because payment is received before the basic tax point (which is 28 May 2012 – date of delivery).

(b)   Balance

4 June 2012: tax at 20% × £750 = £150. This is accounted for on the VAT return to 31 July 2012. The charge arises on 4 June because the invoice was issued within 14 days of the basic tax point of 28 May 2012 (delivery date).

7.3 Miscellaneous points

Goods supplied on sale or return are treated as supplied on the earlier of adoption by the customer or 12 months after despatch.

Continuous supplies of services paid for periodically normally have tax points on the earlier of the receipt of each payment and the issue of each VAT invoice, unless one invoice covering several payments is issued in advance for up to a year. The tax point is then the earlier of each due date or date of actual payment. However, for connected businesses the tax point will be created periodically, in most cases based on 12 month periods.

8 The valuation of supplies

FAST FORWARD

In order to ascertain the amount of VAT on a supply, the supply must be valued. If a discount is offered for prompt payment, VAT is chargeable on the net amount even if the discount is not taken up.

8.1 Value of supply

The value of a supply is the VAT-exclusive price on which VAT is charged. The consideration for a supply is the amount paid in money or money's worth.

Thus with a standard rate of 20%:

Value + VAT = consideration
£100 + £20.00 = £120.00

The VAT proportion of the consideration is known as the 'VAT fraction'. It is:

$$\frac{\text{rate of tax}}{100 + \text{rate of tax}} = \frac{20}{100 + 20} = \frac{1}{6}$$

Provided the consideration for a bargain made at arm's length is paid in money, the value for VAT purposes is the VAT exclusive price charged by the trader. If it is paid in something other than money, as in a barter of some goods or services for others, it must be valued and VAT will be due on the value.

If the price of goods is effectively reduced with money off coupons, the value of the supply is the amount actually received by the taxpayer.

8.2 Discounts

Where a discount is offered for prompt payment, VAT is chargeable on the net amount, regardless of whether the discount is taken up.

When goods are sold to staff at a discount, VAT is only due on the discounted price.

8.3 Miscellaneous

For goods supplied under a hire purchase agreement VAT is chargeable on the cash selling price at the start of the contract.

When goods are permanently taken from a business for non-business purposes VAT must be accounted for on their market value. Where business goods are put to a private or non-business use, the value of the resulting supply of services is the cost to the taxable person of providing the services. If services bought for business purposes are used for non-business purposes (without charge), then VAT must be accounted for on their cost, but the VAT to be accounted for is not allowed to exceed the input tax deductible on the purchase of the services.

9 The deduction of input tax

9.1 Input tax recovery

FAST FORWARD

> Not all input VAT is deductible, eg VAT on most motor cars.

For input tax to be deductible, the payer must be a taxable person, with the supply being to him in the course of his business. In addition a VAT invoice must be held (except for payments of up to £25 including VAT which are for telephone calls or car park fees or which are made through cash operated machines).

Input tax recovery can be denied to any business that does not hold a valid VAT invoice and cannot provide alternative evidence to prove the supply took place.

9.2 Capital items

The distinction between capital and revenue which is important in other areas of tax **does not apply to VAT**. Thus a manufacturer buying plant subject to VAT will be able to obtain a credit for all the VAT immediately. The plant must of course be used to make taxable supplies, and if it is only partly so used only part of the VAT can be reclaimed. Conversely, if plant is sold second-hand then VAT should be charged on the sale and is output tax in the normal way.

9.3 Non-deductible input tax

Exam focus point

> In the F6 exam students are not required to know actual cases where VAT decisions were made. They are included below for your information only.

The following input tax is not deductible even for a taxable person with taxable outputs.

(a) **VAT on motor cars** not used wholly for business purposes. VAT on cars is never reclaimable unless the car is acquired new for resale or is acquired for use in or leasing to a taxi business, a self-drive car hire business or a driving school (see further below).

(b) **VAT on business entertaining** where the cost of the entertaining is not a tax deductible trading expense unless the entertainment is of overseas customers in which case the input tax is deductible.

   If the items bought are used partly for non-deductible entertaining and partly for other purposes, an apportionment of the expenses is required. In *Ernst & Young v CCE* the Tribunal held that staff entertaining was wholly for business purposes and a full input tax recovery was allowed. HMRC accept this decision in respect of staff entertainment but maintain that following the case *KPMG v CCE* input tax on entertaining guests at a staff party is non-deductible.

(c) **VAT on expenses incurred on domestic accommodation for directors.**

(d) **VAT on non-business items passed through the business accounts.** However, when goods are bought partly for business use, the purchaser may:

   (i) Deduct all the input tax, and account for output tax in respect of the private use, or
   (ii) Deduct only the business proportion of the input tax.

   Where services are bought partly for business use, only method (ii) may be used. If services are initially bought for business use but the use then changes, a fair proportion of the input tax (relating to the private use) is reclaimed by HMRC by making the trader account for output tax.

(e) **VAT which does not relate to the** making of supplies by the buyer in the course of a **business**.

9.4 Irrecoverable VAT

Where all (as with many cars) or some (as for partial business use) of the input tax on a purchase is not deductible, the **non-deductible VAT is included in the cost for income tax, corporation tax, capital allowance or capital gains purposes. Deductible VAT is omitted from costs, so that only net amounts are included in accounts. Similarly, sales** (and proceeds in chargeable gains computations) **are shown net of VAT**, because the VAT is paid over to HMRC.

9.5 Motoring expenses

9.5.1 Cars

The VAT incurred on the purchase of a car not used wholly for business purposes is not recoverable (except as mentioned above). If accessories are fitted after the original purchase and a separate invoice is raised then the VAT on the accessories can be treated as input tax so long as the accessories are for business use.

If a car is used wholly for business purposes (including leasing, so long as the charges are at the open market rate), the input tax is recoverable but the buyer must account for VAT when he sells the car. **If a car is leased, the lessor recovered the input tax when the car was purchased and the lessee makes some private use of the car** (for example private use by employees), **the lessee can only recover 50% of the input tax on the lease charges. A hiring of five days or less is assumed to be for wholly business use.**

If a car is used for business purposes then any VAT charged on repair and maintenance costs can be treated as input tax. No apportionment has to be made for private use.

9.5.2 Fuel for business use

The VAT incurred on fuel used for business purposes is fully deductible as input tax. If the fuel is bought by employees who are reimbursed for the actual cost or by a mileage allowance, the employer may deduct the input tax provided he **holds a VAT invoice (or invoices) showing sufficient VAT to cover the input tax claim being made**. Normally there will not be an invoice showing the exact amount of input VAT reclaimed because some of the fuel may have been used by employees for private purposes and only business use is reimbursed (or a mileage allowance is used). It is sufficient to hold invoice(s) showing an amount of input tax on fuel at least equal to the input tax being recovered by the business.

9.5.3 Fuel for private use

FAST FORWARD

If fuel is supplied for private purposes all input VAT incurred on the fuel is allowed but the business must account for output VAT using a set of scale charges.

When fuel is supplied for an individual's private use at less than the cost of that fuel to the business, all input tax incurred on the fuel is allowed, but the business must account for output tax using set scale charges per VAT return period, based on the CO_2 emissions of the car. As for income tax, the CO_2 emissions are rounded down to the nearest 5%. The scale figures will be stated in the exam if required. However, take care to note whether the examiner has given you the VAT inclusive or the VAT exclusive scale figure.

The output tax is the VAT inclusive scale charge × 1/6 or the VAT exclusive scale charge × 20%.

If the employee has to pay the full cost of fuel (or more than its cost) to the employer, the employer must account for VAT on the amount paid, rather than on the scale charge.

Question

Iain is an employee of ABC Ltd. He has the use of a car with CO_2 emissions of 176 g/km for one month and a car with CO_2 emissions of 208 g/km for two months during the quarter ended 31 May 2012.

ABC Ltd pay all the petrol costs in respect of both cars without requiring Iain to make any reimbursement in respect of private fuel. Total petrol costs for the quarter amount to £300 (including VAT).

What is the VAT effect of the above on ABC Ltd?

VAT scale rates (VAT inclusive) for 3 month periods

CO_2 emissions	£
175	394
205	488

Answer

Value for the quarter:

	£
Car 1	
£394 × 1/3 =	131.33
Car 2	
£488 × 2/3 =	325.33
	456.66
Output tax:	
1/6 × £456.66	£76.11
Input tax	
1/6 × £300	£50.00

10 Relief for impairment losses (bad debts)

FAST FORWARD

> Relief for VAT on impairment losses (bad debts) is available if the debt is over six months old (measured from when the payment is due) and has been written off in the trader's accounts.

Where a supplier of goods or services has accounted for VAT on the supply and the customer does not pay, the supplier may claim a refund of VAT on the amount unpaid. **Relief is available for VAT on impairment losses (bad debts) if the debt is over six months old (measured from when payment is due) and has been written off in the creditor's accounts.** Where payments on account have been received, they are attributed to debts in chronological order. If the debtor later pays all or part of the amount owed, a corresponding part of the VAT repaid must be paid back to HMRC.

Impairment loss relief claims must be made within three years of the time the debt became eligible for relief. The creditor must have a copy of the VAT invoice, and records to show that the VAT in question has been accounted for and that the debt has been written off. The VAT is reclaimed on the creditor's VAT return.

A business which has claimed input tax on a supply, but which has not paid the supplier of the goods or services within six months of date of supply (or the date on which the payment is due, if later), must repay the input tax, irrespective of whether the supplier has made a claim for bad debt relief. The input tax will be repaid by making an adjustment to the input tax on the VAT return for the accounting period in which the end of the six months falls.

Exam focus point

Watch out for the six month rule when claiming relief for impairment losses.

Chapter Roundup

- VAT is charged on turnover at each stage in a production process, but in such a way that the burden is borne by the final consumer.

- VAT is chargeable on taxable supplies made by a taxable person in the course or furtherance of any business carried on by him. Supplies may be of goods or services.

- Some supplies are taxable (either standard-rated, reduced-rate or zero-rated). Others are exempt.

- A trader becomes liable to register for VAT if the value of taxable supplies in any period up to 12 months exceeds £73,000 or if there are reasonable grounds for believing that the value of the taxable supplies will exceed £73,000 in the next 30 days alone. A trader may also register voluntarily.

- Two or more companies under common control can register as a group for VAT purposes. A single VAT return and payment are then made by a representative member for a VAT period but all members of the group are jointly and severally liable for VAT due. There is no need to account for VAT on supplies between group members.

- A trader may deregister voluntarily if he expects the value of his taxable supplies in the following one year period will not exceed £71,000. Alternatively, a trader who no longer makes taxable supplies may be compulsorily deregistered.

- VAT is chargeable on all goods and services on hand at the date of deregistration.

- The transfer of a business as a going concern is outside the scope of VAT.

- VAT is administered by HMRC. Appeals are heard by the Tax Tribunal.

- VAT is accounted for on regular returns – most are submitted electronically. Extensive records must be kept.

- The tax point is the deemed date of supply. The basic tax point is the date on which goods are removed or made available to the customer, or the date on which services are completed. If a VAT invoice is issued or payment is received before the basic tax point, the earlier of these dates becomes the actual tax point. If the earlier date rule does not apply, and the VAT invoice is issued within 14 days of the basic tax point, the invoice date becomes the actual tax point.

- In order to ascertain the amount of VAT on a supply, the supply must be valued. If a discount is offered for prompt payment, VAT is chargeable on the net amount even if the discount is not taken up.

- Not all input VAT is deductible, eg VAT on most motor cars.

- If fuel is supplied for private purposes all input VAT incurred on the fuel is allowed but the business must account for output VAT using a set of scale charges.

- Relief for VAT on impairment losses (bad debts) is available if the debt is over six months old (measured from when the payment is due) and has been written off in the trader's accounts.

Quick Quiz

1. On what transactions will VAT be charged?
2. What is a taxable person?
3. What are the two advantages of group registration?
4. When may a person choose to be deregistered?
5. What is the time limit in respect of claiming pre-registration input tax on goods?
6. On what amount is VAT charged if a discount is offered for prompt payment?
7. What input tax is never deductible?
8. What relief is available for impairment losses?

1   VAT is charged on taxable supplies of goods and services made in the UK by a taxable person in the course or furtherance of any business carried on by him.

2   Any 'person' whose taxable turnover exceeds the registration limit. The term 'person' includes individuals, partnerships and companies.

3   The two advantages of group registration are:

    •   saving on administrative costs: only one VAT return needs to be completed for the group
    •   no VAT on supplies between group members

4   A person is eligible for voluntary deregistration if HMRC are satisfied that the value of his taxable supplies in the following year will not exceed £71,000.

5   The VAT must have been incurred in the four years prior to the effective date of registration.

6   VAT is chargeable on the net price, regardless of whether the discount is taken up.

7   VAT on:

    •   motor cars
    •   UK business entertaining
    •   expenses incurred on domestic accommodation for directors
    •   non-business items passed through the accounts
    •   items which do not relate to making business supplies

8   Where a supplier has accounted for VAT on a supply and the customer fails to pay, then the supplier may claim a refund of the VAT accounted for to HMRC but never actually collected from the customer.

Now try the question below from the Exam Question Bank

Number	Level	Marks	Time
Q40	Examination	10	18 mins

Further aspects of VAT

27

Topic list	Syllabus reference
1 VAT invoices and records	G3(c)
2 Penalties	G3(g)
3 Imports, exports, acquisitions and despatches	G3(h)
4 Special schemes	G4(a)-(c)

Introduction

In the previous chapter we looked at the scope of VAT and when businesses must, or may, register for VAT.

In this chapter we consider the contents of a valid VAT invoice and the main penalties used to enforce the VAT system.

VAT needs to be applied to imports, so that people do not have a tax incentive to buy abroad, and VAT is taken off many exports in order to encourage sales abroad. We see how this is achieved for transactions both within and outside the European Union.

Finally we look at the three special schemes which are intended to reduce the administrative burden for small businesses.

This chapter concludes our study of UK taxation and the F6 syllabus.

Study guide

		Intellectual level
G3	**The computation of VAT liabilities**	
(c)	List the information that must be given on a VAT invoice.	1
(g)	Explain the circumstances in which the default surcharge, a penalty for an incorrect VAT return, and default interest will be applied.	1
(h)	Explain the treatment of imports, exports and trade within the European Union	1
G4	**The effect of special schemes**	
(a)	Describe the cash accounting scheme, and recognise when it will be advantageous to use the scheme.	2
(b)	Describe the annual accounting scheme, and recognise when it will be advantageous to use the scheme.	2
(c)	Describe the flat rate scheme, and recognise when it will be advantageous to use the scheme.	2

Exam guide

There will always be at least 10% of the marks in the exam on VAT. Although this will normally be in question 1 or 2 there may be a separate question on VAT. Penalties are an important topic as they are used to enforce the VAT system, but the special schemes are designed to make life simpler for small businesses. You may be asked to advise on the VAT treatment of imports and exports outside the European Union (EU) and on trade within the EU. The flat rate scheme may also lead to a small extra profit for the business, depending on the flat rate percentage and the level of inputs.

1 VAT invoices and records

1.1 VAT invoices

FAST FORWARD

A taxable person making a taxable supply to another registered person must supply a VAT invoice within 30 days.

A taxable person making a taxable supply to another person registered for VAT must supply a VAT invoice within 30 days of the time of supply, and must keep a copy. The invoice must show:

(a) The supplier's name, address and registration number

(b) The date of issue, the tax point and an invoice number

(c) The name and address of the customer

(d) A description of the goods or services supplied, giving for each description the quantity, the unit price, the rate of VAT and the VAT exclusive amount

(e) The rate of any cash discount

(f) The total invoice price excluding VAT (with separate totals for zero-rated and exempt supplies)

(g) Each VAT rate applicable and the total amount of VAT

If an invoice is issued, and a change in price then alters the VAT due, a credit note or debit note to adjust the VAT must be issued.

Credit notes must give the reason for the credit (such as 'returned goods'), and the number and date of the original VAT invoice. If a credit note makes no VAT adjustment, it should state this.

A less detailed VAT invoice may be issued by a retailer where the invoice is for a total including VAT of up to £250. Such an invoice must show:

(a) The supplier's name, address and registration number
(b) The date of the supply
(c) A description of the goods or services supplied
(d) The rate of VAT chargeable
(e) The total amount chargeable including VAT

Zero-rated and exempt supplies must not be included in less detailed invoices.

VAT invoices are not required for payments of up to £25 including VAT which are for telephone calls or car park fees or are made through cash operated machines. In such cases, input tax can be claimed without a VAT invoice.

1.2 Records

FAST FORWARD

Every VAT registered trader must keep records for six years.

Every VAT registered trader must keep records for six years, although HMRC may sometimes grant permission for their earlier destruction. They may be kept on paper, on microfilm or microfiche or on computer. However, there must be adequate facilities for HMRC to inspect records.

All records must be kept up to date and in a way which allows:

- The calculation of VAT due
- Officers of HMRC to check the figures on VAT returns

The following records are needed.

- Copies of VAT invoices, credit notes and debit notes issued
- A summary of supplies made
- VAT invoices, credit notes and debit notes received
- A summary of supplies received
- A VAT account
- Order and delivery notes, correspondence, appointment books, job books, purchases and sales books, cash books, account books, records of takings (such as till rolls), bank paying-in slips, bank statements and annual accounts
- Records of zero-rated and exempt supplies, gifts or loans of goods, taxable self-supplies and any goods taken for non-business use

2 Penalties

2.1 The default surcharge

FAST FORWARD

A default occurs when a trader either submits his VAT return late, or submits the return on time but pays the VAT late. A default surcharge is applied if there is a default on payment during a default surcharge period.

A default occurs when a trader either submits his VAT return late, or submits the return on time but pays the VAT late. If a trader defaults, HMRC will serve a surcharge liability notice on the trader. The notice specifies a surcharge period running from the date of the notice to the anniversary of the end of the period for which the trader is in default.

If a further default occurs in respect of a return period ending during the specified surcharge period, the original surcharge period will be extended to the anniversary of the end of the period to which the new default relates. In addition, if the default involves the late payment of VAT (as opposed to simply a late return) a surcharge is levied.

The surcharge depends on the number of defaults involving late payment of VAT which have occurred in respect of periods ending in the surcharge period, as follows.

Default involving late payment of VAT in the surcharge period	Surcharge as a percentage of the VAT outstanding at the due date
First	2%
Second	5%
Third	10%
Fourth or more	15%

Surcharges at the 2% and 5% rates are not normally demanded unless the amount due would be at least £400 but for surcharges calculated using the 10% or 15% rates there is a minimum amount of £30 payable.

A trader must submit one year's returns on time and pay the VAT shown on them on time in order to break out of the surcharge liability period and the escalation of surcharge percentages.

Question
Default surcharge

Peter Popper has an annual turnover of around £300,000. His VAT return for the quarter to 31.12.10 is late. He then submits returns for the quarters to 30.9.11 and 31.3.12 late as well as making late payment of the tax due of £12,000 and £500 respectively.

Peter's VAT return to 31.3.13 is also late and the VAT due of £1,100 is also paid late. All other VAT returns and VAT payments are made on time. Outline Peter Popper's exposure to default surcharge.

Answer

A surcharge liability notice will be issued after the late filing on the 31.12.10 return outlining a surcharge period extending to 31.12.11.

The late 30.9.11 return is in the surcharge period so the period is extended to 30.9.12. The late VAT payment triggers a 2% penalty. 2% × £12,000 = £240. Since £240 is less than the £400 de minimis limit it is not collected by HMRC.

The late 31.3.12 return is in the surcharge period so the period is now extended to 31.3.13. The late payment triggers a 5% penalty. 5% × £500 = £25. Since £25 is less than the £400 de minimis limit it is not collected by HMRC.

The late 31.03.13 return is in the surcharge period. The period is extended to 31.03.14. The late payment triggers a 10% penalty 10% × £1,100 = £110. This is collected by HMRC since the £400 de minimis does not apply to penalties calculated at the 10% (and 15%) rate.

Peter will have to submit all four quarterly VAT returns to 31.3.14 on time and pay the VAT on time to 'escape' the default surcharge regime.

A default will be ignored for all default surcharge purposes if the trader can show that the return or payment was sent at such a time, and in such a manner, that it was reasonable to expect that HMRC would receive it by the due date. Posting the return and payment first class the day before the due date is generally accepted as meeting this requirement. A default will also be ignored if the trader can demonstrate a reasonable excuse for the late submission or payment.

The application of the default surcharge regime to small businesses is modified. **A small business is one with a turnover below £150,000.** When a small business is late submitting a VAT return or paying VAT it will receive a letter from HMRC offering help. No penalty will be charged. If a further default occurs within 12 months a surcharge liability notice will be issued.

2.2 Penalties for errors

FAST FORWARD

There is a common penalty regime for errors in tax returns, including VAT. Errors in a VAT return up to certain amounts may be corrected in the next return.

2.2.1 Common penalty regime

The common penalty regime for making errors in tax returns discussed earlier in this Text applies for value added tax.

2.2.2 Errors corrected in next return

Errors on a VAT return not exceeding the greater of:

- £10,000 (net under-declaration minus over-declaration); or
- 1% x net VAT turnover for return period (maximum £50,000);

may be **corrected on the next return**.

Other errors should be notified to HMRC in writing eg by letter.

In both cases, a penalty for the error may be imposed. Correction of an error on a later return is not, of itself, an unprompted disclosure of the error and fuller disclosure is required for the penalty to be reduced.

Default interest (see below) on the unpaid VAT as a result of the error is only charged where the limit is exceeded for the error to be corrected on the next VAT return.

2.3 Interest on unpaid VAT (default interest)

FAST FORWARD

Default interest is charged on unpaid VAT if HMRC raise an assessment of VAT or the trader makes a voluntary payment before the assessment is raised. It runs from the date the VAT should have been paid to the actual date of payment but cannot run for more than three years before the assessment or voluntary payment.

Interest (not deductible in computing taxable profits) **is charged on VAT which is the subject of an assessment** (where returns were not made or were incorrect), **or which could have been the subject of an assessment but was paid before the assessment was raised. It runs from the reckonable date until the date of payment.** This interest is sometimes called 'default interest'.

The reckonable date is when the VAT should have been paid (one month from the end of the return period), or in the case of VAT repayments, seven days from the issue of the repayment order. However, where VAT is charged by an assessment, interest does not run from more than three years before the date of the assessment; where the VAT was paid before an assessment was raised, interest does not run for more than three years before the date of payment.

In practice, interest is only charged when there would otherwise be a loss to the Exchequer. It is not, for example, charged when a company failed to charge VAT but if it had done so another company would have been able to recover the VAT.

3 Imports, exports, acquisitions and despatches

3.1 Introduction

The terms **import and export** refer to purchases and sales of goods with countries **outside the European Union (EU)**.

The terms **acquisition and despatch** refer to purchases and sales of goods with countries **in the EU**.

3.2 Trade in goods outside the European Union

FAST FORWARD

> Imports of goods from outside the EU are subject to VAT and exports of goods to outside the EU are zero-rated.

3.2.1 Imports

Goods imported into the UK from outside the EU are effectively treated in the same way as goods that are purchased within the UK. This is because imports are chargeable to VAT if the same goods supplied in the home market by a registered trader would be chargeable to VAT. The rate of VAT is the same as that which would have applied if the supply had been made in the home market.

An importer of goods from outside the EU must calculate VAT on the value of the goods imported and account for it at the point of entry into the UK. He can then deduct the VAT payable as input tax on his next VAT return. HMRC issue monthly certificates to importers showing the VAT paid on imports. VAT is chargeable on the onward sale of the goods in the UK in the normal way.

If security (such as a bank guarantee) can be provided, the deferred payment system can be used whereby VAT is automatically charged to the importer's bank account each month rather than payment being made for each import when the goods arrive in the UK. Approved importers are able to provide reduced (and in some cases zero) security in respect of the deferred payment scheme. Such importers need to seek the approval of HMRC.

3.2.2 Exports

There is a general zero-rating where a person exports goods from the EU.

It is not sufficient merely to export goods. The zero-rating only applies if HMRC 'are satisfied' that the supplier has exported the goods. Evidence of the export must therefore be retained by the trader and must take the form specified by HMRC.

3.3 Trade in goods within the European Union

FAST FORWARD

> Sales of goods to registered traders in other EU states are zero-rated. Taxable acquisitions of goods to the UK from other EU states are subject to VAT in the UK as both output tax and input tax.

3.3.1 Sales (despatches)

Where goods are sold to another EU member state, the supply is zero-rated if the supply is made to a registered trader.

3.3.2 Purchases (acquisitions)

Goods acquired in the UK by a VAT registered person from another EU member state are liable to VAT in the UK. Consequently, output tax has to be accounted for on the relevant VAT return. **The 'tax point' for such acquisitions is the earlier of:**

*   **The fifteenth day of the month following the month of acquisition, and**
*   **The date of issue of an invoice.**

The transaction is entered on the relevant VAT return as an output and an input so the effect is neutral. Thus the trader is in the same position as he would have been if he had acquired the goods from a UK supplier.

The only time that there is a VAT cost is if a business makes exempt supplies, since an exempt business cannot reclaim any input VAT.

Although the end result is the same as with an import from outside the EU, the difference with an EU acquisition is that there is no need to actually pay the VAT subsequent to its recovery as input VAT.

3.4 Supplies of services

FAST FORWARD

Supplies of services are generally subject to VAT in the same way as supplies of goods. However, supplies of services by a UK business to outside the EU are outside the scope of VAT.

3.4.1 Supplies of services within the EU

If a UK VAT registered business is supplied with services from within the European Union, or where a UK VAT registered business supplies services to another VAT registered European Union business, the VAT treatment is generally the same as for a supply of goods.

The tax point for a supply of services within the EU is the earlier of:

- The time the service is completed, and
- The time the service is paid for.

3.4.2 Supplies of services outside the EU

If a UK VAT registered business is supplied with services from outside the European Union, the VAT treatment is generally the same as for a supply of goods.

Supplies of services by a UK business to outside the EU are outside the scope of VAT.

4 Special schemes

FAST FORWARD

Special schemes include the cash accounting scheme, the annual accounting scheme and the optional flat rate scheme. These schemes can make VAT accounting easier and ease cash flow for certain types of trader.

4.1 The cash accounting scheme

The cash accounting scheme enables businesses to account for VAT on the basis of cash paid and received. That is, the date of payment or receipt determines the return in which the transaction is dealt with. This means that the cash accounting scheme gives automatic impairment loss relief (bad debt relief) because VAT is not due on a supply until payment has been received.

The scheme can only be used by a trader whose annual taxable turnover (exclusive of VAT) does not exceed £1,350,000. A trader can join the scheme only if all returns and VAT payments are up to date (or arrangements have been made to pay outstanding VAT by instalments).

If the value of taxable supplies exceeds £1,600,000 in the 12 months to the end of a VAT period a trader must leave the cash accounting scheme immediately.

Businesses which leave the scheme (either voluntarily or because they have breached the £1,600,000 limit) can account for any outstanding VAT due under the scheme on a cash basis for a further six months.

4.2 The annual accounting scheme

The annual accounting scheme is only available to traders who regularly pay VAT to HMRC, not to traders who normally receive repayments. It is available for traders **whose taxable turnover (exclusive of VAT) for the 12 months starting on their application to join the scheme is not expected to exceed £1,350,000**.

Under the annual accounting scheme traders file annual VAT returns but throughout the year they must make payments on account of their VAT liability by direct debit. The year for which each return is made may end at the end of any calendar month. Unless HMRC agree otherwise, the trader must pay 90% of the previous year's net VAT liability during the year by means of nine monthly payments commencing at the end of the fourth month of the year. The balance of the year's VAT is then paid with the annual return. There is an option for businesses to pay three larger interim instalments.

Late payment of instalments is not a default for the purposes of the default surcharge.

An annual VAT return must be submitted to HMRC along with any balancing payment due within two months of the end of the year.

It is not possible to use the annual accounting scheme if input tax exceeded output tax in the year prior to application. In addition, all returns must have been made up to date.

If the expected value of a trader's taxable supplies exceeds £1,600,000, notice must be given to HMRC within 30 days and he may then be required to leave the scheme. If the £1,600,000 limit is in fact exceeded, the trader must leave the scheme.

If a trader fails to make the regular payments required by the scheme or the final payment for a year, or has not paid all VAT shown on returns made before joining the scheme, he may be expelled from the scheme. HMRC can also prevent a trader using the scheme 'if they consider it necessary to do so for the protection of the revenue'.

Advantages of annual accounting:

- Only one VAT return each year so fewer occasions to trigger a default surcharge
- Ability to manage cash flow more accurately
- Avoids need for quarterly calculations for input tax recovery

Disadvantages of annual accounting:

- Need to monitor future taxable supplies to ensure turnover limit not exceeded

- Timing of payments have less correlation to turnover (and hence cash received) by business

- Payments based on previous year's turnover may not reflect current year turnover which may be a problem if the scale of activities has reduced

4.3 Flat rate scheme

The optional flat rate scheme enables businesses to calculate VAT due simply by applying a flat rate percentage to their turnover.

Under the scheme, businesses calculate VAT by applying a fixed percentage to their tax inclusive turnover, ie the total turnover, including all reduced rate, zero-rated and exempt income.

The percentage depends upon the trade sector into which a business falls. It ranges from 4% for retailing food, confectionery or newspapers to 14.5% for accountancy and book-keeping services.

A 1% reduction off the flat rate % can be made by businesses in their first year of VAT registration.

Exam focus point	The flat rate percentage will be given to you in your examination.

Businesses using the scheme must issue VAT invoices to their VAT registered customers but they do not have to record all the details of the invoices issued or purchase invoices received to calculate the VAT due. Invoices issued will show VAT at the normal rate rather than the flat rate.

To join the flat rate scheme businesses must have a VAT exclusive annual taxable turnover of up to £150,000.

A business must leave the flat rate scheme if the total value of its VAT inclusive supplies in the year (excluding sales of capital assets) is more than £230,000.

4.4 Example: flat rate scheme

An accountant undertakes work for individuals and for business clients. In a VAT year, the business client work amounts to £35,000 and the accountant will issue VAT invoices totalling £42,000 (£35,000 plus VAT at 20%). Turnover from work for individuals totals £18,000, including VAT. Total gross sales are therefore £60,000. The flat rate percentage for an accountancy businesses is 14.5%.

VAT due to HMRC will be 14.5% × £60,000 = £8,700

Under the normal VAT rules the output tax due would be:

	£
£35,000 × 20%	7,000
£18,000 × 1/6	3,000
	10,000

Whether the accountant is better off under the scheme depends on the amount of input tax incurred as this would be offset, under normal rules, from output tax due.

Chapter Roundup

- A taxable person making a taxable supply to another registered person must supply a VAT invoice within 30 days.

- Every VAT registered trader must keep records for six years.

- A default occurs when a trader either submits his VAT return late, or submits the return on time but pays the VAT late. A default surcharge is applied if there is a default on payment during a default surcharge period.

- There is a common penalty regime for errors in tax returns, including VAT. Errors in a VAT return up to certain amounts may be corrected in the next return.

- Default interest is charged on unpaid VAT if HMRC raise an assessment of VAT or the trader makes a voluntary payment before the assessment is raised. It runs from the date the VAT should have been paid to the actual date of payment but cannot run for more than three years before the assessment or voluntary payment.

- Imports of goods from outside the EU are subject to VAT and exports of goods to outside the EU are zero-rated.

- Sales of goods to registered traders in other EU states are zero-rated. Taxable acquisitions of goods to the UK from other EU states are subject to VAT in the UK as both output tax and input tax.

- Supplies of services are generally subject to VAT in the same way as supplies of goods. However, supplies of services by a UK business to outside the EU are outside the scope of VAT.

- Special schemes include the cash accounting scheme, the annual accounting scheme and the optional flat rate scheme. These schemes can make VAT accounting easier and ease cash flow for certain types of trader.

Quick Quiz

1   How long must a VAT trader keep records?

2   What is a default?

3   Dylan makes an error in his VAT for the quarter ending 31 March 2012 which results in a net under-declaration of £5,000. His net VAT turnover for the period is £150,000. How can Dylan correct the error?

4   Are goods despatched to the EU standard-rated or zero-rated?

5   Mr Higgins is registered for VAT in the UK. Mr Higgins is supplied with services by a French business on 1 September 2011. The value of the supply is £50,000. What are the VAT consequences of the supply?

6   How does the cash accounting scheme operate?

7   The turnover limits for the annual accounting scheme are not exceeding £_____m to join the scheme and once turnover exceeds £_____m the trade must leave the scheme. Fill in the blanks.

8   What is the optional flat rate scheme?

Answers to Quick Quiz

1   A VAT trader must keep records for 6 years.

2   A default occurs when a trader either submits his VAT return late or submits the return on time but pays the VAT late.

3   Dylan can correct the error in his VAT return for the quarter ending 30 June 2012. This is because the error is less than £10,000 and also less than 1% of his net VAT turnover for the return period.

4   In general, despatches to the EU are zero-rated.

5   Mr Higgins will have to account for output tax of £50,000 x 20% = £10,000 on the supply and also £10,000 of input tax. The reverse charge is therefore tax neutral for him.

6   The cash accounting scheme operates by a trader accounting for VAT on the basis of cash paid and received (rather than invoices). The date of payment or receipt determines the return in which the transaction is dealt with. The scheme gives automatic impairment loss relief because VAT on a supply is not due until payment is received.

7   The turnover limits for the annual accounting scheme are not exceeding **£1.35m** to join the scheme and once turnover exceeds **£1.6 m** the trade must leave the scheme

8   The optional flat rate scheme enables businesses to calculate VAT simply by applying a percentage to their tax-inclusive turnover. Under the scheme, businesses calculate VAT due by applying a flat rate percentage to their tax inclusive turnover, ie the total turnover generated, including all reduced-rate, zero-rated and exempt income. The percentage depends upon the trade sector in which a business falls.

Now try the questions below from the Exam Question Bank

Number	Level	Marks	Time
Q41	Examination	10	18 mins
Q42	Examination	10	18 mins
Q43	Examination	10	18 mins

Exam question and answer bank

1 Mary and Luke

22 mins

(a) Mary (aged 25) has partnership trading income of £15,500. She also receives building society interest of £6,400 (net), dividends of £1,800 (net), and pays interest of £2,500 each year on a loan to purchase an interest in the partnership.

Required

Calculate how much cash Mary will have available to spend in 2011/12. Ignore national insurance.

(7 marks)

(b) Luke is aged 78. In 2011/12, he has pension income of £21,200 and receives bank interest of £4,000.

Required

Calculate Luke's tax liability for 2011/12.

(5 marks)

(Total = 12 marks)

2 Mr and Mrs Lowrie

27 mins

John Lowrie and Helen Lowrie who are both in their thirties are a married couple. Mr and Mrs Lowrie received the following income in 2011/12.

	Mr Lowrie	Mrs Lowrie
	£	£
Salary (gross)	44,540	21,000
PAYE tax deducted	7,800	2,600
Dividends (amount received)	1,090	2,538
Bank deposit interest (amount received)	600	76
Building society interest (amount received)	592	420

Required

Compute the tax payable by Mr Lowrie and by Mrs Lowrie for 2011/12.

(15 marks)

3 Michael and Josie

27 mins

Michael Selby (aged 45) and Josie Selby (aged 47) received the following income in 2011/12.

	Michael	Josie
	£	£
Salary (gross)	163,540	100,000
PAYE tax deducted	57,400	33,000
Dividends (amount received)	10,900	2,538
Bank deposit interest (amount received)	6,000	760
Building society interest (amount received)	5,920	4,200

Josie made a gift aid donation of £1,600 in December 2011.

Required

Compute the tax payable or repayable by Michael Selby and by Josie Selby for 2011/12.

(15 marks)

4 Employment and self-employment

27 mins

Discuss the factors to be taken into consideration when deciding whether a person is employed or self-employed for the purposes of income tax.

(15 marks)

5 Azure plc

The following items have been provided by a UK company, Azure plc, to employees earning more than £8,500 a year.

(a)   A loan of £16,000 at 1% a year to Mr Andrews on 6 October 2011 which has been used to improve his private residence.

(b)   A £1,000 interest free loan to Mrs Preece on 6 April 2011 which was used to finance her daughter's wedding.

(c)   The loan of a TV and video system to Mr Charles from 6 June 2011, the asset having cost the company £800 in 2009 and having had a market value of £500 in June 2011.

(d)   A long service award in December 2011 to Mrs Davies, the company secretary, comprising a gold wrist watch costing £400. Mrs Davies has been employed by the company since December 1986.

(e)   The loan of a petrol engined BMW motor car to Mr Edgar from 6 April 2011. The car had a list price of £23,000. The car emits CO_2 of 124g/km. The company pays all running costs, including fuel.

(f)   The exclusive private use of a company flat in central London, by Mr Ford, the managing director. The company acquired the flat in February 2009 for £100,000 and Mr Ford has used it since that date. The flat is fully furnished at a cost of £5,000 and the council tax paid by the company amounted to £500. The annual value is £900. The running costs of the flat amounting to £1,200 for 2011/12 were paid directly by Mr Ford.

(g)   Removal expenses of £9,500 to Miss Jackson in September 2011 who moved from Plymouth to Liverpool to take up a new position in the Liverpool office in July 2011.

(h)   The provision of two mobile phones to Mr Long on 6 April 2011 both of which were available for private use as well as business use. Azure Ltd paid £120 for the hire of each of the mobile phones for the tax year. The market value of each of the phones was £500. The cost of the calls made during the year was £300 for one of the phones and £400 for the other phone. HMRC have agreed that 70% of these expenses related to business use.

Required

State in detail how each of the above items would be treated for 2011/12, computing the amount of any taxable benefit.   **(15 marks)**

6 Gary, George and Geraldine

(a)   Gary had employment income of £55,000 for 2011/12. He paid £4,000 (net) into his personal pension scheme in 2011/12. This was the first year in which he had been a member of a registered pension scheme.

Required

Calculate Gary's income tax payable.   **(2 marks)**

(b)   George had employment income of £45,000 for 2011/12. He paid £39,200 (net) into his personal pension scheme in 2011/12. This was the first year in which he had been a member of a registered pension scheme.

Required

Calculate George's income tax payable.   **(2 marks)**

(c)   Geraldine had trading income of £60,000 for 2011/12. She paid £25,000 (net) into her personal pension scheme in 2011/12. This was the first year in which she had been a member of a registered pension scheme. She estimates that she will have trading income of £130,000 in 2012/13.

Required

Explain the maximum net personal pension contribution that Geraldine will be able to make in 2012/13.

(2 marks)

(Total = 6 marks)

7 Mr Lee   27 mins

You have received the following e-mail from a client, Mr Lee:

'I have just started a new job and thought that I ought to start making some pension provision now that I am in my mid-30s. My initial salary is £40,000 a year, but I am hoping that, with bonuses, it may increase in the next few years.

My employer operates a pension scheme and I have been given a booklet about it. The booklet says that the scheme is a 'money purchase' scheme. If I join the scheme, my employer will make contributions to the scheme in addition to the amount that I pay into it.

Could you answer the following questions:

(1)   Do I have to join my employer's pension scheme or can I make other pension arrangements? What is a 'money purchase' scheme?

(2)   If I join my employer's pension scheme, how much can I contribute to the scheme and how much can my employer contribute? The booklet refers to an annual limit and a lifetime limit. How do these work?

(3)   I have heard that there is tax relief on my contributions to a pension scheme. How does that work if I join my employer's pension scheme?

Required

Draft an e-mail in response.   **(15 marks)**

8 Rafe   27 mins

On 1 May 2011, Rafe started to invest in rented properties. He bought three houses in the first three months, as follows.

House 1

Rafe bought house 1 for £62,000 on 1 May 2011. It needed a new roof before it was fit to be let out. Rafe paid £5,000 for the work to be done in May. He then let it unfurnished for £600 a month from 1 June to 30 November 2011. The first tenant then left, and the house was empty throughout December 2011. On 1 January 2012, a new tenant moved in. The house was again let unfurnished. The rent was £6,000 a year, payable annually in advance.

Rafe paid water rates of £320 for the period from 1 May 2011 to 5 April 2012 and a buildings insurance premium of £480 for the period from 1 June 2011 to 31 May 2012.

House 2

Rafe bought house 2 for £84,000 on 1 June 2011. He immediately bought furniture for £4,300, and let the house fully furnished for £5,000 a year from 1 August 2011. The rent was payable quarterly in arrears. Rafe paid water rates of £240 for the period from 1 June 2011 to 5 April 2012. He claimed the wear and tear allowance for furniture.

House 3

Rafe bought house 3 for £45,000 on 1 July 2011. He spent £1,200 on routine redecoration and £2,300 on furniture in July, and let the house fully furnished from 1 August 2011 for £7,800 a year, payable annually in advance. Rafe paid water rates of £360 for the period from 1 July 2011 to 5 April 2012, a buildings insurance premium of £440 for the period from 1 July 2011 to 30 June 2012 and a contents insurance premium of £180 for the period from 1 August 2011 to 31 July 2012. He claimed the wear and tear allowance for furniture.

During 2011/12 Rafe also rented out one furnished room of his main residence. He received £4,600 and incurred allowable expenses of £875.

Required

Compute Rafe's property business income for 2011/12. **(15 marks)**

9 A Trader

27 mins

A Trader's income statement for the year to 31 March 2012 was as follows.

	£	£
Gross profit		246,250
Other income		
Impairment losses recovered (previously written off)	373	
Profit on sale of office	5,265	
Building society interest	1,900	
		7,538
Expenses		
General expenses	73,611	
Repairs and renewals	15,000	
Legal and accountancy charges	1,200	
Subscriptions and donations	7,000	
Impairment losses (trade)	500	
Salaries and wages	30,000	
Travel	8,000	
Depreciation	15,000	
Rent and rates	1,500	
		(151,811)
Net profit		101,977

Notes

(1) *General expenses include the following.*

	£
Entertaining staff	1,000
Entertaining suppliers	600

(2) *Repairs and renewals include the following.*

	£
Redecorating existing premises	300
Renovations to new premises to remedy wear and tear of previous owner (the premises were usable before these renovations)	500

(3) *Legal and accountancy charges are made up as follows.*

	£
Debt collection service	200
Staff service agreements	50
Tax consultant's fees for special advice	30
45 year lease on new premises	100
Audit and accountancy	820
	1,200

(4) *Subscriptions and donations include the following.*

	£
Donations under the gift aid scheme	5,200
Donation to a political party	500
Sports facilities for staff	600
Subscription to trade association	100

(5) Travel expenses included A Trader's motoring expenses of £2,000. 25% of his use of his car was for private purposes.

(6) Capital allowances amounted to £2,200.

Required

Compute A Trader's taxable trading profit for the accounting period to 31 March 2012. You should start with net profit figure of £101,977 and you should indicate by the use of zero (0) any items which do not require adjustment. **(15 marks)**

10 Tom Hardy

27 mins

Tom Hardy makes accounts to 30 June. Despite substantial investment in new equipment, business has been indifferent and he will cease trading on 31 December 2015. His last accounts will be prepared for the six months to 31 December 2015.

The tax written down values at 1 July 2011 were as follows.

	£
Main pool	31,500
Short life asset (acquired 1.5.11)	4,400

Additions and disposals have been as follows.

		£
20.9.11	Plant cost	102,000
15.7.12	Car for own use cost	13,400
14.7.14	Plant sold for	340
10.5.15	Short life asset sold for	2,900

Private use of the car was 20% for all years. The car emits CO_2 of 125g/km.

At the end of 2015, the plant will be worth £24,000 and the car £10,600.

Required

Calculate the capital allowances for the periods from 1 July 2011 to 31 December 2015, assuming the capital allowances rates for 2011/12 apply throughout. **(15 marks)**

11 Saruman
14 mins

Saruman is the sole proprietor of a small engineering business. He prepares accounts annually to 5 April and has been in business since 6 April 2004.

Main pool brought forward on 6 April 2011	£52,000
Tax written down value of motor car for Saruman's use on 6 April 2011	£600

Private use of this car is 25%.

The following events occurred during the year ended 5 April 2012.

Disposals:	20 April 2011	–	Plant £12,000 (original cost £10,000)
	21 May 2011	–	Motor car for Saruman's own use £920 (original cost £1,896)
	20 June 2011	–	Plant £800 (original cost £3,000)
Additions:	21 May 2011	–	New car for Saruman's use £19,000 CO_2 emissions 170 g/km
	1 October 2011	–	Car for use by sales representative £4,800 CO_2 emissions 120 g/km

Required

Calculate Saruman's capital allowances for the year ended 5 April 2012. **(8 marks)**

12 Mr Cobbler
27 mins

Mr Cobbler starts a business as a sole trader on 1 January 2012.

His business plan shows that his monthly profits are likely to be as follows.

January 2012 to June 2012 (inclusive)	£800	a month
July 2012 to December 2012 (inclusive)	£1,200	a month
Thereafter	£2,000	a month

Mr Cobbler is considering two alternative accounting dates, 31 March and 30 April, in each case commencing with a period ending in 2012.

Required

Show the taxable trading profits which will arise for each of the first four tax years under each of the two alternative accounting dates, and recommend an accounting date. **(15 marks)**

13 Miss Farrington
27 mins

Miss Farrington started to trade as a baker on 1 January 2012 and made up her first accounts to 30 April 2013. Adjusted profits before capital allowances are as follows.

	£
Period to 30 April 2013	137,144
Year to 30 April 2014	24,829

Miss Farrington incurred the following expenditure on plant and machinery.

Date	Item	£
1.1.12	Desk and other office furniture	10,500
4.1.12	General plant	32,280
1.3.12	Second-hand oven acquired from Miss Farrington's father	21,200
25.3.12	Delivery van	21,800
15.4.12	General plant	34,220
15.5.12	Car for Miss Farrington	6,600
30.1.14	General plant	10,000
30.4.14	Mixer	1,200

The private use of the car is 35%. The car has CO_2 emissions of 123g/km.

Required

Calculate the taxable profits for the first four tax years and the overlap profits carried forward. Assume that the capital allowances rates applicable in 2011/12 apply throughout. **(15 marks)**

14 Langland   27 mins

Langland started to trade on 1 February 2007 and decided to retire on 31 October 2012. His accounts show the following profits as adjusted for income tax purposes.

	£
P/e 30 April 2008	12,000
Y/e 30 April 2009	6,000
Y/e 30 April 2010	8,000
Y/e 30 April 2011	10,000
Y/e 30 April 2012	6,000
P/e 31 October 2012	4,000

Required

Calculate the trading assessments for all tax years in question. **(15 marks)**

15 Morgan   27 mins

Morgan started to trade on 6 April 2007. His business has the following results.

Year ending 5 April		£
2008	Profit	12,000
2009	Profit	16,000
2010	Profit	18,000
2011	Profit	15,000
2012	Loss	(32,000)

It is expected that the business will show healthy profits thereafter. In addition to his business Morgan has gross investment income of £8,000 a year.

Required

(a)   Outline the ways in which Morgan could obtain relief for his loss. **(5 marks)**

(b)   Prepare a statement showing how the loss would be relieved assuming that relief were to be claimed as soon as possible. Comment on whether this is likely to be the best relief. **(5 marks)**

(c)   Describe briefly how the situation would alter if Morgan were to cease trading on 5 April 2012. **(5 marks)**

(Total = 15 marks)

16 Adam, Bert and Charlie   27 mins

Adam, Bert and Charlie started in partnership as secondhand car dealers on 6 April 2008, sharing profits in the ratio 2:2:1, after charging annual salaries of £15,000, £12,000 and £10,000 respectively.

On 5 July 2009 Adam retired and Bert and Charlie continue, taking the same salaries as before, but dividing the balance of the profits in the ratio 3:2.

On 6 May 2011 Donald is admitted as a partner on the terms that he received a salary of £18,000 a year, that the salaries of Bert and Charlie should be increased to £18,000 a year each and that of the balance of the profits, Donald should take one tenth, Bert six tenths and Charlie three tenths.

The trade profits of the partnership as adjusted for tax purposes are as follows.

Year ending 5 April	Profits £
2009	102,000
2010	208,000
2011	126,000
2012	180,000

Required

Show the taxable trade profits for each partner for 2008/09 to 2011/12 inclusive. **(15 marks)**

17 Partnerships

27 mins

(a) Required

Briefly explain the basis by which partners are assessed in respect of their share of a partnership's taxable trading profit. **(3 marks)**

(b) Anne and Betty have been in partnership since 1 January 2005 sharing profits equally. On 30 June 2011 Betty resigned as a partner, and was replaced on 1 July 2011 by Chloe. Profit continued to be shared equally. The partnership's taxable trading profits are as follows:

	£
Year ended 31 December 2011	60,000
Year ended 31 December 2012	72,000

As at 6 April 2011 Anne and Betty each have unrelieved overlap profits of £3,000.

Required

Calculate the taxable trading profits of Anne, Betty and Chloe for 2011/12. **(6 marks)**

(c) Daniel and Edward have been in partnership since 6 April 2003, making up accounts to 5 April. On 31 December 2011 Edward resigned as a partner, and was replaced on 1 January 2012 by Frank. For the year ended 5 April 2012 the partnership made a trading loss of £40,000. This was allocated between the partners as follows.

	£
Daniel	20,000
Edward	15,000
Frank	5,000

Each of the partners has investment income. None of them have any capital gains.

Required

State the possible ways in which Daniel, Edward and Frank can relieve their trading losses for 2011/12. **(6 marks)**

(Total = 15 marks)

18 Denise

18 mins

Denise started business on 6 April 2011 as a designer dressmaker. Her trading profits in her first year of trading were £45,000. She expects her profits to rise in future years.

Required

(a)   Outline briefly what payments Denise could make into a personal pension scheme and the tax relief such payments would receive. You should outline the restrictions of the annual allowance and the lifetime allowance.   **(7 marks)**

(b)   Show the Class 2 and Class 4 contributions payable by Denise in 2011/12.   **(3 marks)**

Assume 2011/12 tax rates and allowances apply throughout.

(Total = 10 marks)

19 Sasha Shah

27 mins

Sasha Shah is a computer programmer. Until 5 April 2011 she was employed by Net Computers plc, but since then has worked independently from home. Sasha's income for the year ended 5 April 2012 is £60,000. All of this relates to work done for Net Computers plc. Her expenditure for the year ended 5 April 2012 is as follows:

(1)   The business proportion of light, heat and telephone for Sasha's home is £800.

(2)   Computer equipment was purchased on 6 April 2011 for £4,000.

(3)   A motor car was purchased on 6 April 2011 for £10,000 with CO_2 of 145g/km. Motor expenses for the year ended 5 April 2012 amount to £3,500, of which 40% relate to journeys between home and the premises of Net Computers plc. The other 60% relate to private mileage.

Required

(a)   List eight factors that will indicate that a worker should be treated as an employee rather than as self-employed.   **(4 marks)**

(b)   (i)   Calculate the amount of taxable trading profits if Sasha is treated as self-employed during 2011/12.

(ii)   Calculate the amount of Sasha's taxable earnings if she is treated as an employee during 2011/12.   **(7 marks)**

(c)   (i)   Calculate Sasha's liability to Class 2 and Class 4 NIC if she is treated as self-employed during 2011/12.

(ii)   Calculate Sasha's liability to Class 1 NIC if she is treated as an employee during 2011/12.   **(4 marks)**

(Total = 15 marks)

20 Peter Robinson

18 mins

Peter Robinson made the following disposals of assets during the tax year 2011/12.

30 June 2011

Investment property for £150,000 less costs of disposal £1,280. Acquired for £79,000.

27 July 2011

Part of a plot of land. The proceeds of sale were £35,000. The costs of disposal were £700. The original cost of the land was £54,000. The remainder of the land is worth £70,000.

1 September 2011

A vase which was destroyed. It cost £12,000. Compensation of £20,000 was received on 30 September 2011. Peter bought a new vase as a replacement for £17,000 on 21 December 2011.

Peter had taxable income of £30,600 in 2011/12.

Required

Calculate Peter's capital gains tax payable for the year 2011/12. **(10 marks)**

21 John Harley

18 mins

(a) John Harley purchased a property in England on 1 August 1989 for £40,000 and lived in it until 31 May 1990 when he moved overseas to take up an offer of employment. He returned to the UK on 1 August 1994 and took employment in Scotland until 31 October 2000. During these periods he lived in rented accommodation. On 1 November 2000 he moved back into his own house until he moved out permanently on 30 June 2003. The house was then put up for sale and was finally sold on 30 November 2011 for £120,000. At all times when John was not in the house it remained empty.

Required

Prepare a schedule of periods of exemption and non-exemption, together with the reasons where applicable. **(5 marks)**

(b) Elsie Phillips made the following disposals of assets during the tax year 2011/12.

July 2011

An oil painting for £5,000 (net of £400 commission). She had purchased this at a cost of £11,500.

February 2012

A crystal chandelier for £7,500. She had purchased this for £4,000.

Required

Calculate Elsie's chargeable gains or allowable losses on these two transactions. **(5 marks)**

(Total = 10 marks)

22 The White family

25 mins

(a) Mr White is a sole trader. He bought a factory for use in his trade on 10 July 2006 for £150,000.

On 1 December 2011, Mr White gave the factory to his son, Gary. The market value of the factory at that time was £260,000.

Required

Show the chargeable gains (if any) for Mr White for 2011/12 assuming that any claims to defer gains are made. **(3 marks)**

(b) Gary sells the factory to a developer on 1 March 2012 for £320,000.

Required

Compute the chargeable gain on the sale for Gary. **(2 marks)**

(c) Mrs White is also a sole trader. She acquired a freehold shop for use in the business in May 2004 for £40,000 and sold it in August 2011 for £80,000.

Mrs White is considering buying a new shop. She has located two possible shops. One is a small freehold shop which would cost £72,000. The other is a larger leasehold shop with a lease of 55 years. The cost of the lease would be £90,000.

Required

Explain the tax consequences of acquiring each of the shops. **(9 marks)**

(Total = 14 marks)

23 Alice 9 mins

Alice decided to incorporate her sole trader business on 9 January 2012. She started this business in 1993. All of the business assets were transferred to the new company. The consideration consisted of 200,000 £1 ordinary shares valued at £200,000 and £100,000 in cash. The transfer of the business assets resulted in total gains of £120,000.

Required

Calculate the gain arising on the transfer. Also show the cost of the shares for future disposals.

(5 marks)

24 Kai 18 mins

Kai started in business as a sole trader in August 2005. He acquired a freehold shop for £80,000 and a warehouse for £150,000.

Kai sold his business as a going concern to Jibran in December 2011 and received £50,000 for goodwill, £90,000 for the shop and £180,000 for the warehouse. Kai also sold a plot of land to Jibran which he had not used in his business. The land cost £10,000 and Jibran paid £25,500 for it.

Other than those listed above, Kai had never undertaken any transactions which were relevant for capital gains tax purposes.

Kai's taxable income in 2011/12 was £20,000.

Required

Compute the capital gains tax payable by Kai for 2011/12. **(10 marks)**

25 Melissa 18 mins

Melissa bought shares in Fisher plc as follows:

12 July 2002	6,000 shares for £21,000
14 December 2007	2,000 shares for £6,500
11 July 2011	4,000 shares for £16,000

She sold 10,000 shares for £42,000 on 2 July 2011.

Required

Compute Melissa's gain on sale. **(10 marks)**

26 Tim

15 mins

Tim is a medical consultant. His total tax liability for 2010/11 was £16,800. Of this £7,200 was paid under the PAYE system, £800 was withheld at source from bank interest and £200 was suffered on dividends received during the year.

Tim's total tax liability for 2011/12 was £22,000. £7,100 of this was paid under PAYE system, £900 was withheld at source from bank interest and there was a £250 tax credit on dividends.

Tim did not make any claim in respect of his payments on account for 2011/12. HM Revenue and Customs issued a 2011/12 tax return to Tim on 5 May 2012.

Required

State what payments Tim was required to make in respect of his 2011/12 tax liability and the due dates for the payment of these amounts.

(8 marks)

27 Lai Chan

45 mins

Until 31 December 2011 Lai Chan was employed by Put-it-Right plc as a management consultant. The following information relates to the period of employment from 6 April to 31 December 2011.

(1) Lai was paid a gross salary of £3,250 per month.

(2) She contributed 6% of her gross salary into Put-it-right plc's registered occupational pension scheme. The company contributed a further 6%.

(3) Put-it-Right plc provided Lai with a motor car with a list price of £26,400. The motor car's CO_2 emissions were 175g/km. Lai paid Put-it-Right plc £130 per month for the use of the motor car.

Put-it-Right plc paid for the petrol in respect of all the mileage done by Lai during 2011/12. She paid the company £30 per month towards the cost of her private petrol.

The motor car was returned to Put-it-Right plc on 31 December 2011.

(4) Put-it-Right plc provided Lai with an interest free loan of £30,000 on 1 January 2008. She repaid £20,000 of the loan on 30 June 2011 with the balance of £10,000 being repaid on 31 December 2011.

On 1 January 2012 Lai commenced in self-employment running a music recording studio. The following information relates to the period of self-employment from 1 January to 5 April 2012.

(1) The trading profit for the period 1 January to 5 April 2012 is £44,500. This figure is *before* taking account of capital allowances.

(2) Lai purchased the following assets:

1 January 2012	Recording equipment	£20,000
15 January 2012	Motor car CO_2 emissions 175g/km	£18,800
20 February 2012	Motor car CO_2 emissions 145g/km	£10,400
4 March 2012	Mixing desk	£6,500

The motor car purchased on 15 January 2012 is used by Lai, and 40% of the mileage is for private purposes. The motor car purchased on 20 February 2012 is used by an employee, and 10% of the mileage is for private purposes.

The mixing desk purchased on 4 March 2012 is to be treated as a short-life asset.

(3) Since becoming self-employed Lai has paid £256 (net) per month into a personal pension scheme. Payments are made on the 20th of each month.

Required

(a) Calculate Lai's income tax liability for 2011/12. **(20 marks)**

(b) Briefly explain how Lai's income tax liability for 2011/12 will be paid to the HM Revenue and Customs.

(5 marks)

(Total = 25 marks)

28 Colin

27 mins

Colin died on 20 December 2011. During his lifetime, he used his annual exemption in April each year and also made the following gifts.

Date	Gift	Recipient
21.1.07	Cash of £300,000	Trustees (Colin paid the IHT)
20.8.08	Shares worth £30,000 (value at 20.12.11 £200,000)	Daughter
19.6.09	Shares worth £103,000 (value at 20.12.11 £150,000)	Trustees (Trustees paid the IHT)
1.9.11	Cash of £200,000	Wife

Required

(a) Explain the inheritance tax implications of these gifts during Colin's lifetime, computing any inheritance due. State the due dates for payment of the tax. **(7 marks)**

Nil rate bands for previous years

2006/07	£285,000
2008/09	£312,000
2009/10	£325,000

(b) Explain the inheritance tax position on these gifts as a result of Colin's death, computing any inheritance tax due. State the due dates for payment of the tax. **(5 marks)**

(c) It is March 2012. Colin's cousin wishes to give £50,000 to his daughter. His daughter is likely to get married in May 2012. Colin's cousin has not made any recent gifts.

What advice would you give Colin's cousin? **(3 marks)**

(Total = 15 marks)

29 Marissa

27 mins

Marissa made the following lifetime transfers:

10 August 2000   Gift of house worth £200,000 to her son

15 July 2006   Gift of unquoted shares to her daughter. The gift was of 5,000 shares valued at £50,000. Before the gift, Marissa owned 8,000 shares valued at £160,000. After the gift Marissa owned 3,000 shares valued at £22,500.

Marissa died on 25 November 2011, leaving the following assets:

	£
Shares in MS plc	320,000
Life assurance policy	see note
House in UK	175,000
Villa in Spain	80,000
Household furniture	20,000
Cash in bank	17,750
Car	5,000

Marissa also had the following debts at her death

	£
Bank loan secured on UK house	10,000
Credit card bills	7,000
Income tax	3,000
Gas bill	250

Note

The value of the insurance policy immediately before Marissa's death was £60,000. The proceeds payable as a result of Marissa's death were £250,000.

The personal representative of Marissa's estate paid funeral expenses of £2,500.

Marissa was widowed in September 2007. Her husband left £20,000 to his sister and the rest of his estate to Marissa. He had not made any lifetime gifts. The nil rate band for 2007/08 was £300,000. Marissa remarried in April 2010.

In her will, Marissa left her house in the UK to her second husband and the remainder of her estate to her children.

Required

(a) Explain the inheritance tax implications of the lifetime gifts made by Marissa **(9 marks)**

(b) Compute Marissa's death estate and the inheritance tax due on it. State who is liable to pay the tax due and the due date for payment. **(6 marks)**

(Total = 15 marks)

30 Elderflower Ltd

27 mins

Elderflower Ltd is a UK resident company which trades as a manufacturer of specialist soft drinks. The company's income statement for the year ended 31 March 2012 is as follows:

	£	£
Gross profit		510,000
Other income		
Profit on disposal of office building (note 1)		54,000
Bank interest (note 2)		7,000
Expenses		
Depreciation	54,690	
Professional fees (note 3)	22,000	
Repairs and renewals (note 4)	29,700	
Other expenses (note 5)	24,400	
		(130,790)
Finance costs		
Interest payable (note 6)		(23,000)
Profit before taxation		417,210

Notes

(1) *Disposal of office building*

The profit of £54,000 is in respect of a freehold office building that was sold on 30 June 2011 for £380,000. The chargeable gain on sale has been computed to be £50,690.

(2) *Bank interest received*

The bank interest was received on 31 March 2012 and is the amount accrued to that date. The bank deposit is held for non-trading purposes.

(3)   *Professional fees*

Professional fees are as follows:

	£
Accountancy and audit fee	4,600
Legal fees in connection with the issue of share capital	8,800
Legal fees in connection with the issue of loan notes (see note 6)	6,400
Legal fees in connection with breach of contract by supplier	1,300
Legal fees in connection with fine for breach of health and safety legislation	900
	22,000

(4)   *Repairs and renewals*

The figure of £29,700 for repairs includes £9,700 for constructing an extension to the company's manufacturing premises and £5,400 for repainting the interior of the company's offices.

(5)   *Other expenses*

Other expenses include £2,310 for entertaining customers, £1,600 for entertaining employees and a Gift Aid donation of £500.

(6)   *Interest payable*

Elderflower Ltd issued loan notes on 1 October 2011. The capital raised was used for trading purposes. Interest of £23,000 in respect of the first six months of the loan was paid on 31 March 2012.

(7)   *Plant and machinery*

On 1 April 2011 the tax written down values of plant and machinery were as follows:

	£
Main pool	27,500
Expensive motor car (acquired in 2005)	14,700

The following transactions took place during the year ended 31 March 2012:

		Cost/(Proceeds) £
10 May 2011	Purchased plant	30,200
5 January 2012	Sold the expensive motor car	(9,700)
20 March 2012	Sold a delivery van	(11,600)
31 March 2012	Purchased a motor car CO_2 emissions 137g/km	9,600

The van sold on 20 March 2012 for £11,600 originally cost £18,500. The motor car purchased on 31 March 2012 is used by the sales manager: 25% of the mileage is for private journeys.

Required

(a)   Calculate Elderflower Ltd's trading profit for the year ended 31 March 2012. Your answer should commence with the profit before taxation figure of £417,210 and should list all of the items in the income statement indicating by the use of a zero (0) any items that do not require adjustment. You should assume that the company claims the maximum available capital allowances.   **(13 marks)**

(b)   Calculate Elderflower Ltd's taxable total profits for the year ended 31 March 2012.   **(2 marks)**

(Total = 15 marks)

31 Tree Ltd

27 mins

(a)   Tree Ltd, a company with no associated companies, had the following results for the twelve
months to 31 March 2012:

	£
Trading profits	180,000
Chargeable gain	105,000
Gift aid donation	27,000
Bank interest received	36,000
Dividend received	29,700

The bank interest accrued evenly over the period.

Required

Compute the corporation tax liability for the year ended 31 March 2012.   **(7 marks)**

(b)   Dealers plc, a company with no associated companies, had taxable total profits of £420,000 for its
six month accounting period ended 31 March 2012. No dividends were received by the company
during the year.

Required

Compute Dealers plc's corporation tax liability for the period.   **(3 marks)**

(c)   Springer Ltd had profits chargeable to corporation tax of £600,000 in the year to 31 December
2011. It received a dividend of £27,000 on 1 September 2011.

Required

Calculate Springer Ltd's corporation tax liability for the year ended 31 December 2011.

(5 marks)

(Total = 15 marks)

32 Righteous plc

18 mins

Righteous plc used to make its accounts up to 31 December. A decision has been made to change its year
end to 31 May. The following information relates to the period of account from 1 January 2010 to 31 May
2011.

	£
Trading profits	500,000
Bank interest accrued and received	
30.6.10	15,000
31.12.10	6,000
31.5.11	2,500
Capital gain on property sold on	
1.5.11	5,000
Gift Aid donations paid	
28.2.10	15,000
31.8.10	15,000
28.2.11	40,000

No capital allowances are claimed.

Required

Calculate the corporation tax liability.   **(10 marks)**

33 E Ltd
9 mins

E Ltd disposed of assets as follows.

(a) On 1 January 2011 it sold a car which had been used by a company director at a loss of £10,700.
(b) On 28 February 2011 it sold some shares at a loss of £16,400.
(c) On 1 May 2011 it sold some shares and realised a gain of £17,700.
(d) On 1 October 2011 it sold some shares at a loss of £6,000.
(e) On 1 December 2011 it sold a picture to a collector for £50,000, making a gain of £3,000.

Required

What loss, if any, is available to be carried forward at the end of its year ended 31 March 2012? **(5 marks)**

34 Hardup Ltd
27 mins

Hardup Ltd made the following disposals in the year ended 31 March 2012.

(a) On 31 May 2011 it sold an office block for £120,000. The company had bought the offices for £65,000 on 1 July 1993. The company had invested £100,000 in another office block on 1 May 2010.

(b) On 18 June 2011 it sold a plot of land for £69,000. It had bought it for £20,000 on 1 April 1986 and had spent £4,000 on defending its title to the land in July 1990.

(c) On 25 June 2011 the company exchanged contracts for the sale of a workshop for £173,000. Completion took place on 24 July 2011. It had bought the workshop for £65,000 on 16 October 1988.

Required

Compute Hardup Ltd's chargeable gains for the year end 31 March 2012.   **(15 marks)**

Assume retail prices index

May 2011 = 233.9   July 1993 = 140.7
June 2011 = 234.5   July 1990 = 126.8
July 2011 = 234.9   October 1988 = 109.5
                                    April 1986 = 97.67

35 Ferraro Ltd
27 mins

Ferraro Ltd has the following results.

	y/e 31.3.09 £	y/e 31.3.10 £	9m to 31.12.10 £	y/e 31.12.11 £
Trading profit (loss)	34,480	6,200	4,320	(100,000)
Bank deposit interest accrued	200	80	240	260
Rents receivable	1,200	1,420	1,440	1,600
Capital gain			12,680	
Allowable capital loss	5,000			9,423
Gift aid donation paid (gross)	1,000	0	1,000	1,500

Required

Compute all taxable total profits, claiming loss reliefs as early as possible. State any amounts carried forward as at 31 December 2011.   **(15 marks)**

36 P Ltd
27 mins

P Ltd owns the following holdings in ordinary shares in other companies, which are all UK resident.

Q Ltd	83%
R Ltd	77%
S Ltd	67%
M Ltd	80%
T Ltd	70%

In each case, the conditions for claiming group relief, where appropriate, are satisfied.

The following are the results of the above companies for the year ended 31 March 2012.

	M Ltd £	P Ltd £	Q Ltd £	R Ltd £	S Ltd £	T Ltd £
Trading profit	20,000	0	64,000	260,000	0	70,000
Trading loss	0	226,000	0	0	8,000	0
Property business income	0	6,000	4,000	0	0	0
Gift aid donation paid	4,000	4,500	2,000	5,000	0	0

Required

(a) Compute the corporation tax payable for the above accounting period by each of the above companies. Assume that group relief is claimed where appropriate and the most tax efficient manner.

(b) Advise the board of P Ltd of the advantages of increasing its holding in S Ltd, a company likely to sustain trading losses for the next two years before becoming profitable. P Ltd itself is likely only to break even in the next few years.

(15 marks)

37 Apple Ltd
27 mins

Apple Ltd owns 100% of the ordinary share capital of Banana Ltd and Cherry Ltd. The results of each company for the year ended 31 March 2012 are as follows:

	Apple Ltd £	Banana Ltd £	Cherry Ltd £
Tax adjusted trading profit/(loss)	(125,000)	650,000	130,000
Capital gain/(loss)	188,000	(8,000)	–

Apple Ltd's capital gain arose from the sale of a freehold warehouse on 15 April 2011 for £418,000. Cherry Ltd purchased a freehold office building for £290,000 on 10 January 2012.

Required

(a) Explain the group relationship that must exist in order that group relief can be claimed. **(3 marks)**

(b) Explain how group relief should be allocated between the respective claimant companies in order to maximise the potential benefit obtained from the relief. **(4 marks)**

(c) Assuming that reliefs are claimed in the most favourable manner, calculate the corporation tax liabilities of Apple Ltd, Banana Ltd and Cherry Ltd for the year ended 31 March 2012. **(8 marks)**

(Total = 15 marks)

38 M Ltd

18 mins

M Ltd is a UK resident company which owns controlling interests in four other UK resident companies and has three overseas branches.

In the year to 31 March 2012 the branches had the following results:

Branch	After tax profits	Foreign tax paid
	£	£
A	170,000	30,000
B	150,000	50,000
C	120,000	67,500

M Ltd had experienced a prolonged period of poor trading and, as a result of losses brought forward from earlier years, its adjusted trading profits for the year ended 31 March 2012 are only £20,000.

During the year, a gift aid donation of £75,000 had been paid to charity and this had been added back in arriving at the adjusted taxable trading profits.

Required

Compute the corporation tax payable by M Ltd in respect of the year ended 31 March 2012. Your answer should show clearly your treatment of the gift aid payment and of the foreign taxes suffered. You should explain why you are dealing with items in a particular way and you should use a columnar layout.

(10 marks)

39 Hogg Ltd

9 mins

(a) Hogg Ltd prepares accounts for the year to 31 March 2012. Its taxable total profits for the year will be £1,750,000. The company has always paid corporation tax at the main rate.

Required

State the amounts and due dates for the payment of corporation tax by Hogg Ltd in respect of the year to 31 March 2012. **(3 marks)**

(b) State the due date for submission of Hogg Ltd's corporation tax return assuming a notice to file the return is issued on:

(i)   12 April 2012

(ii)   12 February 2013 **(2 marks)**

(Total = 5 marks)

40 Newcomer Ltd and Au Revoir Ltd

18 mins

(a) Newcomer Ltd commenced trading on 1 October 2011. Its forecast sales are as follows.

		£
2011	October	12,500
	November	16,200
	December	23,400
2012	January	21,300
	February	15,700
	March	1,200

The company's sales are all standard-rated, and the above figures are exclusive of VAT.

Required

Explain when Newcomer Ltd will be required to compulsorily register for VAT. **(6 marks)**

(b)   Au Revoir Ltd has been registered for VAT since 1996, and its sales are all standard-rated. The company has recently seen a downturn in its business activities, and sales for the years ended 31 October 2011 and 2012 are forecast to be £69,000 and £66,500 respectively. Both of these figures are exclusive of VAT.

Required

Explain why Au Revoir Ltd will be permitted to voluntarily deregister for VAT, and from what date deregistration will be effective.   **(4 marks)**

(Total = 10 marks)

41 Justin   18 mins

Justin has the following transactions in the quarter ended 31 December 2011. All amounts exclude any VAT unless otherwise stated.

	£
Purchases (all standard-rated)	
Furniture for resale	275,000
Computer for use in the business	2,400
Restaurant bills: entertaining customers	1,900
Petrol for cars owned by Justin and used only by his employees	2,800
Sales	
Furniture (standard-rated)	490,000
Books on interior design (zero-rated)	2,400

Only one employee's car has petrol for private motoring provided by Justin (the appropriate fuel scale charge for the quarter is £378 inclusive of VAT).

Required

Calculate the amount of VAT which Justin must pay to HM Revenue and Customs for the quarter.

(10 marks)

42 Ongoing Ltd   18 mins

Ongoing Ltd is registered for VAT, and its sales and purchases are all standard-rated. The following information relates to the company's VAT return for the quarter ended 30 April 2011:

(1)   Standard-rated sales amounted to £120,000. Ongoing Ltd offers its customers a 5% discount for prompt payment, and this discount is taken by half of the customers.

(2)   Standard-rated purchases and expenses amounted to £35,640. This figure includes £480 for entertaining UK customers.

(3)   On 15 April 2011 the company wrote off impairment losses (bad debts) of £2,100 and £840 in respect of invoices due for payment on 10 August 2010 and 5 December 2010 respectively.

(4)   On 30 April 2011 the company purchased a motor car at a cost of £16,450 for the use of a salesperson, and machinery at a cost of £21,150. Both these figures are inclusive of VAT. The motor car is used for both business and private mileage.

Unless stated otherwise, all of the above figures are exclusive of VAT. Ongoing Ltd does not operate the cash accounting scheme.

Required

Calculate the amount of VAT payable by Ongoing Ltd for the quarter ended 30 April 2011.

(10 marks)

43 Jason
18 mins

Jason is a sole trader who has recently registered for value added tax (VAT). He buys and sells goods and services to other businesses in the European Union (EU) and outside the EU.

Required

(a) State how supplies of goods made by Jason to a VAT registered trader in another EU state will be treated for VAT. **(1 mark)**

(b) Explain how Jason will deal with the VAT implications of buying goods from a VAT registered trader in another EU state. State the tax point for acquisitions of goods in the UK from other VAT registered businesses in the EU. **(5 marks)**

(c) Explain how Jason will deal with the VAT implications of importing goods from outside the EU. You may assume that Jason is not a regular importer of goods from outside the EU. **(3 marks)**

(d) State how the supply of services by Jason outside the EU will be dealt with for VAT **(1 mark)**

(Total = 10 marks)

44 Industrial Ltd
45 mins

Industrial Ltd is a UK resident company that manufactures furniture. The company's results for the year ended 31 March 2012 are summarised as follows:

	£
Trading profit (as adjusted for taxation but before taking account of capital allowances)	1,810,000
Income from property (note 1)	110,400
Bank interest received (note 2)	8,000
Loan interest received (note 3)	36,000
Profit on disposal of quoted shares (note 4)	90,622
Donation to charity (note 5)	(1,500)

Note 1 – Income from property

Since 1 January 2012 Industrial Ltd has leased an office building that is surplus to requirements. On that date the company received a premium of £80,000 for the grant of a ten-year lease, and the annual rent of £30,400 which is payable in advance.

Note 2 – Bank interest received

The bank interest was received on 31 March 2012. The bank deposits are held for non-trading purposes. There were no accruals of bank interest at the beginning or end of the year.

Note 3 – Loan interest received

The loan interest was received on 31 March 2012. The loan was made for non-trading purposes to another UK company. There were no accruals of loan interest at the beginning or end of the year.

Note 4 – Profit on disposal of quoted shares

The profit on disposal of quoted shares is in respect of a shareholding that was sold on 15 January 2012 for £236,696. The shareholding was purchased on 1 April 2006 for £135,800. The indexation allowance from April 2006 to January 2012 is £27,974.

At 1 April 2011 Industrial Ltd had unused capital losses brought forward of £10,800.

Note 5 – Donation to charity

The donation to charity was the amount paid under the gift aid scheme.

Note 6 – Plant and machinery

On 1 April 2011 the tax written down values of plant and machinery were as follows:

	£
Main pool	84,600
Expensive motor car (acquired May 2007)	15,400

The expensive motor car was sold on 31 August 2011 for £19,600.
The following assets were purchased during the year ended 31 March 2012.

		£
15 June 2011	Machinery	3,400
15 August 2011	Motor car (CO$_2$ emissions 170g/km)	17,200
30 September 2011	Heating system for factory	62,800
30 September 2011	Fire alarm system for factory	7,200
12 October 2011	Lorry	32,000
10 December 2011	General plant	27,000

Note 7 – Other information

Industrial Ltd has no associated companies. For the year ended 31 March 2011 Industrial Ltd had taxable total profits of £1,650,000.

Required

(a) Calculate the corporation tax payable by Industrial Ltd for the year ended 31 March 2012.

(21 marks)

(b) (i) Explain why Industrial Ltd is required to make quarterly instalment payments in respect of its corporation tax liability for the year ended 31 March 2012. **(2 marks)**

(ii) State the relevant due dates for payment of the corporation tax liability. **(2 marks)**

(Total = 25 marks)

Approaching the answer

You should read through the requirement before working through and annotating the question as we have so that you know what you are looking for.

Industrial Ltd is a UK resident company that manufactures furniture. The company's results for the year

> ALL in FY 11

ended 31 March 2012 are summarised as follows:

	£
Trading profit (as adjusted for taxation but before taking account of capital allowances)	1,810,000
Income from property (note 1)	110,400
Bank interest received (note 2)	8,000
Loan interest received (note 3)	36,000
Profit on disposal of quoted shares (note 4)	90,622
Donation to charity (note 5)	(1,500)

Note 1 – Income from property

Since 1 January 2012 Industrial Ltd has leased an office building that is surplus to requirements. On that

date the company received a premium of £80,000 for the grant of a ten-year lease, and the annual rent of

> Prorate × $^3/_{12}$

£30,400 which is payable in advance.

> Property income charge on short leases

Note 2 – Bank interest received

The bank interest was received on 31 March 2012. The bank deposits are held for non-trading purposes.

There were no accruals of bank interest at the beginning or end of the year.

> Investment income received

Note 3 – Loan interest received

The loan interest was received on 31 March 2012. The loan was made for non-trading purposes to another UK company. There were no accruals of loan interest at the beginning or end of the year.

> Received gross

> Also investment income

Note 4 – Profit on disposal of quoted shares

The profit on disposal of quoted shares is in respect of a shareholding that was sold on 15 January 2012 for £236,696. The shareholding was purchased on 1 April 2006 for £135,800. The indexation allowance from April 2006 to January 2012 is £27,974.

> Set off capital loss b/f against gain

At 1 April 2011 Industrial Ltd had unused capital losses brought forward of £10,800.

Note 5 – Donation to charity

The donation to charity was the amount paid under the gift aid scheme.

> Deduct from total profits

Note 6 – Plant and machinery

On 1 April 2011 the tax written down values of plant and machinery were as follows:

	£
Main pool	84,600
Expensive motor car (acquired May 2007)	15,400

The expensive motor car was sold on 31 August 2011 for £19,600

> Balancing charge

The following assets were purchased during the year ended 31 March 2012.

		£
15 June 2011	Machinery	3,400
15 August 2011	Motor car (CO$_2$ emissions 170g/km)	17,200
30 September 2011	Heating system for factory	62,800
30 September 2011	Fire alarm system for factory	7,200
12 October 2011	Lorry	32,000
10 December 2011	General plant	27,000

> AIA best use

Note 7 – Other information

Industrial Ltd has no associated companies. For the year ended 31 March 2011 Industrial Ltd had taxable total profits of £1,650,000.

> Paid CT at main rate

Required

(a) Calculate the corporation tax payable by Industrial Ltd for the year ended 31 March 2012.

(21 marks)

(b) (i) Explain why Industrial Ltd is required to make quarterly instalment payments in respect of its corporation tax liability for the year ended 31 March 2012. **(2 marks)**

(ii) State the relevant due dates for payment of the corporation tax liability. **(2 marks)**

Instalment dates

(Total = 25 marks)

45 Carolyn Kraft

45 mins

Carolyn Kraft is aged 34. She is employed as a buyer for a large retail group of companies. She is married to Mike.

In the tax year 2011/12, Carolyn was paid a salary of £37,000 (PAYE £5,900). Carolyn also received bank interest of £8,000 in 2011/12. On 14 November 2011 Carolyn made a donation under Gift Aid to Cancer Research UK of £800.

Mike undertakes a business from home. His accounts for the year ended 31 December 2011 show an adjusted profit of £57,500. He is also entitled to capital allowances of £1,600. Mike had owned a freehold shop which he had used in his business. He had acquired the shop on 10 April 2010 for £53,300 and sold it for £85,000 in August 2011. He is considering acquiring another shop to replace this one.

Mike also received dividends of £9,000 in 2011/12 and makes a contribution of £200 each month to his personal pension.

Carolyn bought a flat in August 2009 for £180,000. Carolyn arranged for renovation work to be undertaken, which cost £30,000 in January 2011. Carolyn sold the flat for £250,000 in December 2011. The flat was unoccupied between the date of purchase and the date of sale.

Required

(a) Calculate both Carolyn and Mike's income tax payable for 2011/12 and state when it is payable.

(11 marks)

(b) Calculate the amount of national insurance contributions payable by both Carolyn and Mike for 2011/12. **(4 marks)**

(c) Calculate Carolyn's and Mike's 2011/12 capital gains tax liability stating the due date. Assume Mike does not acquire another shop. **(7 marks)**

(d) Briefly explain the relief available to Mike if he does acquire another shop. **(3 marks)**

(Total = 25 marks)

Approaching the answer

You should read through the requirement before working through and annotating the question as we have so that you know what you are looking for.

Carolyn Kraft is aged 34. She is employed as a buyer for a large retail group of companies. She is married to Mike.

In the tax year 2011/12, Carolyn was paid a salary of £37,000 (PAYE £5,900). Carolyn also received bank interest of £8,000 in 2011/12. On 14 November 2011 Carolyn made a donation under Gift Aid to Cancer Research UK of £800.

> Increases basic rate limit

Mike undertakes a business from home. His accounts for the year ended 31 December 2011 show an adjusted profit of £57,500. He is also entitled to capital allowances of £1,600. Mike had owned a freehold shop which he had used in his business. He had acquired the shop on 10 April 2010 for £53,300 and sold it for £85,000 in August 2011. He is considering acquiring another shop to replace this one.

> Self employment

> Looks like rollover relief

Mike also received dividends of £9,000 in 2011/12 and makes a contribution of £200 each month to his personal pension.

> Increases basic rate limit

Carolyn bought a flat in August 2009 for £180,000. Carolyn arranged for renovation work to be undertaken, which cost £30,000 in January 2011. Carolyn sold the flat for £250,000 in December 2011. The flat was unoccupied between the date of purchase and the date of sale.

> Enhancement expenditure

> CGT

> No PPR

> Easy marks

Required

(a) Calculate both Carolyn and Mike's income tax due for 2011/12 and state when it is due.

(11 marks)

(b) Calculate the amount of national insurance contributions payable by both Carolyn and Mike for 2011/12.

(4 marks)

(c) Calculate Carolyn's and Mike's 2011/12 capital gains tax liability stating the due date. Assume Mike does not acquire another shop.

> Easy marks

(8 marks)

(d) Briefly explain the relief available to Mike if he does acquire another shop.

(2 marks)

(Total = 25 marks)

> Follow instructions: make your answer brief!

1 Mary and Luke

Tutorial note. If you get into the habit of setting up your income tax computations with three columns like this you should have a good chance of getting them right. Remember that the savings income starting rate only applies if non-savings income is less than £2,560. Dividend income under the basic rate limit is taxed at 10%.

(a)   Mary 2011/12

	Non-savings income	Savings income	Dividend income	Total
	£	£	£	£
Trading income	15,500			
Building society interest × 100/80		8,000		
Dividends × 100/90			2,000	
Total income	15,500	8,000	2,000	
Less interest paid	(2,500)	0	0	
Net income	13,000	8,000	2,000	23,000
Less personal allowance	(7,475)	0	0	
Taxable income	5,525	8,000	2,000	15,525

	£
Non-savings income	
£5,525 × 20%	1,105
Savings income	
£8,000 × 20%	1,600
Dividend income	
£2,000 × 10%	200
	2,905
Less tax credit on dividend income	(200)
tax suffered on building society interest	(1,600)
Balance of tax still to pay	1,105

	£	£
Profits received		15,500
Building society interest received		6,400
Dividend received		1,800
		23,700
Less interest paid on loan	2,500	
income tax to pay	1,105	
		(3,605)
Available to spend		20,095

(b)   *Luke 2011/12*

	Non-savings income £	Savings income £	Total £
Pension income	21,200		
Bank interest × 100/80		5,000	
Net income	21,200	5,000	26,200
Less: age allowance (W)	(8,990)		
Taxable income	12,210	5,000	17,210

	£
Non-savings income	
£12,210 × 20%	2,442
Savings income	
£5,000 × 20%	1,000
Tax liability	3,442

Working

	£
Net income	26,200
Less income limit	(24,000)
Excess	2,200
Age allowance (75+)	10,090
Less half excess £2,200 × ½	(1,100)
Revised age allowance	8,990

2 Mr and Mrs Lowrie

> **Tutorial note**. Mr Lowrie's dividend income is between the basic rate limit and the higher rate limit, so it is taxed at 32.5%. Mrs Lowrie's dividends, however, fall below the basic rate limit and are consequently taxed at 10%.

Mr Lowrie	Non-savings income £	Savings income £	Dividend income £	Total £
Employment income	44,540			
Dividends × 100/90			1,211	
Bank deposit interest × 100/80		750		
Building society interest × 100/80		740		
Net income	44,540	1,490	1,211	47,241
Less personal allowance	(7,475)			
Taxable income	37,065	1,490	1,211	39,766

	£	£
Non savings income		
£35,000 × 20%		7,000
£2,065 × 40%		826
Savings income		
£1,490 × 40%		596
Dividend income		
£1,211 × 32.5%		394
		8,816
Less: tax credit on dividend	121	
tax suffered on savings income	298	
PAYE	7,800	
		(8,219)
Tax payable		597

	Non-savings income £	Savings income £	Dividend income £	Total £
Mrs Lowrie				
Employment income	21,000			
Dividends × 100/90			2,820	
Bank deposit interest × 100/80		95		
Building society interest × 100/80		525		
Net income	21,000	620	2,820	24,440
Less personal allowance	(7,475)			
Taxable income	13,525	620	2,820	16,965

	£	£
Non-savings income		
£13,525 × 20%		2,705
Savings income		
£620 × 20%		124
Dividend income		
£2,820 × 10%		282
Tax liability		3,111
Less: tax credit on dividends	282	
tax suffered on savings income	124	
PAYE	2,600	
		(3,006)
Tax payable		105

3 Michael and Josie

> **Tutorial note**. Michael is not entitled to a personal allowance because his net income is more than £114,950. Josie is entitled to a reduced personal allowance because her adjusted net income is between £100,000 and £114,950.

Michael Selby	Non-savings income £	Savings income £	Dividend income £	Total £
Employment income	163,540			
Dividends × 100/90			12,111	
Bank deposit interest × 100/80		7,500		
Building society interest × 100/80		7,400		
Net income/Taxable income	163,540	14,900	12,111	190,551

Non-savings income 7,000 £(150,000 − 35,000) = 115,000 × 40%

	46,000
£13,540 × 50%	6,770
Savings income	
£14,900 × 50%	7,450
Dividend income	
£12,111 × 42.5%	5,147
	72,367
Less: tax credit on dividend	1,211
tax suffered on savings income	2,980
PAYE	57,400
	(61,591)
Tax payable	10,776

Josie Selby	Non-savings income £	Savings income £	Dividend income £	Total £
Employment income	100,000			
Dividends × 100/90			2,820	
Bank deposit interest × 100/80		950		
Building society interest × 100/80		5,250		
Net income	100,000	6,200	2,820	109,020
Less personal allowance (W)	(3,965)			
Taxable income	96,035	6,200	2,820	105,055

	£	£
Non-savings income		
£35,000 × 20%		7,000
£2,000 × 20% (increased basic rate limit)		400
£59,035 × 40%		23,614
Savings income		
£6,200 × 40%		2,480
Dividend income		
£2,820 × 32.5%		916
Tax liability		34,410
Less: tax credit on dividends	282	
tax suffered on savings income	1,240	
PAYE	33,000	
		(34,522)
Tax repayable		(112)

Working

	£
Net income	109,020
Less gross gift aid donation £1,600 × 100/80	(2,000)
Adjusted net income	107,020
Less income limit	(100,000)
Excess	7,020
Personal allowance	7,475
Less half excess £7,020 × ½	(3,510)
Revised age allowance	3,965

4 Employment and self-employment

> **Tutorial note**. In general, individuals prefer self-employment to employment because NICs are lower and the rules on the deductibility of expenses are less onerous. HM Revenue and Customs will decide any particular case of employment or self-employment by looking at all the relevant facts.
>
> You are unlikely to get a full question with no computation in the exam but do ensure that you are comfortable providing brief written answers.

The factors to consider in deciding whether someone is employed or self-employed for income tax purposes are as follows.

(a) How much control is exercised over the way work is done? The greater the control, the more likely it is that the worker is an employee.

(b) Does the worker provide his own equipment? If so, that would indicate self-employment.

(c) If the worker hires his own helpers, that indicates self-employment.

(d) If the worker can profit by his own sound management, or lose money through errors, that indicates self-employment.

(e) If there is a continuing obligation to provide work for the worker, and an obligation on the worker to do whatever job is offered next, that indicates employment.

(f) If the worker accepts work from independent sources, that indicates self-employment.

(g) If the worker can work whenever he chooses, that indicates self-employment.

These tests are summed up in the general rule that there is employment when there is a contract **of** service, and self-employment when is a contract **for** services.

5 Azure plc

> **Tutorial note**. The calculation of benefits is particularly important for exam purposes. Ensure that you pro-rate the benefits if they are not available for the entire year.

(a)   A taxable benefit must be computed for Mr Andrews. The benefit will equal the difference between the interest which would have arisen at the official rate and the actual interest paid. The benefit for 2011/12 is therefore £16,000 × (4 − 1)% × 6/12 months = £240.

(b)   The loan to Mrs Preece is less than £5,000, so the taxable benefit is nil.

(c)   Mr Charles will have a taxable benefit of the annual value of the TV and video system, which will be computed as 20% of the value of the asset when first provided as a benefit to any employee. If the system had been lent to an employee when it was bought, the benefit for 2011/12 would be £800 × 20% = £160 × 10/12 = £133. If the system was first provided as a benefit in June 2011, the benefit would be £500 × 20% = £100 × 10/12 = £83.

(d)   Long service awards of tangible property to employees with at least 20 years service are not taxed provided the cost to the employer does not exceed £50 for each year of service and no similar award has been made to the same person within the previous ten years. In Mrs Davies's case the limit on value would be £50 × 25 = £1,250, so there will be no taxable benefit.

(e)   The car benefit and fuel scale benefit will apply to the car provided for Mr Edgar. The car benefit is calculated as price of car × %. The % depends on the CO_2 emissions of the car.

   (i)   Because CO_2 emissions are 124g/km the percentage is 15%. This is below the 125g/km baseline but more than 120g/km so the percentage is 15%.

   (ii)   The fuel scale benefit will be at £18,800 multiplied by the percentage used in calculating the car benefit, in this case 15%.

   (iii)   The charges will not be reduced on a time basis because the car was provided for the whole of 2011/12.

   The taxable benefit will therefore be as follows.

	£
Car £23,000 × 15%	3,450
Fuel £18,800 × 15%	2,820
	6,270

(f)   Mr Ford will be taxed on the annual value of the flat and of the furniture. The company's payment of his council tax will also be a taxable benefit.

   The following rules will apply.

   (i)   There will be a basic accommodation benefit equal to the annual value.

   (ii)   There will be an additional accommodation benefit equal to the excess of the flat's cost over £75,000, multiplied by the official rate of interest at the start of the tax year.

   (iii)   There will be a benefit in respect of the use of the furniture, equal to 20% of its value when first provided as a benefit to any employee.

   The taxable benefit will therefore be as follows.

	£
Flat: annual value	900
additional charge £(100,000 − 75,000) × 4%	1,000
	1,900
Furniture £5,000 × 20%	1,000
Council tax	500
	3,400

(g)   The first £8,000 of removal expenses payable to Miss Jackson will be an exempt benefit because:

(i)   She does not already live within a reasonable daily travelling distance of her new place of employment, but will do so after moving, and

(ii)   the expenses are incurred or the benefits provided by the end of the tax year following the tax year of the start of employment at the new location.

Miss Jackson will be taxable on the excess removal expenses £(9,500 – 8,000) = £1,500.

(h)   The private use of one mobile phone is an exempt benefit. The private use of the second phone is a taxable benefit Mr Long can choose which phone is exempt and should therefore choose the one which has the higher phone charges.

The taxable benefit on the second phone is calculated as follows.

	£
Greater of:	
20% of market value (20% × £500 = £100)	
Hire charge £120	
ie	120
Cost of calls	300
	420
Private use taxable benefit £420 × 30%	126

6 Gary, George and Geraldine

> **Tutorial note.** Tax relief is available on pension contributions up to the higher of relevant earnings and the basic amount (£3,600). However, tax relief on contributions in excess of the annual allowance are clawed back by the excess contributions charge.

(a)   Gary 2011/12

	Non-savings income
	£
Employment income	55,000
Less personal allowance	(7,475)
Taxable income	47,525

Tax

	£
£35,000 × 20%	7,000
£5,000 (£4,000 × $^{100}/_{80}$) × 20% (extended basic limit)	1,000
£7,525 × 40%	3,010
47,525	11,010

(b)   As George's earnings are only £45,000 for 2011/12 the maximum net contribution entitled to tax relief would be £45,000 × 80% = £36,000. Therefore the remaining £3,200 (£39,200 - £36,000) would not qualify for tax relief.

George 2011/12

	Non-savings income
	£
Employment income	45,000
Less personal allowance	(7,475)
Taxable income	37,525

His income tax liability will be:

		£
£35,000 × 20%		7,000
£ 2,525 × 20%		505
37,525		7,505

Note the basic rate limit is increased by £45,000, but the tax relievable contribution falls below this limit.

(c) In 2011/12, Geraldine has made a gross contribution of £(25,000 x 100/80) = £31,250. She therefore has an unused annual allowance of (50,000 – 31,250) = £18,750. This will be carried forward and added to her annual allowance of £50,000 for 2012/13, giving a total of £(18,750 + 50,000) = £68,750. The net equivalent (ie the amount she would actually pay) is £68,750 x 80% = £55,000.

7 Mr Lee

Tutorial note. You are writing an e-mail to a client and you should aim to be clear but concise.

To: Mr Lee@red.co.uk
From: An Advisor@taxadvice.co.uk
Date: [   ]
Re: Pension advice

Thank you for your e-mail about pension advice. My answers to your questions are as follows:

(1) You do not have to join your new employer's pension scheme. Instead you could start a pension with a financial institution such as a bank or insurance company. However, your employer may not want to contribute to private pension arrangements so you need to bear this in mind when considering whether or not to join your employer's scheme.

A money purchase scheme is one where the value of your pension benefits depends on the value of the investments in the pension scheme at the date that you set aside ('vest') funds to produce those benefits. This is distinct from a defined benefits scheme where the benefits are defined from the outset. If you decide to use private pension arrangements, these are also likely to be money purchase arrangements.

(2) You can contribute an amount up to your earnings into the pension scheme and obtain tax-relief on those contributions. You can also make any amount of further contributions, for example out of capital, but these will not obtain initial tax relief. However, since there is no income tax or capital gains tax payable by a pension fund, it may still be beneficial for such extra contributions to be made into this tax-exempt fund.

In addition, your employer can make any amount of contributions provided that the tax authorities are happy that such contributions are not excessive and so not for the purposes of the employer's trade.

The annual allowance limits the inputs that can be put into the pension fund. For 2011/12, this limit is £50,000. The amounts that you contribute **and** obtain tax relief on, plus any contributions made by your employer, will count towards the annual allowance. If those contributions exceed the annual allowance, there will be a tax charge on the excess which is primarily payable by you. This might be relevant in later years when your earnings may be above the annual allowance limit.

The lifetime allowance limit is the maximum value of the pension fund that you are allowed to build up to provide pension benefits without incurring adverse tax consequences. The lifetime allowance is £1,800,000 in 2011/12. This limit is tested against the value of your pension fund when you vest pension benefits. If your fund exceeds the lifetime allowance at that time, there will be a tax charge of 55% on funds vested to provide a lump sum and 25% on funds vested to provide a pension income. Although there are no adverse tax consequences if your pension fund exceeds the lifetime allowance other than at the time that pension benefits are vested, it would be wise to keep an eye on how your fund is growing so that you can adjust your contributions accordingly so as to keep within the lifetime allowance.

(3)   Your employer will deduct your pension contributions gross from your pay before applying PAYE. This means that tax relief is given automatically at your highest rate of tax and no adjustment is needed in your tax return. As an example, if you contribute £1,000 to your pension and that amount of income would have been taxed at 40%, your pay will be reduced by £1,000 but the amount of tax that would be deducted from your pay would be reduced by £400, so that the net amount of the contribution payable by you would be £600.

The above is only an outline of the basics of pension provision as this is very complex area, so I suggest that we meet once you have decided how you wish to proceed.

AN Advisor

8 Rafe

> **Tutorial note.** Remember to accrue the rents receivable and expenses payable for the tax year. Where you disallow an expense, such as the new roof, note this in your computation to show that you have considered it.

	£	£
Rent		
House 1: first letting £600 × 6		3,600
House 1: second letting £6,000 × 3/12		1,500
House 2: £5,000 × 8/12		3,333
House 3: £7,800 × 8/12		5,200
		13,633
Expenses		
House 1: new roof, disallowable because capital	0	
House 1: water rates	320	
House 1: buildings insurance £480 × 10/12	400	
House 2: water rates	240	
House 2: wear and tear £(3,333 – 240) × 10%	309	
House 3: redecoration	1,200	
House 3: water rates	360	
House 3: buildings insurance £440 × 9/12	330	
House 3: contents insurance £180 × 8/12	120	
House 3: wear and tear £(5,200 – 360) × 10%	484	
		(3,763)
Income from houses		9,870
Rent a room (*Working*)		350
Total property business income		10,220

Working

Rafe should claim rent a room relief in respect of the letting of the furnished room in his main residence, since this is more beneficial than the normal basis of assessment (£4,600 – £875 = £3,725). This means that Rafe will be taxed on an additional £350 (£4,600 – £4,250) of property business income.

9 A Trader

> **Tutorial note.** You are extremely likely to be required to adjust accounts profit in your exam to arrive at taxable trading profits. The best way to familiarise yourself with the adjustments required is to practise plenty of questions like this.

		£	£
Net profit			101,977
Add:	general expenses: entertaining staff	0	
	general expenses: entertaining suppliers	600	
	repairs and renewals: redecoration	0	
	repairs and renewals: renovation	0	
	legal and accountancy: debt collection	0	
	legal and accountancy: staff service agreements	0	
	legal and accountancy: tax consultancy	30	
	legal and accountancy: grant of short lease on new premises	100	
	legal and accountancy: audit and accountancy	0	
	subscription and donations: gift aid donation	5,200	
	subscription and donations: political donation	500	
	subscription and donations: trade association	0	
	subscription and donations: sports facilities for staff	0	
	Impairment losses (trade)	0	
	salaries and wages	0	
	travel: private travel expenses 25% × £2,000	500	
	depreciation	15,000	
	rent and rates	0	
			21,930
Less:	profit on sale of office	5,265	
	impairment losses recovered	0	
	capital allowances	2,200	
	building society interest	1,900	
			(9,365)
Taxable trading profit			114,542

10 Tom Hardy

	AIA £	Main Pool £	Private Use car (80%) £	Short life asset £	Allowances £
1.7.11 – 30.6.12					
Brought forward		31,500		4,400	
Addition qualifying for AIA					
Plant	102,000				
AIA	(100,000)				100,000
	2,000				
Balance to pool	(2,000)	2,000			
		33,500			
WDA @ 20%		(6,700)		(880)	7,580
Carried forward		26,800		3,520	
Allowances					107,580
1.7.12 – 30.6.13					
Addition (not AIA)			13,400		
WDA @ 20%		(5,360)	(2,680) ×80%	(704)	8,208
Carried forward		21,440	10,720	2,816	
Allowances					8,208
1.7.13 – 30.6.14					
WDA @ 20%		(4,288)	(2,144) ×80%	(563)	6,566
Carried forward		17,152	8,576	2,253	
Allowances					6,566
1.7.14 – 30.6.15					
Disposals		(340)		(2,900)	
		16,812		(647)	
Balancing charge				647	(647)
WDA @ 20%		(3,362)	(1,715) ×80%		4,734
Carried forward		13,450	6,861		
Allowances					4,087
1.7.15 – 31.12.15					
Disposals		(24,000)	(10,600)		
		(10,550)	(3,739)		
Balancing charges		10,550	3,739 ×80%		(13,541)

11 Saruman

> **Tutorial note.** Balancing adjustments where there has been private use of the asset are restricted to the business use element.

Capital allowances computation for year ended 5 April 2012

	Main Pool £	Saruman's car (75%) £	Allowances/ (charges) £
TWDV b/f	52,000	600	
Addition (no AIA on car)	4,800		
Disposals (10,000 + 800)	(10,800)	(920)	
	46,000		
Balancing charge		(320) × 75%	(240)
Private use car		19,000	
WDA 20%	(9,200)		9,200
WDA 10%		(1,900) × 75%	1,425
TWDV c/f	36,800	17,100	
Allowances			10,385

12 Mr Cobbler

> **Tutorial note.** Significant cash flow advantages can be gained with a careful choice of accounting date.

TAXABLE PROFITS FOR THE FOUR YEARS 2011/12 TO 2014/15

The accounts profits will be as follows.

		Accounting date	
Period ending in	Working	31 March £	30 April £
2012	3 × £800	2,400	
	4 × £800		3,200
2013	3 × £800 + 6 × £1,200 + 3 × £2,000	15,600	
	2 × £800 + 6 × £1,200 + 4 × £2,000		16,800
2014	12 × £2,000	24,000	24,000
2015	12 × £2,000	24,000	24,000

The taxable profits will be as follows.

		Accounting date	
		31 March £	30 April £
2011/12	Actual basis	2,400	
	£3,200 × 3/4		2,400
2012/13	Year to 31.3.13	15,600	
	First 12 months		
	£3,200 + £16,800 × 8/12		14,400
2013/14	Year to 31.3.14	24,000	
	Year to 30.4.13		16,800
2014/15	Year to 31.3.15	24,000	
	Year to 30.4.14		24,000
		66,000	57,600

30 April is the better choice of accounting date as it will give a considerable cash flow advantage.

13 Miss Farrington

> **Tutorial note**. In a question like this, work out the capital allowances for each period of account before you think about allocating profits to tax years.
>
> Writing down allowances and the annual investment allowance are time apportioned in a long period of account.

We must first work out the capital allowances.

	AIA £	Main Pool £	Private use Car (65%) £	Allowances £
1.1.12 – 30.4.13				
Additions qualifying for AIA				
Desk and office furniture (1.1.12)	10,500			
General plant (4.1.12)	32,280			
Secondhand oven (1.3.12)	21,200			
Delivery van (25.3.12)	21,800			
General plant (15.4.12)	34,220			
	120,000			
AIA £100,000 × 16/12 = £133,333	(120,000)			120,000
Addition not qualifying for AIA				
Car (15.5.12)			6,600	
WDA @ 20% × 16/12			(1,760) × 65%	1,144
Carried forward		0	4,840	
Allowances				121,144
1.5.13 – 30.4.14				
Additions qualifying for AIA				
General plant (30.1.14)	10,000			
Mixer (30.4.14)	1,200			
	11,200			
AIA	(11,200)			11,200
WDA @ 20%			(968) × 65%	629
Carried forward			3,872	
Allowances				11,829

Profits are as follows.

Period	Profit £	Capital allowances £	Adjusted profit £
1.1.12 – 30.4.13	137,144	121,144	16,000
1.5.13 – 30.4.14	24,829	11,829	13,000

The taxable profits are as follows.

Year	Basis period	Working	Taxable profit £
2011/12	1.1.12 – 5.4.12	£16,000 × 3/16	3,000
2012/13	6.4.12 – 5.4.13	£16,000 × 12/16	12,000
2013/14	1.5.12 – 30.4.13	£16,000 × 12/16	12,000
2014/15	1.5.13 – 30.4.14		13,000

The overlap profits are the profits from 1 May 2012 to 5 April 2013: £16,000 × 11/16 = £11,000.

14 Langland

Tutorial note. Work out the tax years which the trading covers, then allocate the profits to the relevant years. Don't forget overlap profits. A good check is to add up the profits throughout the life of the business: the result should be the same as the total of the profits assessed in each tax year.

			£
2006/07	1.2.07 – 5.4.07		1,600
	$(12,000 \times \frac{2}{15})$		
2007/08	6.4.07 – 5.4.08		9,600
	$(12,000 \times \frac{12}{15})$		
2008/09	12m to 30.4.08		9,600
	$(12,000 \times \frac{12}{15})$		
2009/10	Y/e 30.4.09		6,000
2010/11	Y/e 30.4.10		8,000
2011/12	Y/e 30.4.11		10,000

			£
2012/13	Y/e 30.4.12		6,000
	P/e 31.10.12		4,000
			10,000
	Less: Overlap profits		
	1.5.07 to 5.4.08		
	$\left(\frac{11}{15} \times 12,000\right)$		(8,800)
			1,200

15 Morgan

Tutorial note. In a losses question take care to consider all available reliefs. When deciding on the best relief you must consider both the rate of tax saved and the timing of the relief.

(a)   Loss relief could be claimed:

(i)   against general income of the year of loss (2011/12), the investment income of £8,000;

against general income of the preceding year (2010/11). This would be trading profits of £15,000 plus investment income of £8,000;

against the first available future profits of the same trade.

(b) The quickest claim

The quickest way to obtain relief would be for Morgan to use loss relief against general income in both years. The tax computations would then be as follows.

	2010/11 £	2011/12 £
Trading profits	15,000	0
Investment income	8,000	8,000
Total income	23,000	8,000
Less loss relief against general income	(23,000)	(8,000)
Net income	0	0

The balance of the loss, £1,000, would be carried forward and relieved against future trading income.

Although this proposal produces loss relief quickly, it has the disadvantage of wasting Morgan's personal allowance in both years. Morgan could, if he chose, delay his relief by carrying the loss forward. The loss would then be set off only against trading income, with the investment income using his personal allowance.

(c) On a cessation, terminal loss relief would be available. The loss could be set against profits taxable in the tax year of cessation and the three preceding tax years, later years first. This would probably be the best claim for Morgan. The effect would be as follows.

Year	Original £	Loss relief £	Revised £
2011/12	0	0	0
2010/11	15,000	(15,000)	0
2009/10	18,000	(17,000)	1,000
2008/09	16,000	0	16,000

Tutorial note. Because of Morgan's choice of accounting date, no overlap profits arose on commencement.

16 Adam, Bert and Charlie

	Total £	A £	B £	C £	D £
Year ending 5 April 2009					
Salaries	37,000	15,000	12,000	10,000	
PSR (balance)	65,000	26,000	26,000	13,000	
Total	102,000	41,000	38,000	23,000	
Year ending 5 April 2010					
6 April to 5 July					
Salaries	9,250	3,750	3,000	2,500	
PSR (balance)	42,750	17,100	17,100	8,550	
Total	52,000	20,850	20,100	11,050	
6 July to 5 April					
Salaries	16,500		9,000	7,500	
PSR (balance)	139,500		83,700	55,800	
Total	156,000		92,700	63,300	
Totals for the year	208,000	20,850	112,800	74,350	
Year ending 5 April 2011					
Salaries	22,000		12,000	10,000	
PSR (balance)	104,000		62,400	41,600	
Total	126,000		74,400	51,600	
Year ending 5 April 2012					
6 April to 5 May					
Salaries	1,833		1,000	833	
Balance	13,167		7,900	5,267	
Total	15,000		8,900	6,100	
6 May to 5 April					
Salaries	49,500		16,500	16,500	16,500
Balance	115,500		69,300	34,650	11,550
Total	165,000		85,800	51,150	28,050
Totals for the year	180,000		94,700	57,250	28,050

Taxable trade profits are as follows.

	A £	B £	C £	D £
Year				
2008/09	41,000	38,000	23,000	
2009/10	20,850	112,800	74,350	
2010/11		74,400	51,600	
2011/12		94,700	57,250	28,050

17 Partnerships

> **Tutorial note.** This is a comprehensive question as it asks you to explain how partners are taxed, followed by a computation including joining and retiring partners, and finishes with a discussion of losses.
>
> Overlap profits are relieved either on a change of accounting date or on a cessation. Each partner obtains relief for their own overlap profits and their own losses.

(a)   Each partner is taxed like a sole trader who runs a business which starts when he joins the partnership, finishes when he leaves the partnership, has the same periods of account as the partnership, and makes profits or losses equal to the partner's share of the partnership profits or losses.

(b)

	Total £	Anne £	Betty £	Chloe £
1.1.11 – 31.12.11				
January to June	30,000	15,000	15,000	
July to December	30,000	15,000	–	15,000
Totals	60,000	30,000	15,000	15,000
1.1.12 – 31.12.12	72,000	36,000	–	36,000

Trading profit assessments 2011/12

	Anne £	Betty £	Chloe £
Profits y/e 31.12.11	30,000		
Profits 1.1.11 – 30.6.11		15,000	
Profits 1.7.11 – 31.12.11			15,000
Profits 1.1.12 – 5.4.12			
3/12 × £36,000			9,000
	30,000	15,000	24,000
Less overlap relief for Betty on cessation		(3,000)	
Profits assessable 2011/12	30,000	12,000	24,000

(c)   (i)   *Daniel*

Daniel can use his £20,000 loss:

- against general income of 2011/12 and/or of 2010/11
- against future trading profits

(ii)   *Edward*

Edward can use his £15,000 loss:

- against general income of 2011/12 and/or of 2010/11

- if there is a terminal loss in the last 12 months of trading, against trading profits of the tax year of cessation and the three preceding years, later years first

(iii)   *Frank*

Frank can use his loss of £5,000:

- against general income of 2011/12 and/or 2010/11
- against general income of 2008/09, 2009/10 and 2010/11 (early years loss relief)
- against future trading profits

18 Denise

> **Tutorial note**. It is important that you can calculate and distinguish NICs for the self-employed and employed individuals. Here both Class 2 and Class 4 were required for a self-employed individual.

(a) Denise can contribute a gross amount up to her earnings into a personal pension scheme and obtain tax relief on those contributions ie up to £45,000 for 2011/12. She can also make any amount of further contributions, for example out of capital, but these will not obtain initial tax relief. However, since there is no income tax or capital gains tax payable by a pension fund, it may still be beneficial for such extra contributions to be made into this tax exempt fund.

However, there are two limits that Denise needs to be aware of. First, there is an annual allowance which limits the inputs that can be put into the pension fund. For 2011/12, this limit is £50,000. The amounts that Denise contributes and obtains tax relief on will count towards the annual allowance. If those contributions exceed the annual allowance, there will be a tax charge on the excess computed in relation to the other income that Denise has in the tax year. This might be relevant in later years when Denise's earnings may be above the annual allowance limit. However, if Denise does not use her annual allowance in full in a tax year, any unused amount can be carried forward up to three years and used against contributions in those years.

The second limit is the lifetime allowance limit. This is the maximum value of the pension fund that Denise is allowed to build up to provide pension benefits without incurring adverse tax consequences. The lifetime allowance is £1,800,000 in 2011/12. This limit is tested against the value of her pension fund at the date she sets aside (vests) the fund to provide these benefits. If her fund exceeds the lifetime allowance at that time, there will be a tax charge of 55% on funds vested to provide a lump sum and 25% on funds vested to provide a pension income.

Personal pension contributions are entitled to tax relief at source. The pension payments made will be treated as being net of basic rate tax at 20%. If she is a higher rate tax payer, she will then need to claim higher rate tax relief of an additional 20% through her tax return. Thus for a gross contribution of £1,000, Denise would pay £800 to the pension provider and then she would claim an additional £200 through her tax return.

(b)

	£
Class 2 NICs	
£2.50 × 52	130

	£
Class 4 NICs	
£(42,475 – 7,225) × 9%	3,172
£(45,000 – 42,475) × 2%	50
	3,222

19 Sasha Shah

Tutorial notes.

1 Strictly, expenses are only deductible in calculating net taxable earnings if they are incurred wholly, necessarily and exclusively in the performance of the duties. In practice, however, HM Revenue and Customs allow an apportionment between private and business use as here.

2 Capital allowances are available to an employee who provides plant and machinery necessarily for use in the performance of his duties, in the same way as a sole trader.

3 The use of the car for travel between home and work is ordinary commuting and not business use.

4 'Earnings' for Class 4 NIC purposes are trading profits. However, earnings for Class 1 NIC purposes are gross earnings before the deductions of any expenses.

(a) Factors that will indicate that a worker should be treated as an employee rather than as self-employed are:

(i) control by employer over employee's work;

(ii) employee must accept further work if offered (and employer must offer work);

(iii) employee does not provide own equipment;

(iv) employee does not hire own helpers;

(v) employee does not take substantial financial risk;

(vi) employee does not have responsibility for investment and management of business and cannot benefit from sound management;

(vii) employee cannot work when he chooses but when an employer tells him to work;

(viii) described as an employee in any agreement between parties.

(b) (i) *Income assessable as trading profits*

	£	£
Gross income		60,000
Less: business expenses on heating etc	800	
computer – AIA	4,000	
business expenses re car (£3,500 × 40%)	1,400	
WDA @ 20% on business car (CO_2 less than 160g/km)		
£10,000 × 20% × 40% (business proportion)	800	(7,000)
Assessable as trading profits		53,000

(ii) *Net taxable earnings*

	£	£
Gross income		60,000
Less: business expenses on heating etc	800	
computer – AIA	4,000	(4,800)
Net taxable earnings		55,200

(c) (i) *Class 2 and Class 4 NIC*

		£
Class 2	£2.50 × 52	130
Class 4	£(42,475 – 7,225) × 9%	3,172
	£(53,000 – 42,475) × 2%	210
Total		3,512

	£
£(42,475 − 7,225) × 12%	4,230
£(60,000 − 42,475) × 2%	350
Total	4,580

20 Peter Robinson

> **Tutorial note.** The first disposal is a basic computation. The second disposal tests the A/(A+B) formula and the third part tests compensation for the destruction of an asset

Peter Robinson CGT payable 2011/12

Summary

	£
Investment property (W1)	69,720
Land (W2)	16,300
Destroyed asset (W3)	3,000
	89,020
Less: annual exempt amount	(10,600)
Taxable gains	78,420
CGT	
£(35,000 − 30,600) = £4,400 @ 18% (W4)	792
£(78,420 − 4,400) = £74,020 @ 28%	20,726
CGT 2011/12	21,518

Workings

1   *Investment property*

	£
Proceeds	150,000
Less cost of disposal	(1,280)
Net proceeds	148,720
Less cost	(79,000)
Gain	69,720

2   *Land*

	£
Proceeds	35,000
Less cost of disposal	(700)
Net proceeds	34,300
Less cost	
$£54,000 \times \dfrac{35,000}{35,000 + 70,000}$	(18,000)
Gain	16,300

3   *Vase*

	£
Proceeds	20,000
Less cost	(12,000)
Gain	8,000
Gain immediately chargeable £(20,000 – 17,000)	3,000

Remainder rolled into base cost of new vase (£8,000 – £3,000 = £5,000)

4   *Determination of rates of CGT*

	£
Taxable income	30,600
Taxable gains	78,420
	109,020

The gains will be taxed at 18% up to the basic rate limit and at 28% thereafter.

21 John Harley

> **Tutorial note**. Part (a) is a typical question examining principal private residence relief. You are asked to present your answer as a schedule (ie table) showing periods of exemption and non-exemption with reasons (ie explanation of your application of the rules). To obtain good marks you must comply with these instructions.

(a)   **John Harley – Gain on house**

	Chargeable months	Exempt months
1.8.89 – 31.5.90 – actual residence		10
1.6.90 – 31.7.94 – employed abroad any period		50
1.8.94 – 31.7.98 – up to 4 years work elsewhere		48
1.8.98 – 31.10.00 – up to 3 years any reason		27
1.11.00 – 30.6.03 – actual residence		32
1.7.03 – 30.11.08 – absent	65	
1.12.08 – 30.11.11 – last 3 years ownership for any reason		36
Totals	65	203

(b)   **Elsie Phillips**

(i)   Painting

	£
Proceeds (deemed)	6,000
Less costs of disposal	(400)
Gain	5,600
Less: cost	(11,500)
Loss	(5,900)

(ii)   Chandelier

	£
Proceeds	7,500
Less: cost	(4,000)
Gain	3,500
Cannot exceed £(7,500 – 6,000) × 5/3	2,500

22 The White family

> **Tutorial note.** In an exam question you should watch out for the CGT reliefs. When dealing with rollover relief look out for depreciating assets.

(a) *2011/12*

Gift relief can apply to the gift of the factory because it is an asset used in the trade of the donor. Full relief is available as no payment is made by Gary ie it is an outright gift.

	£
Market value at gift	260,000
Less cost	(150,000)
Gain heldover	110,000

(b) Gary's gain on sale is:

	£
Proceeds	320,000
Less cost £(260,000 – 110,000)	(150,000)
Gain	170,000

(c) Mrs White has made a gain of £40,000 (£80,000 – 40,000) on the sale of the shop. If she acquires a replacement shop within 3 years of the sale, she can claim rollover relief.

Freehold Shop

Less than the full proceeds have been reinvested. A gain equal to the amount not reinvested (£80,000 – £72,000 = £8,000) will remain in charge.

The remainder of the gain of £32,000 can be rolled over into the base cost of the freehold shop. The base cost will therefore be £72,000 – £32,000 = £40,000 for the purposes of computing a gain on its disposal.

Leasehold Shop

Full deferral of the gain is available as the whole of the proceeds of sale are reinvested.

The leasehold shop is a depreciating asset as the lease has less than 60 years to run. The gain is not deducted from the base cost of the leasehold shop, but is deferred until the earliest of the disposal of the leasehold shop, ceasing to use it in the business or 10 years from its acquisition. The gain which will come into charge at that date will be £40,000.

If a non depreciating asset is acquired before the gain crystallises it can be rolled over into that new asset.

23 Alice

> **Tutorial note.** Remember that incorporation relief only applies to the extent that shares are received in exchange for the assets transferred to the company.

	£
Gains on incorporation	120,000
Less: incorporation relief $\dfrac{200,000}{200,000 + 100,000} \times £120,000$	(80,000)
Gain chargeable in 2011/12	40,000
Base cost of shares £(200,000 – 80,000)	£120,000

24 Kai

Tutorial note. Gains qualifying for entrepreneurs' relief use up the basic rate band in priority to gains not qualifying for the relief.

	Gains £	Gains £	CGT £
Gains qualifying for entrepreneurs' relief			
Goodwill		50,000	
Shop	90,000		
Less cost	(80,000)		
Gain		10,000	
Warehouse	180,000		
Less cost	(150,000)		
Warehouse		30,000	
Taxable gains		90,000	
CGT @ 10% on £90,000			9,000
Gains not qualifying for entrepreneurs' relief			
Land	25,500		
Less cost	(10,000)		
Gain		15,500	
Less: annual exempt amount (best use)		(10,600)	
Taxable gain		4,900	
CGT @ 28% on £4,900 (N)			1,372
Total CGT due			10,372

Note

Total of taxable income and gains is £(20,000 + 90,000 + 4,900) = £114,900. The basic rate band is used first by income (£20,000), then by gains qualifying for entrepreneurs' relief (£90,000). The remaining gain is therefore above the basic rate limit and so taxable at 28%.

25 Melissa

Tutorial note. The matching rules are very important and must be learnt.

First match the disposal with the acquisition in the next 30 days:

	£	£
Proceeds $\frac{4,000}{10,000} \times £42,000$	16,800	
Less: cost	(16,000)	800

Next match the remaining shares with the share pool:

	£	£
Proceeds $\frac{6,000}{10,000} \times £42,000$	25,200	
Less: cost (W)	(20,625)	4,575
Total gains		5,375

Working

	No. of shares	Cost
12 July 2002 acquisition	6,000	21,000
14 December 2007 acquisition	2,000	6,500
	8,000	27,500
2 July 2011 disposal	(6,000)	(20,625)
c/f	2,000	6,875

26 Tim

> **Tutorial note**. Three payments of income tax may need to be made in respect of a tax year. Two payments on account are normally made on 31 January in the tax year and on the following 31 July. These are based on the prior year tax payable under self assessment. A final balancing payment of the income tax due for a year is normally made on the 31 January following the year.

Tim's payments on account for 2011/12 were based on the excess of his 2010/11 tax liability over amounts deducted under the PAYE system, amounts deducted at source and tax credits on dividends:

	£
2010/11 tax liability	16,800
Less: PAYE	(7,200)
tax deducted at source	(800)
tax credit on dividends	(200)
Total payments on account for 2011/12	8,600

Two equal payments on account of £4,300 (£8,600/2) were required. The due dates for these payments were 31 January 2012 and 31 July 2012 respectively.

The final payment in respect of Tim's 2011/12 tax liability was due on 31 January 2013 and was calculated as follows:

	£
2011/12 tax liability	22,000
Less: PAYE	(7,100)
tax deducted at source	(900)
tax credit on dividends	(250)
	13,750
Less payments on account	(8,600)
Final payment due 31 January 2013	5,150

27 Lai Chan

Tutorial notes. This is a good example of the type of question that you might find as Question 1 of the exam.

1   For capital allowance purposes the AIA and WDA are restricted by the length of the basis period.

2   There is no capital allowance restriction in respect of the private use of an asset by an employee.

3   The basic rate limit is increased by the gross amount of personal pension contributions made. Occupational pension contributions are, however, deducted in computing employment income.

4   There is no taxable benefit in respect of the company's contribution to the occupational pension scheme.

(a)   *Income tax liability*

	£	Non-savings income £
Gross salary 9 × £3,250	29,250	
Less pension contribution (6%)	(1,755)	
	27,495	
Car benefit (W1)	3,780	
Fuel benefit (W2)	3,525	
Taxable cheap loan (W3)	500	
Employment income		35,300
Trading profit	44,500	
Less Capital allowances (W4)	(25,877)	
Taxable trading profit		18,623
Net income		53,923
Less personal allowance		(7,475)
Taxable income		46,448

Tax

	£
£35,000 × 20%	7,000
£960 × 20% (W5)	192
£10,488 (46,448 − 35,500 − 960) × 40%	4,195
Tax liability	11,387

Workings

1   *Car benefit*

	£
25% × £26,400 × 9/12 (note)	4,950
Less contribution £130 × 9	(1,170)
	3,780

Note. The % depends on the CO_2 emissions of the car.

CO_2 emissions = 175 g/km

Amount above baseline figure 175 − 125 = 50 g/km

Divide by 5 = 10 g/km

Taxable percentage = 15% + 10% = 25%

The benefit is time apportioned as the car is available for only nine months of the year.

2   *Fuel benefit*

£18,800 × 25% × 9/12 = £3,525

No reduction for partial reimbursement of private fuel cost. The benefit is time apportioned as the car was available for only nine months of the year.

The taxable percentage used in calculating the fuel benefit is the same as the percentage used in calculating the car benefit.

3   *Taxable cheap loan*

Average method

$$4\% \times \frac{30,000 + 10,000}{2} \times 9/12 = £600$$

Alternative method (strict method)

	£
£30,000 × 3/12 × 4% =	300
£10,000 × 6/12 × 4% =	200
	500

Elect for strict method

4

	AIA £	Main pool £	Private use car (60%) £	Short life asset £	Allowances £
Additions qualifying for AIA					
1 January 2012	20,000				
AIA £100,000 × 3/12 = £25,000	(20,000)				20,000
4 March 2012	6,500				
AIA £(25,000 − 20,000)	(5,000)				5,000
	1,500				
Balance to SLA	(1,500)			1,500	
Additions not qualifying for AIA					
15 January 2012			18,800		
20 February 2012		10,400			
		10,400	18,800	1,500	
WDA @ 20% × 3/12		(520)		(75)	595
WDA @ 10% × 3/12			(470) × 60%		282
TWDV c/f		9,880	18,330	1,425	
Allowances					25,877

5   Basic rate limit

The limit is increased by (£256 × 100/80 × 3) = £960

(b)   Up to 31.12.11 PAYE will have been deducted from Lai Chan's salary. It is likely that her PAYE code was adjusted to take account of her benefits. Further tax payable (or tax repayable) will be dealt with under the self-assessment system.

As Lai Chan was employed before starting in business on her own account, she is unlikely to have made any payments on account for 2011/12. Therefore, the tax on her trading profit will be collected in full on 31 January 2013 under the self assessment system.

28 Colin

> **Tutorial note.** This answer follows the 'steps' set out within the text but in a streamlined format which is equally acceptable in the exam.

(a) **IHT implications during Colin's lifetime**

21.1.07

No chargeable transfers were made in the seven years prior to 21.1.07 so all of the nil band of £285,000 remained available for use.

	£
Net transfer of value	300,000

IHT			£
	£285,000	× 0% =	Nil
	£ 15,000	× 20/80 =	3,750
	£300,000		3,750

The gross chargeable was: £300,000 + £3,750 = £303,750.

Check: tax £(303,750 − 285,000) = £18,750 × 20% = £3,750.

The IHT was due on 31 July 2007.

20.8.08

	£
Potentially exempt transfer	30,000

This was a PET so no lifetime tax was due. The transfer is treated as exempt during Colin's lifetime so no lifetime tax was due and the transfer does not enter into cumulation whilst Colin is alive.

19.6.09

Gross chargeable transfers of £303,750 had been made in the seven years prior to 19.6.09. The nil rate band remaining for use was £(325,000 - 303,750) = £21,250. The trustees pay the IHT due so no grossing up is required.

	£
Gross transfer of value	103,000

IHT			£
	£21,250	× 0% =	Nil
	£ 81,750	× 20% =	16,350
	£103,000		16,350

The IHT was due on 30 April 2010.

1.9.11

This was an exempt transfer to Colin's spouse so no lifetime tax was due and the transfer does not enter into cumulation.

(b) **IHT position as a result of Colin's death**

21.1.07

Gross transfer of value	£303,750

No gross chargeable transfers were made in the seven years prior to 21.1.07 so all of the nil band at death of £325,000 remains available for use.

No death IHT payable because the transfer is within the available nil rate band (but there is no refund of lifetime tax).

20.8.08

Gross chargeable transfers of £303,750 have been made in the seven years prior to 20.8.08. The nil rate band remaining for use is £(325,000 - 303,750) = £21,250.

The value of the PET is the value at the date of the gift, not the value at the death of the donor.

Gross transfer of value				£30,000
				£
IHT	£21,250	× 0% =		Nil
	£8,750	× 40% =		3,500
	£30,000			3,500
Less taper relief @ 20% (3-4 years)				(700)
IHT payable				2,800

The IHT is due on 30 June 2012.

19.6.09

Gross chargeable transfers of £(303,750 + 30,000) = £333,750 have been made in the seven years prior to 19.6.09 so there is no nil band available to set against this transfer. There is no effect on the value of the transfer as a result of the increase in value of the asset between the lifetime transfer and the death of the donor.

Gross chargeable transfer	£103,000
	£
£103,000 × 40% =	41,200
Less lifetime tax	(16,350)
Tax due on death	24,850

No taper relief as death occurs within 3 years of the gift.

The IHT is due on 30 June 2012.

1.9.11

No IHT arises on an exempt transfer to a spouse so death of Colin has no effect on this transfer.

(c) Colin's cousin should make a transfer of £6,000 to his daughter before 6 April 2012 in order to use his annual exemptions for 2011/12 and 2010/11.

Colin's cousin should then give his daughter the remaining £44,000 on her marriage so that he can utilise the marriage exemption. For a parent the exemption is £5,000. The annual exemption of £3,000 for 2012/13 will also be available. The rest of the gift of £36,000 will be a potentially exempt transfer.

29 Marissa

(a) **IHT implications of lifetime gifts by Marissa**

10 August 2000

The transfer of value on this gift is £200,000. £6,000 of the transfer will be exempt due to the annual exemptions for 2000/01 and 1999/00. The remaining £(200,000 – 6,000) = £194,000 is a potentially exempt transfer. This is treated as exempt during Marissa's lifetime. Since Marissa survives 7 years from making this transfer, it remains exempt on her death and so no IHT is payable on it and it does not enter into cumulation.

15 July 2006

The transfer of value is the diminution of Marissa's estate as a result of the gift:

	£
Before the gift:	160,000
After the gift:	(22,500)
Diminution in value	137,500

£6,000 of this transfer will be exempt due to the annual exemptions for 2006/07 and 2005/06. The remaining £(137,500 – 6,000) = £131,500 is a potentially exempt transfer. This is treated as exempt during Marissa's lifetime. Since Marissa does not survive 7 years from making this transfer, it becomes chargeable on her death. As there are no chargeable transfers in the 7 years before 15 July 2006, the full Marissa's nil rate band at death is available.

Marissa's first husband had an unused nil rate band of £(300,000 – 20,000) = £280,000. In terms of the nil rate band at Marissa's death, the unused proportion is:

$$\frac{280,000}{300,000} \times £325,000 = £303,333$$

Marissa's personal representatives can elect to transfer this unused nil rate band to Marissa. The total nil rate band available to calculate death tax on Marissa's lifetime transfers and on her death estate is therefore £(325,000 + 303,333) = £628,333 and so no IHT is chargeable on this lifetime transfer. However, it uses up £131,500 of the nil rate band available leaving £(628,333 – 131,500) = £496,833 available to set against the death estate

(b) **Marissa's death estate**

	£	£
Shares in MS plc		320,000
Life assurance policy (amount of proceeds payable as result of death)		250,000
House in UK	175,000	
Less: loan secured on house	(10,000)	
		165,000
Villa in Spain		80,000
Household furniture		20,000
Cash in bank		17,750
Car		5,000
Less: credit card bills	7,000	
income tax	3,000	
gas bill	250	
funeral expenses	2,500	(12,750)
Net death estate		845,000
Less: spouse exemption (net value of UK house)		(165,000)
Chargeable death estate		680,000

The IHT on Marissa's death estate is:

	£
£(680,000 – 496,833) = £183,167 @ 40%	73,267

This is payable by the personal representatives of Marissa's estate on the earlier of 31 May 2012 and the date on which they file their inheritance tax account.

30 Elderflower Ltd

> **Tutorial notes.** You must use the layout shown when adjusting profits for taxation. The notes have been added for tutorial purposes.

(a) **Trading profit for y/e 31 March 2012**

	£	£
Profit before taxation		417,210
Add:		
Depreciation	54,690	
Accountancy and audit	0	
Legal fees – share capital (N1)	8,800	
Legal fees – loan notes (N1)	0	
Legal fees – breach of contract	0	
Legal fees – health and safety (N1)	900	
Repairs and renewals: extension (N2)	9,700	
Repairs and renewals: repainting (N2)	0	
Other expenses: entertaining customers	2,310	
Other expenses: entertaining employees	0	
Other expenses: gift aid	500	
Interest payable (N3)	0	
		76,900
Deduct:		
Office building profit	54,000	
Bank interest	7,000	
Capital allowances (W)	40,300	
		(101,300)
Profit adjusted for tax purposes		392,810

Notes

1   Costs relating to share capital need to be added back as they relate to a capital expense. However, the fees relating to the debentures are a loan relationship expense and thus deductible as a trading expense because the debenture is for trade purposes. Legal fees in relation to fine are not deductible as the fine is a payment contrary to public policy.

2   The cost of the extension has been added back as a capital expense but the cost of repainting is allowable as it is a repair and therefore a revenue expense.

3   No adjustment is needed for the interest because it relates to a trade purpose loan.

Working

Capital allowances on plant and machinery

	AIA £	Main pool £	Exp. Car £	Allowances £
TWDV b/f		27,500	14,700	
Additions qualifying for AIA				
10.5.11 Equipment	30,200			
AIA	(30,200)			30,200
Additions not qualifying for AIA				
5.2.12 Car				
31.3.12 Car		9,600		
Disposals				
5.1.12 Car			(9,700)	
Balancing allowance			5,000	5,000
20.3.12 Van		(11,600)		
		25,500		
WDA @ 20%		(5,100)		5,100
TWDVs c/f		20,400		
Allowances				40,300

Note. The private use of the car by the employee is not relevant for capital allowance purposes. No adjustment is ever made to a company's capital allowances to reflect the private use of an asset.

(b) **Total taxable profits y/e 31 March 2012**

	£
Trading profits	392,810
Chargeable gain	50,690
Investment income	7,000
Total profits	450,500
Less: Gift aid donation	(500)
Taxable total profits	450,000

31 Tree Ltd

Tutorial note. You need to calculate both taxable total profits and augmented profits. Augmented profits determine which tax rate applies, but the tax rate is applied to taxable total profits.

(a) Tree Ltd

	Year to 31.3.12 £
Trading profits	180,000
Chargeable gain	105,000
Investment income	36,000
Total profits	321,000
Less: Gift aid donation	(27,000)
Taxable total profits	294,000
FII: £29,700 × 100/90	33,000

Augmented profits	327,000

Marginal relief applies

Year to 31.3.12

	£
Corporation tax (FY 11)	
£294,000 × 26%	76,440
Less 3/200 (1,500,000 − 327,000) × $\dfrac{294,000}{327,000}$	(15,819)
	60,621

(b) Dealers plc's augmented profits are £420,000 so marginal relief applies.

	6 months to 31.3.12
	£
Taxable total profits	420,000
Augmented profits	420,000
Upper limit £1,500,000 × 6/12	750,000
Lower limit £300,000 × 6/12	150,000

	£
Corporation tax (FY 11)	
£420,000 × 26%	109,200
Less marginal relief	
£(750,000 − 420,000) × 3/200	(4,950)
	104,250

(c) Springer Ltd's accounting period to 31 December 2011 falls partly in FY10 and partly in FY11.

	£
Taxable total profits	600,000
FII: £27,000 × 100/90	30,000
Augmented profits	630,000

Marginal relief applies in both FY10 and FY11

	£
FY10 (1.1.11 to 31.3.11 – 3 months)	
£600,000 × 3/12 × 28%	42,000
Less marginal relief	
£(1,500,000 − 630,000) × 600,000/630,000 × 7/400 × 3/12	(3,625)
FY10 (1.4.11 to 31.12.11 – 9 months)	
£600,000 × 9/12 × 26%	117,000
Less marginal relief	
£(1,500,000 − 630,000) × 600,000/630,000 × 3/200 × 9/12	(9,321)
Corporation tax liability for y/e 31 December 2011	146,054

32 Righteous plc

	1.1.10- 31.12.10 (12m) £	1.1. 11 - 31.5.11 (5m) £
Trading income (12:5)	352,941	147,059
Investment income (15,000 + 6,000)	21,000	2,500
Chargeable gain	–	5,000
Total profits	373,941	154,559
Less: gift aid donations (15,000 + 15,000)	(30,000)	(40,000)
Taxable total profits	343,941	114,559

Lower limit: £300,000 x 5/12 = 125,000

Upper limit: £1,500,000 x 5/12 = 625,000

Therefore marginal relief applies for the first 12 month accounting period and small profits rate applies for the 5 month accounting period.

12 m/e 31.12.10

Although the first 12 month accounting period straddles two financial years, there is no change in the rates between FY09 and FY10, so no apportionment is needed.

FY09 and FY10

	£
£343,941 × 28%	96,303
Less: £(1,500,000 − 343,941) × $^7/_{400}$	(20,231)
Tax due for y/e. 31.12.10	76,072

5 m/e 31.5.11

	£114,559
Taxable total profits/augmented profits	

Small profits rate applies for both FY10 (1.1.11 to 31.3.11 − 3 months) and FY11 (1.2.11 to 31.5.11 − 2 months).

	£
FY 10 £114,559 × $^3/_5$ = £68,735 × 21%	14,434
FY 11 £114,559 × $^2/_5$ = £45,824 × 20%	9,165
Total tax due for p/e 31.5.11	23,599

33 E Ltd

Motor cars are exempt assets, so the loss brought forward from the year ended 31 March 2011 is £16,400.

The position for the year ended 31 March 2012 is as follows.

	£
Gains	
Shares	17,700
Picture	3,000
	20,700
Less loss on shares	(6,000)
	14,700
Less loss brought forward	(14,700)
Chargeable gains	Nil

The loss carried forward at 31 March 2012 is £(16,400 − 14,700) = £1,700.

34 Hardup Ltd

> **Tutorial note**. The date of disposal for chargeable gains purposes is the date that the disposal becomes unconditional. In this case the date of exchange, not the date of completion.
>
> Rollover relief is not available to defer the gain arising on the sale of the office block, because the reinvestment was not made in the qualifying period, commencing one year before and ending three years after the disposal.

CAPITAL GAINS COMPUTATION

	£
Office block (W1)	11,970
Plot of land (W2)	13,584
Workshop (W3)	33,770
Chargeable gains	59,324

Workings

1   *The office block*

	£
Proceeds	120,000
Less cost	(65,000)
	55,000
Less indexation allowance $\frac{233.9 - 140.7}{140.7}$ (0.662) × £65,000	(43,030)
	11,970

Rollover relief is not available as replacement asset acquired outside the qualifying period.

2   *The plot of land*

		£
Proceeds		69,000
Less cost		(20,000)
expenditure in July 1990		(4,000)
		45,000
Less indexation allowance		
$\dfrac{234.5 - 97.67}{97.67}$ $(1.401) \times £20,000$		(28,020)
$\dfrac{234.5 - 126.8}{126.8}$ $(0.849) \times £4,000$		(3,396)
		13,584

3 *The workshop*

	£
Proceeds	173,000
Less cost	(65,000)
	108,000
Less indexation allowance $\dfrac{234.5 - 109.5}{109.5}$ $(1.142) \times £65,000$	(74,230)
	33,770

35 Ferraro Ltd

> **Tutorial note**. The pro-forma for loss relief is important. If you learn the proforma you should find that the figures slot into place. Note that the result of a losses claim may be that, as here, gift aid donations become unrelieved.

	Accounting periods			
	12m to 31.3.09	12m to 31.3.10	9m to 31.12.10	12m to 31.12.11
	£	£	£	£
Trading profits	34,480	6,200	4,320	0
Investment income	200	80	240	260
Property business income	1,200	1,420	1,440	1,600
Chargeable gain (12,680 – 5,000)	0	0	7,680	0
Total profits	35,880	7,700	13,680	1,860
Less current period loss relief	0	0	0	(1,860)
	35,880	7,700	13,680	0
Less carry back loss relief	0	(1,925)	(13,680)	(0)
Less Gift Aid donations	(1,000)	(0)	(0)	(0)
Taxable total profits	34,880	5,775	0	0
Unrelieved Gift Aid donations			1,000	1,500

Loss memo	£
Loss of y/e 31.12.11	100,000
Less used y/e 31.12.11	(1,860)
	98,140
Less used 9m/e 31.12.10	(13,680)
	84,460
Less used 3m/12 × £7,700	(1,925)
c/f	82,535

The allowable capital loss of £9,423 during the year ended 31 December 2011 is carried forward against future chargeable gains.

The gift aid donation made in the 9 months to 31 December 2010 remains unrelieved. Similarly the gift aid donation in the year to 31 December 2011 remains unrelieved.

> **Tutorial note.** The loss is carried back to set against profits arising in the previous 12 months. This means that the set off in the y/e 31.3.10 is restricted to 3/12 × £7,700 = £1,925.

36 P Ltd

> **Tutorial note.** You are asked to use group relief in the most efficient manner. This means giving it first to companies in the marginal relief band, then to companies paying tax at the main rate.

(a) There are six associated companies, so the lower and upper limits are £50,000 and £250,000 respectively.

S Ltd and T Ltd are outside the P Ltd group for group relief purposes. P Ltd's loss should be surrendered to Q Ltd, to bring its total taxable profits down to £50,000, and to R Ltd to bring its total taxable profits down to £50,000. The balance of £5,000 should be surrendered to either M Ltd, Q Ltd or R Ltd. In this case M Ltd has been selected. A claim by P Ltd against its own profits would have wasted gift aid and carrying the loss forward would not obtain relief for several years.

	M Ltd £	P Ltd £	Q Ltd £	R Ltd £	S Ltd £	T Ltd £
Trading profits	20,000	0	64,000	260,000	0	70,000
Property business income	0	6,000	4,000	0	0	0
Total profits	20,000	6,000	68,000	260,000	0	70,000
Less Gift aid donation	(4,000)	(4,500)	(2,000)	(5,000)	0	0
	16,000	1,500	66,000	255,000	0	70,000
Less group relief	(5,000)	0	(16,000)	(205,000)	0	0
Taxable total profits	11,000	1,500	50,000	50,000	0	70,000
Corporation tax:						
at 20%	2,200	300	10,000	10,000	0	
at 26%						18,200
Less marginal relief						
3/200 (£250,000 − 70,000)						(2,700)
Corporation tax payable	2,200	300	10,000	10,000	0	15,500

(b) If P Ltd were to acquire another 8% of the share capital of S Ltd, bringing the total holding to 75%, S Ltd's losses could be surrendered to P Ltd, Q Ltd, R Ltd or M Ltd.

37 Apple Ltd

> **Tutorial note.** The marginal rate of tax of 27.5% is an effective tax rate only. It is never actually used in working out corporation tax.

(a) Group relief is available within a 75% group. This is one where one company is a 75% subsidiary of another company or both are 75% subsidiaries of a third company. The holding company must have at least 75% of the ordinary share capital of the subsidiary, a right to at least 75% of the distributable income of the subsidiary, and the right to at least 75% of the net assets of the subsidiary were it to be wound up.

Two companies are in a group only if there is a 75% effective interest eg if Company A holds 90% of Company B which holds 90% of Company C, all three companies are in a group because 90% × 90% = 81%.

(b) Losses should be allocated to the company with the highest marginal rate of tax. This is Cherry Ltd and Apple Ltd to the extent that taxable total profits exceed £100,000 since the small profits rate lower limit is £300,000 ÷ 3 = £100,000. Such profits are taxed at the marginal rate of 27.5%. Then, the remainder of the loss should be set against the total profits of Banana Ltd which bears tax at 26%.

(c) Rollover relief for part of Apple Ltd's gain can be claimed in respect of the investment by Cherry Ltd. The excess of amount of proceeds over the amount invested remains in charge ie £(418,000 – 290,000) = £128,000.

An election should be made so that the capital loss by Banana Ltd is transferred to Apple Ltd. Apple Ltd will then be able to offset the loss of £8,000 against the gain of £128,000, leaving £120,000 chargeable.

Apple Ltd should then make a current year loss relief claim to bring its profits down to £100,000.

	Apple Ltd £	Banana Ltd £	Cherry Ltd £
Trading profits	–	650,000	130,000
Net capital gain	120,000	–	–
Total profits	120,000	650,000	130,000
Less: loss relief against total profits	(20,000)		
group relief		(75,000)	(30,000)
Taxable total profits	100,000	575,000	100,000
Tax @ 20%	20,000		20,000
Tax @ 26%		149,500	

Note that the upper limit is £1,500,000 ÷ 3 = £500,000.

38 M Ltd

> **Tutorial note**. In order to maximise the set off of double tax relief, gift aid payments are allocated firstly to UK profits and then to overseas sources of income that have suffered the lowest rate of overseas tax.
>
> There are five associated companies so the main rate of corporation tax applies.

Year ended 31 March 2012

	Total £	UK £	A £	B £	C £
Trading profits: UK	20,000	20,000			
Trading profits: overseas (W1)	587,500	–	200,000	200,000	187,500
Total profits	607,500	20,000	200,000	200,000	187,500
Less Gift aid donations	(75,000)	(20,000)	(55,000)	–	–
Taxable total profits	532,500	–	145,000	200,000	187,500
CT @ 26%	138,450	–	37,700	52,000	48,750
Less DTR (W2)	(128,750)	–	(30,000)	(50,000)	(48,750)
Corporation tax	9,700	–	7,700	2,000	–

Workings

1 *Overseas profits*

		Net £	Tax paid £	Gross £
A	15% tax suffered	170,000	30,000	200,000
B	25% tax suffered	150,000	50,000	200,000
C	36% tax suffered	120,000	67,500	187,500

2   *Double tax relief*

		A	B	C
		£	£	£
Lower of				
(i)	UK tax	37,700	52,000	48,750
(ii)	Overseas tax	30,000	50,000	67,500
		£30,000	£50,000	£48,750

39 Hogg Ltd

> **Tutorial note**. Companies paying corporation tax at the main rate must pay their CT liabilities in quarterly instalments.

(a)   Hogg Ltd's corporation tax liability for the year is £1,750,000 × 26% = £455,000. The due dates for the payment of corporation tax by Hogg Ltd in respect of the year to 31.3.12 are:

	£
14 October 2011 1/4 × £455,000	113,750
14 January 2012 1/4 × £455,000	113,750
14 April 2012 1/4 × £455,000	113,750
14 July 2012 1/4 × £455,000	113,750
Total	455,000

(b)   (i)   31 March 2013 – 12 months after the end of the accounting period.
      (ii)   12 May 2013 – 3 months after the notice to file the return.

40 Newcomer Ltd and Au Revoir Ltd

> **Tutorial note**. This question is a typical question on registration and deregistration. Note the importance of the dates.

(a)   The registration threshold is £73,000 during any consecutive 12 month period.

This is exceeded in January 2012:

		£
2011	October	12,500
	November	16,200
	December	23,400
2012	January	21,300
		73,400

Therefore, Newcomer Ltd must register within 30 days of the end of the month the threshold was exceeded, ie by 1 March 2012 (since 2012 is a leap year and there are 29 days in February 2012).

Newcomer Ltd will be registered from 1 March 2012 or an earlier date agreed between the company and HM Revenue and Customs.

(b)   A person is eligible for voluntary deregistration if HM Revenue and Customs are satisfied that the amount of his taxable supplies (net of VAT) in the following one year period will not exceed £71,000. However, voluntary deregistration will not be allowed if the reasons for the expected fall in value of taxable supplies is the cessation of taxable supplies or the suspension of taxable supplies for a period of 30 days or more in that following year. HM Revenue and Customs will cancel a person's registration from the date the request is made or an agreed later date.

41 Justin

	£	£
Output VAT		
Furniture: £490,000 × 20%	98,000	
Books: £2,400 × 0%	0	
Petrol (VAT scale charge): £378 × 1/6	63	
		98,063
Input VAT		
Furniture: £275,000 × 20%	55,000	
Computer: £2,400 × 20%	480	
Entertaining: irrecoverable	0	
Petrol: £2,800 × 20%	560	
		(56,040)
VAT to account for quarter ending 31 December 2011		42,023

42 Ongoing Ltd

	£	£
Output tax		
£120,000 × 95% = 114,000 × 20% (note 1)		22,800
Input tax		
£(35,640 − 480) = 35,160 × 20% (note 2)	7,032	
£(2,100 × 95%) = £1,995 × 20% (note 3)	399	
£21,150 × 1/6 (note 4)	3,525	(10,956)
VAT payable for quarter ending 30 April 2011		11,844

Notes

1   VAT is calculated after the deduction of the prompt payment discount.

2   UK entertaining is not an expense on which input tax can be recovered.

3   The debt must be 6 months old to claim bad debt relief. The output tax accounted for on the supply was net of the 5% discount for prompt payment even though the discount was obviously not taken up. The same amount of input tax can therefore be recovered under bad debt relief.

4   Input tax on motor cars is blocked.

43 Jason

(a)   As Jason is an UK VAT registered business, when he supplies goods to another VAT registered business within the European Union, the supply is zero-rated.

(b)   When Jason acquires goods from a VAT-registered trader in another EU member state, he is liable to VAT in the UK.

He will enter the transaction on his VAT return as an output and an input so the effect is neutral.

This means that Jason is in the same position as he would have been if he had acquired the goods from a UK supplier.

The 'tax point' is the earlier of:

(i)   The fifteenth day of the month following the month of acquisition, and
(ii)   The date of issue of an invoice.

(c)   Jason must account for VAT on the goods imported from outside the EU account at the point of entry into the UK.

Jason can then deduct the VAT payable as input tax on his next VAT return.

This means that Jason is in the same overall position as he would have been if he had acquired the goods from a UK supplier.

(d)   Supplies of services by a UK business to outside the EU are outside the scope of VAT.

44 Industrial Ltd

(a)   Corporation tax payable y/e 31.3.12

	£	£
Trading profit	1,810,000	
Less: capital allowances on plant and machinery (W2)	(120,920)	
Trading profit		1,689,080
Investment income	8,000	
Loan interest received	36,000	44,000
Property business income (W3)		73,200
Chargeable gains (W4)		62,122
Total profits		1,868,402
Less: Gift aid donation		(1,500)
Taxable total profits		1,866,902

Main rate of CT applies

Tax

£1,866,902 × 26% = £485,395

Workings

1   *Plant and machinery*

	AIA £	Main pool £	Special rate pool £	Expensive car £	Allowances £
TWDVs b/f		84,600		15,400	
Additions qualifying for AIA					
Heating system	62,800				
Less: AIA	(62,800)				62,800
Machinery	3,400				
Fire alarm system	7,200				
Lorry	32,000				
General plant	27,000				
	69,600				
Less: AIA (balance)	(37,200)				37,200
	32,400				
Transfer balance	(32,400)	32,400			
		117,000			
Addition not qualifying for AIA					
Car			17,200		
Disposal					
Car				(19,600)	
Balancing charge				4,200	(4,200)
WDA @ 10%			(1,720)		1,720
WDA @ 20%		(23,400)			23,400
TWDVs c/f		93,600	15,480		
Allowances					120,920

> Use against special rate pool first

3   *Property business profit*

	£	£
Premium		
Amount received	80,000	
Less 2% × (10 − 1) × 80,000	(14,400)	
Assessable as property income		65,600
Rental (3/12 × £30,400)		7,600
Property business profit		73,200

> Don't forget to add the rental income

4   *Capital gain on sale of shares*

	£
Proceeds	
Less cost	(135,800)
Unindexed gain	100,896
Less indexation allowance	(27,974)
Indexed gain	72,922
Less loss b/f	(10,800)
Net gains	62,122

> No annual exempt amount for companies!

(b) (i) Industrial Ltd pays corporation tax at the main rate and did so in the previous year. Therefore it is required to make quarterly payments on account of corporation tax.

(ii) Industrial Ltd must pay its liability in four equal instalments. These are due on: 14 October 2011; 14 January 2012; 14 April 2012 and 14 July 2012.

45 Carolyn Kraft

Tutorial note. The requirement is already helpfully broken down, so first of all deal with the part you know best to pick up marks early on and boost your confidence. You can really improve your presentation by starting each requirement on a new page. However, do not spend too much time on any one requirement – use the mark allocation as an indication of how much time to spend on each. Finally, do not miss out on the easy marks available for stating payment dates – you could even answer these parts of the relevant requirements first so you don't forget.

(a) *Income tax calculations 2011/12*

Carolyn

	Non-savings income £	Savings income £
Salary	37,000	
Bank interest £8,000 × 100/80		10,000
Net income	37,000	10,000
Less personal allowance	(7,475)	
Taxable income	29,525	10,000

Don't forget to gross up net income

	£
Tax	
£29,525 × 20%	5,905
£5,475 × 20%	1,095
£1,000 × 20% (W1)	200
£3,525 × 40%	1,410
Total tax liability	8,610
Less tax credits	
(i) PAYE	(5,900)
(ii) Interest: £10,000 @ 20%	(2,000)
Tax payable by 31 January 2013	710

Do a working to show the increase in basic rate limit

Always state the due dates – it's a good habit to get into

Mike

	Non-savings income £	Dividend income £
Trade profit (W2)	55,900	
Dividends £9,000 × 100/90		10,000
Net income	55,900	10,000
Less personal allowance	(7,475)	
Taxable income	48,425	10,000

	£
Tax	
£35,000 × 20%	7,000
£3,000 × 20% (W3)	600
£10,425 × 40%	4,170
£10,000 × 32.5%	3,250
Total tax liability	15,020
Less tax credit on dividends: £10,000 @ 10%	(1,000)
Tax payable	14,020

> Consider POAs for anyone whose tax is not all collected at source

Mike also needs to make payments on account as, being self-employed, it is likely that more than 80% of his tax for the prior year was **not** collected at source. The liability for 2011/12 is paid in two POA on 31 January 2012 and 31 July 2012 (each based on half of the prior year's tax payable), with a balancing payment on 31 January 2013.

Workings

1   *Carolyn's basic rate limit*

Increase by gross donation: £800 × 100/80 = £1,000

2   *Mike's taxable trading profits*

	£
Adjusted profit	57,500
Less capital allowances	(1,600)
Taxable trade profits	55,900

3   *Mike's basic rate limit*

Increase by gross pension contribution: (£200 × 12) × 100/80 = £3,000

(b)   *National Insurance contributions 2011/12*

(i)   *Carolyn*

Class 1 primary contributions

First   £7,225 @ 0%
        £29,775 @ 12% = £3,573
        £37,000 (below UEL)

(ii) *Mike*

Class 2

£2.50 × 52 = £130

Class 4

	£
£(42,475 – 7,225) = £35,250 @ 9%	3,172
£(55,900 – 42,475) = £13,425 @ 2%	268
	3,440

(c) **Capital gains tax**

(i) *Carolyn*

	£
Proceeds	250,000
Less cost	(180,000)
renovation (enhancement expenditure)	(30,000)
Gain	40,000
Less annual exempt amount	(10,600)
Taxable gain	29,400

Don't forget to get the easy marks!

CGT @ 28% due 31 January 2013: £8,232

(ii) *Mike*

	£
Proceeds	85,000
Less cost	(53,300)
Gain	31,700
Less annual exempt amount	(10,600)
Taxable gain	21,100

CGT @ 28% due 31 January 2013: £5,908

(d) **Available relief**

Be brief. Make your sentences snappy. Use bullet points for clarity.

(i) Mike can claim 'rollover' relief for reinvestment into replacement business assets.

(ii) He must invest in the new shop within three years of the disposal of the original shop.

(iii) If any proceeds are not reinvested they will be chargeable immediately and only the balance of the gain can be deferred.

Tax tables

SUPPLEMENTARY INFORMATION

1. Calculations and workings need only be made to the nearest £.
2. All apportionments may be made to the nearest month.
3. All workings should be shown.

TAX RATES AND ALLOWANCES

The following tax rates and allowances are to be used in answering the questions.

Income tax

		Normal rates	Dividend rates
		%	%
Basic rate	£1 – £35,000	20	10
Higher rate	£35,001 to £150,000	40	32.5
Additional rate	£150,001 and over	50	42.5

A starting rate of 10% applies to savings income where it falls within the first £2,560 of taxable income.

Personal allowances

		£
Personal allowance	Standard	7,475
Personal allowance	65 – 74	9,940
Personal allowance	75 and over	10,090
Income limit for age related allowances		24,000
Income limit for standard personal allowance		100,000

Car benefit percentage

The base level of CO_2 emissions is 125 grams per kilometre.

A rate of 5% applies to petrol cars with CO_2 emissions of 75 grams per kilometre or less, and a rate of 10% applies where emissions are between 76 and 120 grams per kilometre.

Car fuel benefit

The base figure for calculating the car fuel benefit is £18,800.

Individual savings accounts (ISAs)

The overall investment limit is £10,680, of which £5,340 can be invested in a cash ISA.

Pension scheme limits

Annual allowance	£50,000

The maximum contribution that can qualify for tax relief without any earnings is £3,600.

Authorised mileage allowances: cars

Up to 10,000 miles	45p
Over 10,000 miles	25p

Capital allowances: rates of allowance

Plant and machinery	%
Main pool	20
Special rate pool	10

Motor cars (purchases since 6 April 2009 (1 April 2009 for limited companies))	
New cars with CO_2 emissions up to 110 grams per kilometre	100
CO_2 emissions between 111 and 160 grams per kilometre	20
CO_2 emissions over 160 grams per kilometre	10

Annual investment allowance	
First £100,000 of expenditure	100

Corporation tax

Financial year	2009	2010	2011
Small profits rate	21%	21%	20%
Main rate	28%	28%	26%
Lower limit	300,000	300,000	300,000
Upper limit	1,500,000	1,500,000	1,500,000
Standard fraction	7/400	7/400	3/200

Marginal relief

Standard fraction × (U − A) × N/A

Value Added Tax

Standard rate	20.0%
Registration limit	£73,000
Deregistration limit	£71,000

Inheritance tax: tax rates

£1 – £325,000		Nil
Excess	– Death rate	40%
	– Lifetime rate	20%

Inheritance tax: taper relief

Years before death	% reduction
Over 3 but less than 4 years	20
Over 4 but less than 5 years	40
Over 5 but less than 6 years	60
Over 6 but less than 7 years	80

Capital gains tax

Rates of tax	– Lower rate	18%
	– Higher rate	28%
Annual exempt amount		£10,600
Entrepreneurs' relief	– Lifetime limit	£10,000,000
	– Rate of tax	10%

National insurance contributions
(Not contracted-out rates)

		%
Class 1 Employee	£1 – £7,225 per year	Nil
	£7,226 – £42,475 per year	12.0
	£42,476 and above per year	2.0
Class 1 Employer	£1 – £7,072 per year	Nil
	£7,073 and above per year	13.8
Class 1A		13.8
Class 2	£2.50 per week	
	Small earnings exception	£5,315
Class 4	£1 – £7,225 per year	Nil
	£7,226 – £42,475 per year	9.0
	£42,476 and above per year	2.0

Rates of Interest (assumed)

Official rate of interest	4.0%
Rate of interest on underpaid tax	3.0%
Rate of interest on overpaid tax	0.5%

Index

Review Form – Paper F6(Taxation) Finance Act 2011 (10/11)

Please help us to ensure that the ACCA learning materials we produce remain as accurate and user-friendly as possible. We cannot promise to answer every submission we receive, but we do promise that it will be read and taken into account when we update this Study Text.

Name: _____   Address: _____

_____

_____

How have you used this Study Text?
(Tick one box only)

☐ Home study (book only)

☐ On a course: college _____

☐ With 'correspondence' package

☐ Other _____

Why did you decide to purchase this Study Text? *(Tick one box only)*

☐ Have used BPP Texts in the past

☐ Recommendation by friend/colleague

☐ Recommendation by a lecturer at college

☐ Saw information on BPP website

☐ Saw advertising

☐ Other _____

During the past six months do you recall seeing/receiving any of the following?
(Tick as many boxes as are relevant)

☐ Our advertisement in *ACCA Student Accountant*

☐ Our advertisement in *Pass*

☐ Our advertisement in *PQ*

☐ Our brochure with a letter through the post

☐ Our website www.bpp.com

Which (if any) aspects of our advertising do you find useful?
(Tick as many boxes as are relevant)

☐ Prices and publication dates of new editions

☐ Information on Text content

☐ Facility to order books off-the-page

☐ None of the above

Which BPP products have you used?

Text	☑	Success CD	☐
Kit	☐	i-Pass	☐
Passcard	☐	Interactive Passcard	☐

Your ratings, comments and suggestions would be appreciated on the following areas.

	Very useful	Useful	Not useful
Introductory section	☐	☐	☐
Chapter introductions	☐	☐	☐
Key terms	☐	☐	☐
Quality of explanations	☐	☐	☐
Case studies and other examples	☐	☐	☐
Exam focus points	☐	☐	☐
Questions and answers in each chapter	☐	☐	☐
Fast forwards and chapter roundups	☐	☐	☐
Quick quizzes	☐	☐	☐
Question Bank	☐	☐	☐
Answer Bank	☐	☐	☐
Index	☐	☐	☐

	Excellent	Good	Adequate	Poor
Overall opinion of this Study Text	☐	☐	☐	☐

Do you intend to continue using BPP products?   Yes ☐   No ☐

On the reverse of this page is space for you to write your comments about our Study Text. We welcome your feedback.

The BPP Learning Media author of this edition can be e-mailed at: AlisonPriest@bpp.com

Please return this form to: Lesley Buick, ACCA Publishing Manager, BPP Learning Media Ltd, FREEPOST, London, W12 8BR

TELL US WHAT YOU THINK

Please note any further comments and suggestions/errors below. For example, was the text accurate, readable, concise, user-friendly and comprehensive?